JACOBY

DESCENT INTO DISCOURSE

CRITICAL PERSPECTIVES

ON THE PAST

A series edited by

Susan Porter Benson

Stephen Brier

Roy Rosenzweig

Descent into Discourse

THE REIFICATION OF LANGUAGE AND

THE WRITING OF SOCIAL HISTORY

Bryan D. Palmer

 TEMPLE UNIVERSITY PRESS | PHILADELPHIA

Temple University Press, Philadelphia 19122
Copyright © 1990 by Temple University. All rights reserved
Published 1990
Printed in the United States of America

The paper used in this publication meets the minimum
requirements of American National Standard for Information
Sciences—Permanence of Paper for Printed Library Materials,
ANSI Z39.48-1984

Library of Congress Cataloging-in-Publication Data
Palmer, Bryan D.
    Descent into discourse : the reification of language and the
writing of social history / Bryan D. Palmer.
        p.   cm.—(Critical perspectives on the past)
    Includes index.
    ISBN 0-87722-678-4 (alk. paper)
    1. Language and history.   2. Historical materialism.   3. Discourse
analysis.   4. Criticism.   5. Historiography.   I. Title.
II. Series.
P41.P35   1990
401'.41—dc20   89-5080
                                                                    CIP

For Automatic Slim, Razor Totin' Jim,
Fast Talkin' Fannie, Butcher-Knife Totin' Annie,
Pistol Pete, Shakin' Box-Car Joe,
Washboard Sam, Last Decision Red,
and Cooler Crawlin' Ed
(who keep me company)

For Charlie and Joyce
(who indulge my excesses)

For Greg
(who is doing real research)

And for Beth
(who makes my world go round . . . and round)

The problem of descending from the world of thoughts to the actual world is turned into the problem of descending from language to life.

—*Marx and Engels,*
   The German Ideology *(1845–1846)*

Contents

Preface

THE WORLD AS IT IS AND THE WORLD AS IT IS CONCEIVED TO be never seem quite to coincide. There are understandable reasons for this, not the least of which is that specific interests make sure that this divergence occurs and continues. Those, like myself, who began looking at the world seriously in the late 1960s and early 1970s know well the vocabulary of this process, reared as we were on the relationships of theory and practice, words that we drummed into our political lives, at times with mind-numbing persistence.

To consider the world of writing in 1989 is to confront this problem immediately. Theoretically, innovative works in criticism have attempted to destabilize our understanding of what is at stake in writing, emphasizing the shifting nature of meaning, the determinative power of language, the autonomy of texts, the problematic nature of authorial intention, indeed the death of authorship itself. Practically, it is nevertheless all too apparent that meanings can be read unambiguously, that power, often of a brutal and terroristic sort, is able to overstep language, and that authors, their intentions, and the consequences of their writing are in fact tangible features of an unfolding history of class struggles, political economy, and international relations.

The truly terrifying response of Islamic fundamentalism to Salman Rushdie's *Satanic Verses* (1988), a novel published as this book was going to press, made this all too clear. *The Satanic Verses* offended premodern power with its depiction of the prophet Mohammed, just as Martin Scorsese's *Last Temptation of Christ* drew the ire of Christian zealots. From Ayatollah Khomeini's decree of Rushdie's death and his promise of martyrdom and earthly reward for any successful assassin to the score and more who have died in protesting the publication of Rushdie's book in Pakistan and India, the importance of meaning and authority were clarified in blood. The ugly mixture of Muslim clerical reaction, Western chauvinism, opportunistic media manipulation, and concessions to the strategically pivotal mullahs by the state offices of capital and actually existing socialism threatened to ignite an explosion of racist backlash that would target the large and highly differentiated Muslim communities of North America and Europe. As governments and capitalist outlets backtracked, Western religious figureheads called for the *extension* of Victorian blasphemy laws, and Rushdie and his wife went underground, it would have been rather outlandish to argue that there is nothing outside of the text and that authors do not exist.

This is not to say that *The Satanic Verses* could not be subjected to a poststructuralist, deconstructive reading. Nor is it to claim that there can be no connection between such a reading and the politics of the event. Indeed, when protesting authors donned placards proclaiming "I am Rushdie," they were no doubt adopting a slogan eminently compatible with the premises of deconstruction. My contention, then, is not that this reading of the Rushdie case is wrong, only that an interpretation of this text and its fundamentally political and material consequences demands more. *The Satanic Verses* and Islamic fundamentalism's frightening response to it are representative of a wide range of past and ongoing processes and events that historians and others seek to interpret. In that analytic search for meaning historians have recently been drawn to literary theory and poststructuralist thought. This book was conceived as an introduction to how this body of critical writing, which posits the centrality of discourse or language in constructing being, power, and consciousness, is used in historical circles, most especially in social history.

North American social history is actually something of a new arrival in the discipline. To be sure, it existed in the interwar period in the "New History" of Schlesinger, Barnes, and Fox, but this project never really "took." Only over the past twenty years has social history gained a strong foothold in departments, consolidated course offerings, and established its own journals and legitimacy. As such, social history's arrival paralleled the post-1960 expansion of the universities and the loose set of radical challenges growing out of the ferment of the 1960s. In this climate, social history and historical materialism simultaneously engaged the attention and allegiance of many radical scholars. As social history flourished, becoming something of a major growth industry, many saw it as a bid for academic hegemony, an overt attempt to displace other fields—intellectual, political, diplomatic, economic—and score a coup for the left. Although this was by no means what was happening, the convergence of social history and historical materialism, as well as animosities from the politically hostile or the intellectually insecure, provide the background to attacks on social history in the later 1980s, whether launched from overt conservatives or the camps of discontented specialists.[1] With the times moving decidedly and decisively to the right, a disciplinary field and orientation associated with a generation and a period identified, however loosely, with the left was certain to be subject to specific assaults and particular pressures.

Precisely because this challenge from conservatism and the territorially threatened surfaced at the very moment that discourse theory was being promoted as a specific interpretive answer to the perceived analytic difficulties within social history, the issues of debate have become, in some circles, complex. Lawrence Stone, no friend of a social history guided by historical materialism, and long a polemicist against the intrusions of Marxism into an empirically orchestrated narrative-ordered discipline,[2] struck an early blow against "the growing army of enemies of rationality." By that he meant the followers of "the fashionable cult of absolute relativism, emerging from philosophy, linguistics, semiotics, and deconstructionism."[3]

Like Stone, I have my complaints. But unlike him, my polemic against historians' much-heralded utilization of what has come to be known as critical theory rests on the conviction that historical materialism remains the theoretical foundation upon which studies of the past must be erected. This does not necessarily mean I see no value in literary theory as a guide to the reading of texts. It does mean that I am suspicious of those historians, many of them once adherents of historical materialism, who now hold to the primacy of language, stressing its nonreferentiality and its determinative capacity.

Most social historians who champion discourse theory are only superficially acquainted with critical theory and its problematic historical formation and construction. As a result, their histories are undertheorized and insufficiently attentive to the often one-sided way in which they develop their readings of the texts, broadly defined, of the past. One aim of this book is to introduce historians more fully to the theoretical writing that many are alluding to and drawing from rather cavalierly.

But I do not simply claim that historians are gravitating to discourse in ways that are ill informed. I also stand against the adoption of critical theory as a means of rejecting or subverting historical materialism. Much of the current attraction to language seems to necessitate downplaying the importance of historical forces such as class and class struggle. Another purpose of this book, then, is to argue for the centrality of these processes, as categories of analysis and essential components of lived experience.

I am also interested in why and how social historians once committed to historical materialism as a way of understanding the world of the past and the present have come to embrace theories and perspectives that often stand in opposition to a Marxist analysis of social relations and structures. Beyond the sociological and political explanations of why this has happened, there are also intellectual currents that have played their part. And here is where the two-sidedness of specific texts of historical materialism is of considerable importance, producing ironic consequences and developments in paving the way for the reception of critical theory among those who might have been expected to resist what I call the descent into discourse. I insist on recognition of the ways that certain writings of historical materialism have dealt with language and enhanced our understanding of the past, paying particular attention to works that have broken decisively from vulgar materialism to sketch theoretically and empirically how human agency and structural determination connect with one another. Yet I also suggest that in this writing, with its attempt to supersede the mechanical content of the theoretical edifice of historical materialism and its metaphor of base and superstructure, lay a problematic blurring of differentiations. The result is an increasing drift toward idealism and movement away from materialism. The current focus on language and discourse is but a part of this larger trajectory.

Critical theory is no substitute for historical materialism; language is not life. That, bluntly, is the argument of this book. Left to its own devices, poststructuralist theory will always stop short of interpretive clarity and a relationship to the past premised on political integrity and a contextualized situating of historical agents within structures of determination. Whatever insight can be gleaned from discourse theory and its privileging of language needs to be balanced with other appreciations drawn from more resolutely historical and materialist traditions. Without this balance, interpretation descends into discourse. This book has been written because analysis seems to be following this trajectory in the 1980s. It tries to be clear in the midst of much that is not.

Literary theorists and poststructuralist thinkers are not the main intended audience for this book. Most of these types are decidedly uninterested in a dialogue between their own esoteric theoretical fields and another discipline such as history. Instead, it seeks to inform historians, especially those now serving apprenticeships, of the potential and problem posed by the current theoretical implosion around language. Others, in such disciplines as politics, philosophy, literature, Romance languages, cultural studies, sociology, and even geography, where discourse, poststructuralism, and postmodernism are now much in vogue, may also follow the argument productively.

In the opening chapter I survey the discovery of language, charting the rise and perpetual revision of theories turning on the centrality of discourse. Next, I consider works of historical materialism that are attentive to this realm of language but predate or exist outside of what I refer to as the implosion of theory that forced language to the forefront in the 1970s and 1980s. In this initial engagement with texts of historical materialism I focus singlemindedly on their positive contributions, leaving their problematic consequences to a later discussion. As these contributions are universally unacknowledged among both the post-structuralist community and within circles of social history where discourse is now a fashionable interpretive panacea, this seems a necessary point of departure. I then turn, in succeeding chapters, to themes of broad relevance—politics, class, and gender.

Within each of these historically situated realms, discourse and materialism relate to one another differently, forcing me to vary slightly the tone and perspective of each chapter. Class, for instance, is all too curtly dismissed in much of the recent writing of social history informed by discourse theory, and, as a consequence, my discussions of some of the literature addressing politics and labor take a decidedly polemical turn. Gender, however, seems a realm more open to the interpretive possibilities afforded by critical theory, in which the capacities of discourse to construct meaning and identity are more pronounced. This does not mean that I accept the curt dismissal of historical materialism espoused by some feminist advocates of language, or that I discount the role of economic determination in the making of gendered experience. Nor does it suggest that gender is historically or analytically a unique case. Rather, within the generalized adherence to my argument, I see gender as a site where the case for discourse can be made with more force, albeit problematically, and where the lacunae of historical materialism are admittedly more pronounced. For these reasons my discussion of gender is perhaps both more respectful and less polemical than are my attentions to politics and class.

Finally, I address the politics of theory and historical interpretation, recognizing that parts of critical theory offer potential insights to historians, allowing discourse a place in interpretation. But I am ultimately insistent that the limits and limiting refusals of this theoretical moment be exposed. As well, I ask why this interpretive direction has been taken, offering answers that draw on the sociology and politics of the 1980s, looking to the ways in which the pioneering social histories and cultural studies discussed in the second chapter have unwittingly conditioned a climate congenial to the reification of language. I conclude with a discussion of the basic opposition that, critical theory's refusal of such binary pairings aside, can hardly be avoided: discourse versus materialism.

This book would never have happened without others' involving themselves, however innocently, in my writing. Helmut Gruber long ago asked me to respond to Joan Scott in the pages of *International Labor and Working-Class History*. Because of the appearance of that small article I was exposed to the problem of language more forcefully than otherwise would have been the case. And I exposed myself. My crude formulations and polemical (if respectful) zeal drew me to the attention of three editors—Steve Brier, Roy Rosenzweig, and Susan Porter Benson—who, with a bit of cajoling, enlisted me in their cause. I would still probably never have written this book had not Pamela Divinsky kept telling me that I must, even though she could hardly fathom what I might say. Many people also offered sources and suggestions, among them Harold Mah, Allen Seager, Rick Gruneau, Robert Malcolmson, Peter Baxter, Bob Shenton, Christie Brown, and Charles Freedeman. Members of the Historians Interested in Political Economy Group at Queen's University read parts of the manuscript and offered me their criticisms. I am indebted to Jean-Christophe Agnew, who anonymously assessed my original brief proposal to Temple University Press and then provided an encouraging and thoughtful reflection on a first draft of the manuscript. Deborah Kaplan's commentary on parts of the text forced me to clarify certain passages and restructure my language. At Temple, Janet Francendese was always interested and interesting, by far the most involved editor I have encountered in academic publishing. Nelcya Delanoë read the entire manuscript and was too gentle with her critical suggestions.

I can perhaps best introduce this book with the conclusion from another. In his assessment of Derrida, Lacan, Lyotard, and Foucault, Peter Dews notes that poststructuralist thought is a mosaic of theories covering similar ground. These theories, he suggests, collectively reject belief in an integrated critical standpoint and equate acceptance of such a political center with "repressive totalization." Dews argues that this poststructuralist premise hardly frees interpretation from specific and much-maligned illusions, nor does it provide "a more powerful illumination of the contemporary world." He ends his important study, *The Logics of Disintegration: Post-structuralist Thought and the Claims of Critical Theory* (1987) with the conclusion that critique is not simply a question of the arbitrary and coercive espousal of premises, precepts, and categories, but rests instead on the kinds of coherent thought that can actually lead to the emancipation of humanity.[4] I could not agree more.

In this refusal of the theoretical claims of poststructuralism Dews situates himself within the achievements of the modern world, denying implicitly the attainment of some postmodernist order in which all has been overturned and transformed. To place oneself within such a set of refusals and denials is to swim against the stream of contemporary intellectual obscurantism. It is to align oneself with the achievements of the past, intellectually and politically, so that the attainments of the future can be realized.

History is indeed at a specific crossroads, but it is not the self-indulgent unintelligibility of a postmodernist late-twentieth-century swirl of excess, waste, and disaccumulation depicted in some ostensibly theoretical texts.[5] Rather, capitalism is impaled on its own contradictions. Production falters in the advanced capitalist West as the rate of profit spirals downward, revived only by the short-term exploitative possibilities open to an imperialism that will reap accumulative spoils out of umbrellas from Taiwan or cocaine from Columbia. Peace can supposedly be secured only by the buildup of Armageddon's nuclear arsenals. Science and knowledge are increasingly challenged by superstition and fundamentalist faith. Bourgeois democracy's promise of equality falters persistently in orgies of chauvinism and bigotry, with the unambiguous revitalization of fascism and racism providing abundant evidence of the political and social consequences of economic stagnation and the entrenchment in power of the New Right. The way out of this impasse is not, theoretically or practically, to buy into it and its logic of disintegration. Whatever small part the writing of social history can play in insuring that this road is not taken will happen only if some refusals and denials begin to be made. This book attempts to explore how that might be done.

DESCENT INTO DISCOURSE

1 *The Discovery/Deconstruction of the Word/Sign*

In the beginning was the Word; the word was in God's presence, and the word was God.

—*John 1:1*

The Formalists show a fast ripening religiousness. They are followers of St. John. They believe that "In the beginning was the Word." But we believe that in the beginning was the deed. The word followed, as its phonetic shadow.

—*Leon Trotsky,* Literature and Revolution *(1924)*

ANY BEGINNING IS AN ACT OF DIFFERENTIATION.[1] MY BEGINning is not with a divine origin, but with a profane concern: a current trend in the writing of social history. To locate and explore this trend is not, of course, to imply that social history ever was or is now an entirely homogeneous entity. But it is to suggest that the field has moved of late, is being subjected to pressures of a new and unique sort. I will call this the linguistic turn, or, more polemically, the descent into discourse.

Simply put, this motion, seemingly perpetual, is driven by the premise/promise that language, broadly conceived as systems of signification that extend well beyond mere words to include the symbols and structures of all ways of communicating (from the articulated to the subliminal), is the essential ground within which social life is embedded. Language thus constructs being: it orders the relations of classes and genders, ever attentive to specific hierarchies; it is the stage on which consciousness makes its historical entrance and politics is scripted. As its own master, moreover, language is nonreferential, and

3

there can be no reduction of its beginnings and meanings "to some primal anterior reality."[2]

Social historians have not made this turn quickly and, indeed, have lagged behind trends in other fields. In philosophy, for instance, it could be argued that the linguistic turn has orchestrated the trajectory of the discipline in the twentieth century.[3] Fifteen years ago Roland Barthes, writing from the ambiguity of a space that defied disciplinary conventionality, noted that:

> The present emphasis on problems of language irritates some, who regard it as an excessive fashion. Yet they will have to resign themselves to the inevitable: we are probably only beginning to speak of language: along with other sciences which tend, today, to be attached to it, linguistics is entering the dawn of its history.[4]

Less austere, but perhaps no less revealing, are the fictional utterances of Malcolm Bradbury:

> It is proving beyond doubt that we find ourselves in *the age of the floating signifier*, when word no longer attaches properly to thing, and no highbonding glues can help us. . . . The undermining of the illusion of presence indeed goes back to the early days of the tendency, and was famously developed by Roland Barthes in his great essay of 1968 on the Death of the Author. . . . What writes books is in fact nothing other than history, culture, or to be more precise, *language itself.* Indeed so effective is language that it has frequently arrived early in the morning, sat down at the typewriter, and as good as completed half a day's work before the average so-called author has even showered, dressed and got through his breakfast croissant.[5]

Coming slowly as it did to practitioners of history, a contingent known for its attachment to tradition and resistance to theory, it is perhaps not surprising that this discovery of language by historians is now being promoted with such messianic zeal. The entrepreneurial marketing of language has become the hallmark of a spate of recent texts. Historians are exhorted to "study the production of interest, identification, grievance, and aspiration within political languages themselves" and warned of the dangers of "refusal to consider theories which have attempted to confront the implications of landmarks in twentieth century linguistics for the study of the social."[6] Such well-placed calls to attend to language have not gone unheeded. Recent writing focuses on the languages of work, factory reform, class, politics, markets, professionalism, and gender. Many of these texts use the word *discourse* as a signifier of intellectual sophistication and fashion, and it is not surprising that a recent collection of essays contains the introductory remark, "Historians are also beginning to learn much from students of the primary medium of culture, namely language."[7]

This is not an entirely pernicious development. Attention to language is clearly vital to any historical practice. Documents demand nuanced readings, and there are abundant indications that historians can use all the help they can get in making sense of them. There is nothing wrong with interrogating, and drawing insight from, theories of language or texts—in philosophy, literary theory, and other realms—that can illuminate meanings and suggest ways of situating historical experience within the kinds of limitations that language undoubtedly imposes. *Discourse* is not a word, or a process, that needs to be avoided because of some taint or contamination.[8] I am not upset that we now have endless discourses working their way into the various moments of historical scrutiny: discourses of sexuality, of quackery, of reform, of community and political economy, of paternalism, of social history itself.[9] This is all to the good.

What I question, what I refuse, what I mark out as my own differentiation from the linguistic turn, is all that is lost in the tendency to reify language, objectifying it as unmediated discourse, placing it beyond social, economic, and political relations, and in the process displacing essential structures and formations to the historical sidelines. At stake is nothing less than many of the gains that historical materialism, as *theory,* and social history, as *practice,* however constrained and contradictory, were thought to have registered over the course of the last decades. For in the current fixation on language a materialist understanding of the past is all too often sacrificed on the altar of an idealized reading of discourse and its influence. Such reading, while thoroughly in step with current developments in literary theory, ironically often owes less to the increasing analytic sophistication of social historians than it does to a partial and selective making of the linguistic turn. The way forward, however, lies not in establishing the tyranny of language as some prior, determining feature of human relations, but in excavating, and hence materializing, the relations of economy and culture, necessity and agency, structure and process, that language mediates incessantly.

To do this, however, demands an elementary beginning. It is a beginning that the advocates of the linguistic turn in social history have made, if at all, very poorly. For all the exhortations and prefatory gestures toward language and its complexities, those social historians who champion a history informed by discourse (or critical/literary/linguistic) theory seldom betray much of an interest in the very key that they contend can open the hermeneutic door to the past.

The remainder of this chapter attempts to forge a facsimile of that key, which is nothing less than the development of linguistic and literary theory over the last century. By the late 1970s and into the 1980s such developments would culminate in a conceptual implosion, in which a host of contending approaches to discourse—deconstruction in its Derridean and Yale variants, reader-oriented perspectives, Lacanian psychoanalytic attention to the subject and the unconscious, and Marxist and feminist hermeneutics, among others—fractured the discovery of the word/sign along a multitude of new lines of inquiry.[10] The initiation of this process is no doubt buried in antiquity, but a dual opening out into one set of beginnings lies in the different orientations to language of Nietzsche and Saussure.

▶   ### The Wild and the Innocent

Hermeneutics—the explication of the principles and methods of interpretation—broke free of theology and its confinement to biblical texts only when the material unfolding of capitalism's relentless appetite for change turned nineteenth-century society into something radically different than ever before imagined. Abundance and want, freedom and exploitation, walked hand-in-hand. Christian ideals of the soul's integrity and the will to truth withered as the death of God was proclaimed and the will to power was unmasked as the dominating trajectory of the modern world. In the words of the *Communist Manifesto:*

> All fixed, fast-frozen relations, with their train of ancient and venerable prejudices, are swept away, all new-formed ones become antiquated before they can ossify. All that is solid melts into air, all that is holy is profaned, and man is at last compelled to face with sober senses, his real conditions of life, and his relations with his kind.[11]

Capital's capacity to mystify and obscure this process was, however, considerable. Marx and Engels struggled constantly to expose "the rational kernel within the mystical shell," to confront controlling metaphors of appearance and reality with their own counter-readings.[12]

Nietzsche, like Marx and Engels, appreciated the ironic and dialectical drift of history, as well as the possibility of utopia. In *Beyond Good and Evil* (1882) he articulated the same sense of crisis and imperative that animated the founders of historical materialism. His words, more opaque and ornate, captured the spirit of the age but left his language of interpretation floating in a metaphorical sea untroubled by the only force that could tame its undulating turbulence—a program.

> At these turning points in history there shows itself, juxtaposed and often entangled with one another, a magnificent, manifold, jungle-like growing and striving, a sort of tropical tempo in rivalry of

development, and an enormous destruction and self-destruction, thanks to egoisms violently opposed to one another, exploding, battling each other for sun and light, unable to find any limitation, any check, any considerateness within the morality at their disposal. . . . Nothing but new "wherefores," no longer any communal formulas; a new allegiance of misunderstanding and mutual disrespect; decay, vice, and the most superior designs gruesomely bound up with one another, the genius of the race welling up over the cornucopias of good and ill; a fateful simultaneity of spring and autumn. . . . Again there is danger, the mother of morality—great danger—but this time displaced onto the individual, onto the nearest and dearest, onto the street, onto one's own child, one's own heart, one's own innermost secret recesses of wish and will.[13]

In distancing itself from materialism and focusing on submerged individualism, Nietzsche's text can be read as the outcome of a process of intellectual domestication, a cry of anguish from the bowels of bourgeois society.

In terms of language, Nietzsche stands as an important strand in the unraveling of what Allan Megill denotes *aestheticism*. Breaking from the conventional meaning of this term, which implies enclosure within a self-contained realm of aesthetic objects and sensations and isolation from a real world of objects, Megill uses the term *aestheticism* to "refer to a tendency to see 'art' or 'language' or 'discourse' or 'text' as constituting the primary realm of human experience." Nietzsche would claim that "it is only as an *aesthetic phenomenon* that existence and the world are eternally justified," and that facts and things are created by the human act of interpretation itself. Language does not so much imitate nature as displace it. Essentially figurative and nonreferential for Nietzsche, language is incapable of conveying objective historical knowledge, which cannot possibly exist.[14] Yet, more than any other product of human society, language imprisons men and women, defining them by the chains with which it binds humanity.[15]

Simultaneously pessimistic, hedonistic, and dismissive of collective, as opposed to individual, genius, Nietzsche could plead for a cure for society's liberation from the vice of crisis while being unable to chart a way forward. As J. G. Merquior has noted:

Nietzsche found himself torn between the following theoretical alternatives: *either* he was to undertake an "immanent critique" of philosophical reason, in an attempt to rescue it from the shortcomings of historicist thought . . . *or* he could ditch philosophy's rational programme altogether. Nietzsche chose the latter course. He adopted a paradoxical strategy of subverting reason. Boldly flaunting an uncompromising irrationalism, he denounced reason as a

> form of will-to-power and deprived value judgements of all cogni-
> tive force. In so doing Nietzsche was not only the first to give a
> conceptual form to modernist aesthetics as a ludic, Dionysian mode
> of change and self-denial: he also built an alluring *aesthetocentric*
> redefinition of thought. . . . On the one hand, he contemplated the
> possibility of a new, sceptic history, a starkly critical genealogy of
> morals freed from every illusion about objective truth. On the other
> hand, he countenanced a critique of metaphysical assumptions that
> was still faithful to the idea of philosophy as a higher knowledge.

As we will see, these paths mark out important directions taken in the
implosion of theory. More important, Nietzsche charted the first steps
of the hedonistic freewheeling descent into discourse that the worst
elements of critical theory would embrace in the 1980s. "Theory itself,"
concludes Merquior, "disparaged sustained logical analysis for the sake
of 'life' and wild insight."[16]

Unlike Nietzsche, the generally acknowledged father of linguistic
theory Ferdinand de Saussure seldom walked on the wild side, prefer-
ring instead the innocent scholasticism of the detached intellectual.
Living out his life in relative obscurity, the Swiss linguist developed
rather than discovered the field, but he did so with a clarity that was to
prove enticing to future generations. It is one of the ironies of the
production of theory that Saussure, whose influence reaches across the
twentieth century in ways that infiltrate virtually every recess of contemporary critical theory, wrote little of significance himself. His much
alluded-to major work, *Course in General Linguistics*, was not only
published but written posthumously, a compilation of Saussure's lecture notes undertaken by several of his students.[17]

Saussure stressed the fundamental distinction between language system, called *langue*, upon which we all draw unconsciously as speakers,
and the individual utterances we make, or *parole*. It was *langue* that
interested Saussure, the system or structure that governed *parole* and
those who were bound within its forms of determination. He rejected
the idea that language is a simple sum total of its vocabulary, a quantitative piling up of words. Instead he stressed that words are signs, composed of two parts: signifiers, either written or spoken, are the form that
language assumes on the page or in speech, an arbitrary set of letters or
sounds that bears no necessary relationship to the object they denote;
and the signified, a concept that is thought as the signifier is visualized
or verbalized. Finally, Saussure introduced the terms *synchronic* and
diachronic. Synchronic scrutiny of a language system attended to a
particular linguistic state, without reference to time, development, or
historical evolution. Diachronic study, which was the ruling orthodoxy
before Saussure, was concerned with language's evolution over time. At

pains to break decisively from nineteenth-century linguistics, which had lost interest in the word as sign/representation, focusing instead on its historical evolution and relations, Saussure stressed the necessity of a synchronic study of language in which the meaning of words and signs was exposed through examination of an essential structure of differentiations.[18]

Saussure's linguistics thus rested firmly on sets of oppositions: *langue/parole*; signifier/signified; synchronic/diachronic. Just these kinds of oppositions would figure prominently in later developments in critical theory. The oppositions were on occasion illusory, however much heuristic value they contained. Distinguishing *langue* and *parole* has proven more than a little difficult. In some languages signifiers and signified are more intimately related than they are in others. Although the sign as a unity of signifier and signified *was* arbitrary, the concept being eminently detachable from its acoustic or formal image, meaning was acquired only within the differentiations of *langue* as a structure or system. Within language as a system of nonreferential signs, then, lay buried a critical referential axis.[19] Similarly, Saussure's synchronic/diachronic dichotomy actually works precisely because his insistence on freezing analysis of language systems within a particular time rests upon a profound appreciation of the essentially historical character of language. Since the sign is arbitrary, it is nothing less than the product of history. To study its constantly evolving motion, therefore, would be to fail to grasp its systematic logic in the world of the present.[20]

As Sebastiano Timpanaro and Perry Anderson have emphasized, Saussure proposed his linguistic course cautiously, with due regard for the singularity of language. Convinced that language was "a human institution of such a kind that all the other human institutions, with the exception of writing, can only deceive us as to its real essence if we trust in their analogy," Saussure warned that "whoever sets foot on the terrain of language can be said to be bereft of all the analogies of heaven and earth." He was adamant that other human systems—he specifically named kinship and economy—were not comparable to language. The unmistakable implication is that his linguistic system, for all his gestures toward the imperialistic nature of a science of signs, a semiology that he recognized did not yet exist, was necessarily limited in its applicability.[21] Saussure was the last of his kind who could claim innocence.

▶ **Revolution and the Word**

Saussure died in 1913. The Bolshevik revolutionary seizure of power in 1917 was, for many, a new beginning for humankind, a shattering of what was left of innocence. It was a beginning, to be sure, powered by words, but it was the revolutionary act, or deed, that transformed social relations on a world scale. And, as Trotsky had noted, many words followed. One part of the "phonetic shadow" cast by the revolution was a dynamic dialogue about language and literary scholarship.

The word/sign entered into the mainstream of revolutionary theoretical pronouncement via two related, but distinct, channels. First, and of less concern here, was the revolutionary proletarian assault on Russian formalism and its futurist allies. Prominent in Russian literary studies since about 1916, formalism's predominant emphasis, in Raymond Williams's words, "was on the specific, intrinsic characteristics of a literary work, which required analysis 'in its own terms' before any other kind of discussion, and especially social or ideological analysis was relevant or even possible."[22] The working-class rejection of formalism was initiated and sustained at its best by the polemical challenge of Trotsky and, more problematically, in the practical contribution of Aleksandr Konstantinovich Voronskii and the literary circle he gathered around the "thick" journal *Red Virgin Soil* in the creative and open years 1921–1928.[23] Second, was the emergence of a Marxist critique of Saussure.

Distancing itself from the idealism and metaphysical underpinnings of formalism/futurism, as well as the populism/patriotism of the often peasant-fixated "literary fellow travelers," the critical current associated with Trotsky and Voronskii was riveted to a program of realism at the same time that it could acknowledge the contribution of its antagonists:

> The methods of formal analysis are necessary, but insufficient. You may count up the alliterations in popular proverbs, classify metaphors, count up the number of vowels and consonants in a wedding song. It will undoubtedly enrich our knowledge of folk art, in one way or another; but if you don't know the peasant system of sowing, and the life that is based on it, if you don't know the part the scythe plays, and if you have not mastered the meaning of the church calendar to the peasant, of the time when the peasant marries, or when the peasant women give birth, you will have only understood the outer shell of folk art, but the kernel will not have been reached.[24]

Others adopted a more blunt and moralistic tone, and by the mid-to-late 1920s the language of exile had been imposed on the formalists by the consolidating Stalinist state.[25]

As the official attack on "aesthetic gourmandizing" grew more vitriolic, it swept the futurist theoretician and head of the formalist school Victor Shklovsky into an ever-quickening pace of compromise, retreat, and ultimate recantation. By 1930, with the publication of Shklovsky's "Monument to a Scientific Error," formalism was dead at the same time that its central figure, through a series of opportunistic public self-denunciations, survived.[26] Trotsky, Voronskii, and others fared less well. In the reciprocal race of revolution and the word in the Soviet 1920s, as social and intellectual transformation gave way to degeneration, the political and literary voices of Bolshevism, more so than formalism, had to be silenced. Expelled in 1927 from the party he had helped to lead to power, Trotsky would soon note that Voronskii, in the company of other old Bolsheviks, was among several hundred dissidents arrested early in 1928.[27]

The critique of formalism initiated by Trotsky and Voronskii was carried to its conclusion by a contingent of philosophers and literary theorists headed by Mikhail Bakhtin, V. N. Volosinov, and P. N. Medvedev.[28] Running parallel to their critique of the formalists was the Bakhtin circle's sustained opposition to Saussure. Saussurean linguistics was judged objectivist and abstract, the conjuring up of an ahistorical, illusory synchronic system governed by an unworldly formalism and stability. In Volosinov's *Marxism and the Philosophy of Language* (1929), Saussure's *langue* took a back seat to the concrete and socially contextualized character of language. The word/sign was less a fixed, neutral, nonreferential, arbitrary unit than it was an active, historically changing, constantly modified component of communication, its meaning conveyed by tones and contexts that were themselves always products of struggles and conflicts among classes, social groups, individuals, and discourses. The word/sign, in short, was weighted down with referentiality. Against the set of Saussurean oppositions Bakhtin, Medvedev, and Volosinov posed the historical, multiaccentual, referential nature of language.[29]

All of this did nothing to negate the relative autonomy of language, which Volosinov argued was, as a socially constructed sign system, a material reality. More than mere reflection, language was itself a means of production, in which meaning was created within the materiality of the sign through a process of social conflict and differentiation:

> Existence reflected in the sign is not merely reflected but refracted. How is this refraction of existence in the ideological sign determined? By an intersecting of differently oriented social interests within one and the same sign community, i.e. by the class struggle. Class does not coincide with the sign community, i.e. with the community which is the totality of users of the same set of signs for ideological communication. Thus various different classes will use one and the same language. As a result, differently oriented accents

intersect in every ideological sign. Sign becomes an arena of class struggle. This social multiaccentuality of the ideological sign is a very crucial aspect. . . . A sign that has been withdrawn from the pressures of the social struggle—which, so to speak, crosses beyond the pale of the class struggle—inevitably loses force, degenerating into allegory and becoming the object not of live social intelligibility but of philological comprehension.[30]

In this passage, with its stress on multiaccentuality and class struggle, lay a radical opposition to the tenets of Saussurean linguistics and its future reception in the rise of structuralism.

Within the Soviet Union itself, however, the continuing degeneration of the revolutionary state and the march of the ideology of "socialism in one country" obscured this reading of language in the social chauvinism of Stalin's reductionist *Marxism and Linguistics* (1951). Upon the appearance of a study of Dostoevsky in 1929, Bakhtin went the way of Voronskii: exiled to Kazakhstan for six years, a dissertation on Rabelais rejected, he would experience intellectual rehabilitation, not so much in his Soviet homeland, but among Western intellectuals. Volosinov, meanwhile, "disappeared" sometime in the 1930s.[31]

► **Exile on Main Street:**
Jakobson and the Signs of Structuralism
Not all Russian formalists made their peace with Stalinism. Some stuck to their literary guns and took their leave of class struggle, exiling themselves from the revolutionary project at the very beginning. One such figure was Roman Jakobson, founder of the Moscow Linguistic Circle and, next to Shklovsky, the most dazzling formalist of his day. His earliest projects derived from Shklovsky and reveled in the Nietzschean subversiveness of futurist poetry. If meaning was always primary with Jakobson, who insisted on recognition of the social, political, and cultural underpinnings of the texts he chose to work with, this analytic and materialistic sensitivity was often overwhelmed by his penchant for form and linguistic pyrotechnics. This no doubt left him somewhat outside of developments within the Soviet Union, and he departed Russia for Prague in 1920. There he was destined to play an influential role in launching the Prague Circle, breeding ground of structuralism in linguistics.[32]

Jakobson never quite shed his formalist skin, and his emergence as an interwar member of the Czech structuralist community highlighted the existence of a subtle divide. On the one side of an undeclared differentiation stood those, led by Jakobson, who adhered to an unrepentant formalism outfitted with the categories of Saussurean linguistics. Others, with Jan Mukarovsky their most able representative, cultivated an awareness of the linguistic sign that went beyond formalism in its balanced appreciation of form and reality, style and culture, art and history, grounded in a sense of the social context of literature that had significant resonance with the work of Bakhtin.

This Jakobson/Mukarovsky contrast lay inert in the face of the Prague School's common vocabulary, rooted in the formalist concept of "defamiliarization" and the peculiarly Czech notion of "the dominant." Defamiliarization guided critics to acknowledge the material process of language which, in works of art, estranges and undermines conventional sign systems, thereby opening up a historically and constantly changing set of perceptions and transformations of consciousness. Within this artistic permanent revolution,[33] Prague aesthetics stressed the critical importance of the structural unity of texts, which it saw focused through the dominant, a particular level of the literary work that exercised a determining or deforming influence, drawing all other levels into its own orbit. Finally, Jakobson pioneered the study of phonology, which focused on the physiology of signifying language and thus broke from phonetics in its stress on the distinctive "negatively" differentiating sounds of language. Phonology was regarded as the great achievement of Czech structural linguistics in the late 1920s and 1930s, and Jakobson's contribution to this area no doubt clothed his aesthetics in an authority that must have muffled disagreements within the Prague Circle and understated the fundamental separation of his orientation from that of Mukarovsky.[34] But once loosed from the Prague linguistic community by his World War II Scandinavian exile and eventual migration to America, Jakobson's rigidly formalistic and phonologically revised Saussureanism came to the fore in a series of literary pronouncements, masked by linguistic "scientism."[35]

In the process what was lost was Mukarovsky's view of literature as a set of social signs, his liberation of literary criticism from the fetishism of form, and his insistence that aesthetics strive to recover an appreciation of the social contexts and meanings of literary production.[36] Instead, Jakobson, whose American critical theory came to reside in the aggressive reduction of poetry to a linguistic dominant, retreated into Saussurean categorizations and distinctions. The medium *was* the message: poetry and literature were, at base, a play with language; and such a play was as little referential as possible. In the words of Merquior, Jakobson had contributed immeasurably to the rise of a literary formalistic structuralism in which "the first commandment of criticism became: never treat literature as if it were about anything except language."[37] It was but a short step to take the logic behind such a commandment—the independence of the sign—and universalize and canonize it in an interpretive movement known as *structuralism*.

▶   ***Interpretive Promiscuity and the***
Birth of Structuralism

Structuralism developed out of the merger of Saussurean-Jakobsonian linguistics and the social anthropology of Claude Lévi-Strauss. This coming together of specific interpretive systems took place in New York, when Jakobson and Lévi-Strauss found themselves at the New School for Social Research during the dislocations of World War II. Central to the making of structuralism was what Perry Anderson has referred to as the *"exorbitation of language,"* and the launching of this interpretive innovation took place appropriately in the pages of *Word*, an authoritative linguistics journal, under the commanding title "Structural analysis in linguistics and anthropology." The new structuralism would prove ambitious beyond prediction and, with its maturing, would entice and cajole whole realms of contemporary thought into joining its intellectual cause.[38]

Members of the Prague Circle, in congealing linguistics and aesthetics in a specific articulation of literary theory, remained within Saussurean boundaries, albeit ones they stretched a little. As Lévi-Strauss abolished such boundaries in an interpretive promiscuity, universalizing the Saussurean conception of the system or structure of *langue* through his insistence that *all* human systems, with communication at their core, were subject to the same operative structural laws, structuralism was launched as theory writ large. Along the way the reification of language was assured, Lévi-Strauss being quick to comment that "the real question is the question of language."[39]

Structuralism's beginnings, and their relation to language, thus represented an important shift and a fundamental movement toward aestheticism. In universalizing Saussurean premises about *langue*, imposing them on economies, kinship systems, and exchange relations within "primitive" societies, Lévi-Strauss forced language out of the confines within which Saussure himself willingly placed it, literally initiating an interpretive moment in which any and all signifiers floated free of the referential constraints of material moorings. Saussure had warned of the folly of this very project, acknowledging that the arbitrary, nonreferential nature of the relationship of signifier and signified within language was unique. Any analysis of human systems in which value figured, however conceived, must, according to Saussure, be developed in ways essentially different than those employed in linguistics. Precisely because value is historically rooted and materially grounded, it inevitably obliterated the distinction between synchrony and diachrony that Saussurean linguistics proclaimed:

> For a science concerned with values the distinction is a practical necessity and sometimes an absolute one. In these fields scholars cannot organize their research rigorously without . . . making a distinction between the system of values per se and the same values as they relate to time. This distinction has to be heeded by the linguist above all others for language is a system of pure values which are determined by nothing except the momentary arrangement of its terms. A value—so long as it is somehow rooted in things and in their natural relations, as happens with economics (the value of a plot of ground, for instance, is related to its productivity)—can to some extent be traced in time if we remember that it depends at each moment upon a system of co-existing values. Its link with things gives it, perforce, a natural basis, and the judgments that we base on such values are therefore never completely arbitrary; their variability is limited. But we have just seen that natural data have no place in linguistics.[40]

Lévi-Strauss's structuralism was able to race past this recognition of the material world because his fixation on the scientific explication of structure was a mere facade obscuring an idealist commitment to the primacy of the mind.

At a 1953 conference of anthropologists and linguists, Lévi-Strauss declared: "we have not been sufficiently aware of the fact that *both* language and culture are the product of activities which are basically similar. I am now referring to this uninvited guest which has been seated during this Conference beside us, and which is *the human mind*."[41] Regardless of the "empirical" focus of his investigations, Lévi-Strauss has always been concerned primarily with revelation of the mind's penchant for orchestration: structuralism, in its Lévi-Straussian origins, is a *psycho*logical ethnology covering "reality with several grids of classification."[42]

For all his antagonism to metaphysics, Lévi-Strauss's structural anthropology, proceeding from a particular view of language's privileged and tyrannizing stature, is thus strikingly metaphysical. "Language, an unreflecting totalization," declares Lévi-Strauss in *The Savage Mind,* "is human reason which has its reasons and of which man knows nothing."[43] This kind of strident assertion of language's absoluteness sanctioned an intrepid relativism. His study of totemism rises and falls on the aggressive insistence that anthropology is nothing more than the assertion of "a homology of structure between human thought in action and the human object to which it is applied . . . between method and reality."[44] It does not matter if his interpretation of myth is right or wrong, so long as his pursuit of "drawing up an inventory of mental patterns," of reducing "apparently arbitrary data to some kind of order," and attaining "a level at which a kind of necessity becomes apparent" is fullfilled:

> What does it matter? For if the final aim of anthropology is to contribute to a better knowledge of objectified thought and its mechanisms, it is in the last resort immaterial whether in this book the thought processes of the South American Indians take shape through the medium of my thought, or whether mine take place throught the medium of theirs. What matters is that the human mind, regardless of the identity of those who happen to be giving it expression, should display an increasingly intelligible structure as a result of the doubly reflexive forward movement of two thought processes acting one upon the other, either of which can in turn provide the spark or tinder whose conjunction will shed light on both.[45]

Small wonder that Lévi-Straussian structuralism echoes a curiously nonchalant concern with history, "that irreducible contingency without which necessity would be inconceivable." History, after all, "may lead to anything, provided you get out of it." Nor is it at all surprising that explanation is so little valued within a structuralist project that begins, in Lévi-Strauss's words, by submitting itself to "the powerful inanity of events."[46]

In the structuralist end, according to Edward Said's perception, these features of the Lévi-Straussian agenda are pushed in worrying directions. One example will suffice: Lévi-Strauss's reading of kinship relations as put forward in an article, "Language and the Analysis of Social Laws." He commences with the argument that "language is a phenomenon fully qualified to satisfy the demands of mathematicians" for scientific analysis since it "goes back a considerable distance and furnishes long enough runs," making it "difficult to see why certain linguistic problems could not be solved by modern calculating machines." Then, by treating marriage regulations and kinship systems as a kind of language, in which communication is taking place among groups and individuals, Lévi-Strauss proposes "that the mediating factor . . . should be the *women of the group,* who are *circulated* between classes, lineages, or families, in place of the *words of the group,* which are *circulated* between individuals." Of course the women are not merely signs, "for words do not speak, while women do; as producers of signs, women can never be reduced to the status of symbols or tokens." Nevertheless, women "may afford us a workable image of the type of relationships that could have existed at a very early period in the development of language, between human beings and their words."[47] To pose the problem of kinship in this way is to reduce life to language, to obliterate the relations of power, exploitation, and inequality that order, not only gender relations, but human history itself. It is to close the interpretive circle in a rather perverse way, for surely the question that needs asking, even granting all of Lévi-Strauss's assumptions, is "what happened that necessitated the utilization of one part of humanity as a sign for another?" The effacement of that kind of questioning, Said points out, is the culmination of structuralism's removal of "the authority of a privileged Origin that commands, guarantees, and perpetuates meaning." The beginnings of structuralism, intimately related to the acceptance of "a dominantly linguistic apprehension of reality," thus mark a critical conjuncture, in which linguistics and social science merged in a descent into discourse.[48]

▶ **Barthes and the Political Descent of Discourse**
Structuralism's concerns and assumptions thrived in many quarters not all that attentive to Lévi-Strauss. Semiotics emerged as a virtual captive of structuralist method. Pioneered by the American philosopher Charles Sanders Peirce, who wrote before Saussure and differentiated himself from the Swiss linguist in his examination of the sign's representational qualities, its subjective content, and the capacity of the signified to generate a series of meanings, semiotics also drew heavily on the Prague Circle's understanding of "defamiliarization" and was developed in part by Jakobson. Its impact would be felt most acutely in media studies and film criticism, although literary texts, too, would be scrutinized with a semiotic gaze.[49] If semiotics was truly internationalist in its origins and impact, Paris was its most congenial stomping grounds, a locale where the whirl of theoretical innovation proceeded with a dizzying pace and unanticipated, sometimes shockingly abrupt, conceptual and political realignments. In the person of Roland Barthes, the process of post–World War II structuralism ran its course, exposing the best and the worst that discourse had to offer.

Structuralism's political vocabulary in the 1950s and early 1960s was by no means hostile to Marxism.[50] Volosinov had argued:

> The ruling class strives to impart a supraclass, eternal character to the ideological sign, to extinguish or drive inward the struggle between social value judgements which occurs in it, to make the sign unaccentual. In actual fact, each living ideological sign has two faces, like Janus. Any current curse word can become a word of praise, any current truth must inevitably sound to many people as the greatest lie. This inner dialectical quality of the sign comes out

fully in the open only in times of social crisis or revolutionary change.[51]

This was, in some ways, exactly what Barthes was taking pains to explore and reveal in his writing of the late 1950s, most emphatically in *Mythologies* but also, no doubt, in his association with the heretical pseudo-Marxist journal *Arguments*. His structuralism was a semiological mode of analysis of cultural artifacts that was grounded loosely and eclectically in the methods of contemporary linguistics.[52] Convinced that language was a boundary, style the mark of individuality, and writing an act of historical choice and solidarity, Barthes's early project was one of historicizing literature and exposing the way in which the language of myth was nothing more than the vocabulary of ideology, an excising of historical reality and its ever-present modes of domination.[53]

Mythologies stands as something of the semiological political exception proving the rule of structuralist aestheticism. It subjected myth to a relentless debunking, cutting away the luxuriant foliage of ideology to reveal the stark class purpose of the denial of history through the manipulative substitutionism of prettifying essences:

> And just as bourgeois ideology is defined by the abandonment of the name "bourgeois," myth is constituted by the loss of the historical quality of things: in it, things lose the memory that they once were made. The world enters language as a dialectical relation between activities, between human actions; it comes out of myth as a harmonious display of essences. A conjuring trick has taken place; it has turned reality inside out, it has emptied it of history and has filled it with nature, it has removed from things their human meaning so as to make them signify a human insignificance. The function of myth is to empty reality: it is, literally, a ceaseless flowing out, a haemorrhage, or perhaps an evaporation, in short a perceptible absence. . . . Myth deprives the object of which it speaks of all History. . . . We can see all the disturbing things which this felicitous figure removes from sight: both determinism and freedom. Nothing is produced, nothing is chosen: all one has to do is possess these new objects from which all soiling trace of origin or choice has been removed.

For Barthes, then, the only language that could not be reduced to mythology was the language of labor, of production, through which "man speaks in order to transform reality and no longer to preserve it as an image."[54]

This was a curiously voluntarist reading of language's capacities to step resolutely outside of the determinations of class relations, conveniently innocent of the extent to which producerism, as an ideology, was capable of masking class antagonisms at particular historical stages of development.[55] Along with Barthes's rather wooden posturing concerning the right's monopoly on myth, this kind of blind spot undercut the analytic power of *Mythologies*, leading J. G. Merquior to claim that the Barthes of this period "breathes the air of the *bien-pensant* left . . . a blinkered believer in the most conventional revolutionary socialism. . . . [feeding] on the unexamined assumptions of glib radical sociology."[56]

Be that as it may, Barthes's kind of social criticism was rare in the Parisian structuralist circles of the late 1950s and has been resisted ever since. Frank Lentricchia can perhaps be forgiven his enthusiasms:

> The immense force of [Barthes's] point is perhaps matched only by the near universality with which it has been resisted in the contemporary critical theory community. By reminding us of the artificiality and undeniably arbitrary status of semiological systems—and we can add to his examples the discourse of literature and literary critics—Barthes reminds us not only of their unnatural status (they are modes of discourse given to us neither by God nor by the nature of things) but also of the much-avoided (because uncomfortable) corollary that these systems are put into operation, put into force, *by force*. Vast, diffuse, and nearly anonymous "deciding groups," establishments of power, in so elaborating the perimeters and structures of a language, define our ways of thinking and behaving and our norms of value: the individual has no say, and neither does that sentimental construction called "the people." After Barthes, the various formalist notions of a free and unconstrained self, and of a free, autonomous literary language, are revealed for what they are: the fantasies of the repressed and . . . the prized ideals of bourgeois culture.[57]

Mixed unmistakably with a politics of refusal/resistance, however, were abundant signs of incorporation within the aestheticism of structuralism's project. How else could Barthes propose that "the best weapon against myth is perhaps to mythify it in its turn, and to produce an artificial myth: and this reconstituted myth will in fact be a mythology? Since myth robs language of something, why not rob myth? All that is needed is to use it as the departure point for a third semiological chain, to take its signification as the first term of a second myth." A passage such as this indicated how imprisoned Barthes was in the categories and analytic modes of structuralism as an interpretive movement, how the reification of language culminated in a rarefied politics. As a program for the materialist transformation of class relations and the undermining of bourgeois ideology—by Barthes's own account, the only possible means of challenging myth—it left much to be desired.[58]

Barthes's effectiveness, indeed celebrity-like status, as a critic of French popular fetishes in the mid-1950s (striptease, wrestling, steak and chips) lay in his politicization of the "popular." He decoded the commonplace with unusual sensitivity to relations of authority and their need to be cloaked in acceptability. His semiology bore all the formalistic marks of Saussurean "science," but he refused the true believer's closure and opted instead for attending to both the synchronic and diachronic dimensions of the language of myth:

> Semiology is a science of forms, since it studies significations apart from their content. I should like to say one word about the necessity and limits of such a formal science. . . . It may well be that on the plane of "life," there is but a totality where structures and forms cannot be separated. But science has no use for the ineffable: it must speak about "life" if it wants to transform it. . . . Less terrorized by the specter of "formalism," historical criticism might have been less sterile; it would have understood that the specific study of forms does not in any way contradict the necessary principles of totality and History. . . . The danger, on the contrary, is to consider forms as ambiguous objects, half form and half substance, to endow form with a substance of form. . . . Semiology, once its limits are settled, is not a metaphysical trap: it is a science among others, necessary but not sufficient. The important thing is to see that the unity of an explanation cannot be based on the amputation of one or other of its approaches, but, as Engels said, on the dialectical coordination of the particular sciences it makes use of. This is the case with mythology: it is a part both of semiology inasmuch as it is a formal science, and of ideology inasmuch as it is a historical science: it studies ideas-in-form.

This entry of life/history/transformation into the structuralist agenda was realized, ultimately, in Barthes's politicized semiology, exemplified in his famous reading of the imperialistic imagery and mythology of a *Paris-Match* cover adorned with the photograph of a Negro in French uniform saluting the tricolor.[59] But the political moment of semiological discourse was not to last.

There is some controversy dating the transformation of Barthes and locating the timing of his movement away from a politicized semiology. One reason for this is his theoretical looseness and, in spite of rigorous assertions to the contrary, his eclectic deployment of Saussurean categories. As Merquoir and the French semiologist Georges Mounin have pointed out, Barthes's semiological texts rarely dealt with Saussurean signs, as arbitrary coded representations, but rather focused on symbols (in which the relation between signifier and signified is natural) or indices (perceptible facts indicating something not readily grasped).[60]

Whatever the conceptual confusion, the early 1960s saw a subtle shifting of Barthesian concern away from writing as an act of political engagement and politics as a matter of unmasking the exploitations and oppressions of class structure and colonialism. Not surprisingly, the drift took a linguistic turn: Barthes's writings increasingly stressed the structured determinations of language; his politics of demystifying authority's rationalizing and legitimating mythologies gave way before the new imperative of invoking and interrogating the codes of a text's unfolding structure.[61]

Within this movement, which saw Barthes's texts alternate between the literary (Racine and Balzac) and the cultural (clothing as sign, fashion as *written* meaning), Lévi-Strauss figures centrally. He apparently advised Barthes in a way that prompted the semiological detour into fashion that would result in *Système de la Mode* (1967). And in *Critique et Vérité* (1966) Barthes voiced a repudiation of his earlier historicist project in words that are reminiscent of Lévi-Strauss's mythologies rather than his own:

> Thus begins, at the heart of the critical work, the dialogue of two histories and two subjectivities, the author's and the critic's. But this dialogue is egoistically shifted toward the present: criticism is not an homage to the truth of the past or to the truth of "others"—it is a construction of the intelligibility of our own time.[62]

This fit easily and self-consciously with an increasing Barthesian fixation on authorship. As early as 1960 he was bemoaning the hybridization of the author-writer, which forcibly blurred the priestly author and the clerical writer in an institutionalization of subjectivity. By 1968 he had proclaimed the death of the author.[63]

Such views coincided with the Barthesian proclamation of high structuralism in *S/Z* (1970), his "scientific, textual analysis" of Balzac's novella *Sarrasine*. Breaking up the text into "galaxies of signifiers," Barthes also constructs a grid of classificatory codes: thirty pages of art give rise to some two hundred pages of digressive "science." Waging war against a strawman-like realism with the arsenal of "a liberating theory of the Signifier" informed by a crude Freudianism reduced to the castration complex, *S/Z* soars to new heights of structuralist potency.[64] What is most telling, for our purposes, however, is Barthes's metaphorical mixing of movements, for this ultimate statement of structuralism is full of the seeds of its own opposition.

Prefacing this rigidly coded reading of Balzac is a downplaying of the individuality of texts and an endorsement of their "play," governed by "the infinite paradigm of difference." The back cover of *S/Z* hails the "pluralization of criticism."[65] From the vantage of hindsight, it is now all too easy to see these pronouncements as the signs of a structuralism in disarray, a gesture toward the newly consolidating challenge of deconstruction associated with the rising star of Derrida and the *Tel Quel* group with which Barthes had long interacted. Barthes helped to ignite the implosion of theory; he would prove to be one of its most tragic casualties.

For this sorry end, Barthes had no one to blame but himself. In his writings in the mid-to-late 1970s he distanced himself willfully from all that he had been a part of before, openly (and perhaps honestly) deflating his linguistic competence, redefining semiology as concerned primarily with "the impurity of language," and championing a Nietzschean hedonism that took potshots at the left and Marxism. Overtaken by a libertine narcissism, he oscillated between self-promotion and literary introspection, which he elevated to a guide for the kind of proper reading that could elicit pleasurable (euphoric and comfortable) and blissful (unsettling of cultural expectations) texts.[66]

The supreme irony was that Barthes's peculiar descent ended up pitting *discourse* against language. Overturning with a vengeance all of his structuralist thought of the mid-to-late 1960s, Barthes railed against the totalitarian stranglehold of language, which he categorized as *"fascist"*! Only the voice of the self, or discourse, could redeem words, but writing itself then forcibly returned discourse to the terrain of language and its relentless determinations. The sign was christened with an increasingly moral virtue, its arbitrary, nonreferential essence secured by the resolute insistence that the signifier floated free of the signified: recognizing signs wherever they appeared and refusing to mistake them for natural phenomena became, for Barthes, the fundamental ethical problem of our time. As the world, site of a never-ending proliferation and naturalization of signs, was weighted down with meaning, the desire to make everything signify and affirm meaning paradoxically subverted meaning. Meaning was thus obliterated for Barthes. It took on the status of a force to be conquered rather than received, an intrusion of extratextuality when each text had to be seen intertextually. Barthes argued that as "a mirror of other texts, both past and future, literary semiosis—the process of literary sign-making and signifying— was to be regarded as an *open* structure, a structure governed less by (deep) rules than by ever-missing elements: structure became a work in progress forever in thrall to an undetermined future." As Merquior, perhaps too quick to create a unity of the early and late Barthes, concludes: "In the end, Barthes made formalism speak the joyful idiom of libertinism; alas, all the bliss in it was merely the dark night of the blind sign, drifting away from the concerns of humanity."[67]

▶ *Structuralism, Idealist Marxism,*
and the Althusserian Interlude

As Barthes stumbled, then raced, down the path from structuralism to poststructuralism, critical theory propelled by Saussurean linguistics inched increasingly close to a rapprochement with Nietzsche. There were, of course, structuralist spheres immune from such a trajectory, but they would be, predictably, those realms where language had not commanded the analytic heights.

Althusser's structuralist Marxism, for instance, never, for all of its sins, plummeted to the depths of Barthes's self-indulgences. In the implosion of theory it would be but one iconoclastic fragment among many, distinctive in its gesture toward rather than avoidance of "structural causality" and notable for its homage to Marx and Lenin.[68]

In this Althusserian structural Marxist interlude there was an awkward tension that simultaneously separated this analytic fragment out from the trajectory of discourse-oriented thought and linked it tenuously to the new Parisian-based theoretical carnival. This tension turned on the fundamental Althusserian understanding of ideology, a process superficially not unrelated to the increasing theoretical focus on discourse. Althusser struggled to reconcile the resolutely *negative* reading of ideology that permeated Marx's own writings with the more *positive* assessment of ideological possibility in Lenin's understanding of the unfolding of the revolutionary class struggle.[69] For Marx, ideology was nothing less than concealment and mystification, the process whereby bourgeois society inverted the realities that lay submerged and obfuscated at its exploitative and oppressive economic foundations.[70] After Marx, however, many in the revolutionary tradition laid increasing emphasis on the ways in which ideology was both the exercise of class domination *and* class resistance. By the time of Lenin, this conceptual slippage had solidified to the point that ideology was virtually equatable with the political consciousness of the great contending classes: bourgeois ideology sustained capitalist relations and authority; proletarian or socialist ideology was a potent weapon in the class struggle, a necessary, if not sufficient, condition for the realization of working-class power. Althusser combined aspects of these conceptions of ideology, distinguishing a theory of ideology *in general*, in which ideology secures social cohesion, from a theory of *particular* ideologies, in which, through the process of overdetermination, the general is superseded by the particular class needs of domination.[71]

The Althusserian understanding of ideology was sufficiently embedded in two contradictory camps—orthodox Marxism and its conception of materialism and determination versus discourse and its groping toward the discursive nature of construction (heavily influenced by Lacan, to be discussed below)—that it ended up uneasily astride an uncomfortable theoretical fence. On the one hand, the Althusserian reading of ideology was unambiguously rooted in a conception of class "interests" that discourse theory would come to reject as "fictioned." On the other hand, in its presentation of ideology as "a representation of the imaginary relationship of individuals to their real conditions of existence," Althusserianism adopted the language of discourse and gravitated toward its aestheticism in passages such as this:

> the forms of the "imaginary" cannot arise spontaneously from the subject (that would convert recognition into *imagination* and restore the constitutive subject), equally, they cannot be given by "reality" (that would restore a simple reflection theory). The forms of the imaginary should, if these positions were to be avoided, have the status of *significations*, representations which are reducible neither to a represented which is beyond them, nor to an origin in a subject, but which are effects of the action of means of representation.[72]

The striking ambivalence of the Althusserian interlude was resolved in what E. P. Thompson and Norman Geras dubbed "the final idealism."[73] Ideology, weighted down with a discourse-denied "interest," nevertheless was adapted to the dictates of reified language by stripping it of any relationship to the political practice of the working class. Althusser divorced ideology from material life, declaring it autonomous from class formations and struggles. What was positive in ideology was its development as science, as valid knowledge, a process dependent upon the Althusserian "realization" that the "only interests at work in the development of knowledge are interests internal to knowledge." As Geras concluded, "When knowledge celebrates its autonomy, the philosophers celebrate their dominance."[74]

In his quest to uncover "the logic of the conditions of the production of knowledges, whether they belong to the history of a branch of still ideological knowledge, or to a branch of knowledge attempting to constitute itself as a science or already established as a science," Althusser gravitated instinctually toward the major figure who confirmed at important levels his conception of knowledge, Michel Foucault. There he found *a* history congruent with his own premises, a construction of "*the concept of history*" that broke loose of a "content" empirically weighted down with "the vacuity of events." Not entirely of discourse, the Althusserian interlude was nevertheless captivated by its possibilities.[75]

▶ *Foucault and the Discourse of Power*

Foucault was something of an aestheticist Judas, given to denying his Christ in passionate outbursts of vehement separation: "in France, certain half-witted 'commentators' persist in labelling me a 'structuralist.' I have been unable to get it into their tiny minds that I have used none of the methods, concepts, or key terms that characterize structural analysis."[76] Foucault's distancing himself from structuralism is useful to recognize, not the least because he never concerned himself seriously with modern linguistics, opting instead for conscious identification with a Nietzschean lineage. Yet he protests too much. As Megill argues, Foucault's writings of the 1960s encounter structuralism in diverse ways and, for our purposes, most especially in the preoccupation with language that, in his 1970s publications, focuses resolutely on the relationship of power and discourse.[77] As the perfect embodiment of a structuralist marriage of heaven and hell, what Merquior refers to as an unholy alliance of formalism and Nietzsche, Foucault was well suited to follow the implosion of theory in the direction of poststructuralism.[78]

Foucault's work evolved from a focus on experience *itself*, evidenced in the phenomenological premises of *History of Madness* (1961) and *Birth of the Clinic* (1963), to an overt repudiation of the possibility and necessity of grasping "the thing itself." Indeed, there is no more pristine instance of the movement into the determination of discourse than the Foucault of the period 1961–1969, his *Archaeology of Knowledge* (1969) standing as an unashamed statement of authorial immersion in language, conceived as primary and decisive:

> There can be no question of interpreting discourse with a view to writing a history of the referent. . . . What, in short, we wish to do is to dispense with "things.". . . I would like to show that discourse is not a slender surface of contact, or confrontation, between a reality and a language (*langue*) the intrication of a lexicon and an experience; I would like to show with precise examples that in analysing discourses themselves one sees the loosening of the embrace, apparently so tight, of words and things, and the emergence of a group of rules proper to discursive practices. These rules define not the dumb existence of a reality, nor the canonical use of a vocabulary, but the ordering of objects. . . . practices that systematically form the objects of which they speak.[79]

Or, more bluntly:

> Expressing their thoughts in words of which they are not the masters, enclosing them in verbal forms whose historical dimensions they are unaware of, men believe that their speech is their servant

> and do not realize that they are submitting themselves to its de-
> mands. The grammatical arrangements of a language are the *a priori*
> of what can be expressed in it.[80]

The gulf separating the Foucault of *The Birth of the Clinic* from the
Foucault of *The Archaeology* is superficially obvious in the texts's very
beginnings, the former opening with a statement on "Spaces and
Classes" (objectified/materialistic), the latter introduced by "The Uni-
ties of Discourse," an aestheticized interrogation of "the statement/
event."

This suppression of the subject was in fact not as dramatic a rupture
as, at first glance, it appeared. For Foucault, at his phenomenological
best, never paid all that much attention to experience as social context,
consciously dwelling instead on the "attitudinal codes towards insan-
ity, systems of cognitive a prioris, regimes of punishment and sexual
ethics in a *formalist vein*, invariably choosing 'immanent analysis'
against more textual approaches."[81] As Foucault concluded in *The Birth
of the Clinic*, "What counts in the things said by men is not so much
what they may have thought or the extent to which these things represent their thoughts, as that which systematizes them from the outset,
thus making them endlessly accessible to new discourses and open to
the task of transforming them."[82]

What therefore marks the movement of Foucault is the increasingly
self-conscious attempt to differentiate language, as an experience recognizing itself as the world, and discourse, a representational will-to-
power that exercised dominance in periods/spheres of the past and
holds forth radical activist possibilities in the present and future. In the
shift from his pseudo-historical archaeologies to his politico-moral ge-
nealogies, Foucault adopts a Barthesian politics of countering myth
with myth, of making, as Edward Said has pointed out, "discourse
visible not as a historical task but as a political one":

> The longer I continue, the more it seems to me that the formation of
> discourses and the genealogy of knowledge need to be analysed, not
> in terms of types of consciousness, modes of perception and forms
> of ideology, but in terms of tactics and strategies of power. Tactics
> and strategies deployed through implantations, distributions, de-
> marcations, control of territories, and organisations of domains
> which could well make up a sort of geopolitics.[83]

Archaeology, in which discourse is conceived broadly, aims at revealing
how discourse overdetermines the social order and governs the production of culture; genealogy preserves much of the archaeological method
but narrows the understanding of discourse and focuses the purpose of

Foucault's project in a politics of Nietzschean rejection that betrays little interest in causation.

With the publication of *Discipline and Punish* (1975) Foucault's genealogical drift and its implications were apparent. Engaged in "histories" that he now frankly confessed were "fictioned," Foucault, Nietzsche-like, Lévi-Strauss—like, disclaimed any attempt to achieve objective historical knowledge. Instead, "One 'fictions' history on the basis of a political reality that makes it true, one 'fictions' a politics not yet in existence on the basis of an historical truth."[84] His study of the birth of the prison was proclaimed "a correlative history of the modern soul and of a new power to judge; a genealogy of the present scientifico-legal complex from which the power to punish derives its bases, justifications and rules, from which it extends its effects and by which it masks its exorbitant singularity."[85]

As attractive as this exposure of power's rawness and its merger in past/present is to radical sensibilities, there remain many problems. Most relate to Foucault's entrapment, self-confessed, within discourse, the tyrannical formalism that continues, throughout his phenomenological, archaeological, and genealogical periods, to remove the subject and obliterate human agency in history.[86] "One remains within the dimension of discourse," he confessed in *The Archaeology of Knowledge*, a confinement exposed most illuminatingly in the perverse reductionism of the Foucauldian account of nineteenth-century parricide, *I, Pierre Rivière, having slaughtered my mother, my sister, and my brother. . . .* There an ensemble of social relations, caught up in the intense materialism of production and reproduction, ideology and state power, is collapsed into "a strange contest, a confrontation, a power relation, a battle among discourses and through discourses."[87]

What *Pierre Rivière* reveals is Foucault's anarchistic hostility to all order and his refusal to conceive a counter-order, a point on which he has been forcefully challenged by Noam Chomsky.[88] This relates directly to his conception of power and knowledge as constructed discursively, flowing out of and penetrating all realms. Given this "understanding" of power's pervasiveness and the resulting refusal of any center of power, it is apparent that all theory that attempts to locate such force is suspect. It is but a small step, after such premises have been accepted, to a kind of Foucauldian interpretive nihilism: "Reject all theory and all forms of general discourse," he proclaimed in 1971. "This need for theory is still part of the system we reject."[89] The consequence of this kind of absolutism is the avoidance of explanation in general and hostility to one theoretical form, historical materialism, in particular. Both relentless critics of Foucault, such as Merquior, and cautious advocates, such as Edward Said, have pointed to the glaring holes this leaves in the successive texts of radical archaeology/genealogy. Attentive to power, Foucault's discourse is nevertheless "passive and sterile" on critical questions of "how and why power is gained, used, and held on to." Privileging the exercise of power and its strategic dissemination, Foucault understates the locales of power (be they class, gender, or nation state) and bypasses the historically situated motive forces that ground the will to power in concrete acquisitions, conquests, and needs.[90]

In denying the concreteness of the referent and rejecting the notion that there is a "reality" that precedes language and allows entry to a prediscursive "explanation" of historical statements and events, Foucault's descent into a discourse of power was relentless. "Wherever Foucault looks," comments Hayden White, "he finds nothing but discourse; and wherever discourse arises, he finds a struggle between those groups which claim the 'right' to discourse and those which are denied the right to their own discourse."[91]

Devoid of subject and strategic direction, Foucault's discourses offer no exit from the dominations and subjugations of successive regimes of power. They construct a history without a center, beyond meaning save that of the constant motion of the revolving door in which all of humanity is forever trapped in the repetitive linkage of discourse/power/knowledge. Within the shifting possibilities of these forces, always locked in the prison-house of language, Foucault struck his blows at structuralism, insisting that "what is at stake in discourse is not only the signified but who speaks it and under what conditions."[92] Yet he remained a captive of formalism, his authorial hands self-bound by his insistence on the structured determinations of language. His archaeologies/genealogies were one fragment in the implosion of theory that ushered in the age of poststructuralism, implying but never being capable of delivering a history of subjectivity/agency/activity, within which power was undoubtedly lived. Small wonder that another fragment would be the Lacanian quest for what had simultaneously been summoned and suppressed in the Foucauldian *oeuvre*: the subject.

▶   *Poststructuralism's Psychoanalytic Moment*

Linguistic structuralism entered psychoanalysis, albeit awkwardly and incompletely, with the personage of Jacques Lacan. High priest of a Parisian cult that touched most of the major figures of structuralism and poststructuralism (Foucault, Althusser, Barthes, and Derrida attended his lectures), Lacan invaded semiotic, literary, film, and feminist criticism and has arguably been the most influential psychotheorist since Jung if not Freud.[93] Juliet Flower MacCannell concludes that Lacan is "much more effective as a plague than Freud ever was, . . . [he] is everywhere and nowhere, like a contagion."[94]

Lacan "Saussureanized" psychoanalysis, marching to the drum of structuralist dictate with his marketing—complete with the two-minute session—of the decree that the unconscious was structured like a language. "It is our task to demonstrate that these concepts assume their full sense only when oriented in the domain of Language, only when ordered in relation to the function of the Word," he declared, adding that "the unconscious is the discourse of the other . . . the symptom resolves itself entirely in a Language analysis, because the symptom itself is structured like a Language, because the symptom is a Language from which the Word must be liberated."[95]

Lacanian thought turned on the signifier, and its divorce from the real: the signifier "father" bore no relation to actual paternal entities, nor did the supporting signifying "phallus." While language was not the only source of signifiers—which could be generated by a Barthesian plethora of conventions, rituals, ceremonies, and fetishes—it was the privileged point at which signification was mediated:

> Symbols . . . envelop the life of man in a network so total that they join together, before he comes into the world, those who are going to engender him "by flesh and blood"; so total that they give the words that will make him faithful or renegade, the law of the acts that will follow him right to the very place where he *is* not yet and even beyond his death; and so total that through them his end finds its meaning in the last judgement, where the Word absolves his being or condemns it.[96]

Small wonder, then, that for Lacan the Symbolic Order assumed ultimate significance as a discourse of the unconscious in which powerful systems transcend, predate, and preorder human subjectivity. Men and women are less makers and masters of symbols than they are the servants of the symbolic, a slippery slope on which all clarity of meaning fades and evaporates.[97] "The meaning of meaning in *my* practice," stated Lacan, "can be grasped in the fact that it runs away: in the sense of something leaking from a barrel, not in the sense of 'making tracks.' It is because it runs away (in the barrel sense) that a discourse assumes a meaning, in other words: by virtue of the fact that its effects are impossible to calculate."[98]

Because of the illusiveness and impenetrability of the symbolic, Lacan's language-structured unconscious exhibits an "incessant sliding of the signified *under* the signifier."[99] As countless critics have pointed out, this assertion of the primacy of the signifier is nothing less that a violent break with Saussurean principles, necessitated by the fundamental unlanguage-like character of the unconscious. Language is learned; the unconscious is not. The linguistic sign is arbitrary, unmotivated, and capable of conveying simple meaning; Freudian symbols are deeply the opposite. Finally, language is parochial and articulated within particular national cultures; the unconscious is universal.[100] Less a language than a linguistically influenced site, the Lacanian unconscious, as Merquior perceives, "invokes Saussure's structuralism yet has no structures—and therefore provided French theory with a powerful rationale for going post-structuralist."[101] This conditioned a particular relationship to history, with the purpose of Lacanian analysis being to restore the subject to a past that is not remembered, but rewritten or reconstructed. History, for Lacan, is never just *there*: it is "that present synthesis of the past," which forms "the centre of gravity of the subject."[102] Lacan thus articulated a qualified respect, highly abstracted and emphatically selective, for the importance of historical determinations.

Yet as a decidedly relativist strain within poststructuralism, Lacanian psychoanalysis degenerated into an endless and meaningless system of playing with words, a punning "carnival, a fad, a dazzling display of fireworks. Rockets went off in every direction. And the meaning evaporated." As his sympathetic and long-supporting advocate Catherine Clément reported:

> A day came when the puns became an end in themselves. . . . Rhetoric overwhelmed him to the point where it hindered his conceptual imagination. . . . And the more he lived as a "leader," the more polished his rhetoric became. From rhetoric he moved on to pure celebration, to compulsive word play—a logical trajectory. Language got the better of him.

The consequences were debilitating: "Lacan created monsters in the proper sense of the word: creatures turned away from their true function. Creatures of style."[103]

Lacan's "problem" was not that he had nothing to say, or that it was all always facade and banal. Nor was it that he identified with the pathologies he depicted, as some feminists suggest. Even less was it that he charted the terrain of the unconscious, rather than privileging the realm of overt struggle or the material unfolding of economic/class formations.[104] As MacCannell and Clement show, Lacan's insights into sexuality and the fundamental inequalities of the gender order are profound *and* profoundly radical. They force a decisive rupture from the psychoanalytic tradition's reliance upon "Nature" as an explanation of sexuality's differential hold over men, women, and children. Instead, with Lacan, the fragilities, complexities, and subjectivities of sexuality are basic processes of a constructed and historically formed unconscious. Unlike his most notable disciple, Julia Kristeva, Lacan never accepted the ultimate power of the word and its capacity to enclose human relations but instead sought to cure his patients and teach his students through a rejection of the absoluteness of the circle. Feminine sexuality and pleasure, for instance, is conceived in the Lacanian framework as potentiality, its repressions and inhibitions regarded as fundamental to the Symbolic Order.[105] There was, and is, much to learn from Lacan.

That has unfortunately been obscured in the appropriation and promotion of Lacan's poststructuralist surrender of signification to the mystifications of signifiers forever broken from any relation to reality. This overdetermined Lacan's fate, pitching him into the wild playfulness of discourse that produced some of the most unfathomable prose known in the annals of critical theory and that made words the prison-house of subjects ultimately detached from the real. The Lacanian rereading of Freud thus produced some odd pages:

> We therefore invariably rediscover our double reference to the Word and to Language. In order to liberate the subject's Word, we introduce him into the Language of his desire, that is, into the *primary Language*, in which, beyond what he tells us of himself, he is already talking to us unbeknownst to him, and in the symbols of the symptom in the first place. . . . The Word is in fact a gift of Language, and Language is not immaterial. It is a subtle body, but body it is. Words are trapped in all the corporeal images whch captivate the subject; they can make the hysteric pregnant, be identified with the object of *penis-neid*, represent the flood of urine of urethral ambition, or the retained faeces of avaricious *jouissance*.[106]

In Lacan the psychoanalytic implosion of poststructuralist theory re-imploded, in Catherine Clément's phrase "setting itself ablaze on a pyre of its own excrement."[107] "Words, that's all," continues Clément in another comment, "and all this theatre has become nothing but language."[108]

▶ *Poststructuralism's* **Lider Maximo:**
Derrida and Deconstruction

The history of ideas, however much intellectual historians would like to make it so, is never entirely divorced from the politics of the times within which it develops. Structuralism's implosion was no exception and, inasmuch as Paris was its post–World War II home, Parisian events and politics figured forcefully in the making of the poststructuralist avant-garde. Most importantly, the *gauchiste,* libertarian revolt of May 1968 rewrote the structuralist text. It was a moment of decisive importance in the remaking of a European left, exposing the sclerotic ossification of the Communist party and reformulating orthodoxies of tactics and strategies that had long been central to an understanding of how socialism would be made.[109] Within the structuralist milieu 1968 pushed Barthes into his hedonistic headiness and Foucault toward a sycophantic embrace of any and all rebelliousness that confirmed his own critique of power.[110]

"Structuralism is dead!" screamed the walls of the Sorbonne, and with Lévi-Strauss and Althusser silenced by an upheaval they could neither have predicted nor understood, classical Parisian theory stood at an obvious impasse. Eagleton alludes to the meaning of the moment:

> Post-structuralism was a product of that blend of euphoria and disillusionment, liberation and dissipation, carnival and catastrophe, which was 1968. Unable to break the structures of state power, post-structuralism found it possible instead to subvert the structures of language. . . . The student movement was flushed off the streets and driven underground into discourse. . . . the system had proved too powerful . . . and the "total" critique offered of it by a heavily Stalinized Marxism had been exposed as part of the problem, not the solution. All such total systematic thought was now suspect as terroristic: conceptual meaning itself, as opposed to libidinal gesture and anarchist spontaneity, was feared as repressive. . . . The only forms of political action now felt to be acceptable were of a local, diffused, strategic kind: work with prisoners and other marginalized social groups, particular projects in culture and education. The women's movement, hostile to the classical forms of left-wing organization, developed libertarian, "decentered" alternatives and in some quarters rejected systematic theory as male. For many post-structuralists, the worst error was to believe that such local projects and particular engagements should be brought together within an overall understanding of the working of monopoly capitalism, which could only be as oppressively "total" as the very system it opposed.[111]

Some, to be sure, resisted, but for the most part their politics collapsed into an uncritical Maoism, a short-lived flirtation with the dialectics of contradiction and cultural revolution that, as with the crowd gathered around the Parisian journal of poststructuralism *Tel Quel,* all too quickly degenerated into euphoria for mysticism and things American.[112] Jacques Lacan, with characteristic acerbity and ambiguity, delivered the ultimate message to a Vincennes student radical in 1969: "What you as a revolutionary aspire to is a master. You will have one."[113]

Indeed, the master had already arrived.[114] His name was Jacques Derrida, until the late 1960s a relatively undistinguished French philosopher who no doubt considered himself confined within the stasis of the Gaullist republic and structuralist orthodoxy. He made his debut far from the barricades and seminar rooms of Paris—in part no doubt because French academe had done its bit to repress him—choosing to launch himself from that bastion of liberty, the American university. In 1966 he appeared at a conference at Johns Hopkins and proclaimed the end of structuralism, of structure itself. His paper, "Structure, Sign and Play in the Discourse of the Human Sciences," opened with the statement, "We need to interpret interpretations more than to interpret things," and proceeded to "decenter" Western thought in ways that would eventually enrage other pillars of the poststructuralist community such as Foucault.[115]

As Peter Dews has recently suggested, the novelty of Derridean argument and its radical break with all previous discussion of interpretation is much overstated, Derrida's thought being anticipated, in some ways, within the hermeneutic tradition by Schleiermacher and others.[116] But for our purposes, it is undeniable that Derrida's writings promoted discourse to new heights of determination:

> It was necessary to begin thinking that there was no center, that the center could not be thought in the form of a present-being, that the center had no natural site, that it was not a fixed locus but a function, a sort of nonlocus in which an infinite number of sign-substitutions came into play. This was the moment when language invaded the universal problematic, the moment when, in the absence of center or origin, everything became discourse—provided we can agree on this word—that is to say, a system in which the central signified, the original or transcendental signified, is never absolutely present outside a system of differences. The absence of the transcendental signified extends the domain and the play of signification indefinitely.

Empiricism, oddly associated with the work of Lévi-Strauss, was of course castigated, and Derrida privileged thought and language in a way that sidestepped history—"a detour between two presences"—neatly: "the passage beyond philosophy does not consist in turning the page of philosophy (which usually amounts to philosophizing badly), but in continuing to read philosophers *in a certain way.*" The decentered world was one in which the play of signification was limitless, an endless circle of discourse's dependencies, which lie as an undeclared trace between the lines of all writing: "we can pronounce not a single destructive proposition which has not already had to slip into the form, the logic, and the implicit postulations of precisely what it seeks to contest." Meaning was understandably reduced to insignificance, a fleeting product of words or signifiers that inevitably shifted and were inherently unstable. What was critical, for Derrida, thus became the play itself: "Being must be conceived as presence or absence on the basis of the possibility of play and not the other way around." Derrida literally reveled in the loss of presence and origin, championing a Nietzschean ontology:

> Turned towards the lost or impossible presence of the absent origin, this structuralist thematic of broken immediacy is therefore the saddened, *negative,* nostalgic, guilty, Rousseauistic side of the thinking of play whose other side would be the Nietzschean *affirmation,* that is the joyous affirmation of the play of the world and of the innocence of becoming, the affirmation of a world of signs without fault, without truth, and without origin which is offered to an active interpretation. *This affirmation then determines the noncenter otherwise than as loss of the center.* And it plays without security. For there is a *sure* play: that which is limited to the *substitution* of *given* and *existing, present* pieces. In absolute chance, affirmation also surrenders itself to *genetic* indetermination, to the *seminal* adventure of the trace.[117]

Perry Anderson has seen in such passages the conception of the poststructuralist project, defined by the capsizing of structure into a subjectivism without a subject.[118]

One year later Derrida arrived with a vengeance, his works rolling off the presses in an avalanche of rhetorical skepticism. *Of Grammatology, Writing and Difference,* and *Speech and Phenomena* all appeared in 1967, Year I of the Derridean intellectual coup d'état. His arsenal was built around the differentiations of speech and writing; his aim, to depose the Western tradition's privileging of the former at the expense of the latter. The problem of language was nothing less than the supreme matter of investigation, having invaded "the global horizon of the most diverse researches and the most heterogeneous discourses." As a sign inflated above all others, language had captured humanity, necessitating that the "historico-metaphysical epoch *must* finally determine as language the totality of its problematic horizon." Escaping from the infinite play of language was now exposed as a blunt impossibility, the desire or attempt to do so a fantastic utopianism. What could be done was, through incessant attention to the course by which language had adventurously and willfully misled thought, which on specific levels therefore had no weight and meant nothing, push language toward its point of exhaustion, force it in the direction of "a new situation for speech, of its subordination within a structure of which it will no longer be the archon." Writing, for Derrida, thus assumed new stature, over and above exhausted and exhausting speech: "The constitution of a science or a philosophy of writing is a necessary and difficult task. . . . Thinking is what we already know we have not yet begun; measured against the shape of writing, it is *broached* only in the *episteme*."[119]

This, the Derridean grammatology, would still be walled in within the logocentrism of the Western tradition, but it reformulated the sign/word so as to capture its making as a reconstituted and complex, rather than solitary, presence.[120] Grammatology thus forced a confrontation with Saussure. Insistent that writing, traditionally conceived as "sign of a sign," is in fact not a supplementary adjunct to speech, but a series of stress points that resist reduction to a single-*voiced* truth, grammatology champions writing in a Nietzschean affirmation of play that stands as an overt repudiation of Saussure's suspicions and depictions of writing as a veil masking language in disguise. Derridean grammatology exposed the contradiction at the core of linguistic theory's elevation of speech and denigration of writing. Saussure's conception of the arbitrary nature of the sign, the denial that any *natural* relation existed between signifier and signified, a proposition that structured Lévi-Straussian anthropology and Barthesian literary/cultural criticism in specific ways, is regarded as curiously inconsistent with his prejudicial pampering of phonology, wherein signifier and signified are mystically bonded in a natural unity of sound and sense. Saussurean linguistics, premised on meaning's composition in difference, unravels logically in a problematic drift that Derrida locates within Saussure's desperate attempt to preserve speech as self-presence and reduce writing to a tyrannizing pathology.[121]

Writing is thus at the core of the grammatological project. Texts are its medium and its message, the destabilization of philosophical systems its aim. Striking out at the cherished mainstays of bourgeois philosophy, Derrida questions relentlessly the self-evidence of recurring binary oppositions (nature/culture, inside/outside, male/female, sensible/intelligible) and resists the quest for fixed grounds of reference. Deconstruction's project is to uncover the systematic incoherences within texts rather than to capture any unified meanings.[122] Ironically this often means that strict attention to a text, deference to its integrity and totality, is anathema to grammatology. For all the Derridean bravado of the exclamation that "there is nothing outside of the text," grammatology often proceeded by skirting the text, attending to its marginalia rather than to its meaning. As Jonathan Culler observes of Derrida's reading of Rousseau: "it omits most of the contents of every text it mentions and fails to identify a thematic unity or a distinctive meaning for any of Rousseau's writings." Those frustrated with the exercise have been predictably quick to dismiss this "degradation of meaning," attacking grammatology as "less a philosophy than the decadence of a philosophy." Leaving the world unapproached, Derrida is christened a "logomaniac," pronounced "a professional scribbler"; he proceeds through his "mantric rituals, rather as an indulgent grown-up might wait dumbly upon the whims of an autistic child."[123]

Such dismissive hostility to the early Derrida was understandable, but overstated and unnecessarily shrill. Year I of the Derridean coup, inaugurated on the ceremonial platform of Nietzschean aestheticism and running its course as part of structuralist theory's implosion and descent into discourse, was, to be sure, a year of living dangerously. Yet there was a radical kernel buried within grammatology, a fundamentally materialist and historicizing cry for the need to reexamine the way in which the Western tradition reconstitutes itself and perpetuates hierarchy. It can be argued that this is what Derrida meant with his comment "There is nothing outside of the text," which he proclaimed the "axial proposition" of grammatology.[124] Not the tyranny of intertextuality, then, but the ultimate determination of the historical moment, arises from the grammatological project.

That this endeavor *could* thus have been turned away from the margins of canonical texts and brought to bear on analyses of power and inequality is no doubt the reason that Derrida has been championed by some on the left as vigorously as he has been castigated by others. But the effort has proven rather hollow precisely because the attempt to proclaim Derridean philosophy complementary to Marxism has been carried out under the banner of a populistic anarcho-communism. Raging against the sins of Leninism, worshiping at the altar of every radical chic popular movement, however impotent and accommodated to the bourgeois order, this reading of Derrida is as premised on its slippage away from Marxism as it is on its appreciation of the radical kernel buried within *On Grammatology* and other texts. This construction of the articulation or complementarity of Marx and Derrida has been primarily the work of Michael Ryan, although Gayatri Chakrovaorty Spivak has also involved herself in this project.[125]

As Barbara Foley has argued forcefully, the Ryan-Spivak assimilation of Marxism and deconstruction rests on the *methodological* rapprochement of these separate traditions: both Marx and Derrida decenter the presuppositions of bourgeois ideology. The consequence is that there is supposedly a striking similarity in the ways in which they critique positivism, idealism, naturalism, and objectivism. Foley begs to differ, drawing a fundamental distinction between Marx, the dialectician, and Derrida, the deconstructionist. For Marx the critical opposition—wage labor/capital—is posed *in movement*, rather than as a static, metaphysical category, precisely because it is located in the real oppositions of material life and its consequent class struggles. Out of this clash of oppositions comes the possibility and potential of change, in which new sets of opposition open out into entirely new, and historically situated, differentiations. The historical subject, in Marx, is the material constrictions and liberations of human potential. In Derridean deconstruction, Foley suggests, binary oppositions are separated from their historical moment, formalized, and, in the process, undecidability is elevated "to the status of historical subject." Both Marx and Derrida are thus radical in their break from bourgeois ideology, but while the former is embedded in a conception and advocacy of historical change, the latter is immobilized in a refusal of any process originating within binary oppositions. Deconstruction fetishizes a "refusal of mastery" and actively "blocks the possibility of resolution or synthesis," in effect stepping outside of a history of change that is always castigated as "linear."[126]

All of this is not unrelated to the ways in which this Ryan-Spivak articulation of Marxism and deconstruction unfolds in terms of its relation to many of the basic premises and concepts of historical materialism. Spivak's recent "Scattered Speculations on the Question of Value" is a curious mix of orthodox reiteration of the labor theory of value and an understatement of the importance of class. In another essay she states that " 'class' is not, after all, an inalienable description of a human reality."[127] As Foley notes, Spivak's concerns revolve far more consciously around women, the Third World, and capitalism's many victims than they relate to class. Ryan's embrace of post-Leninist Marxism and its espousal and uncritical enthusiasm for the struggles of women, students, the unemployed, and the "new" class of social/service workers is premised on the Italian Autonomy Movement's appropriation of the Derridean axiom "the margins are at the center." Class thus gets displaced rather easily in a rejection of what Ryan terms "the traditional leninist centrality of "productive workers.' "[128] Within this Ryan-Spivak reading of Marx and Derrida, then, lurks what Foley identifies as a radicalized leftist pluralism. Hostile to centralism, distanced from class, it is not unproblematically grafted onto the writings of Marx, especially if we consider not only Marx's texts but his politics as well. It is, however, a sign of the political times.[129]

Deconstruction and Marxism are thus not as compatible as Ryan-Spivak would suggest. Within deconstruction the radical rupture with bourgeois ideology was always encased within an aestheticized shell. Between Derrida and Marx stands Nietzsche. The problem would be that the radical kernel would come to be overwhelmed by the thoroughly aestheticized and Nietzschean husk.[130] Indeed, it is perhaps not out of line to suggest that this husk, so much more visible and luxuriant than the kernel, overdetermined the Derridean project. Sensitive critics of Derrida have appreciated this duality.[131] Derrida himself has done his part to keep it alive, addressing in passing Marxist texts and their relationship to his kind of reading in *Positions* (1972) and using the public platform to explore, not the playful limitlessness of discourse, but the concrete construction of authority.[132] So, too, have feminist critics, whose understandable attachment to the Derridean formulation of difference/*différance* and whose appropriation of the Freudian concept of displacement have culminated in recent readings of gender and the "discourse of woman" that necessarily reach past texts, signs, language, and discourse toward the sociohistorical relations of power and domination.[133]

Year II of the Derridean coup, 1972, would suffocate the radical kernel of possibility present in grammatology and alive in these critical endeavors in the cancerous expansion of the husk. This was the year of *Dissemination, Marges de la philosophie,* and *Positions,* a slim volume of interviews that underscored Derrida's newly consolidated celebrity status. It was also the year of that signifier of European stature, the American appointment, and Derrida would henceforth divide his teaching time between Paris and regular visiting professorships at Yale and Johns Hopkins. If he arrived in 1966–1967, he was now, five years later, set up.

Derrida's notion of dissemination depicted language as "endlessly unbalanced and out of equilibrium. . . . In *dissemination,* language reveals an anarchic and unpredictable level of functioning, subversive of all rigid proper meanings on the ordinary socially controlled level." The grammatological project gave way to the age of deconstruction, and in the process what Merquior refers to as "the relatively austere sign problematic of the grammatological period" succumbed to the dizzying imperatives of the signifier let loose.[134] As Dews concludes, "The majority of Derrida's interpreters have, of course, resisted this implication of his position: Derrida is portrayed as merely suggesting that meaning is far more insecure, elusive, undecidable than philosophers had previously imagined. Yet the logical consequence of his argument is not the volatilization of meaning, but its destruction."[135]

By Derrida's own admission, deconstruction was a relatively modest proposal, an approach to texts that stressed the need of being alert to the implications of "the historical sedimentation of the language we use."[136] But it always had its wilder, Nietzschean side, and in the deconstructionist free-for-all of the post-1972 years it was this unrestrained aestheticism that prevailed, often against what one senses must have been Derrida's own better judgment. But the master was not without blame. Problematic denials of meaning, present in Derrida's grammatology, were replaced by blunter statements in the early 1970s. "I do not know where I am going," he once replied to a questioner and, throughout a proliferation of texts, he insisted on their meaninglessness.[137]

Language as play overtook his writing, evidenced in the title of one work, *The Archeology of the Frivolous* (1973), in which Derrida, reading the French *philosophe* Condillac, issued a deconstructionist declaration: "Mastery, *if there is any,* does not exist. . . . The sign's active essence, its energy, is freedom." That freedom licensed *Glas* (1974). Hailed by many as a masterpiece, this transposition of Jean Genet and Hegel puns its way through hundreds of pages of whimsical commentary. Deconstruction came, unmistakably, to the sorry end of textuality. As Derrida explained in "Living On: Border Lines" (1979), it is "no longer a finished corpus of writing, some content enclosed in a book or its margins, but a differential network, a fabric of traces referring endlessly to something other than itself." In *The Postcard from Socrates to Freud and Beyond* (1980), the notion that all of Derrida's texts are mere prefaces to works yet to be written is introduced, mounted on a burlesque celebration of the comic. A joke, of course, is not always simply a joke, but sometimes it is just that. It is hard not to conclude that, like Lacan, Derrida has been gotten the better of by language. The Emperor of Deconstruction seems in need of some clothes. But then the very metaphor of clothing was always a repugnant one to Derrida, suggestive as it was of a dichotomy that allowed meaning to be grasped through the kind of differentiation that Derrida hails theologically at the same time as he denies it in his insistence on the constancy of interpenetration:

> Writing, sensible matter and artificial exteriority: a "clothing." It has sometimes been contested that speech clothed thought. . . . But has it ever been doubted that writing was the clothing of speech. For Saussure it is even a garment of perversion and debauchery, a dress of corruption and disguise, a festival mask that must be exorcised, that is to say warded off, by the good word: "Writing veils the appearance of language; it is not a guise for language but a disguise." Strange "image." One already suspects that if writing is "image" and exterior "figuration" this representation is not innocent. The outside bears with the inside a relationship that is, as usual, anything but simple exteriority. The meaning of the outside was always present within the inside, imprisoned outside the outside, and vice versa.

Always vice versa![138]

It is this, the Derrida of the undoing of hermeneutics, who has captivated sectors of American criticism and pushed them headlong in the direction of the ultimate undecidability of the text, lending himself to the unrepressed affirmation of freedom, joy, and the erotic pleasures of reading. Among the Yale deconstructionists (Hartman, de Man, Miller, and to a lesser extent Bloom), as well as in Fishian pronouncements, this impulse has run amuck in a series of denials—historical constraint and authorial intention primary among them—that collapse textual reality into an amorphous orgy of yarn spinning, rationalized as scholarship by dichotomizing good and bad yarns/readings.[139] However much Derrida distances himself from this free fall into discourse's hedonisms with reminders that he is no pluralist and that he recognizes the determinate forces of author, intention, and historical conditions in the making of meaning, it is all too little too late. The statement that "it is by touching solid structures, 'material' institutions, and not merely discourses or significant representations, that deconstruction distinguishes itself from analysis or 'criticism'" is useful as academic corrective, but it is nevertheless entirely academic.[140] There have been too many other declarations, such as Derrida's confession that "before me, the signifier on its own says more than I believe that I meant to say, and in relation to it, my meaning-to-say is submissive rather than active." As Richard Harland notes, in this reading of writing, "even the writer is just another reader. . . . language constitutes the human world and the human world constitutes the whole world." Deconstruction is nothing less than a "philosophy of the world *as* language."[141] The damage has been done, and no amount of innovative use of deconstruction within literary criticism is likely to salvage poststructuralism's Derridean postmortem.[142]

In the implosion of theory Derrida has been something of a *lider maximo*. He commanded an army that he was incapable of leading and controlling, indeed, that he had no desire to direct. In the long march of deconstruction, it was inevitable that many would take the fundamental ambiguities of the context, mutiny, and plunge critical theory even further into the abyss of aestheticism.[143] This has been the trajectory of the critical community's appropriation of Derrida in America, where it has been possible for a deconstructionist godfather such as Paul de Man to imply that empirical events themselves—wars and revolutions—do not really exist except as "texts" masquerading as "the real." "Textual privatization" of this sort unleashed a terroristic assault on reality and a violent repudiation of history in which "all that threaten[ed] or promise[d] to remain [was] the pure negativity and circularity of a will to demystify, standing playfully and demonically on its own." There were, fortunately, those who said no to this discourse.[144]

▶ *Dissenting Discourses*

Many voices were raised against the descent into discourse, voices arising from bodies grounded in recognition of the importance of the word/sign. Among those who opposed the drift of linguistic and critical theory, refusing to bow to the initial Saussurean *coup de force* separating *langue* from the social conditions of its making and use were, for instance, Pierre Macherey and Pierre Bourdieu. The former espoused a theory of literary *production* that stressed the manifold determinations that set the table on which texts were laid and consumed: "Through its relationship to the theoretical and ideological uses of language, the text is also influenced by the formal function of the writer and by the problems of his individual existence; finally, specific literary works are determined by the history of literary production from which they receive the means of their own realisation. . . . men have to *produce* [works], not by magic but by a real labour of production."[145] In Bourdieu this productivist orientation was displaced by metaphorical concern with the market, in which a "law of price formation" separated those with access to linguistic capital from those subaltern classes defined by their many deprivations. Within the social relations of production and exchange inequality is perpetual, the symbolic violence of the market order evident in

> all the corrections, momentary or long-lasting, to which dominated speakers, in a desperate effort towards correction, consciously or unconsciously subject the stigmatized aspects of their pronunciation, their vocabulary (with all the forms of euphemism) and their syntax; or in the confusion which makes them "lose their means," rendering them incapable of "finding their words," as if they had been suddenly dispossessed of their own language.

Where Saussure recoiled in horror from the "pathologies" of class-constituted language, Bourdieu used it to explore the construction of hegemony.[146]

Macherey and Bourdieu epitomized an epistemological break with discourse as the *dominant* that remained within a French idiom. In the United States dissenting discourses would speak with different accents. Edward Said's exploration of Orientalism as a servile discourse created and sustained in the interests of imperialistic authority employed "close textual readings whose goal [was] to reveal the dialectic between individual text or writer and the complex collective formation to which [the work was] a contribution." This formed a necessary background for a more generalized demand for secular criticism, a call that took direct aim at the proud stand of American literary theory for a textuality that refused "to appropriate anything . . . worldly, circumstantial, or socially contaminated," insuring criticism's antithesis to and displacement of history. Said's impressive political blend of cosmopolitanism and common sense raked across the complacency of the textualist bed of literary theory:

> My position is that texts are worldly, to some degree they are events, and, even when they appear to deny it, they are nevertheless a part of the social world, human life, and of course the historical moments in which they are located and interpreted. . . . it is no accident that the emergence of so narrowly defined a philosophy of pure textuality and critical noninterference has coincided with the ascendancy of Reaganism, or for that matter with a new cold war, increased militarism and defense spending, and a massive turn to the right on matters touching the economy, social services, and organized labor. . . . The realities of power and authority—as well as the resistances offered by men, women, and social movements to institutions, authorities, and orthodoxies—are the realities that make texts possible, that deliver them to their readers, that solicit the attention of critics. I propose that these realities are what should be taken account of by criticism and the critical consciousness.[147]

No less grating were the resolutely polemical and historical refusals of literary theory's avant-garde by Frank Lentricchia, whose acerbic pillorying of the patriarchs of American deconstruction earned him the— for Marxists at least—distinction of a threatened lawsuit. Not afraid of the traditional—"We Marxists have always lived in tradition," Trotsky affirmed—Lentricchia gives no ground in his insistence that class, so often seen as one of the many "disappeared" of Reagan's America, matters, and that those critics, such as Kenneth Burke, who recognized this remain relevant in the Age of the New Critic. His criticism, like Said's, is rooted in specific beginnings, his own class background. He consequently never forgets the need for and possibility of change: "For me to ignore the possibility and reality of change is for me to betray who I am and where I've come from. I'm not going to do that."[148] For all the strengths of their dissenting discourses, Said and Lentricchia employ, not the vocabulary of Marxism, but the sentences and structuring logic of a radicalism bounded by liberalism and populism.

The most visible American Marxist figure in the struggle to force discourse out of its downwardly spiraling descent, leading literary criticism out of the hubristic wilderness of unreason, is Fredric Jameson.[149] More than fifteen years ago he offered a mild disclaimer against the drift of literary theory: "Even if ours is a critical age, it does not seem to me very becoming in critics to exalt their activity to the level of literary creation, as is loosely done in France today."[150] His own early appreciation and ultimate rejection of structuralism and poststructuralism, *The Prison-House of Language* (1972), was an even-handed denial of the absolutization of discourse/interpretation. It called for reopening texts and analytic processes alike "to all the winds of history." Against the mainstay of linguistic theory's twentieth-century r/evolution, language's reification according to the principle of nonreferentiality, Jameson offers the persistent injunction, "Always historicize!"[151]

There is no question that this blunt slogan, hailed as "the transhistorical imperative of all dialectical thought," is aimed at the new hedonists of literary theory, where it finds its mark. Nor is there any question of Jameson's self-conscious identification with Marxism in an American field uncomfortably unreceptive to historical materialism at the best of times, and these are not the best of times.[152] At a recent meeting that brought together most of the left critical theorists active in the United States, Jameson felt the need to declare that "during this Marxist conference I have frequently had the feeling that I am one of the few Marxists left."[153]

Yet for all of his Marxist, historical materialist intention, Jameson, as a number of critics have pointed out, has been unable to break out of the enclosures of the contemporary scene of critical theory. Valiantly struggling against the forces of active direction and inertia that mobilize the descent into discourse, he seems nailed to its course, a reluctant sign of the power of this interpretive trend. His own penchant for style— Eagleton describes his prose as carrying an "intense libidinal charge"— coupled with an eclectic Hegelianism "capable of raiding, embracing, and subsuming a wide range of other theoretical positions" have insured that Jameson's Marxist hermeneutics retain more than a little of the theory and formalism that it seems mandatory to shed.[154] Structuralism's "rethinking everything through once again in terms of linguistics" is thus rejected forcefully, but somewhat rhetorically.[155]

This Jamesonian dilemma emerges most clearly in the pages of *The Political Unconscious*. At its best in elaborating a conception of how material reality, located in the mode of production, mediates culture, the book pits itself against the windless closure of formalism and textuality:

> It would be desirable for those who celebrate the discovery of the Symbolic to reflect on the historical conditions of possibility of this new and specifically modern sense of the linguistic, semiotic, textual construction of reality. The "discovery" of Language is at one with its structural abstraction from concrete experience, with its hypostasis as an autonomous object, power, or activity. . . . The

> paradox disappears only if we make a radical break with the idea that language always functions in one way, always serves the same purpose: to convey thoughts.

But Jameson concludes with a historicist and materialist statement alive with Derridean vocabulary:

> So it is that a Marxist hermeneutic—the decipherment by historical materialism of the cultural monuments and traces of the past— must come to terms with the certainty that all the works of class history as they have survived and been transmitted to people, the various museums, canons, and "traditions" of our own time, are all in one way or another profoundly ideological, have all had a vested interest in and a functional relationship to social formations based on violence and exploitation; and that, finally, the restoration of the meaning of the greatest cultural monuments cannot be separated from a passionate and partisan assessment of everything that is oppressive in them and that knows complicity with privilege and class domination, stained with the guilt not merely of culture in particular but of History itself as one long nightmare.[156]

The problem here is not so much the one-sided character of history in Jameson's pessimistic reading, although that should cause some pause for thought, even in today's bleak milieu. Rather, it is the "overtextualization" of history that lies behind this judgment:

> History is therefore the experience of Necessity, and it is this alone which can forestall its thematization or reification as a mere object of representation or as one master code among many others. Necessity is not in that sense a type of content, but rather the inexorable *form* of events; it is therefore a narrative category in the enlarged sense of some properly narrative political unconscious which has been argued here, a retextualization of History which does not propose the latter as some new representation of "vision," some new content, but as . . . "an absent cause."[157]

As Jim Merod has argued forcefully, this abstraction dissolves experience, certainly, and possibly even possibility itself. In following the Althusserian dictate that experience is inhabited utterly by "the imaginary relationship of individuals to their real conditions of existence," by *ideology* unchallenged and unchallengable, Jameson understandably searches out the site of this experiential entrapment. He locates it in the literary text and the broader "text" of culture, locales of "the production of false consciousness." This is not wrong, absolutely, but it is one-sided and culminates in just the kind of aestheticism that Jameson's entire *oeuvre* ostensibly rejects. The world becomes a matter of decoding an infinite extension of texts and, by implication, the way forward to transformation must inevitably lie on the path of reconstituting countertexts: we are back with the Barthes of *Mythologies*. What gets lost, in Merod's words, is the centrality of the question "How are texts and interpretations used within the interactions of institutions? How do they generate and participate in the relations of power and ordering?"[158]

Motivated by the priority he places on a political reading of texts, and well aware of the extent to which historical materialism has been denied and denigrated within the politics of reading, Jameson challenges much that is dear to the critical theory community. But his style and eclecticism, in which the rancor and polemic of a Lentricchia or the unmistakable clarity and openness of a Said seldom, if ever, appear, seem self-conscious adaptations to the critical mainstream, a concession to academic pluralism in the interests of legitimizing Marxism. One can understand the tactic. But the strategic consequences are costly, insuring that Jameson remains one component, albeit a critical one—in both senses of the word—in the implosion of theory. Like his English counterpart and the only Marxist critic alive to rival Jameson in reach and influence, Terry Eagleton, Fredric Jameson remains both inside and outside the descent into discourse.[159]

▶   *Born under a Bad Sign*

We have traveled a considerable distance. And yet what remains is not much more than a gloss on the development of linguistics and literary criticism in the twentieth century, a gesture toward some of the landmarks in the discovery of the word/sign. So much more could be said, and many other exemplary figures introduced. But a purpose has been achieved. It should be evident that language is not some unproblematic entity. At each and every turn in its discovery there have appeared new and previously unanticipated halts, realignments, and analytic detours. The essential and highly influential premises of Nietzschean and Saussurean approaches to language, as play or science unfolding within their own universes of nonreferentiality, were never without their difficulties and detractors. In this sense language's birth in the twentieth century took place under a troubled, if not bad, sign. It has grown with that sign, shadowing it for the better part of one hundred years.

However irrelevant to an assessment of language and the way various readings of it have structured critical theory and its implosion, it is difficult to avert one's gaze from the tragedy, or worse, that seems to stalk the personnel of structuralism and poststructuralism: Barthes's sad end in a Parisian street; the striking down of Foucault by the apocalyptic plague of our times; Althusser's terrible inner turmoil and the prices it exacted in ultimate human terms;[160] the dark secret of de

Man's "war" of 1940–1942, in which an "ambiguous," at best, relation to fascism was forged, later to be papered over with a shameful "text" of lies and evasions.

It is this latter process, opening out so necessarily into the political realm, that is the most disturbing, potentially if not actually, sign of all. In a book on poststructuralism and its claims that predated the de Man issue, Peter Dews identified this political thorn in the side of critical theory, prefacing his study with the blunt reminder that a major limitation "of the Anglo-Saxon reception of post-structuralist thought has been a continuing lack of clarity about the political consequences of its characteristic positions." Dews correctly noted that "there has sometimes been little attempt to think through the ultimate compatibility of progressive political commitments with the dissolution of the subject, or a totalizing suspicion of the concept of truth."[161]

The deconstructionist project, of course, is not forever repudiated and scandalized by de Man's long hidden history, for no individual failure, however horrendous, can bear such socio-intellectual weight. What happened almost fifty years ago, involving a single individual uninvolved in anything approximating his later theoretical project, who went on, by all accounts, to break decisively from his own compromising history with a Nazism he preferred not to name, hardly serves to repudiate deconstruction and its advocates. But the incontestable evidence of de Man's writing for newspapers associated with Nazism in Belgium during World War II provides precisely the kind of historical background to his texts that American deconstructionists have made it their priority to deny and subvert. It allows a particular kind of reading of *Blindness and Insight*, where the Nietzschean conception and rejection of pasts that are so threatening they must be forgotten in purgatory acts of criticism figures centrally in "Literary History and Literary Modernity." A sensitive contextualization of this history and its own deconstruction has been lost in the swirl of journalistic exploitation of the de Man revelations and the lining up of academic forces on the respective sides of a special kind of barricade.[162] Derrida has brought to the issue a rare rigor, exemplary in its thorough reading of the de Man articles, but excessive in its capacity to understate and obscure the politics of de Man's moment of involvement in the fascist reconstruction of Europe.[163]

When one considers that Heidegger, a pivotal thinker in the making of structuralism/poststructuralism, with whom Derrida once confessed to "eat, sleep, and breathe," and whom he has now confronted explicitly and politically,[164] is now more widely known to have been little better than a Nazi, propagating fascist ideology and engaging in active support for the Hitler regime, it is apparent that the discovery of the word/sign has licensed more than a little objectionable politics.[165] Foucault's political apostasy and Kristeva's even more blatant accommodation to the right merely underscore the point.[166] Whatever Althusser's relation to Stalinism—agent or antagonist, depending on whether you follow Thompson or Jameson—he was most emphatically in motion toward Maoism, which was a neo-Stalinism if ever there was one.[167] Bad signs. Compared with them, Lacan's cranky idiosyncrasy, his dissolution of his school and retreat into egocentric insularity—"I don't need many people. And there are people I don't need"—appears positively benign.[168] All of this, while it *does* weigh like a nightmare on the brain of living discourse theorists, is still not necessarily the end of their project. But it stands as an important and unhealthily protracted process demanding and stimulating reconsiderations of meaning, referentiality, and the role of language.

Those kinds of reconsiderations will necessarily look to the ways in which language and discourse mediate the material, historically ordered world of sociopolitical relations. They will draw on much that has been surveyed above. They will seek to make the sign under which language has labored for so long good rather than bad. In that project there may well be something to be learned from social histories and cultural studies guided by the theory, not of linguistic determination, but of historical materialism. This does not mean that language's importance must be denied and refused; it does mean that it cannot be simply assumed, gestured at cavalierly as if there is a theoretical certainty behind the very pronouncement of linguistic centrality. Yet, as we shall see, this is precisely how social historians making the linguistic turn, or urging others to do so, often operate. In their hurry to descend into discourse, they ignore, all too innocently, what has been going on in a part of their own backyard for some time.

2 *Historical Materialism*

Life's but a walking shadow, a poor player
That struts and frets his hour upon the stage,
And then is heard no more; it is a tale
Told by an idiot, full of sound and fury,
Signifying nothing.

—Macbeth, V, v, 17

DISCOURSE, NOT SURPRISINGLY, HAS TRADITIONALLY BEEN the terrain of intellectual history. Small wonder that among many intellectual historians the linguistic turn has been made with a sharpness, velocity, and acute self-consciousness rare in other fields of the discipline. Indeed, it is possible to locate important works of intellectual history attentive to language that seem to predate poststructuralism, just as it is also apparent that the attraction of intellectual history to discourse and literary theory has run a certain course yet to be traveled by historians concerned predominantly with the social.[1]

The extent to which literary criticism and linguistic theory have found a receptive audience among intellectual historians is evident in the evolution of Hayden White and the arrival of Dominick LaCapra.[2] White, whose writings of the mid-1970s betrayed a curious ambivalence to critical theory, is now far less guarded in his advocacy. His early discussions of "the absurdist moment" of literary criticism praised aspects of the carnival of the implosion of theory but did not shy away from some rather blunt assaults on the pretense of the Derridean project:

> Derrida's philosophy—if it can be legitimately called that—represents nothing more than the hypostatization of the theory of discourse underlying and sanctioning the structuralist activity. He regards his own philosophy as a transcendence of the structuralist problematic, but he is wrong: it is its fetishization. . . . He may

criticize Lévi-Strauss for his failure to demythologize his own thought; but Derrida is no less a mythologue when he reflects on the nature of what he calls "the interpretation of interpretation.". . . Here criticism becomes the celebration of an as yet unborn and therefore unnameable "monstrosity." . . . Derrida not only thinks the unthinkable but turns it into an idol. . . . Derrida sees himself as a critic of structuralism, but . . . [he] is the minotaur imprisoned in structuralism's hypostatized labyrinth of language.[3]

A decade later White situates himself more respectfully and more circumspectly in relation to Derrida.[4] For LaCapra, little in the way of distancing or caution with respect to Derrida, whom he often chooses to "echo," is required.[5]

LaCapra provides a useful point of departure in any discussion of discourse and social history because his own project of "rethinking intellectual history" appears motivated by a concern located at the conjuncture where intellectual history, social history, and language meet. As he states in *History and Criticism*:

I am especially interested in the relations between intellectual history, which must develop modes of critical and self-critical interpretation, and social history, which has been preoccupied with the attempt to elaborate methods to investigate the contexts of interpretation. I continue to believe that historians have much to learn from disciplines such as literary criticism and philosophy where debates over the nature of interpretation have been particularly lively in the recent past. I would like to help bring historiography to the point at which it is able to enter those debates in a more even-handed way—not simply as a repository of facts or a neopositivistic stepchild of social science, and certainly not as mythologized locus of some prediscursive image of "reality," but as a critical voice in the discipline's addressing of problems of understanding and explanation.[6]

This loudly proclaimed opening statement of good will is subverted softly by the very characterizations of social history that follow immediately after it. In its overgeneralized lumping of social history into a particular congealed intellectual mass, as well as in its condescension and patronizing superiority, this seemingly bland passage hints at some far from innocuous signs of hostility. LaCapra is perhaps the most pronounced advocate of a deconstructive history in North American intellectual circles, and what is all too obvious to a social historian is the shocking foundational animosities of his crusade.

That LaCapra is engaged in a willful assault on a social history he perceives as ascendant is evident in the form that his remarks often take. Behind the postured high purpose of calling attention to the problematic nature of context, the complexities of texts, and pursuing a criticism capable of grasping history as "the situated uses of language constitutive of significant texts"[7] lie a series of childlike outbursts against social history's apparent attempt to steal all of the disciplinary marbles:

> The very idea of a "total history" has often been little more than a blind behind which social history could be transformed into the mother hen of historiography in general.

> Social historians have of course been particularly notable exponents of a scientific and at times a positivistic idea of history. Until recently, the influential Annales school tended to view narrative as superficial, to stress a socio-scientific conception of "serious" history with an emphasis upon statistical series and exhaustive archival research, and to hold forth the ideal of a "total history" in which social history had the privileged position of basic ground or essential indicator of fundamental reality. One often heard—and still occasionally hears—phrases such as "the need to root problems in social reality." Total history itself might serve as a Trojan horse for a social metaphysic in the understanding of the past and a pretension to preeminence in the present organization of the historical profession.

> The archival sociocultural historian is a busy little ant that is not afraid to dirty its "hands" with real labor as it stores up real knowledge. The intellectual historian who does not emulate it is a relaxed parasite who does little more than dilettantish, after-dinner reading.[8]

Passages such as these expose an embarrassing moment of intellectual insecurity. They are a testament to the perils of a professionalism that lusts after place, reputation, and recognition, all of which are conceived within a mercantilist world view of finite spoils to be hoarded within the boundaries of a particular field.

This is not to argue that LaCapra has nothing to say to social historians. His conception of language as a signifying practice that "undercuts the dichotomy between text and context and underscores their sometimes ambivalent interaction" and his persistent insistence on the irreducibility of context to a simplistic accumulation of documentary texts leads toward some fruitful metacommentary. Placed against the hedonistic Nietzscheanism of the American deconstructive literary community, LaCapra often seems a fount of sober wisdom: "Meaning is indeed context-bound, but context is not itself bound in any simple or unproblematic way."[9]

What is troubling is LaCapra's capacity to lose control of his argument when social histories are at stake, flailing away at figures such as

Carlo Ginzburg and Robert Darnton. These authors rouse his ire because they apparently "effect an uncritical assimilation of intellectual
and social history," displacing concern with "society as a whole" and
the canonical texts that supposedly illuminate such a fiction to the
margins of a populistic romanticism enclosed by class or the limitations of particularistic levels of "culture." Such a procedure then becomes identifiable as social history's essence:

> Contemporary sociocultural history was in part motivated by a
> justifiable revolt against an abstracted history of ideas. But it has
> often tended simply to reverse the latter's assumptions (through
> reductionism) and to replicate its documentary treatment of ar-
> tifacts (as symptoms of society or economy rather than mind). It has
> also replicated an all-too-prevalent social reaction to intellectual
> history's objects of study (both artifacts and artists or intellectuals).
> For it has responded to the anxiety of transference through pro-
> cesses of reduction or exclusion that amount to at least method-
> ological scapegoating if not anti-intellectualism, and it has thereby
> tended to deny the contestatory dimensions of high culture and the
> challenge of forging new links between it and popular culture—a
> challenge that confronts historians themselves in the very language
> they use to interpret aspects of culture. Sociocultural history has
> sometimes proceeded under the banner of a populism ("history from
> the bottom up") that has become less political and increasingly
> methodological, taking social research in directions that are of little
> significance or even diversionary both for the oppressed in society
> and for those attempting to develop a critical historiography. In any
> event, its populism often repeats rather blindly the scapegoating
> propensities of populism in society. The result is prepossessing and
> intimidating when social history claims to be a "total history" or at
> least the cynosure to which all other historical approaches must be
> referred.[10]

There are a number of points that need making about this remarkable
passage. The first is that it captures *something* about the directions that
specific social histories have taken in the last decade. Darnton, in
particular, is an easy target, representing much that is problematic in a
social history where power and structural determination recede from
view. But that said, what deserves notice are the layers of qualification
that LaCapra buries his critique beneath: "in part motivated by . . . often
tended simply . . . tended to deny . . . sometimes proceeded under the
banner . . . often repeats rather blindly. . . ." Indeed, this kind of caution
is mandatory precisely because of the limitations within which La-
Capra's critique unfolds. Dressed in the garb of generality, this assault
marches forward as if the reader is to witness *the* fashionable trajectory
of social history—the chapter in which these views are espoused is

illuminatingly entitled, "Is Everyone a *Mentalité* Case?"—which La-
Capra identifies as "an almost oneiric reliance on the concept of culture." Yet for all the totalizing facade of his critical commentary on
social history, it is informed by a previous chapter's challenge to
Ginzburg's *The Cheese and the Worms*, engagement with a single text
of Carl Schorske and scrutiny of some of the writings of Darnton. That
these authors/works can stand for social history as a whole is, of course,
an act of gross substitutionism/reductionism.[11]

It also makes painfully obvious LaCapra's lack of awareness of what is
going on within social history. Heated debates about culture are now
rather old hat.[12] Virtually no one, save rather innocent refugees from
the American New Leftism of the 1960s, champions "history from the
bottom up," and the dangers of a depoliticized social history have been
apparent for some time.[13] In the 1980s the "problem" of social history
appears to be far removed from LaCapra's much-feared populistic romanticism, clearly fading fast in the presence of new trends, not the
least of which is the very focus on discourse this book is attempting to
address. More powerful, and pernicious, is the stilted empiricism over-
taking the field: it dictates a detached charting of the cold confinements
of subordinate groups, in which any remnant of utopianism/romanti-
cism/human agency is dispatched coolly in a tidy bow to political
pragmatism and scholastic rigor. With the response of the New Profes-
sionals to the posthumously published essays of Herbert Gutman,
Power and Culture, this is all too apparent.[14] Nor can anyone, after
Gutman's *Slavery and the Numbers Game*, seriously contend that
social historians are not aware of the fetishization of method evident in
quantitative history's advertisements for itself.[15] Finally, it is surely
bordering on the offensive for LaCapra to imply that social history often
proves diversionary for both the oppressed and for those interested in a
critical historiography when his own project remains so self-satisfy-
ingly unconcerned with social change.

All of this is not meant to slide away from the necessity of a critique
of social history. Rather, it is to insist that such a scrutiny of the field be
much more than a caricature, attending to the differentiations and
debates that have figured centrally in the historical practice of the last
decade and more. This chapter introduces some texts of social history,
historical materialism, and cultural criticism in an effort to impress
upon those who mount their call for a "linguistic turn" on a cavalier
dismissal of an entire way of conceiving the world that all of these mere
tales do indeed signify something.

By historical materialism, I do not mean that "economic conditions
are the sole active cause and everything else mere passive effect." But,
rather, as Engels would stress in the 1890s, that there is "interaction on

the basis of a prevailing economic necessity in the last instance." This economic last instance is a profoundly historical phenomenon, and "men make their history themselves, but in a given milieu which conditions them; they do this on the basis of pre-existing relations, amongst which the economic are decisive in the last instance, though they may be influenced by other relations, political and ideological." As Marx wrote to Annenkov in 1846:

> The productive forces are therefore the result of practical human energy; but this energy is itself conditioned by the circumstances in which men find themselves, by the productive forces already won, by the social form which exists before they do, which they do not create, which is the product of the former generation. Because of this simple fact that every succeeding generation finds itself in possession of the productive forces won by the previous generation which serve it as the raw material for new production, a connection arises in human history, a history of humanity takes shape which has become all the more a history of humanity since the productive forces of man and therefore his social relations have been extended. Hence it necessarily follows: the social history of men is never anything but the history of their individual development, whether they are conscious of it or not. Their material relations are the basis of all their relations. These material relations are only the necessary forms in which their material and individual activity is realised.

The coming together of social history, historical materialism, and cultural criticism is anticipated nicely in the *Theses on Feuerbach*: "The chief defect of all previous materialism—that of Feuerbach included— is that the thing, reality, sensuousness, is conceived only in the form of the object, or of contemplation, but not as sensuous human activity, practice, not subjectively. . . . Social life is essentially *practical*. All mysteries which mislead theory to mysticism find their rational solution in human practice and in the comprehension of this practice."[16] But to make these points of connection bluntly and briefly within the present context of a concern with discourse, the following commentary focuses, not on the many accomplishments of specific texts informed by historical materialism, but rather on the extent to which they do in fact have something to say about *language*.

▶ **Marx and the Margins**

Among those historians, such as White and LaCapra, who have taken historical representation as their chosen theme, a long-favored text is Marx's *The Eighteenth Brumaire of Louis Bonaparte*.[17] White is, characteristically, the more sophisticated, reaching toward an appreciation of the subtle interplay of narrative, explanation, political purpose, and biting appreciation of the farcical unfolding of bourgeois order in what he refers to as "a masterful interpretation of a complex historical situation." For LaCapra the issue is more easily reduced to form: "the importance of rhetorical and stylistic considerations in their relation to the 'theses' for which Marx has become famous or infamous."

Fixated on what he takes to be the abusive, aggressive, negative tone of *The Eighteenth Brumaire*, LaCapra dislikes Marx's animosity toward the *lumpenproletariat* and is suspicious of his displacement of peasant interests. Marx's attempt to analyze the French events of 1848–1852 in class terms draws LaCapra into a repudiation of proletarian power that relies on rather amateurish psychologizing:

> The intensity of Marx's polemical animus against the lumpenproletariat and other groups blocking revolution might be seen as a function of a concealed or even repressed fear that the proletariat itself is not the revolutionary agent Marx wishes it to be and that other groups do not hold out the transformative promise he seeks. In *The Eighteenth Brumaire*, Marx seems to be on the verge of the dilemma that would confront radical intellectuals in the twentieth century when they were to face the possiblity that modern societies did not offer a more or less ready-made group analogous to the classical revolutionary subject. Marx's own account of the ease with which the proletariat was repressed in June 1848 and duped into taking to the streets in June 1849 creates suspicion concerning the proletariat's fitness to assume the heroic role in which Marx would cast it.

White, at least, is more open in his antagonism to proletarian power, declaring his opposition to revolutionary change forthrightly rather than hiding behind some pseudo-Freudian couch. In the end, LaCapra's reading of *The Eighteenth Brumaire* is predictably mundane, reducing the complex weave of politics, history, and conceptualization that constitute the text into a language of "living labor" meant to critique the social order and change it as well. This will come as small surprise to those who have taken the elementary trouble to read the *Theses on Feuerbach*.[18]

What is puzzling in this reading of *The Eighteenth Brumaire* is what is missed, passed over in silence. For social historians working within the tradition of historical materialism have long located the essential theoretical statement of this text in its opening passage:

> Men make their own history, but they do not make it just as they please; they do not make it under circumstances chosen by themselves, but under circumstances directly encountered, given and transmitted from the past. The tradition of all the dead generations

weighs like a nightmare on the brain of the living. And just when they seem engaged in revolutionising themselves and things, in creating something that has never yet existed, precisely in such periods of revolutionary crisis they anxiously conjure up the spirits of the past to their service and borrow from them names, battle cries and costumes in order to present the new scene of world history in this time-honoured disguise and this borrowed language.[19]

It is this materialistic situating of human agency, always constrained by the limitations of so many factors, not the least of which are ideology and language, that is fundamental to Marx's reading of the French events of 1848–1852. And it is understanding of this that is increasingly central to the project of a social history guided by historical materialism. On one level, but only one, this passage from the first page of *The Eighteenth Brumaire* is easily assimilated to Derrida's insistent recognition of the historical sedimentation of language. Marx, too, even if he failed to name it, recognized the trace and the cost it could extract in moments of potential revolutionary change.

Indeed, what is apparent from a counterposed set of readings—of Marx of the events of 1848–1852 and of LaCapra of Marx's text—is how far the advocate of a deconstructive history is from practicing what he preaches. Attention to metaphor, which abounds in *The Eighteenth Brumaire*, especially in Marx's assimilation of the nation-state and its politics to the conventionalities associated with true womanhood, is noticeably lacking.[20] Little attention is paid to Marx's profound reliance upon binary oppositions to structure the unfolding of the bourgeois order as farce.[21] And there is, more seriously, no substantive engagement with the confusing swirl of meaning arising out of a moment of upheaval in which language and actions contended in an awkward communication of indecision and ambivalence:

> In no period do we, therefore, find a more confused mixture of high-flown phrases and actual uncertainty and clumsiness, of more enthusiastic striving for innovation and more deeply-rooted domination of the old routine, of more apparent harmony of the whole society and more profound estrangement of its elements.[22]

Instead of addressing this, the way in which the accumulated residue of the political signs and language of the past helps to structure the possibility of the present and the future,[23] LaCapra offers us deeply politicized homilies of the proletariat's incapacities. Overdetermined by its own politics of opposition, LaCapra's reading of Marx's *Eighteenth Brumaire* comes to the profound conclusion that a text of politics is a political text. If this is intellectual history, it is more than a little bereft of ideas.

Marx, however much he is shunted aside in a rude reductionism, could never be conceived as marginal. He lies at the acknowledged center of nineteenth-century thought and practice. Not so the Third World, which has predictably figured peripherally, if at all, in the making of the linguistic turn within intellectual history or the call for this turn to be made in the writing of social history. Yet the connections among the various worlds, forged through the coercive and consensual bonds of imperialism and "development," are critical to all histories, whatever their focus.24 It is appropriate, then, to move off the tracks the likes of White and LaCapra lay for us, to consider two texts of cultural criticism born of the experience of imperialism, where the exploitations of class and the oppressions of race fused in their own language of subordination. "Language," wrote the fifteenth-century Spanish grammarian Elio Antonio de Nebrija, "has always been the consort of empire, and forever shall remain its mate. Together they come into being, together they grow and flower, and together they decline."25

There is perhaps no figure that exemplifies the connectedness of the worlds of empire and colony better than C. L. R. James. His historical writing, such as *The Black Jacobins*, links these worlds at their point of political rupture in revolution; and his reach across literary criticism, political theory, and philosophy may be interpreted similarly, as can his own life of dissident Marxism, touching down on continents as his contemporaries did on countries, even counties. James's impact is felt in the West Indies, Britain, Italy, Africa, and the United States, his authority recognized in the fields of literature, politics, art, history, and sport. Whatever differences one has with James, they are of the sort that matter.26

It is odd that James has received so little attention from the critical theory community. Born in 1901 in Trinidad, he was a scholarship student who early involved himself in two Caribbean literary magazines—*Trinidad* and *The Beacon*—to which he contributed short fiction and criticism. A passion for cricket took him to England in 1932, where he wrote on the sport for the *Manchester Guardian* and *Glasgow Herald*. He also championed West Indian and African independence, authored a novel and a play about Touissaint L'Ouverture in which he acted beside Paul Robeson, and examined the San Domingo slave revolution. Drawn to Trotskyism, he moved to the United States in 1938 where he worked with the Socialist Workers Party for a time before a series of breaks from orthodoxy plunged him into the confusions of Third Campism. At the height of the McCarthyite witchhunt he was interned on Ellis Island, where he wrote much of a study of Herman Melville, *Mariners, Renegades and Castaways*. Focusing on *Moby-Dick* and Ahab, with commentary on other texts, the book is an exploration of the totalitarian mind, scaffolded on James's conception of the way capitalism culminates in the horrors of fascism, the atrocities of Stalinism, the barbarism of destructive innovation, and the debasement of work.

The ship *Pequod* is nothing less than modern industry, which totalitarianism aims to tame: "In its symbolism of men turned into devils, of an industrial civilization on fire and plunging blindly into darkness, it is the world of massed bombers, of cities in flames, of Hiroshima and Nagasaki, the world in which we live, the world of Ahab, which he hates and which he will organize or destroy." But the essential humanity of work stands in the way, a sign of the brake—however unconscious and circumscribed—of limitation placed on barbarism. That work, however, is orchestrated by the power of language and the symbols that drape it in an authority all the more encompassing for its terrifying isolation:

> What is the bitterest personal cry of Ahab? It is his isolation, the isolation inseparable from the function of authority in the modern world. . . . On the *Pequod*, Ahab's word is law and it is this which paralyses resistance. . . . Ahab's dinner-table is the symbol of his social isolation. . . . It is the relations between men at work that shape human character. And the most decisive relation on board ship is the relation between officers and men.

To read James on Melville is to appreciate the possibilities of a criticism informed by political sensibility and historical materialism. Indeed, what James has to say about Melville can well stand as a comment on James himself: "Yet how light in the scales is the contemporary mountain of self-examination and self-pity against the warmth, the humour, the sanity, the anonymous but unfailing humanity of the renegades and castaways and savages of the *Pequod*, rooted in the whole historical past of man, doing what they have to do, facing what they have to face."[27]

Mariners, Renegades, and Castaways reveals James as a historical materialist capable of dealing with language and signification, but it is another text, *Beyond a Boundary*, that I want to use to further develop this theme.[28] Ostensibly and obviously about cricket, it begins with the question "What do they know of cricket who only cricket know?" Indeed, cricket, in contemporary critical theory's terms, is treated as a "text," a "language." It is a language James was convinced that his political comrades in the United States, for all the vocabulary they shared with him, could not understand.[29] Unfolding within his departure from Trotskyism, *Beyond a Boundary*, like all of C. L. R. James's writing, demands a political reading that addresses its content in terms of the debates that raged within the workers' movement at the time. Here I settle for something less.

Writing *Beyond a Boundary* appeared a pressing necessity because of a rather mundane sports scandal in 1950. University basketball teams had been bought by bookmakers, paid to fix games. James had always restrained himself, coming as he did from another culture, another way of life, and he never questioned American mores, suppressing his instinctual opposition to what he regarded as the strangeness of much that was done: "If they played that way that was their way." Yet as the daily press broke the news of the corruption of young basketball players, James proved incapable of maintaining his reserve, lapsing into a questioning that increasingly took on a judgmental tone. Reared within the code of Trinidadian public-school cricket, James simply could not fathom the lack of loyalty that the basketball scandal signified: "That young men playing for school or university should behave in this way on such a scale was utterly shocking to me." Yet that shock was not to be seen on the countenances of his comrades: "The boys were wrong in being caught, that was all. The school? Why should they put 'the school' above what they wanted." Within the confines of an ostensibly revolutionary movement, where all spoke the same language, read the same books, and adhered to the same program, opened up an immense gulf between James and the people to whom he was bound closely. And out of all of this came James's fixation on what he thought his history and his politics did not seem to address: "What did men live by? What did they want? What did history show that they had wanted? Had they wanted then what they wanted now? . . . What exactly was art and what exactly culture?"[30]

For James, "A glance at the world showed that when the common people were not at work, one thing they wanted was organized sports and games. They wanted them greedily, passionately." And they wanted them against the devotion of the "politicians," the disciples of culture, the patronizing of the aesthetes, the smug superiority of the churches. They wanted to partake in the spectacle of sport, the professionalization of athletics, and the patriotism of championship contests at precisely the historical moment that popular democracy was being struggled for and secured. They wanted these games in the slums of the industrial capitalist First World and in the outer reaches of empire, to which they were rigorously exported and promoted. Amidst the liberalization of class relations associated with the decline of Chartism, the reformist legislation of the third quarter of the nineteenth century, and the consolidation of an enormous proletarian and clerical urban public, games, too, were what was wanted, as well as factory acts and franchise extension and trade union rights. The human component of the Industrial Revolution, engaged in a ubiquitous defensive quest for improved wages and conditions, managed, as well, to win "for themselves one great victory, freedom on Saturday afternoon. They were 'waiting to be amused.' "[31]

This process could be read as a deflection from politics. James refused this view. Instead, his pre-Derridean deconstruction of the language of cricket took hold of the two-sidedness of the sport. There was no escaping the confinements of this culture, brought to the "natives" dripping with racial and class prejudice, rigidly locked into the established structures of subordination that it undoubtedly reinforced. But another dimension existed: the game's potential as a lever of liberation, its capacity to *force* recognition of basic inequities. "The conflict and rivalries which arose out of the conditions I have described gripped me," reported James. "My Puritan soul burnt with indignation at injustice in the sphere of sport. . . . Cricket had plunged me into politics long before I was aware of it. When I did turn to politics I did not have too much to learn." Robert Lipsyte captures some of the meaning of *Beyond a Boundary* in his preface to the American edition:

> In a cranny of Sports World stands the black Tanapuna Cricket Club, racist, classist memento and victim of British imperialism. Impeccably attired, stiffly contained, the Saturday heroes strut on a stage that is also their cage; the Tunapuna C.C. seems at first an easy metaphor for oppression in sports.
>
> Yet the matches held on this pitch, and the anticipation, gossip, and analysis that swirl around them, are also the joy of Tunapuna, a small town eight miles from Trinidad's capital, Port of Spain. Cricket heroes are not only entertainers here, they seem to offer promise and possibility. The metaphor becomes cloudy. There is liberation, too. . . . C. L. R. James gets to the root of the exhilarating liberation from class and race and future that exists during the transcendent moments of play; but he never forgets that this liberation exists only within the boundaries of the game. . . . Each club represented an economic level, a skin hue, a social stratum. The rivalries were so intense that cricket became an unending allegory. Leading players were symbols of a drama that would have become literally murderous had it been played out beyond the boundary. . . . even cricket was not always cricket.[32]

The language of cricket thus illuminates class and race relations in a colonial setting. It speaks with a dialect understandably divided against itself through the clash of resignation and rebellion. But it always resonates, in *Beyond a Boundary*, with actual historical experience, captured in the lives of the players themselves. From the crude and vulgar Matthew Bondman, mired in wretched poverty and "good for nothing except to play cricket," and that only for a time, to the stoic Bowler John, who faced injustice in scowling silence and responded to a remark from white authority that he looked dejected with a curt reminder that "My face is my own and I'll do what I like with it," the actors in James's cricket game are engaged in a dramatic spectacle. Their lines are scripted by the game, to be sure, but they also have their origins in and mediate realms of power, oppression, and subordination. Like James himself, they are all "on a stage in which the parts were set in advance."[33] We are back to *The Eighteenth Brumaire*.

The cricket field thus provided a locale where the oppressions of race and the limitations of class could be overcome, however briefly and episodically. Beyond the boundaries of the field, however, the social relations of subordination and the structures of power remained. James explores how this dualism played itself out in the Trinidadian public school, where the fictional overcoming of boundaries is lived for a time in the equality of black and white on the field. But once the field is left behind and the old school tie fades beyond the boundary, the hard presence of class and race reappears. Ultimately human links are forged between members of the same class or caste.[34]

Yet the possibilities that, for generations, seemed present on the field are not easily forgotten. When C. L. R. James returned to the West Indies in 1958, after twenty-six years of absence, his manuscript on cricket under his arm, he plunged into the politics of West Indian self-determination. The language of cricket still spoke of imperialist authority, of the racial exclusion of blacks from captaincies of teams, of the maneuverings of West Indian officialdom in the preservation of things that "were not cricket," of international scandals and the severity of local umpires on Trinidad players. The old colonial code, by which true "sports" never protested discrimination, was tossed aside in the newly politicized nationalist crusade. James played a pivotal role in waging a popular campaign to break the color barrier against blacks captaining international teams, and the Trinidadian Frank Worrell was appointed captain of the West Indian team that was to tour Australia in 1960. The language of cricket and the discourse of politics now seemed as one, merged in the crucible of mobilization and change:

> All art, science, philosophy, are modes of apprehending the world, history and society. As one of these, cricket in the West Indies at least could hold its own. . . . In the inevitable integration into a national community, one of the most urgent needs, sport, and particulary cricket, has played and will play a great role. There is no one in the West Indies who will not subscribe to the aphorism: what do they know of cricket who only cricket know?[35]

And in his appreciation of how this process unfolded, James adopts a formulation quite compatible with one of his favored texts. Again, we are back with *The Eighteenth Brumaire*: "So there we are, all tangled up together, the old barriers breaking down and the new ones not yet established, a time of transition, always and inescapably turbulent."[36]

James wrote well before the implosion of theory and outside of any awareness of the stress on language that would figure forcefully in structuralism and poststructuralism. Ariel Dorfman's *The Empire's Old Clothes: What the Lone Ranger, Babar, and Other Innocent Heroes Do to Our Minds* can hardly be fitted into the same prelinguistic space, for Dorfman quotes Barthes and is certainly aware of recent developments in critical theory. Yet for all of this, it is not the linguistic turn that dominates Dorfman's reading of the central figures of popular culture, but more orthodox associations grounded in a historical materialist world view. Much like the early Barthes, Dorfman probes the cultural symbols of our time to uncover the ahistorical, prettifying ways in which ideas and values are manipulated to mask essential relations of inequality, be they lived out between nations (colonialism) or individuals embedded in long-established socioeconomic relations (class exploitation and racial oppression).

Dorfman, like James, begins with the historically determined social relations of inequality, personalized in the case of a Chilean woman slum dweller. She challenged Dorfman's insistence that the illusions of romantic novels adorned with photographic images of handsome actors were hazardous to her political health and future. The woman from the streets had no need of Dorfman's message of purification. "Don't do that to us, *compañerito*," she told him tenderly, "Don't take my dreams away from me." Months later Allende's election restructured politics (Dorfman has, unfortunately, nothing to say about the illusions of that moment of reformist social democracy, and how hazardous it would prove to so many Chileans), and the critic and the slum dweller met again. She announced that she did not read trash anymore. "Now, *compañero*," she added, "we are dreaming reality."

This anecdote is Dorfman's point of departure, setting up the argument that to liquidate hundreds of years of economic and social injustice it is not only mandatory to restructure the commanding heights of the economy but also "to democratize and control a territory more difficult to split up and expropriate, a territory called communication." The woman of the Chilean poor was but one of hundreds of thousands who was being awakened to the possibilities of human life that open out when power is suddenly taken from the few and can be seen as a prerogative of the many. As Dorfman suggests, what that woman and others like her needed was "a new language. The Chilean people and its intellectuals tried to produce that new language, or at least fragments of it, intimations of it. . . . To do so . . . would assist in the elaboration of another sort of communications system which would reject authoritarian and competitive models and provoke doubts, questions, dialogue, real participation, and, eventually, a breakthrough in popular art." This project moved Dorfman to analyze the ways in which the superhero mass literature of the children's comic and the infantilization of knowledge in magazines such as *Reader's Digest* obscured and mystified the systemic domination of everyday life, conditioning a pervasive process of repression, in which reality's unsettling questions were transformed into bland, docile, comforting answers. Children, first, and then men and women, were being formed in part by a language of complacent conventionality: it was right not to rebel.

> And such a process does not happen only in Chile. On the contrary, if people in the so-called Third World are expected to swallow these deformed versions of reality (along with heavier goods and foreign technology), it is because those messages have been produced by the "developed" countries in the first place and injected into their populace in hardly more sophisticated forms. The same methods which the cultural industry uses to narrate, observe, transmit problems in Europe and especially in the U.S. are those which, with minor modifications and at times adaptations, are imported into our miserable and twisted zones.

Third and First world, economic development and popular culture, came together in this making of consumer conventionality.[37]

The Empire's Old Clothes proceeds from this generalized position into case studies of Babar the Elephant, Donald Duck, the Lone Ranger, and *Reader's Digest*. In Babar and the characters of Walt Disney, Dorfman locates the absence of history, the fulfillment of imperialism's colonial dreams, and the masking of capitalism's exploitative essence in the reification of the accumulation process:

> Just as Babar created a kingdom where nature and development were allied, in which civilization and barbarism could be reconciled, so the little ducks present to their readers—children of all ages—the possibility of realizing the most dogged, undying dream of the twentieth century, the dream which led to the founding of the USA, the dream of working and being your own boss at the same time. . . . Such a movement, from inferior to superior, from primitive to urban, from poverty to progress, coincides with the aesthetic experience of reading that the reader has of the world, the way that he vicariously consumes the life of its characters. The reader begins

these cartoons as if he were in an underdeveloped territory, with no control over events, and ends up having acquiesced to illumination, revelation, and success—thereby resolving his tensions and ignorance. The worlds of these "animals" are sheltered from all criticism. It's not just that it's impossible to infiltrate . . . social class and raise a hand to display a photograph of a hungry child, an illiterate person, a military coup taking place, or a violation of human rights. . . . It's that the reader himself has already accepted a formulation about children's literature—it's all harmless fun—which leaves no room for any alternatives. . . . And so, in the end, the reader himself stands at the door to his kingdom like a guardian demon, forbidding entrance to anyone who wants to ask impertinent questions. . . . When the door shuts behind him, leaving him supposedly secure in that magical, saintly space called children's literature, he won't see the blind alley into which he's stumbled, the blind alley which is his past without history and his future without history. He doesn't see it because someone . . . is painting the four infinite walls, the floor and the ceiling, someone is painting on a very hard and very real wall a horizon that does not exist.

As the child grows to adolescence and adulthood, he or she is bombarded with the same message, elephants and ducks giving way to Lone Rangers and Batmen, Hardy Boys and Nancy Drews, *Reader's Digests* and Harlequin romances. These sources teach sex roles, perverse and deformed visions of history, the necessity of adapting to the world as it presently is in order to succeed, and, above and beyond all else, the need not to question. They are comfort itself, enhanced by the rituals surrounding them: "As long as the isolated and scattered faithful renew their faith through the ritual of reading and through that other ritual which is subscription and purchase, the *Digest* is there to reassure them, superior but so close, so familiar, such a good friend, so entertaining, such a part of our lives."[38] Like language itself.

There is no indication that Dorfman has been at all influenced by deconstructive developments, yet his scrutiny of the violent exorcising of history from the pages of popular culture is posed in a language that complements the radical kernel of Derridean readings. When Pontiac is a commodity rolling out of an auto plant rather than a chief of the first American peoples, history has been commercialized and reduced to the dictates of profit. Dorfman is able to read the Lone Ranger in this way, seeing each episode as "an act of omission, a silence, a history book with blank pages . . . [that] purges the violence, erases the conquests, and causes all the strife to settle like the dust on the plains." What is missed is nothing less than the origin of property, the rough, bloody edges of this process of struggle and expropriation that in America ran its course in aboriginal extermination and pacification, smoothed over in a sentimentalized naturalization of ownership as pure in its purpose and "lawful" in its acquisition.

Everything in the subliterary genre is thus the negation of history. Dorfman's book is a tireless assault on the implications of this kind of construction of reality and what it reproduces in its readers:

> The actual fact that humanity is reborn with every baby, and that each new arrival potentially has the right—and I think the duty—to remake the history he or she inherits, is transformed into a purification of that history and that inheritance. To begin at zero, without personal memory, is seized as an occasion for the erasure of collective memory and history; is used to whitewash and forget the past, to which the newest arrival, whether he likes it or not, is linked.[39]

Where this passage breaks from deconstruction and Derrida most decisively, of course, is in its explicit historical materialism, its unashamed espousal of political meaning. There are others whose handling of language grows out of similar imperatives.

► *The History of Language*

It is simply not the case that social historians have avoided discussion of language, although it is true that they have seldom mounted their work on the theoretical introspection demanded by many in line with the linguistic turn. Christopher Hill, for instance, can be held up as an example of how a social historian attentive to writing and ideas in particular contexts can hardly avoid language.[40] But it is Asa Briggs who most clearly confronted language, albeit in ways that avoided even the most cursory gesture to linguistic theory.

Briggs wrote two pioneering articles on the language of class and the language of mass and masses.[41] Anyone with an elementary appreciation of the fine points of poststructuralism's theoretical edifice will have many a quibble with Briggs's approach, attentive as it was to the contextualized emergence of "new verbal frameworks or 'vocabularies' within which experience, old and new, was expressed and communicated."[42] There are almost too many violations of the premises of critical theory in these two lines for discourse's true believers to fathom.

Yet in their attention to the ways in which particular words develop within specific social formations and then begin to help in the reproduction of that politico-economic order, Briggs's articles stand as the beginning point that any history of language avoids at great peril. As a language of ranks, orders, degrees, and interests was succeeded by a language of class and mass, the political economy of eighteenth-century

Britain, a confusing swirl of paternalism, commercialism, agrarianism, and colonialism, gave way to the more focused consolidations of nineteenth-century industrial capitalism. *Class* and *mass* were still used vaguely and metaphorically, but there was a certain understanding of their meanings, and the relationship between them and the structured economics of production and consumption. Words illuminated historical processes, as one late nineteenth-century journalist noted: "Men grope in a kind of linguistic bewilderment until the phrasemonger comes along, and gives them a proper form of expression. Then they are as if a great light had suddenly beamed upon them. The lucky words relieve a strain, and enthusiasm follows."[43]

This kind of discovery appears in the work of Raymond Williams, most explicitly in his discussion of the laborer poet John Clare and what Williams calls "the green language." This green language is the way in which those who lived through the transformation of the country by the incursions of the market, class differentiation, and exploitation managed to survive. In Williams's view, this language connects feelings of human warmth and community at the moment of their dissolution in the dispossessions, evictions, and divisions of the late eighteenth century:

> Bred in a village full of strife and noise,
> Old senseless gossips, and blackguarding boys,
> Ploughmen and threshers, whose discourses led
> To nothing more than labour's rude employs,
> 'Bout work being slack, and rise and fall of bread
> And who were like to die, and who were like to wed.[44]

Language is thus an activity with a history, imprisoned not in some dualistic dichtomized state of synchronic here and diachronic there:

> What we can then define is a dialectical process: the *changing practical consciousness of human beings,* in which both the evolutionary and the historical processes can be given full weight, but also within which they can be distinguished, in the complex variations of actual language use. It is from this theoretical foundation that we can go on to distinguish "literature," in a specific sociohistorical development of writing, from the abstract retrospective concept, so common in orthodox Marxism, which reduces it, like language itself, to a function and then a (superstructural) by-product of collective labour.[45]

From these kinds of premises Williams developed a theory of cultural materialism, increasingly compatible with Marxism, its historical movement steadily leftward, flying in the face of fashion and the canons of literary criticism.[46]

Williams can, of course, be challenged, and especially from the stand-point of Marxism.[47] R. S. Neale has recently argued that Williams understates the determining force of modes of production and their consequent class relations, privileging instead a notion of cultural production that emphasizes language as constitutive, thus threatening to domesticate the materialist conception of history. Against Williams's intuitive attraction to the radical possibilities of language, Neale offers a more pessimistic reading:

> I agree with Williams that human labour is inextricably meshed with the human capacity to produce language as practical consciousness; language *is* always mixed with labour in production— but we differ in our conclusions. In short, *because* language is mixed with labour in production, one might say, under capitalism, and as labour power has two elements—necessary labour and surplus labour—language, as practical consciousness, may also be thought to contain two elements, necessary language and surplus language. In both instances, which are really the same instance, the surplus is appropriated and transformed into a product which stands over and above the labourers (women and men) who possess only a stunted life and a stunted necessary language of labour and everyday life. Marx's concept of alienation encompasses the latter pole, ideology and Gramsci's concept of hegemony the former. And this is to say quite simply that language, like capital, *is* an instrument of domination, a carrier of cultural power.[48]

As a corrective Neale's attack on cultural materialism has value; but it appears, in the face of Williams's contribution, to be one-sided and overly blunt.[49]

For Williams's *oeuvre* is immense, his impact and reach virtually unprecedented. In terms of the ways in which he employed a conception of language and its making over time to reformulate whole arenas of social theory, he stands almost alone.[50] In *Keywords* he began the difficult process of challenging structuralist hegemony within the field of linguistics, an effort that, as Williams himself acknowledged, is not unrelated to the writing of social history:

> Certain crises around certain experiences will occur, which are registered in language in often surprising ways. The result is a notion of language as not merely the creation of arbitrary signs which are then reproduced within groups, which is the structuralist model, but of signs which take on the changeable and often reversed social relations of a given society, so that what enters into them is the contradictory and conflict-ridden social history of the people who speak the language, including all the variations between signs

at any given time. This also involves the rejection of idealist accounts of language as common possession . . . [allowing] us to look at a whole body of social evidence which can be quite precisely studied and related to the rest of social history, but which has never been fully explored. For people who might otherwise have been predisposed to do so have generally assumed that language is merely the instrument or the record of the changes which have happened elsewhere; whereas it seems to me that certain shifts of meaning indicate very interesting periods of confusion and contradiction of outcome, latencies in decision, and other processes of real social history, which can be located rather precisely in this other way and put alongside more familiar kinds of evidence.[51]

From his vitally important discussion of "Base and Superstructure in Marxist Cultural Theory," through commentary on signs and notations in *Marxism and Literature*, to a plethora of articles and chapters structured around concern with writing and authors, Williams, whatever his overt subject, never ventured far from language. For him, with his intense intellectual desire to reconstruct a world wracked by class exploitation and the deformations of imperialism and capitalism, "the field of language and of non-verbal communication" always seemed "a good and practicable place to start."[52] We can question his choice of beginnings, just as we can differ from where they take him. But within Williams's frame of reference there is much to learn.

You would not know this looking at the organs of poststructuralism or reading a manifesto emanating from the corner of the advocates of language. Within such circles Williams, and even more Briggs, are babes in a heavily underbrushed woods of theory. Their materialist and historical "prejudices" confine them in a certain dowdy traditionalism. They produce tales, to be sure, but they apparently signify little.[53] In this regard they are not so different than that well-known story of the making of the English working class.

► ### *Language and* The Making of the
English Working Class

E. P. Thompson has spawned an industry of historiographic criticism. While this industry marketed its wares in the shadow of *The Poverty of Theory* (1978), few of its entrepreneurial activists could avoid the text that influenced a generation of working-class historians and established Thompson as a major figure to be contended with in any serious discussion of historical practice. *The Making of the English Working Class* (1963) is probably one of the most discussed and quoted works of social history ever produced, demanding attention twenty-five years after its original publication and finding its way, through translation and informal academic discussion, into virtually every corner of the modern world.[54]

Noticeably absent in this outpouring of commentary have been literary critics and historians fixated on discourse, at least until quite recently.[55] As Jim Merod, who describes Thompson as an "underutilized figure" in the critical mainstream, notes, the *"Making of the English Working Class* is possibly the most evaded historical or critical 'classic' in the whole of literary study."[56] Hayden White breaks this silence with a four-page discussion of Thompson as tropologist, stressing the extent to which his study of class formation and class consciousness is dependent on language and conceptualization that constructs a "reality" that is supposedly present in a "real historical context" exposed to historical scrutiny by documentary evidence and theoretical suggestion. The discourse of Thompson's text is divided by a logic of "tropological organization" that carries the reader along a relentless progression. For all of Thompson's opposition to the tendency of both positivisitic sociology and vulgar Marxism to assume a predictive law of class formation, White suggests that the trajectory of *The Making of the English Working Class* is predictable in its phases and sequential elaboration: it moves from the vague popular traditions of Part I, "Liberty Tree," through the economic determinations of "The Curse of Adam" and the crystallization of a spirited working-class opposition in "The Working-Class Presence" of Peterloo and beyond in Parts II and III to the class consciousness of the 1820s and 1830s. Stressing Thompson's ironic appreciation of the extent to which class consciousness was made, only to suffer a series of stunning defeats and reverses in the 1830s, White regards the concluding passages of the book as evidence not only of an objective historical process but also, importantly, of authorial self-consciousness. He argues that what Thompson discerned as the making of a class was a pattern as much "imposed upon his data as it was found in them." *The Making of the English Working Class* is thus an unwitting prisoner of the theory of tropes, in which the structure of any self-conscious and self-critical text passes from a naive metaphorical discourse to a more self-critical ironic comprehension of itself. Thompson's English working class is "made" as much in the structure of his narrative discourse as it is in historical "reality," a thoroughly understandable and unsurprising phenomenon for someone who, like White, is committed to a notion of the content of the form.[57]

This all has the ring of intellectual gamesmanship about it, although it is not without its uses. White's metacommentary forces recognition of the elementary point that there is no such thing as unmediated objective reconstruction of the past; it is also suggestive, but by no means conclusive and definitive, in its claim of the ways in which all kinds of discourse are structured by the conventions of form. But in "reading" Thompson in this narrow, indeed reductionist, way, we actually lose more than we gain, even if we restrict the terrain of discussion to language itself. For beyond the metastructure of the text's unfolding does lie page after page of Thompson's own engagement with a history built empirically but conceived through language and in language in ways that allow new appreciations of both past and present. To see *The Making of the English Working Class* as White has seen it is to view the text from a particular Olympian height, in which all kinds of geography are obliterated in a cavalier dismissal of whatever possible integrity the past can hold through a privileging of the determined forms of the mind of the present.[58]

Those who have seen Thompson speak in public will appreciate the extent to which language and its uses are central to his understanding of the past as well as to his own relationship with his audience. Relying upon dialect and accent to convey meaning, reaching into the often carnivalesque contours of plebeian and working-class life as they imprint themselves on historical documents, Thompson's force as an historian is in part his grasp of a Volosinovian sense of the multiaccentuality of language. This allows him not only to decode and refocus evidence that coats the history of subordinate groups in condescension, but also to develop subtle reconsiderations of vital planks in the structure of hegemony: deference and paternalism, for instance, have taken on new meaning on the basis of his attention to the inflections and tones of vocabularies that speak in more than one voice, of signs that encompass resistance as well as resignation. The point could be made with reference to laboring people's internalization of the capitalist discipline of time, or by an exploration of the language and activity of the eighteenth-century crowd, or through a look at the rituals of the wife sale and charivari, or in analysis of the tradition of the threatening letter.[59] It lies at the heart of Thompson's forthcoming studies of plebeian culture in eighteenth-century England, *Customs in Common.*[60] Countless examples, then, could be marshaled. One will suffice, drawn from the linguistic contest between a J. P. and a cloth worker, accused by his employer of neglecting his work:

> *Justice:* Come in Edmund, I have talked with your Master.
> *Edmund:* Not *my Master*, and't please your Worship, I hope I am *my own Master.*
> *Justice:* Well, your Employer, Mr. E. ——, the Clothier: will the word Employer do?
> *Edmund:* Yes, yes, and't please your Worship, any thing, but *Master.*[61]

When Thompson takes the words and tone of a miner to end a review of a book on Methodism and the Durham colliery workers with a blunt "And *fookin'* Amen to that!" he is articulating many things.[62] One of them is the importance of the class-based multiaccentuality of language that he probed substantially in *The Making of the English Working Class.*

To pour over Thompson's text is to confront language, broadly conceived, on literally every page. The book opens with the arrests of Hardy and his comrades in the London Corresponding Society. One of the incarcerated reformers, John Thelwall, recalls his interrogation before the Privy Council, "the whole Dramatis Personae intrenched chin deep in Lectures and manuscripts . . . all scattered about in the utmost confusion":

> *Attorney General* (piano): Mr. Thelwall, what is your Christian name?
> *T.* (somewhat sullenly). John.
> *Att. Gen.* (piano still) . . . With two l's at the end or with one?
> *T.* With two—but it does not signify. (Carelessly, but rather sullen, or so.)

A fourteen-year-old lad was then examined but stood his ground and "entered into a political harangue, in which he used very harsh language against Mr. Pitt, upbraiding him with having taxed the people to an enormous extent." Thompson takes this and other evidence to present, not a view of unrepentant class conflict, but an appreciation of the gropings of the personnel and language of reform and authority toward their appropriate stances: "By the standards of the next 100 years the antagonists appear to be strangely amateurish and uncertain of their roles, rehearsing in curiously personal encounters the massive impersonal encounters of the future."[63]

Then follow explorations of the legacies of the eighteenth century, of "the foundation texts of the English working-class movement," most especially *Pilgrim's Progress.* The chapter "Christian and Apollyon" explores Bunyan's text as a slumbering radicalism awakened in the changed context of the nineteenth century by specific languages of devotion and communitarianism that related to "the positive energy of *Puritanism*" or the "self-preserving retreat of *Dissent.*" These traditions carried a language of common appreciation, whatever the diversity of sects and chapels, and it was through the brotherhood, sisterhood, and enlightenment of the Sunday school, the Old Testament, and *Pilgrim's Progress,* argues Thompson, that the men and women experiencing the Industrial Revolution resolved the tensions between worldly developments and the kingdom within. The evocative images and language of the Old Testament were fundamental to this process and infused the emerging movements of protest with a particular potency that Thompson is at pains to locate empirically and theoretically:

> when we speak of "imagery" we mean much more than figures of speech in which ulterior motives were "clothed." The imagery is itself evidence of powerful subjective motivations, fully as "real" as the objective, fully as effective, as we see repeatedly in the history of Puritanism, in their historical agency. It is the sign of how men felt and hoped, loved and hated, and of how they preserved certain values in the very texture of their language. . . . Whenever we encounter such phenomena, we must try to distinguish between the psychic energy stored—and released—in language, however apocalyptic, and actual psychotic disorder.

Whatever sins one wants to attribute to Thompson, and there is now a lengthy list compiled by his critics, inattention to language is surely not one of them.[64]

Thompson's second foundation-text of the English working-class movement is Paine's *Rights of Man*. Out of it was reforged an invigorated appreciation of the rights of free-born Englishmen. While the political arguments of Paine weighed heavily in all of this, Thompson is aware of Paine's deficiencies as a systematic theorist; it is to the tone of Paine that he turns to reveal his strengths as a publicist. And it is a tone that resonates with a particular historical conjuncture, in which industrial capitalism and its class antagonists have not yet carved themselves indelibly into the political economy. Many of Thompson's critics charge him, implicitly or explicitly, with mythologizing the small producer radicalism of the reform cause he delineates in the pages of *The Making of the English Working Class*.[65] Yet he recognizes the extent to which the *Rights of Man* and the *Wealth of Nations* are companion texts, championing the virtues of an unobstructed economic market: "however hard trade unionists might fight against their employers—industrial capital was assumed to be the fruit of enterprise and beyond reach of political intrusion. Until the 1880s, it was, by and large, within this framework that working-class Radicalism remained transfixed." No advocate of proletarian power, Paine's importance for Thompson lies in his "new rhetoric of radical egalitarianism," in which contempt for monarchical and hereditary principles, unbounded faith in representative political institutions, refusal to accept that human nature contained streaks of viciousness and selfishness, and the relentless appeal to reason all figured forcefully. All of this was expressed, finally, "in an intransigent, brash, even cocksure tone, with the self-educated man's distrust of tradition and institutes of learning . . . and a tendency to avoid complex theoretical problems with a dash of empiricism and an appeal to 'Common Sense.' " Paine's power is captured in this passage from the *Age of Reason,* in which he ridicules the authority of the Bible in a manner calculated to address the life histories of many of the dispossessed:

> the person they call Jesus Christ, begotten, they say, by a ghost, whom they call holy, on the body of a woman engaged in marriage, and afterwards married, and whom they call a virgin seven hundred years after this foolish story was told. . . . Were any girl that is now with child to say . . . that she was gotten with child by a ghost, and that an angel told her so, would she be believed?

This polemical literalness, Thompson argues, structured English radicalism in ways that both propelled and inhibited the working-class movement for a century and more.[66]

To authority, Paine's "indefinite language of delusion" threatened mass agitation. In the proliferation of societies and enthusiasm for revolution that coincided with Paine's rise to popularity and upheaval in France, Thompson locates "a new stridency of republican rhetoric." He provides a detailed narrative of the artisan radicalism of the early-to-mid 1790s, focusing on the Jacobin, John Thelwall, and the rhetorical extension of Paine beyond the sphere of politics per se into the domains of economic and social life. In the language of Thelwall's *The Rights of Nature* (1796), Thompson sees Jacobinism pushed to the borders of socialism and revolution:

> I affirm that *every* man, and *every* woman, and *every* child, ought to obtain something more, in the general distribution of the fruits of labour, than food, and rags, and a wretched hammock with a poor rug to cover it; and that, without working twelve or fourteen hours a day . . . some means of or such information as may lead to an understanding of their rights. . . . Monopoly, and the hideous accumulation of capital in a few hands . . . carry in their own enormity, the seeds of cure. . . . Whatever presses men together . . . though it may generate some vices, is favourable to the diffusion of knowledge, and ultimately promotive of human liberty. . . . Hence every large workshop and manufactory is a sort of political society, which no act of parliament can silence, and no magistrate disperse.

Language such as this nurtured the liberty tree throughout the 1790s, and many seedlings sprouted in unlikely quarters, including, suggests Thompson, among United Irishmen, Scottish weavers, and mutinous seamen. Against the counter-revolutionary panic of the ruling classes, expressed in every part of social life, this language of rights kept Jacobin traditions alive, sustaining internationalism, self-education, and rational criticism at the very moment that they were under seige. "With the bell ringing, and the clamour of the mill, all the vale is disturb'd," noted one visitor to a Yorkshire cotton mill, adding with worry, "treason and leveling systems are the discourse; and rebellion may be near at hand."[67]

The Making of the English Working Class is introduced, then, by a wide-ranging discussion of eighteenth-century popular radicalism that is about nothing if it is not about discourse. While Thompson's attention to language is contextualized, most especially in terms of the political side of political economy, he has struggled most persistently to locate the language of the majority within its own tones, accents, and limitations. This immersion in the words, texts, signs, and inflections of popular discourse proves to be both strength and weakness.

On the one hand, its power is the unprecedented capacity of Thompson's text to convey "the structure of feeling"[68] that linked diverse sections of a plebeian constituency in dissolution and a working class not yet consolidated. However different, the many constituencies of these social groupings found commonalities of experience in the dislocations and debasements of capital's increasing concentration and the political state's repressive response to the threat—domestic and international—of revolution. Yet, on the other hand, as we move from Part I, "The Liberty Tree," to Part II, "The Curse of Adam," it can be argued that Thompson's choice to begin with the language of popular liberty structures, indeed overdetermines, his argument about the experience of economic life.

His discussion of exploitation, for instance, though it gestures toward Marx, concerns itself all too little with the structured extraction of surplus and the accumulation process. Instead, exploitation is defined as it would have been perceived to have been lived by Thelwall and other Jacobins:[69] "the most bitter conflicts of these years turned on issues which are not encompassed by cost-of-living series. The issues which provoked the most intensity of feeling were very often ones in which such values as traditional customs, 'justice,' 'independence,' security, or family-economy were at stake, rather than straight-forward 'bread-and-butter' issues." The exploitive relationship is thus depicted as "more than the sum of grievances and mutual antagonisms . . . which can be seen to take distinct forms in different historical contexts, forms which are related to corresponding forms of ownership and State power." In this exploitive relationship antagonism is accepted as intrinsic; management represses all concern save that with the expropriation of the maximum surplus value from labor. "This is the political economy which Marx anatomised in *Das Kapital*," concludes Thompson, adding, "The worker has become an 'instrument,' or an entry among other items of cost." It is not that this is wrong. Rather, it blurs many different components of the social relations of production together, with the result that Thompson's discussion of exploitation is in fact a melange concerned with alienation, immiseration, and, above all, exposing the extent to which academic scholarship has lost sight of "exploitation" in the empiricist determinism of quantities: "In the scrutiny of credit facilities or of the terms of trade, when each event is explicable and appears also as a self-sufficient cause of other events, we arrive at a *post facto* determinism. The dimension of human agency is lost, and the context of class relations is forgotten."[70]

Thompson's embeddedness in the language of Jacobinism transfers itself into a conception of "exploitation" that understandably predates Marx, exposing not so much the economic extraction of surplus as the trampling of rights. The consequence is a theoretical insistence on human agency and a polemical challenge to received wisdoms of class formation. It is this framework and set of analytic concerns that explain how a chapter on "exploitation" can say so little about the brutal impositions of accumulation and so much about how workers made themselves:

> we should not assume any automatic, or over-direct, correspondence between the dynamic of economic growth and the dynamic of social or cultural life. . . . too much emphasis upon the newness of the cotton-mills can lead to an underestimation of the continuity of political and cultural traditions in the making of working-class communities. . . . The making of the working class is a fact of political and cultural, as much as of economic, history. . . . The working class made itself as much as it was made.

And in all of this there can be no question of the importance of language and of its differentiations of accent and conception: "the Sunderland sailor, the Irish navvy, the Jewish costermonger, the inmate of an East Anglian village workhouse, the compositor on *The Times*—all might be seen by their 'betters' as belonging to the 'lower classes' while they themselves might scarcely understand each others' dialect."[71]

The Making of the English Working Class, however, is no prison-house of language. The remaining chapters in Part II detail how the experiences of field laborers, weavers, artisans, and others touched down on common standards of life and within similar universes of morality, religion, and chialism. In these sections the embeddedness *in* language gives way to an elaboration of deprivation and poverty, constructed through a language whose tone is consistently polemical, butting itself against an academic community too often given to apologetics and cover-ups and historical figures whose sanctimonious purpose it was to "solve" the problems of economic transformation on the backs of the laboring class:

A notable victory for Dr. Kay and Mr. Plum! Twelve able-bodied females made frugal and prudent (perhaps transmogrified from pessimists to optimists?) at a blow!

The "average" working man remained very close to subsistence level at a time when he was surrounded by the evidence of the increase of national wealth, much of it transparently the product of his own labour, and passing, by equally transparent means, into the hands of his employers. In psychological terms, this felt very much like a decline in standards. His own share in the "benefits" of economic "progress" consisted of more potatoes, a few articles of cotton clothing for his family, soap and candles, some tea and sugar, and a great many articles in the *Economic History Review*.

More recently, one writer has surveyed the issue with that air of boredom appropriate to the capacious conscience of the Nuclear Age. The modern reader, he says, "well disciplined by familiarity with concentration camps" is left "comparatively unmoved" by the spectacle of child labour. We may be allowed to reaffirm a more traditional view: that the exploitation of little children, on this scale and with this intensity, was one of the most shameful events in our history.[72]

Thompson begins to move back toward language and signification after this exploration of experience and its consequent polemics. This return to discourse commences with his reconnecting the threads of Puritanism, Dissent, and Nonconformity in the changed context of "exploitation." Methodism proves the crucible in which the laborers are to be turned into their own slave drivers: "The Methodist was taught not only to 'bear his Cross' of poverty and humiliation; the crucifixion was (as Ure saw) the very pattern of his obedience: 'True followers of our bleeding Lamb, Now on Thy daily cross we die. . . .' Work was the Cross from which the 'transformed' industrial worker hung." Thompson then engages in an extraordinary discussion of the symbolism of Wesleyan Methodist hymns, in which a language of maternal, Oedipal, sexual, sado-masochistic, sacrificial imagery twisted human spontaneity into its reverse, constructing grace in the performance of painful, laborious, self-denying tasks. Indoctrinated to submit to this "psychic exploitation," drawn by the comforts of place that church membership bestowed, and consoled by doctrine in the years of counter-revolution, Methodists found themselves in a prison-house of language and symbolism, as real in its ideological confinements as any architectural structure was in its physical restrictions. And yet even here, for all the extremity of his argument, Thompson is cognizant of the class-based tensions inherent in any such process of signification:

> In the Old Testament working people found more than a vengeful authoritarian God; they also found an allegory of their own tribulations. It is this body of symbolism (together with *Pilgrim's Progress*) which was held in common by Chialists, "Johannas," "Jumpers" and orthodox Wesleyans. No ideology is wholly absorbed by its adherents: it breaks down in practice in a thousand ways under the criticism of impulse and of experience: the working-class community injected into the chapels its own values of mutual aid, neighbourliness and solidarity.

Many apparently took to heart "the language of one of the unpaid Ministers of the Independent Methodists of the Newcastle district" when he declared, "The rod of God's strength, which comes out of Zion, is not a rod of oppression."[73]

The presence of community is thus the protective armor shielding the working class from the totality of assaults associated with "exploitation," Methodism, and counter-revolution. It was a community besieged, its entertainments and language constantly under attack as disgusting and demoralizingly obscene. Yet friendly societies and trade unions merged languages of mutuality and brotherhood, just as craft processions articulated a discourse of artisan producerism in their regalia, banners, and slogans. Collectivist values survived, along with what Thompson calls "a definite moral code, with sanctions against the blackleg, the 'tools' of the employer or the unneighbourly, and with an intolerance towards the eccentric or the individualist." In "political theory, trade union ceremonial, moral rhetoric" this working-class culture, with its disciplines and institutions, distinguishes itself from the eighteenth-century plebeian milieu.[74]

The final section of Thompson's text, Part III, "The Working-Class Presence," assumes this community's existence and explores the challenges it mounts against ruling authority, both economically and politically. Much of the story is submerged in the illegalities of opposition and the clandestine character of resistance movements such as Luddism. Neither language nor sign expose themselves readily and self-consciously in this "opaque society," leading Thompson to rely on informers' accounts that he knows tilt the Home Office papers in a distorting direction. He dissects their language in masterful strokes, drawing out the valuable and discarding the contrived. Quoting two spies' reports in 1817, Thompson contrasts their form, and from this outlines a balance sheet of linguistic credibility:

> The first appears to be as credible as any account by an untrained reporter. Clearly, the informer was impressed, despite himself, . . . and he has recorded, more vividly than the "literary" versions usually published in the Radical press, the manner of the democratic

orator. The author of the second is the notorious *provocateur*, John Castle—the "protector" of a brothel madam whose evidence was torn to shreds at the trial of Watson in 1817. But even if we did not know this, his style betrays him in the first line. He is falling over his illiterate pen in an effort to ingratiate himself further with the authorities. This does not mean that every word of his deposition is a lie. It does mean that each word must be critically fumigated before it may be admitted to historical intercourse.[75]

This is a brief, but vitally important, indication of elementary historical method, in which language as evidence is interrogated.

Thompson ends as he began, closing the circle on the language of radicalism with discussion of the libertarian rhetoric that led up to and out of Peterloo, pitting the "people" against the unreformed House of Commons, sustaining demagogues and enshrining journalists and orators in martyrology. This stylized language was consumed eagerly, and its influence in the politics of the age was not without its seamier side: it fostered paid itinerant orators whose trade was to cater to the demands of the crowd, as well as the demagogues of the public house, "whose Radicalism had more froth than body." Those, like Henry "Orator" Hunt, who stood at the pinnacle of this reform crusade, were irksome individualists who manipulated language as much to trade on the emotions of the crowd as to effect a politics of change. They sought the loudest cheer first and enjoyed not so much the principle of the cause as its vanity-enhancing perquisites; they *knew* well that discourse was multiaccented. But in the crowd and on the hustings were also men such as Samuel Bamford, the Middleton weaver who epitomized the political commitment of entire communities. Radical papers proliferated, radiating out from London to the provinces, and small sheets appeared in many unanticipated quarters. "Dustmen and porters read and discuss politics; and labourers, journeymen, and masters speak *one language of disaffection and defiance,*" reported one worried authority. Caps of liberty were donned as a sign of rebelliousness. The Peterloo massing of the reformers gave the cause of universal suffrage an aura of discipline and purposiveness; the Peterloo massacre split the reform movement into constitutionalist and insurrectionary wings, dividing the language of radicalism along lines of emasculation and shadowy conspiratorial intrigue. Within the latter, Bamford found his place. He apparently purchased a pike, and the libertarian rhetoric of constitutional reform gave way to jeering hostility to all constituted authority. At one pike transaction Bamford gave the toast: "May the Tree of Liberty be planted in Hell, and may the bloody Butchers of Manchester be the Fruit of it!" One of his companions added that he would give the Peterloo magistrates "a damn good piking, and he would go home and work, till God damn him, his hands would fly off, and sing Brittania, and the Devil would fetch them all." The language of reform, for some, had run its course; a language of insurrection took over from where it had left off.[76]

This did not last, and the radicalism of the 1820s was brought back into the arena of public discourse by Cobbett. As with Paine, it is form that figures centrally in Thompson's assessment of Cobbett: "It is a matter of tone; and yet, in tone, will be found at least one half of Cobbett's political meaning. . . . [He] brought the rhythms of speech back into prose; but of strenuously argumentative, emphatic speech." Like Paine, he nourished a kind of common-sensical anti-intellectualism that would stay with the British labor movement for a considerable time. And like Paine, he was no advocate of proletarian power, confirmed as he was in his acceptance of property: "He nourished the culture of a class, whose wrongs he felt, but whose remedies he could not understand."[77] When, in the 1830s, the mantle of radicalism passed to Robert Owen, the story would not be all that different.

All of this unfolded against the march of capital and beneath the flag of the state's counter-revolution. The language of radicalism shifted gears in response to many changes, and as it was spoken, or heard, or read, altered its tone and accented new or different features of its content, always drawing on its past and what it had insured and proven:

> Whenever the pressures of the rulers relaxed, men came from the petty workshops or the weavers' hamlets and asserted new claims. They were told that they had no rights, but they knew that they were born free. The Yeomanry rode down their meeting, and the right of public meeting was gained. The pamphleteers were gaoled, and from the gaols they edited pamphlets. The trade unionists were imprisoned and they were attended to prison by processions with bands and union banners. Segregated in this way, their institutions acquired a peculiar toughness and resilience.

And, as *The Making of the English Working Class* reveals so well, this toughness and resilience was forged in part in language. "Orphans we are, and bastards of society," wrote one radical in 1834. Thanks to Thompson we know how these words were meant to be heard: "The tone is not one of resignation but of pride."[78]

▶   ## Deconstructing Thompson

Joan Scott's recently published "Women in *The Making of the English Working Class*" scrutinizes Thompson's text and reads it in ways that concern themselves little with the kinds of issues discussed above. For Scott, attention to discourse demands a set of conclusions about how

Thompson has constructed class; she urges a deconstructive interrogation of this influential text that starts, not with how language is addressed, but with how conceptions of class and consciousness are *gendered*. It is hardly surprising that Scott is uncomfortable with what she refers to as Thompson's location within "a quite orthodox Marxist tradition," given that, as we shall see in a later chapter, her gravitation toward discourse theory is in part sustained by her rejection of the analytic power of historical materialism. But it is nevertheless somewhat grating that she can posit this kind of easy placement without serious scrutiny of the theoretical making of the text itself, its relation to a reconceptualization of base and superstructure and its historical contextualization as a product of the political emergence of a British New Left that was quite different than the American New Left from which Scott herself emerged. Instead, Scott wanders around in an all too ahistorical appropriation of Thompson's political trajectory, which has undergone marked shifts (if not explicit breaks), realigned emphases, and important continuities over the last four decades. She can thus claim, in an essay on *The Making of the English Working Class*, that Thompson insisted that he was not a Marxist, when this distancing from Marxism as theory was well in the future as the study of the working class appeared in 1963. It is also more than a little unsettling to see her address Thompson's problematic account of women and class formation without once alluding to her own writings of the 1970s and 1980s, which were, if anything, far less attentive to realms she now regards as pivotal than was *The Making of the English Working Class*. Scott's first book, and only monograph, was a study of French craftsmen and political action that had little, if anything, to say of women. As late as 1980 she coauthored with Eric Hobsbawm an essay on political shoemakers that studiously avoided gender: the words *wife* or *woman* appear three times—in passing—in the text, while *he/his, craftsmen, tradesmen,* and *journeymen* are marched through the pages incessantly. Critic, deconstruct thyself, one is tempted to say. Instead, a book written during the late 1950s and early 1960s, predating the so-called second wave of feminism, is marked out for its neglect of women artisans.[79]

Scott's substantive critique of Thompson hardly stands or falls on such matters, although a feminism premised on the personal and/is the political might be expected to confront them more explicitly. What Scott does do is address the presumed social "reality" of the "working class." Like Hayden White, she begins from the poststructuralist premise that Thompson has not documented that reality but has instead constructed a conception of class. The strength of his work, in her view (and she is by no means entirely dismissive), is that Thompson's language is that of an advocate of a particular historical memory; his text captures the terms of working-class discourse, endorsing them and reproducing them so that the popular movement's self-conception is actually canonized. As my remarks above on Thompson's relationship to Jacobin language and the consequent problematic reading of exploitation would suggest, I do not think this assessment wrong, and Scott's starting point definitely allows entry into a critical appraisal of *The Making of the English Working Class*.

But the critique does not work. It fails, not because it is insistent that gender's suppression and distortion is at the center of the problematic construction of class in the text, but because this authorial process is read *only as discourse*, and, more fundamentally, as a discourse to be manipulated to force a specific conclusion.

Scott's critique does not proceed from the marshaling of alternative evidence/interpretation, which she does not do or which she does poorly and incompletely. For the deconstructionist true believer, this would not matter.[80] But Scott remains at least in part an historian, and so she orchestrates her reading of Thompson around a set of counter-texts/interpretations. Her favored alternative is Barbara Taylor's writing on the recasting of feminism and utopian socialism, but Taylor's construction of this relationship out of the writings of a handful of Owenite women and an implicit understating of the significance of the activity of the numerically more forceful *communities* of Chartist women is never confronted. Nor is Taylor's caricature of the supposed suppression of women's issues within the later nineteenth-century socialist movement ever questioned, although it rests mainly on assertion.[81] And it is never acknowledged by Scott that Taylor's Owenite women were largely active in a period that post-dates Thompson's chronological context.

Scott also disputes Thompson's analysis of Methodism and its apocalyptic challenges, drawing on the Hobsbawm thesis that, contrary to Thompson, such religious movements coincided with, rather than followed upon the defeats of, revolutionary activism. But she ignores the cautious and suggestive nature of Thompson's rereading of Methodist revivalism, its more millennarian offshoots, and their relationship to political radicalism. So, too, does she bypass empirical evidence he introduces into this debate. And, finally, she forces Thompson into the kinds of binary oppositions that poststructuralists enjoy deconstructing. The basic problem is that the exercise floats above the actual text, bypassing interpretation and its language in a freewheeling, purposive construction of its own, an unchecked progression of assertion. Thus Scott concludes, "The lines between political and religious critiques, between the language of politics and the language of sexuality, seem not to have been as clear as Thompson would have them." Yet while Thompson does at times draw these lines of distinction, he by no means forces the oppositions to the extent that Scott claims. And he explains, patiently, why he has not opted for this course, in a way that undercuts the one-sided reading of his analysis that Scott is promoting: "One reason for this lies in the many tensions at the heart of Wesleyanism. Just as the repressive inhibitions upon sexuality carried the continual danger of provoking the opposite—either in the form of the characteristic Puritan rebel (the forerunner of Lawrence) or in the form of Antinomianism; so the authoritarian doctrines of Methodism at times bred a libertarian antithesis. Methodism (and its evangelical counterparts) were highly politically-conscious religions." The point is a simple one: *The Making of the English Working Class* does not actually say what Scott says it does.[82]

As provocative and at times impressively innovative as is Scott's forceful depiction of the construction of class and consciousness in Thompson's text as *gendered*, this essential matter of what is actually on the page of the book remains. Scott argues that Thompson masculinizes class, not that he ignores women. She contends that he constructs class, as did the nineteenth-century movement, out of an acceptance and elevation of particular sides of sets of oppositions: men/women; political/domestic; rational/expressive. This "worked," in past and present, to marginalize women, to distill class as a male phenomenon, and to insure that the treatment of women and the history of the working class would proceed in an awkward way. If Thompson's text is a "precondition for the socialist-feminist discourse," it is nonetheless, at this conjuncture, as much a barrier to understanding as it is a guide to the necessary project of retheorizing "a different kind of history of working-class politics, one that recasts our knowledge about gender and class."[83]

How does Scott's text address all of this? Put simply, she marshals instances of how Thompson supposedly masculinizes class, most of which are "established" by quotes, often of a single line only, and some of which are, to say the least, employed in ways that defy conventions of criticism. In a central passage Scott considers Thompson's treatment of women workers:

> "Paradoxically," says Thompson, the radicalism of these wage-earning women was an expression of nostalgia for a pre-industrial domestic economy. The women mourned the "loss in status and personal indpendence" of a "way of life centered on the home." Instead of granting this as a valid political position (complementary to, indeed an aspect of, the artisan's longing for a return to his independent status), Thompson depicts it as "paradoxical" and links it to a subordinate status of women in the emerging radical movement.

"Their role was confined to giving moral support to the men, making banners and caps of liberty which were presented with ceremony at reform demonstrations, passing resolutions and addresses, and swelling the numbers at meetings." These women foreshadow "Carlile's womenfolk," described in later pages as those who "underwent trial and imprisonment more out of loyalty than conviction." Since women's independence is cast in terms of a prior domesticity instead of work, their claims and political activities had less weight in the "making" of the class.[84]

All of this *seems* so clear. Words are like that. But let us see what Thompson actually said.

First, the relevant passages in Thompson's text need to be contextualized. On one level, they are located within a broad discussion of the contradictory gendered currents of dependence and independence within the Industrial Revolution, an important and long-recognized reality among historians of the transition to capitalist modes of production that "freed" women in ways that eroded the patriarchal chains of domesticity only to secure the chains of wage labor.[85] On another, these passages, so easily quoted out of context, are situated within discussions that seldom confirm Scott's readings. The actual passage that Scott keys on is prefaced by reference to a strike of 1,500 female card-setters in the West Riding in 1835, and a contemporary radical assessment that reactionary alarmists might well regard such action as menacing to established institutions. Thompson then notes:

> But there is a paradox of feeling even in this advance. The Radicalism of northern working women was compounded of nostalgia for lost status and the assertion of new-found rights. According to conventions which were deeply felt, the woman's status turned upon her success as a housewife in the family economy, in domestic management and forethought, baking and brewing, cleanliness and child-care. The new independence, in the mill or full-time at the loom, which made new claims possible, was felt simultaneously as a loss in status and in personal independence. Women became more dependent upon the employer or labour market, and they looked back to a "golden" past in which home earnings from spinning, poultry, and the like, could be gained around their own door. In good times the domestic economy, like the peasant economy, supported a way of life centred upon the home, in which inner whims and compulsions were more obvious than external discipline. Each stage in industrial differentiation and specialisation struck also at the family economy, disturbing customary relations between husband and wife, parents and children, and differentiating more sharply between "work" and "life." It was to be a full hundred years before this differentiation was to bring returns, in the form of labour-saving de-

vices, back into the working woman's home. Meanwhile, the family was roughly torn apart each morning by the factory bell, and the mother who was also a wage-earner often felt herself to have the worst of both the domestic and the industrial worlds.

Thompson is thus locating a paradox in the historical context, not embracing it the way Scott implies through a judicious misquoting. Moreover, not only is Thompson far from depicting this paradox as grounds for the subordination of women within the radical movement or dichotomizing domesticity/labor so as to understate women's political activities and claims, but on the page opposite this quotation he actually endorses the politics of women's protest. He cites addresses of the Female Reform Societies to William Cobbett, noting the domestically structured abuse their opponents heaped on their limited political activities and exposing the two-sided politics of Cobbett, who held no brief for women's suffrage but who would defend female reformers from the vile attacks of those who sought to suppress the paradoxical consequences of capitalist incursions with the sentimentalized, confining resurrection of women's domestic place. If the role of the female reformers *was* limited in the history, this is not simply authorial construction, although it does need to be pointed out, as has James Epstein, that Thompson understates the role of women in early English radicalism. Finally, as for Scott's statement that these women reformers foreshadow Carlile's compliant womenfolk, this fit is a bit too neat. It fails to acknowledge that Thompson makes his one-line assessment of the limited politics of some of Carlile's incarcerated women within a page-long discussion of other women who defied convention to challenge authority and espouse reform.[86]

Virtually all of Scott's instances of how Thompson constructs class in a gendered way can be challenged through these kinds of basic readings of the text. She notes that Thompson tells us that Susan Thistlewood, companion of the executed Cato Street conspirator Arthur Thistlewood, was "not a cypher" but a "spirited Jacobin in her own right, with a cold and intellectual manner and a readiness to take an active part in [her husband's] defense." Thompson actually wrote that she was active in *the* defense. Editorial insertion/insistence that this must have related only to her husband understates the politics of a woman who acted out of radical commitments that extended beyond wifely duty to take up the cause of publicly defending high treason, however foolhardy, and the ten men that would pay with their lives or transportation. This is small potatoes, but it reveals how Scott is herself engaged in a project of constructing a view of women.

More telling is Scott's unreflective inference that Thompson has suggested that Susan Thistlewood was "not a cypher" precisely because

Thompson and/or his readers think other women were nonentities. In fact, the reference to cyphers is by no means gender specific, but refers to those who aligned themselves with Thistlewood and his conspiracy, suffered for it, and were, as Thompson says, "entitled to condemn him for his folly." As is often the case, the followers of those who advocate insurrection are routinely depicted as deluded and pliant, mindless sheep without principles. In Thistlewood's case, most, certainly, were actually men. Thompson rejects this view of Thistlewood's comrades, whom he says "felt for him the greatest loyalty." They were not cyphers, and neither was Thistlewood's wife. The matter of gender, then, is brought into this discussion only by an interpretive act of violence, a kind of break-and-enter that has little regard for the edifice of textual meaning.[87]

What all of this amounts to is *not* a refusal of Scott's theoretical and critical project. It is a fairly telling repudiation of a part of her method of instancing, however, and a blunt reminder that those who suggest that texts construct can also engage in their own acts of construction, often ones that skew and distort the very language they are deconstructing. But in and of itself this says little about Scott's general proposition that in *The Making of the English Working Class* "the master codes that structure the narrative are gendered in such a way as to confirm rather than challenge the masculine representation of class."[88]

On one, quite basic, level, this is probably true. Any book researched and written three decades ago would necessarily be less attentive to gender than a text that benefited from the empirical and theoretical advances of intervening years, especially given the forward march of women's history, feminist theory, and studies of gender. On another, explicitly political, level, Scott argues that Thompson constructed the *politics* of class out of a masculinist, rational code. She adopts, against the grain of poststructuralist thought, a universalism in which the masculine/feminine opposition is coded as rationalist/expressive, attributing this dichotomy to Thompson. And then she rather wildly locates Thompson's unease with the second New Left's self-indulgent politics of style within this gendered meaning. The supposedly "manly" political tradition with which Thompson identified—both in the past and in his present at the time of publication of the *Making*—is thus for Scott unquestioningly masculinist, hostile to feminism and, even at the point that it embraces Blake, Morris, and the radical romantic tradition, little more than a poetic politics of opposition to feminine expressivity.[89] The political consequence of this is the positing of a universal feminine expressivity and its unquestioning elevation within the discourse of class politics. Joanna Southcott, not Mary Wollstonecraft and Susan Thistlewood, looms large in Scott's deconstruction of Thompson's class politics. It is rather surprising that she makes nothing of the Queen Caroline affair, dripping as it was in the symbolism of purity, womanly virtue, and familial domesticity, all of the quite radical hue and cry over "a woman wronged" voiced in a pronounced expressivity emanating from the largely male Radical milieu.[90]

One comes away from Scott's assessment of women in *The Making of the English Working Class* quite shaken about the politics of a deconstructive feminism.[91] *Real* women, the repositories of sexual *difference*, are expressive, domestic, spiritual, religious, undisciplined, and irrational, coded as feminine. Radical women, secular, combative, and rational, are depicted as the intellectual/political equivalents of men in public drag, coded, for all of their superficial disguise, as masculine. The awkward complexities of *actual* women, often situated within sets of paradoxes and battling against the numerous "constructions" of their lives, remain all too little appreciated in Scott's rereading of Thompson's text. To align oneself with the politics of rationalism, as has Thompson, is to succumb to the masculinist code, to condemn oneself before a court of gender and its reading of the politics of history. And there are no reprieves.

Scott's appraisal of women in *The Making of the English Working Class* thus tilts too problematically toward the determining power of discourse. Her insistence that historians attend to how class is constructed and relate this to the imagery and representation of gender is suggestive and useful. But this, in and of itself, was not the entirety of how class was made, and it will never be adequate as a basis for the unmaking of an historical account such as that offered by Thompson. In its one-sided failure to even gesture toward how all spheres of life were overtaken by capitalism's intensely material drive to accumulate, Scott's construction of the gendered politics of class formation ignores and bypasses too much. It also leaves large questions about just what kind of politics emerge from a history orchestrated by discourses of opposition.[92]

This first sustained effort to deconstruct Thompson, then, falls rather flat. As historical critique it rests on a troubling method of selective instancing that is itself undercut further by obvious misreading and overt distortion. As political critique it assumes an identity of rationalist discourse and masculinity without spelling out clearly just what an ostensibly feminine politics of expressivity entails and leads toward, except an irrationality that, because it flowed "naturally" from women's structured place of oppression, supposedly has more to offer than has been appreciated within the socialist tradition. As theoretical critique it offers insight and a set of guiding questions, many of them quite important and worth attending to, but it also closes off interrogation of a number of other areas beyond discourse that demand attention, including that of material life itself. Scott's historical deconstruction of Thompson is disappointing. But then perhaps it was destined to be. At least one advocate of discourse theory has jettisoned the entire project of rereading "history" in this way. Sande Cohen argues that "historical thought is a manifestation of reactive thinking-about, which blocks the act of thinking-to." Trying to make "history" relevant to critical thinking is an "ill-conceived act." "What actually occurs by means of 'historical thought,'" claims Cohen, "is the destruction of a fully semanticized present."[93] Tales told by idiots, signifying nothing, burp.

▶   I hope the point of all of this is clear enough. It is not a very complicated point. I am aware that the texts treated above could be interrogated to establish other interpretive issues and historical processes of significance. It is also true that they are open—like all texts—to critical challenge, and my refusal of a good deal of Scott's reading of Thompson is by no means a rejection of all of her argument or a repudiation of the project of criticizing texts of historical materialism. Nor, it need be stressed, is it at all the case that these writings—from Marx through James and Dorfman to Thompson—are necessarily compatible in their emphases and analytic directions. The loose grounding of these works in a none-too-rigorously defined tradition of inquiry will no doubt give some skeptics cause for critical pause. Their theoretical poverty, as measured against the much-proclaimed sophistications of contemporary critical theory, will, in some quarters, prompt readers to shunt these works aside with a sneer of indifference.

No matter, the basic point *is* made. All of these writings resist a descent into discourse while attending to language in ways that are instructive. They anticipate, at times, the drift of current theoretical fashion, however much such intellectual trends shout loudly their innovations. At other times they take aspects of language that the recent fetishization of discourse has professed little interest in and illuminate how those unacknowledged features of processes of writing, speaking, and signification tell us much about historical experience. In short, these are tales that signify something, and often quite a lot. They—and many other unmentioned similar texts—demand attention and consideration from precisely those advocates of discourse within the discipline of history who have underutilized them at best, or willfully ignored them at worst. And they provide a measure against which recent texts proclaiming the linguistic turn can be assessed. Let us turn, in the next three chapters, to areas where such writing exists: politics, class, and gender.[94]

3 *Politics*

Not criticism but revolution is the driving force of history.

—*Karl Marx*, The German Ideology *(1845–1846)*

ANALYSIS OF DISCOURSE AND RHETORIC HAS LONG BEEN AS-
sociated with the study of politics. The premises of the new critical
literary theory, however loosely interpreted, find a welcome interpretive home in the sphere of the political. Deconstruction's more extreme
postulates and practices have a certain resonance with the preoccupations of historians focused on political transformation. The assertion
that there is "nothing outside the text" and the privileging of canonical
writings, for instance, take on a rare, if partial, acceptability when
Rousseau and the French Revolution are the subject of inquiry. It is not
surprising, therefore, that it is precisely in the study of the political that
the linguistic turn has been made forcefully and, ironically, that this
revisionist development has taken place with little actual interrogation
of what it means to posit the primacy of language. To explore this
reification of language there are no more instructive cases than that of
recent historical treatments of the French Revolution and American
republicanism.[1]

▶ **The Reinterpretation of the French Revolution**
The French Revolution *is* a text, and one with a wide readership. No
student of modern Europe can ignore it, no theorist and advocate of
revolutionary politics can escape it, and for the French it is a touchstone
of national identity. Its meaning is not inconsequential. One would
expect debate and disagreement about this event, but the surprising
intellectual reality is that interpretive hegemony has historically consolidated quickly, vanquishing analytic opponents with sharp, decisive

polemical strokes that, like the guillotine, hold forth little possibility of reconsiderations and reassessments. Like the revolution itself, these consolidating orthodoxies have passed through phases. What concerns us here is the movement from Jacobinism to Thermidorian Reaction.

There have, of course, been many non-Marxist interpreters of the French Revolution, including Tocqueville. But from World War II to the mid-1960s, a period of important developments in which professional historians adopted new methods and took on a new stature, there can be no question of the dominance of what many have called a Marxist, and others more precisely a Jacobin, conception of the French Revolution.[2] The broad, bold lines of interpretive direction had been drawn by Marx and Engels in the 1840s, although by no means in ways that were devoid of contradiction and ambiguity:

> The revolutions of 1648 and 1789 were not English and French revolutions, they were revolutions of a European type. They did not represent the victory of a particular class of society over the old political order; they proclaimed the political order of the new European society. The bourgeoisie was victorious in these revolutions, but the victory of the bourgeoisie was at that time the victory of a new social order, the victory of bourgeois ownership over feudal ownership, of nationality over provincialism, of competition over the guild, of the division of land over primogeniture, of the rule of the landowner over the domination of the owner by the land, of enlightenment over superstition, of the family over the family name, of industry over heroic idleness, of bourgeois law over medieval privileges.[3]

This interpretive skeleton was fleshed out by Georges Lefebvre and, later, by Albert Soboul, two modern historians who did more than anyone else to establish the orthodoxy of the leftist analysis of the revolution.[4] That orthodoxy insisted on the bourgeois nature of the revolution and, especially with Soboul, laid stress upon the importance of class struggle in the making of 1789 and its aftermath, positing a confrontation in which the bourgeoisie, drawing on the popular classes of town and country, ousted the aristocracy.

Marx's ambiguous acknowledgment that the revolution was not the victory of a particular class but that the bourgeoisie was nonetheless the victor prefaced the ultimate assault that would be waged against Lefebvre and, more violently, Soboul. Alfred Cobban crystallized the early discontent with the Lefebvre-Soboul interpretation in a series of writings. One, "The Myth of the French Revolution," captures nicely the skepticism of what would soon be hailed as the new revisionism:

> In the French Revolution, it is commonly said, the feudal order passed away and the rule of the bourgeoisie took its place. This is,

simply put, the myth which has dominated serious research on the history of the French Revolution during the present century. It is often treated as an exemplification of a scientific law derived from the facts of history. . . . the outline of the story is that there was once a social order called feudalism. This was a terrible ogre and lived in a castle; but for centuries a bourgeois Jack the Giant-killer climbed the beanstalk of economic progress, until finally in the French Revolution he liquidated the old order and put in its place something called alternatively bourgeois society or capitalism. The only divergence from the traditional story is that he did not live happily ever after. I think it would be fair to say that this is the generally accepted myth or theory of the French Revolution.

Cobban then proceeded to argue that feudalism had long since ceased to be an operative social formation well before the outbreak of the French Revolution and that the term *bourgeois*, employed as loosely as that of feudalism, was also meaningless in terms of its explanatory capacity in any search for the origins of the revolution. Rather than a revolutionary bourgeoisie seizing power and banishing a feudal aristocracy from the corridors of state power, Cobban saw the revolution in terms of continuity, not unlike Tocqueville: "the essence of government in France after the Revolution remained where it had been before, in the great and now renewed bureaucratic *cadres*."[5] Cobban has been followed by a seemingly endless parade of well-trained parrots, each mouthing a slightly different rendition of the same rehearsed analytic one-liner. In a recent synthetic discussion of the crisis of class as a concept within historical understanding, William Reddy details the infinite capacity of the new revisionism to reinterpret the origins of the revolution as the result of frustrations among various social strata, rifts and hostilities within a group or institution, or, indeed, as without social causes but, of course, the bearer of many social consequences. Reddy rightly recognizes that a social transformation as significant as the revolution can hardly be reduced to historical accident and petty bickering, acknowledging that the new revisionism has trapped itself within a particular kind of credibility gap. Yet he is a true believer, in large part because the new revisionism's implicit rejection of class as any kind of motive force in history suits so well his intention to write class (and Marxism as the major theoretical edifice dependent upon this term) out of the annals of history: "In the debate over the origins of the French Revolution, the revisionists have clearly carried the day. As recently as the 1950s the bold rebellion of the delegates of the Third Estate, backed by the Paris crowd, against royal absolutism in the summer of 1789 was still seen as a class conflict in which a vigorous capitalist bourgeoisie, allied with the peasants and artisans, had overthrown the declining feudal aristocracy. . . . But now it has become clear that such a class not only had no representatives in the revolutionary assemblies but in effect did not exist. There was no revolutionary bourgeoisie."[6] This is strong statement, admissible only by so defining revolutionary bourgeoisie that it becomes an idealized caricature, marching to a man to the barricades with Adam Smith under its collective arm, proclaiming the Rights of Man, the doctrine of property, and the inalienable pursuit of happiness at every conscious step. History does not work this way, but among historians of France in North America there can be no question that the old left-leaning historiography is now regarded as rather ancient hat.[7]

Against this idealized caricature of a revolutionary bourgeoisie judged not to have existed, Marxist theory has long grappled with the class paradoxes of revolutionary transformation. As his preface to *Contribution to a Critique of Political Economy* made clear, Marx drew no necessary relationship between structural class position and consciousness of that position, which was always a far more confused and ambivalent process than the objective conditions of production (which, admittedly, Marx tended to reduce to a rather simplistic and precisely identifiable factor in history):

> In considering such transformations a distinction should always be made between the material transformation of the economic conditions of production, which can be determined with the precision of natural science, and the legal, political, religious, aesthetic or philosophic—in short, ideological forms in which men become conscious of this conflict and fight it out. Just as our opinion of an individual is not based on what he thinks of himself, so can we not judge of such a period of transformation by its own consciousness; on the contrary, this consciousness must be explained rather from the contradictions of material life, from the existing conflict between the social productive forces and the relations of production.[8]

In the concrete case of the French Revolution, Marx recognized that much of the riddle of the class paradox of transformation lay in Jacobinism, its language and its attempt to revolutionize society politically rather than socially and economically speaking to the class limitations of the 1790s. "If the proletariat brings down the domination of the bourgeoisie," he wrote in 1847, "its victory will be merely ephemeral, only a moment in the service of the bourgeoisie (just like *anno* 1794), so long as within the process of history, within its 'movement,' those material conditions have not been created that make necessary the abolition of the bourgeois mode of production and therefore also the definitive fall of political bourgeois domination."[9]

Trotsky would later embrace a similar position,[10] but the historiography of the revolution, especially after Soboul began to make an impact, treated Jacobinism much more heroically. Gramsci summarized the consolidating "Marxist" sympathy for Jacobinism nicely in his *Prison Notebooks*:

> The Jacobins won their function of "leading" party by a struggle to the death; they literally "imposed" themselves on the French bourgeoisie, leading it into a far more advanced position than the originally strongest bourgeois nuclei would have spontaneously wished to take up, and even far more advanced than that which the historical premises should have permitted—hence the various forms of backlash and the function of Napoleon I. This feature, characteristic of Jacobinism (but before that, also of Cromwell and the "Roundheads") and hence of the entire French Revolution, which consists in (apparently) forcing the situation, in creating irreversible *faits accomplis*, and in a group of extremely energetic and determined men driving the bourgeois forward with kicks in the backside, may be schematized in the following way. The Third Estate was the least homogeneous; it had a very disparate intellectual elite, and a group which was very advanced economically but politically moderate. . . . The representatives of the Third Estate initially only posed those questions which interested the actual physical members of the social group, their immediate "corporate" interests (corporate in the traditional sense, of the immediate and narrowly selfish interests of a particular category). The precursors of the Revolution were in fact moderate reformers, who shouted very loud but actually demanded very little. Gradually a new elite was selected out which did not concern itself solely with "corporate" reforms, but tended to conceive of the bourgeoisie as the hegemonic group of all the popular forces. This selection occurred through the action of two factors: the resistance of the old social forces, and the international threat. . . . The Jacobins, consequently, were the only party of the revolution in progress, in as much as they not only represented the immediate needs and aspirations of the actual physical individuals who constituted the French bourgeoisie, but they also represented the revolutionary movement as a whole, as an integral historical development. For they represented the future needs as well, and, once again, not only the needs of those particular physical individuals, but also of all the national groups which had to be assimilated to the existing fundamental group. . . . They created the bourgeois State, made the bourgeoisie into the leading, hegemonic class of the nation, in other words gave the new State a permanent basis, and created the compact modern French nation.[11]

The divide over Jacobinism separating Marx-Trotsky and Gramsci-Soboul is in fact more apparent than real. An analytic difference of considerable importance does exist, with Marx-Trotsky suspicious of the socioeconomic presence or "reality" of Jacobin class "interests," while Gramsci and Soboul too cavalierly accept the existence of such an historical entity. But on the fundamental political level, this divergence recedes. With it all too clear that proletarian revolution was not on the agenda in the 1790s, Jacobinism represented, in Trotsky's words, "the maximum radicalism which could be produced by bourgeois society," and it is therefore not surprising that subsequent Marxist theoreticians and historians have leaned sympathetically toward the likes of Robespierre and St. Just. Marx himself saw these Jacobins as the tragic victims of confusions and abstractions overdetermined by the material limitations of their times.[12]

The new revisionism seldom pauses to consider such matters. It *knows* class interest expresses itself unambiguously; it *knows*, consequently, that the failure of class interest to proclaim itself articulately and to personalize its presence in identifiable, countable human beings proves that class interest does not actually exist. Marx's basic insight that the French Revolution "did not represent the victory of a particular class . . . [but] proclaimed the political order of the new European society" is thus beyond its conceptual grasp. To be sure, there has been much valuable research by those who have taken aim at the Marxist interpretation of the revolution, and there is no question that their findings must be attended to. Inasmuch as Soboul and others telescoped analysis of the revolution within the confines of class struggle, gesturing only weakly and perhaps wrongly to the structural features of productive life, they bear some responsibility for the new revisionism's discontents. But the tendency to divorce the revolution from material forces, including class alignments, is a retrogressive step. Fueled by the fetishization of quantitative methodology and the rampant anti-Marxism that have infected social science history in the 1970s and 1980s, this analytic action looks persistently to the personnel of the revolution, but not its political outcomes. Indeed, it takes a principled stand against the very consideration of origins and outcomes, unconsciously pulling a leaf from the pages of hedonistic critical theory.[13] A faction of the new revisionist camp, not surprisingly, has opted for the fashionable descent into discourse, seeing the revolution itself as a language in which imagery, rhetoric, and poetics abound, but where classes, material processes of accumulation and struggle, and the consciousness that develop around them are surprisingly silent.[14]

This stress on language and symbolism as the key factor in understanding the making of the French Revolution has its origins in the contentions of the 1790s. Jean-François La Harpe published *Du Fanatisme dans la langue révolutionnaire* (1797) in an attempt to explain the revolution's aberrations as the frenzied spirit of *philosophie* run amok. Henri Grégoire's law on official costume, adopted in 1795, was drawn up within a conception of the importance of signification: "The language of signs has an eloquence of its own; distinctive costumes are part of this idiom for they arouse ideas and sentiments analogous to their object, especially when they take hold of the imagination with their vividness." Revolutionaries who fell during the Terror were seen to have exploited the citizenry through their adroit use of the public platform and the political clubs: "it is by *words* that they accomplished their ends: *words* did everything," reported one shocked observer.[15] Early historians were well aware of this importance of language in the midst of violent political change. "Let no man say that the word is of little use in such moments," argued Michelet with respect to the role of Danton. "Action is here the servant of the word, it follows behind submissively, as on the first day of the world: *He said and the world was*."[16]

There is no denying the importance of language and symbolism in the revolutionary experience, or, indeed, in the interpretation of politics in general, as a number of recent texts, some cast in a Barthesian mold, suggest.[17] Many of these works coexist easily with historical materialism and pay homage to the researches and interpretive direction of Marxist historians such as Soboul. Few make any mention whatsoever of contemporary literary theory. But the imprint of anti-Marxism and critical theory weighs heavily on two revisionist studies.

Perhaps the single most cited text in the much-heralded revisionist reinterpretation of the French Revolution is François Furet's *Interpreting the French Revolution*. Composed of three essays addressing approaches to the history of the revolution and a rambling declarative statement entitled, appropriately and defiantly, "The French Revolution is over," the book is a manifesto for those dissatisfied with the Marxist interpretation of 1789. Two of the four essays are of particular concern here, Furet's assault on Soboul and other Marxists, originally published in *Annales* as "The Revolutionary catechism," and his introductory musings. The first establishes the anti-Marxist essence of the new revisionism, the latter its formal adherence to language.[18]

Furet's "Revolutionary catechism" is a remarkably splenetic piece of scholarship. Commencing as a diatribe against a text written in opposition to Furet and Richet's popularly aimed history of the revolution, it quickly proceeds to argue that three pernicious influences haunt the Marxist-dominated historiography of 1789: the positing of a kinship between the French and Russian revolutions, in which the former serves as mother to the latter; the substitution of a linear, simplistic Marxism for the more subtle, contradictory positions of Marx and Engels on the historical making of the French Revolution; and the consequent entrenchment of a "neo-Jacobinist," "Leninist-populist vulgate" as the sectarian motivation of a "conservative spirit of a historiography that substitutes value judgements for concepts, final ends for causality, argument from authorities for open discussion" and, in the process, insures a ritualistic denunciation of all other interpretation as counter-revolutionary and antinational.[19] (This all sounds fine, until one grasps that Furet's value judgments and appeal to authorities are as blatant as the next Marxist guy's, and that he "solves" the problematic relationship of ends and causes by dismissing the importance of consequences and origins.) My point is not that Furet does not score some hits on an exposed historiography. He does, drawing usefully on Trotsky's distinction in *Our Political Tasks* between proletarian revolution and Jacobinism, correctly pointing to the resulting flaws in analyses that are more rightly considered Jacobin than Marxist and refusing to accept the patriotic reverence that overlays the revolution's historiography. Furet is especially damning of a Marxist historiography—attributable to Soboul—that takes "its bearings from the prevailing ideological consciousness of the period it sets out to explain."[20]

What is so interesting here is Furet's inability to pause and consider the unusual critical inversion he finds himself within, and its own contradictory pulse. On the one hand, he condemns Soboul for adopting an interpretive view of the eighteenth century that is nothing less than the very same perspective put forward by Sièyes in the famous pamphlet *Qu'est-ce que le Tiers Etat?* To write history that takes the image of the past embraced and accepted by its own actors is dismissed as rather small analytic potatoes, and so taken with this condemnation is Furet that he fails to recognize that this is exactly what Marxist historians are all too often urged to do: their histories, it is commonly argued, impose on the past a false and unfittable conceptual agenda drawn from their presentist ideological premises. It is supposedly a high historiographic sin to convey the past as it was lived: "From Soboul's language and ideas, the reader almost feels as if he were participating in the meeting held on the famous night of 4 August 1789." Yet, Furet is undoubtedly uncomfortable with such "criticism" (which many historians would take as high praise) and reaches into the more familiar anti-Marxist bag of charges to draw out a well-worn opposition to "theory." (Theory, of course, is the *only* way to enhance a history of lived experience, extending understanding of the past in ways that can address human activity with an appreciation of the confinements that were not necessarily perceived and fully comprehended by men and women caught within them.) Indeed, on the other hand—which happens to lie on the page to the left—Furet chastises Soboul for just this Marxist sin of theorizing with the condemnation of a mixed metaphor: "Imperturbably Albert Soboul goes about his neo-Aristotelian surgery, in which social classes function as metaphysical categories."[21]

Quoting Kautsky, Furet suggests that Soboul has reduced all historical development within the French Revolution to a class struggle and in so doing has fallen into a mechanical cul-de-sac in which the entire history of the post-1789 years is consumed by "two classes locked in struggle, two compact, homogenous masses, the one revolutionary the other reactionary, those below and those on top." Whatever the analytic failures of Soboul, however, this surely is not high on the list. One wonders if Furet has actually read the historian of the Parisian sans-culottes, for in his treatment of the popular movement Soboul was always at pains to conclude with discussions of contradictions inherent in the composition of the sans-culottes, the failure of class consciousness, and the historic role of a social stratum that pushed bourgeois revolution forward while being incapable of sustaining a social transformation in its own ultimate interests.[22]

As useful as Furet's refusal of a French historiography that has moved "insidiously and permanently, from a Marxism based on the concept of 'mode of production' to one reduced to the class struggle alone" is, his "reading" of the texts of revolutionary historiography is flawed seriously. His conception of "Leninist jargon-mongers" skidding "out of control" is in fact an appropriate autocritique if we simply reword the phrasing to "anti-Leninist." As in so many other instances, anticommunism as a politics has invaded scholarship in the dress of anti-Marxism, as impassioned references to the Gulag and persistent Soviet bashing reveal. The "bourgeois revolution" becomes Furet's old, soiled clothes, and there is no doubt that they demand some laundering given the dirt they have accumulated through recent revisionist research. But though unfashionable, they are not quite yet worthless. We see this much at least as Furet models his new interpretive wardrobe at the end of his essay, substituting the metaphysics of language for the supposed metaphysics of "bourgeois revolution":

> The Revolution was more than the "leap" from one society to another; it was also the conjunction of all the ways in which a civil society, once it had suddenly been "opened up" by a power crisis, let loose all the words and languages it contained. This enormous cultural emancipation, whose meaning society was hard put to "keep within bounds," henceforth fuelled the competition for power conducted through an ever-escalating egalitarian rhetoric. Internalised by the popular masses—or at least by certain sections of them—and all the more ruthless as the people was the only reference mark, indeed the new source of legitimacy, revolutionary

ideology had become the arena *par excellence* of the struggle for power among groups. Through this ideology passed the dialectic of successive schisms within the leadership during 1789–1799, as well as the language assuring continuity of the new elites.

For Furet, language liberates the history of the revolution from the confining orthodoxy of Marxism:

> The revolution was the process by which the collective imaginings of a society became the very fabric of its own history. What, then, can possibly be gained by trying to turn it, willy nilly, into the absolutely inevitable result produced by a single metaphysical essence that unveils one by one, like a set of Russian dolls, the various episodes supposedly contained within it from the very outset? Why try to construct at any cost that fanciful chronology in which an ascending "bourgeois" phase is followed by a period of triumph for the popular classes, to be superseded by a comeback of the bourgeoisie, albeit a "descending" one, since Bonaparte is waiting in the wings? Why this poverty-stricken schema, this resurrection of scholasticism, this dearth of ideas, this passionate obstinacy disguised as Marxism? The vulgate according to . . . Soboul is not grounded in an original approach to the problem, such as might arise from newly acquired knowledge or from a new doctrine; it is but the feeble afterglow of the great shining flame that illuminated the entire history of the Revolution in the days of Michelet or Jaures. The product of a confused encounter between Jacobinism and Leninism, this mixed discourse is unsuited for discovery; it amounts to nothing more than a residual shamanic function destined to comfort any imaginary survivors of Babeuf's utopia.

This is an interpretive language so vitriolic as to be "out of control," a conceptualization as abstract and metaphysical as anything the advocates of "bourgeois revolution" have ever been able to propound. It suggests the need to look closely at Emperor Furet's new clothes.[23]

He wears them in the opening statement of *Interpreting the French Revolution.* They have a certain Parisian look; discerning stylists will readily identify them with the boutiques of poststructuralist radical chic. But Furet is cautiously clandestine and has even gone so far as to remove all designer labels (although he refers, in passing, to Lévi-Strauss), perhaps fearing a backlash from some quarter out of sorts with recent trends. Those in the know, however, are not ones to keep things quiet, as an American reviewer made all too clear in an essay on the original French edition of Furet's book:

> Although Furet never identifies his own theoretical allegiances beyond an occasional reference to the young Marx and much polemical praise of Tocqueville and Cochin, he nonetheless concocts a

fashionable blend of Foucault, Castoriadis, and Derrida. The key words are all here: *le discours, l'imaginaire,* representation, transparency, and the semiotic circuit, and they signal Furet's ambition to make sense of the great Revolution, so long associated with violence, hunger, and the conflict of classes, as a fundamentally semiological event.[24]

In his effort to sink the social interpretation of the revolution, in which class and bourgeois ascent figure so prominently, Furet divorces the political and the social, the representational and the material, elevating discourse to a previously unanticipated hegemonic height.[25]

Interpretively this again relates to the shortcomings of the historiography, with historians of the revolution faulted for taking "the revolutionary discourse at face value because they themselves have remained locked into that discourse. . . . They must therefore believe, since the Revolution says so, that it destroyed the nobility when it negated its principle; that the Revolution founded a new society when it asserted that it did; that the Revolution was a new beginning of history when it spoke of regenerating the human race." Furet pits his entire analytic project against just this kind of "game of mirrors, where the historian and the Revolution believe each other's words literally." Yet as Lynn Hunt has recognized, Furet himself is dependent upon acceptance of revolutionary language at face value in his divorcing the social and the semiotic, in his insistence that there were two revolutions, a "Revolution of interests" that succeeded the more pure revolution of discourse:

> Between 1789 and 9 Thermidor 1794, revolutionary France used the paradox of democracy, explored by Rousseau, as the sole source of power. Society and the State were fused in the discourse of the people's will; and the ultimate manifestations of that obsession with legitimacy were the Terror and the war, both of which were inherent in the ever-escalating rhetoric of the various groups competing for the exclusive right to embody the democratic principle. The Terror refashioned, in a revolutionary mode, a kind of divine right of public authority.
>
> That configuration was broken on 9 Thermidor, when society asserted its independence. Re-emerging with all its unwieldiness, its conflicting interests and its divisions, it attempted to re-establish a law based on the elective representation of the people. In a sense the Revolution was over, for it had renounced its language and admitted that there were specific interests it had to defend.[26]

As in his critique of Soboul, Furet seems to be having it both ways: the historiography is wrong to take the language of revolution at face value; Furet charts new paths of analytic rigor by addressing language, structuring his view of the shifting contours of the revolution around a reading of revolutionary discourse that accepts the revolutionary dichotomization of "interest" and a rhetoric of popular will.

Fixated on the rediscovery of a narrowly, linguistically determined political dimension of the revolution, Furet reifies the language of politics and in the process divorces it from any connection to material life. The result is an analytic agenda in which "we must stop regarding revolutionary consciousness as a more or less 'natural' result of oppression and discontent." If few have ever argued that revolutionary consciousness springs naturally from oppression and discontent, that is not Furet's problem. Nor does it trouble him that oppression and discontent did exist and may have had some role to play in the crisis of the state, the unfolding of revolutionary events, and the consciousness of particular social strata. Instead, Furet hammers mercilessly away at the power of discourse, all the while ignoring the structures of power and the manifold ways that they mediated language and action throughout the 1790s. The result is a totalizing, linguistically orchestrated metaphysics:

> The "people" were defined by their aspirations, and as an indistinct aggregate of individual "right" wills. By that expedient, which precluded representation, the revolutionary consciousness was able to reconstruct an imaginary social cohesion in the name and on the basis of individual wills. That was its way of resolving the eighteenth century's great dilemma, that of conceptualising society in terms of the individual. If indeed the individual was defined in his every aspect by the aims of his political action, a set of goals as simple as a moral code would permit the Revolution to found a new language as well as a new society. Or, rather, to found a new society through a new language: today we would call that a nation; at the time it was celebrated in the *fête de la Federation*.[27]

For Furet the discourse and symbolic system that was operative at the center of political action bears no relation to anything but itself; it was decisive in the struggle for power. And yet there were times, obviously, when discourse and symbolism were not enough, times when the guillotine was necessary, times when specific individuals knew that there was more to revolution than talk and imagery. The loss of a head is a very material historical event.

Furet has an answer for this. Creating conflict and justifying violence was the aristocratic "plot." But if one suggests that this opens the door to the room of class interest, fear not, Furet slams it shut with yet another sleight of discourse's symbolic hand:

> The idea of plot was cut from the same cloth as revolutionary consciousness because it was an essential aspect of the basic nature

of that consciousness: an imaginary discourse on power. That discourse came into being, as we have seen, when the field of power, having become vacant, was taken over by the ideology of pure democracy, that is, by the idea that the people are power, or that power is the people. But the revolutionary consciousness believed in historical action: if its advent was made possible only by the intervention of the people, it was because it had been blocked and continued to be threatened by a counter-power potentially more powerful than power itself: the plot. Hence the plot revived the idea of absolute power, which had been renounced by democratic power. Once the transfer of legitimacy, the very hallmark of the Revolution, had been accomplished, that absolute power became a hidden though formidable threat, while the new one was supreme though fragile. Like the people's will, the plot was the figment of a frenzied preoccupation with power; they were the two facets of what one might call the collectively held image of democratic power.[28]

Power is so easily shunted aside for Furet precisely because he is convinced it "had no objective existence at the social level, it was but a *mental representation of the social sphere* that permeated and dominated the field of politics." A dozen pages later we are told that the Terror was "impossible" after 9 Thermidor "because society had recovered its independence from politics."[29] This kind of position would have some affinity with Marx's and Trotsky's critique of Jacobinism were it rooted in recognition of a specific material context and the ambiguities of class formation. But it is not, and we are left wondering just how such a society loses and recovers its "independence" from politics. We can be excused for suggesting that Marxist orthodoxy is not the only inhabitant of a house of mirrors. Emperor Furet's new clothes, for all their fashionableness, lack more than a little substance: under scrutiny they look increasingly transparent.

Lynn Hunt's *Politics, Culture, and Class in the French Revolution* is less irritatingly opaque than Furet's text, just as it is less polemical. Produced within an American idiom, it is not concerned to distance itself from Marxism, always a subdued intellectual presence in the United States, and more explicit in its acknowledgment of Parisian poststructuralism, which carries more bang for its buck in California than it does in the cafes of the Left Bank, where Hunt's gestures toward Foucault, Barthes, and Derrida would raise few eyebrows. For all of its straighforwardness and its immersion in archival sources, which distance it from the grand posturing of Furet's *Interpreting the French Revolution*, it bears the same marks of anti-Marxism and reification of language.

Like Furet, Hunt privileges the political, especially its symbolic and linguistic components, which she sees as far more than a mere expression of "underlying" economic and social interests. "Revolutionary political culture," she insists, "cannot be deduced from social structures, social conflicts, or the social identity of revolutionaries." Political culture in the revolution was made up "of symbolic practices, such as language, imagery, and gestures." Echoing Furet, whom she quotes as establishing that speech substituted itself for power during the revolution and that "the semiotic circuit [was] the absolute master of politics," Hunt is adamant that language was itself an expression of power, shaping perceptions of interests and reconstituting the social and political world. She proposes to treat this "foremost instrument" of the revolution "as a text in the manner of literary criticism." This method allows her to avoid any interpretive slide into the abyss of "class" politics: as a literary theorist she knows that authorial intention is always uncertain, as was that of the revolutionary text, and she grasps that "the French rhetoric of revolution had to provide its own hermeneutics."[30]

This results, as in Furet, in a totalizing conceptualization of the revolution that rather willfully ignores socioeconomic divisions and that reconstitutes the process of revolution through adherence to linguistic metaphors of the revolutionaries themselves. The Festival of Federation of 14 July 1790 is taken at its word, an expression of national unification and identification demonstrative of the French citizenry's attachment to patriarchy and monarchy: in its celebration of the royal family, "the Festival brought the French family back together again, with the recognition that the father had given in to the pressing demands of his sons." To explain the abrupt shift in the revolution, Hunt turns to Northrop Frye's *Anatomy of Criticism*, arguing that the course of the revolution can be explained by "the transformation of narrative structures that informed revolutionary rhetoric." The "generic plot" of revolution moved from comedy to romance, and in the process the conflictual but reconcilable characters are reconstructed in a set of mythical oppositions, with larger-than-life heroes pitted against cowardly villains. Hence the rise of the Radicals in 1792. Tragedy was around the corner, however, speaking its most dramatic lines in the person of Robespierre, and propelled forward by the revolutionary obsession with the conspiratorial plot. Capital, labor, exploitation, and accumulation were not the orchestrating principles here, but given the discourse of hostility to the aristocracy, Hunt suggests cutely that this may have been a "language of class struggle without class." If you like your revolution neat, this is a drink for you.[31] It is a bit surprising that Crane Brinton's *The Anatomy of Revolution* is not more forcefully presented in the text, so reminiscent of his depiction of revolution is this account of the generic progression of revolutionary plots.[32]

Hunt then moves into a fascinating discussion of political symbolism and ritualism during the revolution. She extends our knowledge of the importance of this realm but oversteps interpretive acceptability with the blunt extremism of her denial of the structural and material substance of power, which is never interrogated, and the force of political ideas and social strata, which are dwarfed by the larger-than-life universe of determining images and representations:

> Political symbols and rituals were not metaphors of power; they were the means and ends of power itself.

> No doubt the women knew they were defending the Revolution when they marched to Versailles, but no speech about "the Revolution" could have mobilized them the way the cockade did.

> Even in these first months of the Revolution, opposing sides in the struggle were given clarity, if they were not actually called into being, by symbols.

> . . . masks and disguises facilitated, if they did not actually bring about, virtually every political and moral evil known to man.

> Taking minutes, sitting in a club meeting, reading a republican poem, wearing a cockade, sewing a banner, singing a song, filling out a form, making a patriotic donation, electing an official—all of these actions converged to produce a republican citizenry and a legitimate government.

> . . . the symbols and rituals of republicanism were tried, tested, and ultimately chosen. Without them, there would have been no collective memory of republicanism and no tradition of revolution.

> The memory of revolution was not carried forward in a book or a document. It was propogated by a few simple slogans, ribbons and caps, and memorable, lifelike figures.[33]

We can appreciate Hunt's suggestive researches and acknowledge the advances her work registers in our understanding of the importance of the symbolic, while distancing ourselves from the ultimate consequences of her reduction of politics to symbolism and imagery. After all, the language of revolutionary republicanism in the 1790s owed something to the long French engagement with Harrington, especially his *Oceana*, as the much-neglected work of S. B. Liljegren shows.[34] Hunt is too quick to accept Robespierre's proclamation that "the theory of revolutionary government is as new as the revolution which brought it into being. It is not necessary to search for it in the books of political writers, who did not foresee this revolution, or in the laws of tyrants, who, content to abuse their power, occupied themselves little with establishing its legitimacy."[35] The result is a book in which the "poli-

tics" of revolution are divorced from ideas, and revolutionaries gal-
vanized solely by cockades and images. So, too, is "politics" considered
outside of any reference to the material factors of work, wages, and
social mobility that Michael Sonenscher has argued were fundamentally related to both the language of labor and the history of the revolution.[36]

The first half of *Politics, Culture, and Class in the French Revolution*
is devoted to this reconsideration of the symbolic; the second concludes
the study with an examination of "The Sociology of Politics." Here the
focus is less on the linguistic and symbolic universe of "politics," and
more on the socioeconomic particularities of place and the culturalist
content of "the new political class." Hunt oscillates between locating
revolutionary politics in the structural attributes of specific geograph-
ical regions—with the left most successful in the regions distant from
Paris, where literacy, urbanization, and wealth were all underdeveloped, and the persistent right concentrated in the rich, literate, agricul-
tural hinterland of Paris, with shifts to conservatism taking place in
certain large peripheral cities—and a generational, family-based, asso-
ciationally rooted network of culture brokers. The result is a rather
confusing abstraction, one part quantification, one part speculation.

She acknowledges that the revolutionary political class that operated
within the symbolic formation of revolutionary rhetoric and image was
indeed "bourgeois":

> The revolutionary political class can be termed "bourgeois" both in
> terms of social position and of class consciousness. The revolution-
> ary officials were the owners of the means of production; they were
> either merchants with capital, professionals with skills, artisans
> with their own shops, or, more rarely, peasants with land. The
> unskilled, the wageworkers, and the landless peasants were not
> found in positions of leadership or even in large numbers among the
> rank and file. The "consciousness" of the revolutionary elite can be
> labeled bourgeois in so far as it was distinctly anti-feudal, anti-
> aristocratic, and anti-absolutist. In their language and imagery, rev-
> olutionaries rejected all reminders of the past, and they included in
> their ranks very few nobles or Old Regime officials. The revolution-
> ary elite was made up of new men dedicated to fashioning a new
> France.[37]

But so hegemonic is the hostility of the new revisionism to any notion
of "bourgeois" revolution that Hunt backtracks, arguing that the term
bourgeois is too general to discriminate between revolutionary mili-
tants and their moderate opponents. It is as if any sense of class frac-
tions within a moment of revolutionary turmoil must be exorcised if
class is to have any meaning.

In the end, Hunt demonstrates the presence of class in the revolution but retreats to the "higher" ground of language, the argument wrapped in circularity: "the left won elections where the Jacobins of the towns and villages were able to develop relationships and organizations favorable to the rhetoric of liberty, equality, and fraternity; and the right won elections where royalists and/or partisans of a republic of order were able to galvanize their clients into movements against the innovating Republic."[38] Convinced that any search for structural origins or outcomes is suspect, Hunt reifies politics and its representations, treating the personnel and principles of the revolution as abstracted, unmediated essences anchored only in their own cultural moment and imagination. The linguistic turn proves a dead end.

Those recent works that address language and the French Revolution in more fruitful ways avoid the pitfalls evident in the Furet and Hunt books precisely because they eschew any descent into discourse and reification of rhetoric and imagery and instead locate language within an ensemble of determinative social, political, and economic forces. William H. Sewell's *Work and Revolution in France*, a study of the language of labor from the Old Regime to 1848, is one such text. Devoid of the antagonism to Marxism that scars Furet and infects Hunt, Sewell denies the ontological priority of economic events but insists that they be treated "as continuous with all other aspects of . . . experience." His "language of labor" is an attempt to explore the vocabularies and representations of many complementary "texts": "This book . . . is . . . not only about workers' utterances or about theoretical discourse on labor, but about the whole range of institutional arrangements, ritual gestures, work practices, methods of struggle, customs and actions that gave the workers' world a comprehensible shape." He thus explores the transformation of language in the context of changed material and political circumstances, examining the ways in which laboring people took an eighteenth-century "corporate idiom" and translated it into the practice of *corporations republicaines* of 1848. In the process a language rooted in the feudal order was reconstituted to espouse a consciousness of labor and its struggles:

> By combining the corporate and revolutionary idioms in this way and by engaging in collective action based on these newly constructed premises, the workers created a new type of opposition to the dominant state and society, an opposition that proclaimed the workers' specific identity as laborers, opposed individualism with an ideal of fraternal solidarity, promised an end to the tyranny of private property, and implied the legitimacy of a revolution to achieve those ends. . . . Although their ideology was elaborated from their particular class perspective, it was stated, like the ideologies of

the Revolution of 1789–1794, in universal terms. As they understood it, theirs was the consciousness of enlightened humanity, not
the consciousness of a class.

A half-century later the language of labor would have shifted again and
"class loyalty," a vocabulary unknown in the Old Regime that would
have been despised as selfish in 1848, would take on the positive con-
notation of devotion to the cause of all proletarians.[39]

In his attention to the contextual inflections of language and of its
referential embeddedness in the material process of long-term social,
economic, and political change, Sewell moves well beyond the conventionalities of linguistic reification. More impressive yet is Michael
Sonenscher's discussion of the sans-culottes' language of labor in the
revolutionary France of the Year II. What distinguishes Sonenscher's
approach is his resolute attempt to uncover the realities of workplace
organization and productive life within the mythical world of the sans-
culottes. This proceeds on the basis of an adamant refusal to take the
representations of this world, as propagated by the sans-culottes themselves and perpetuated by historians such as Soboul, at face value.
Locating a fundamental tension between the staged public discourse of
labor, so influenced by law and state, and the private language of the
workshop, Sonenscher directs attention to the "porous and parasitic
quality of language itself."[40]

Sonenscher's article is premised on an essential refusal. He rejects the
mythic identification of the sans-culottes with small-scale artisan production, arguing on the basis of an impressive rereading of the available
statistical evidence that divisions of labor and *grandes boutiques* were
far more prevalent and influential than previously acknowledged. (He
presents yet more evidence, then, that a bourgeoisie presence, if not a
fully formed class, did indeed exist, although he never frames his argument with this polemical barb at the new revisionists in mind.) The
relations of production, moreover, were a far cry from the classless
harmonies that sometimes are implied in master-journeymen relations
of the time: more than two hundred work disputes erupted in Paris over
the course of the century leading up to the revolution, and in 1791
journeymen secured a two-hour reduction in the working day. Sonenscher uses these kinds of evidence to argue that "substantial and very
durable differences separat[ed] masters and journeymen as collectiv-
ities."[41]

This "rediscovery" of the scale and tension of workshop life poses a
paradox. How was it that the language of the sans-culottes in the Year II
so persistently reproduced a corporate idiom in which the small-scale
nature of production was constantly emphasized? Did the language of

the sans-culottes deliberately misstate reality? In fact it did not, and Sonenscher develops a subtle explanation that attends to how the language of labor was long related to a context of state power that refracted the language of the workshop through the prism of ultimate authority:

> The language of corporate association, rights and privileges fed upon the language of the law and the royal administration. Its terms and propositions supplied master artisans with a vocabulary for engaging with those outside the trades themselves. When brought to bear upon the everyday world of workshop production, it did so in a formally rigid and authoritarian way. The uniformity of the provisions of corporate statutes for the definition of relations between masters and journeymen echoed broader assumptions of hierarchy, subordination, and duty. When challenged, and obliged to present their own claims to the public sphere of royal power, it was to this rhetoric of mercantilist order that master artisans turned.

Sonenscher lays stress on how both masters and journeymen could draw on this old, prerevolutionary public discourse, in which work was duty, but with different intents: "It was a public vocabulary of authority and power upon which masters and journeymen drew in different ways with different inflections."[42]

With the revolutionary decrees of June 1791 outlawing corporations and prohibiting workers' associations—laws passed in the face of increasingly tense workplace relations—the formal idiom of authority that underlay this long-standing language of labor was dismantled. Conventional wisdom then posits that the sans-culottes were swept into a popular movement whose discourse was objectively anchored in the shared commonalities of small-scale production. Sonenscher rejects this explanation, instead turning to the linguistic differentiations that journeymen used throughout the Old Regime to sustain their claims against masters, differentiations in the languages of law and the conduct of a trade. In these languages was articulated a code of conduct that secured journeymen the respect of masters and that acknowledged specific spheres of power, the workshop being the domain of the journeyman, the home that of the master. In their concerns with wage payments and work registration, as well as in their homage to the moral and civic distinctions separating those engaged in the arts and mysteries of a trade from those practicing mere domestic service, both masters and journeymen found themselves impaled on the dilemmas of recognized agreements and irreconcilable differences. Thus the language of the sans-culottes in the Year II bore little relationship to the simplistic cozy convivialities of master and man; instead, it grew out of the conflict-bred negotiations of class interest and productive life:

The language of the Year II drew heavily upon the linguistic and cultural conventions disclosed by the opposition to formal systems of registration in the eighteenth century. The antinomies of the Year II—between equality and deference, natural liberty and arbitrary authority, citizens and lackeys, direct address and obsequious manoeuvre—echoed those of the conventional medium of the mutual evaluation which informed the rhythms of workshop production. In this sense, the metaphor of the *sans-culotte* embodied a certain code of honour which, in varying degrees, journeymen and master artisans were bound to use in their transactions with one another. It was a metaphor charged with those qualities which distinguished masters and journeymen from domestic servants. As a result it was able to provide the language of republicanism with an already meaningful social vocabulary. The metaphor of the *sans-culotte* supplied the language of republicanism with something which it did not have: a range of cultural referents which were meaningful in an urban and artisanal context.[43]

Sonenscher thus provides a rare and welcomed explication of how language develops in the context of material life and its class struggles, and of how it asserts its presence in a moment of political turmoil. Across an ocean, over the course of more than a century, another language of republicanism would also exercise an attraction for historians of labor.

▶   **The Long and Mysterious Life**
    of American Republicanism
No subject has captivated American historiography more than the Revolutionary War for Independence and the meaning and continuity of its republican politics. Compared with the French experience, the American Revolution has little in the way of Marxist interpretive pedigree,[44] but a materialist school of analysis early consolidated around Progressive historians such as Charles A. Beard, who generated shock and outrage on the eve of World War I with the conclusion that the Republic as a political entity was the work "of a consolidated group whose interests knew no state boundaries and were truly national in their scope" and the Constitution "was essentially an economic document based upon the concept that the fundamental private rights of property are anterior to government and morally beyond the reach of popular majorities."[45]

Historians of various methodological and political persuasions have busied themselves with demonstrating that a Beardian fixation on the hegemony of property is insufficient as an analytic starting point in the

consideration of the American Revolution. On the one hand, a distinguished body of scholarship addresses the not inconsiderable role of the
popular classes that Beard saw, simplistically, as dwarfed by revolutionary "interests."[46] An edited collection of documents on the Democratic-
Republican Societies of 1790–1800 is prefaced by a quote from the
Wood's Newark Gazette (19 March 1794): "It must be the mechanics
and farmers, or the poorer class of people (as they are generally called)
that must support the freedom of America; the freedom which they and
their fathers purchased with their blood—the nobility will never do it—
they will be always striving to get the reins of government in their own
hands, and then they can ride the people at pleasure."[47] On the other
hand, not unlike the French reaction to a conception of the revolution as
bourgeois, there has developed in the United States a much-heralded
stress on the consensual ideological origins of the American upheaval, a
stress associated with the work of Bernard Bailyn.[48] None of this work,
however, draws even remotely on the tenets of literary criticism, discourse theory, or poststructuralist thought, of whatever fragment. One
would look hard and long in any attempt to discern a linguistic turn in
this area of American studies.

My concern here is with the subtle incorporation of some of the
conceptual edifice of the reification of discourse into the discussion of
American republicanism's hold over plebeian and proletarian politics in
the nineteenth century. A curious process of intellectual osmosis appears to have been at work over the last decade, with the premises of
areas "high" in theory and ideas flowing to those fields animated by
"lower" concerns: the result is an oddly innocent appropriation of "language" in discussions of the politics of American labor from the time of
Jackson into the Gilded Age. In the midst of a recent exchange of views
on consensus, hegemony, and the so-called new labor history, Mari Jo
Buhle and Paul Buhle suggested that the principal advocate of the labor
historiography produced by those who would associate themselves
with the late Herbert Gutman, Leon Fink, was now "working on fruitful
lines close to the heuristic side of the poststructural dynamic." This
obviously took Fink somewhat by surprise, but his response was by no
means a denial: "While I am happy to be subsumed by Mari Jo Buhle and
Paul Buhle into the poststructural dynamic, I must admit that if I am a
poststructualist it is of the *ex post facto* kind."[49] Fink, known for his
droll sense of humor and Gutmanesque impatience with the pompous-
ness of certain high theoretical pronouncements, may have been tug-
ging at some intellectual legs with his statement, but the last laugh
appears to be on a materialist reading of republicanism.

No recourse to texts alone could possibly explain such a retroactive
theoretical assimilation, for its making lies in many complex quarters,

not the least of which is the political economy of late imperial America
and the sociology of an academically rooted New Left. But the signs of
its gradualist entry into the historiography can be plotted textually and,
this done, interrogated to reveal a particular intellectual substance. Let
us begin with some texts.

There were abundant indications by the early-to-mid 1980s that discussions of popular republicanism in the late eighteenth and nineteenth centuries were about to take a linguistic turn, albeit one that was
not clearly marked by theoretical proclamations. Rhys Isaac's innovative discussion of the transformation of Virginia in the years 1740–1790
closed with "A Discourse on Method" that elaborated a strikingly imaginative conception of how to construct historical meaning ethnograph-
ically. Ostensibly more about anthropology and history than about
literary theory and history, it nevertheless focused on matters entirely
compatible with the poststructuralist attraction to discourse:

> "Translation" is the fundamental task of ethnographers, and in its
> inherent perplexities lies their greatest challenge. A culture may be
> thought of as a related set of languages or as a multichannelled
> system of communication. Consisting of more than just words, it
> also comprises gesture, demeanor, dress, architecture, and all the
> codes by which those who share in the culture convey meanings
> and significance to each other.

Isaac offered stimulating suggestions about how ritual presented statements about the nature of the social universe in eighteenth-century
Virginia and, in particular, how the drama of social interaction within
everyday life could be "read" metaphorically:

> In real life the encounters that are the units of study in action-
> oriented ethnography do not occur—as they may on a page—iso-
> lated from context. The participants must operate within particular
> frames of reference that enable them to orient themselves to one
> another in order to share, exchange, or even contest meanings. It is
> necessary to consider now some systematic approaches to the gen-
> erally available, public symbols and shared meanings through
> which actors relate to, and communicate with, one another. The
> action approach must explicitly take into account some of the ways
> in which culture is composed of interlocking sets of paradigms, or
> metaphors, that shape participants' perceptions by locating diverse
> forms of action on more or less coherent maps of experience. . . . The
> task of the ethnographer begins rather than ends with identifying
> and labeling the metaphors that inform encounters and link them
> together in a patterned system of socially established meanings, or
> *typifications*. . . . Metaphors, then, may be likened to containers
> that must be handled in each case according to their content.

No easily identifiable poststructuralist texts were cited in Isaac's methodological discourse, nor did he allude to any of the accessible literary theory then proliferating among American deconstructionists. He drew instead upon the literature of the sociology of knowledge, phenomenology, and anthropological symbolism and presented "a theater model" of his own construction:

> It will readily be seen that each culture and subculture has its own distinctive dramaturgical kit, consisting of "settings," "props," "costumes," "roles," "script formulas," and, as elusive as they are important, "styles" of action and gesture. The word "role" has become so much a commonplace not only of sociological but of everyday discourse that its origin as a metaphor drawn from the theater has been obscured. . . . The theater model serves to emphasize the formalities that govern so much of social life. . . . Great metaphors of the culture enter into the creation and interpretation of settings; they are a major source of available roles; and they also govern the actors' styles of self-presentation. Above all it is the great metaphors that control the very perception of what constitutes significant action, or drama.

This was not exactly discourse according to Foucault, but it was not that far from it. And yet when Isaac moved into this arena of theoretical congruity, he pulled back: noting at one point that "the 'structuralist' system of Claude Lévi-Strauss" appeared to rear its head, he confessed, "This author deems it prudent not to take a position here with regard to the intense controversies surrounding that theorist."[50]

Isaac's "Discourse," in both its concerns and form, was nevertheless an indication that language, symbolism, and metaphor were on the agenda. Alfred Young had long been at work on an extended discussion of the role and transformation of ritual in Boston during the period leading up to the revolution, and Peter Shaw, a professor of English, had just offered an exposé of the importance of ritual in the American patriot movement.[51] These works represented an equivalent within American revolutionary historiography to Hunt's *Politics, Culture, and Class in the French Revolution*, although they never reified symbol and image to the same extent. They also meshed well with the exciting work on popular politics in eighteenth-century Britain, where John Brewer had recast understanding of the Wilkite agitations with his creative focus on ritual.[52] From another direction, the increasing attraction of American historians to the language of civic virtue associated with J. G. A. Pocock's "Machiavellian Moment" and the transatlantic republican tradition also underscored the arrival of discourse.[53]

Given one historian's confession (however cast) of the ex post facto nature of his integration into the interpretive dynamic of discourse, it is worth pausing to reflect on the meaning of republicanism as it lay poised to enter the nineteenth century. It is not a meaning without its ambiguities and internal contradictions. First, while Bailyn and his followers may lead the way in positing a rational republican consensus, thus marginalizing the "inflamed mobs," "subversive party," "extremists," and others, like Tom Paine, driven by "personal discontent," "passion," and a host of other savage, ignorant, crude, and "slightly insane" impulses,[54] the historiography of the past twenty years establishes that in the turmoil of transformation culminating in American independence, republican ideology was highly contested terrain, fought over and defined and redefined by combatants from differentiated social and economic strata. The crowd, artisans, the yeomanry, blacks, highly mobile elements such as seamen—the list could be extended considerably—all appropriated a piece of the republican pie. Second, although we can recognize this ideological contest over the meaning and social definition and "ownership" of republicanism, it is also apparent that by the 1790s, after the victory over the British and the ratification of the Constitution, republicanism's fissures experienced something of a melt-down in the forced pressure cooker of a consolidating bourgeois social formation. There was some room for republican movement to the left, but not much. A vision of classlessness, in which a society of aspiring men of independence and competence—by which was meant both ability and the wherewithal to pursue ability's potentials and desires—was the "principle of hope" that largely animated republican thought in the ideological consolidation of Jeffersonianism in the closing decade of the eighteenth century. "In so thoroughly embracing the liberal position on private property and economic freedom, the Jeffersonians seemed unable to envision a day when the free exercise of men's wealth-creating talents would produce its own class-divided society," argues Joyce Appleby.[55] When the Philadelphia and New York labor conspiracy trials of 1806 and 1809 exposed this republican hope to the realities of class division and conflict, they "symbolised the issues which had not been solved by political democracy and republicanism."[56] Third, and finally, this republican ideology, as Isaac Kramnick and John Diggins have argued, was always far more integrated into a Lockean accommodation to the market than a Pocock-like fixation on the classlessness of civic virtue is prepared to countenance. Recognition of this ideological reality suggests how the fissured republicanism of the tumultuous 1770s and 1780s gave way to the more overtly capitalistic rationality of later republicanism. As "self-centered economic productivity, not public citizenship, became the badge of virtuous man," the republicanism of the streets and clubs took a back seat to the republicanism of capital and its market society. "When the American spirit was in its youth," Patrick Henry recalled of the momentum and glory of 1776, "the language of America was different: liberty, sir, was then the primary object." As quickly as a decade later, things looked different, and the language of the Constitution reflected republicanism's concern with a more material reality of "interests," "passions," "ambition," "avarice," "pride," "zeal," "jealousy," and other powerful desires that had to be curbed in an obedience that seemed capable of being secured only by recourse to "the most common and durable" needs of "property" and "reward."[57] To date this shift in the content of republicanism precisely is an impossible task, but to imply that it never took place and to carry the illusion of republican radicalism for over a century is surely excessive.

Republicanism and its language were thus premised on an essential schizophrenia, in which the dominant personality of property grew in stature and power as the struggles of the eighteenth century gave way to the consolidations of the nineteenth, all the while nurturing, for its own purposes, the illusive personality of liberty and citizenship. Both, of course, had their class countenances, as is evident from a reading of Sean Wilentz's discussion of artisan republicanism and its political content and symbolism in New York into the Age of Jackson.[58] But as Susan Davis remarks in a perceptive comment on the class dramas of parades in antebellum Philadelphia, "Artisan republicanism was dramatized within events sponsored, produced, and costumed by employers and masters."[59] That the working class wore this mask of republicanism of its own volition came as no surprise to Frederick Engels, who saw, like Marx, that "ideology is the illusion of an epoch." In 1892 Engels wrote to Sorge some prescient words, but ones that are seldom quoted by radical historians of the American working class:

> Here in old Europe things are rather more lively than in your "youthful" country, which still refuses to get quite out of its hobbledehoy stage. It is remarkable, but quite natural, that in such a young country, which has never known feudalism and has grown up on a bourgeois basis from the first, bourgeois prejudices should also be so strongly rooted in the working class. Out of his very opposition to the mother country—which is still clothed in its feudal disguise—the American worker also imagines that the bourgeois regime as traditionally inherited is something progressive and superior by nature and for all time, a *non plus ultra*. Just as in New England, Puritanism, the reason for the whole colony's existence, has become precisely on this account a traditional inheritance, almost inseparable from local patriotism. The Americans can strain and struggle as much as they like, but they cannot realise their future—colossally great as it is—all at once like a bill of exchange;

they must wait for the date on which it becomes due; and just *because* their future is so great their present must mainly occupy itself with preparatory work for the future, and their work, as in every young country, is of a predominantly material nature and determines a certain backwardness of thought, a clinging to traditions connected with the foundation of the new nationality.[60]

Few have been the American historians of labor who have even gestured toward this perspective.[61]

Yet if we stop the clock of historical development at appropriate nineteenth-century moments, when one hand is situated on class struggle and the other on the appropriated language and ideology of republicanism, it is difficult not to see the price American workers paid for a politics that celebrated republican virtue and championed republican rights. The incompatibility of class interests and the embrace of a republican model of citizenship, however radical, is evident in the conspiracy trials of the first decade of the century, the agitations of the 1830s, the drowning of elementary class awareness in the nativist agitations of the 1850s,[62] the waning of radical republicanism in the face of the class conflicts of the 1860s and 1870s,[63] and the burgeoning expansion of class institutions and awareness during the Great Upheaval of the 1880s. One of the architects of those momentous advances, labor reformer George E. McNeill, stated in the 1870s that the workers' movement "declare[d] an inevitable and irresistible conflict between the wage-system of labor and the republican system of government."[64] This breakthrough in political recognition was by no means generalized throughout the working class. When the Great Upheaval subsided, and its major institutional expression, the Knights of Labor, succumbed to employer hostility, factional intrigue, and confrontation, the corporatist carrots of state patronage and reform, and the dislocations of economic depression, more isolated and radical enclaves of working-class resistance never quite refashioned the widespread "moral universality" of the Gilded Age's "nineteenth-century language" of opposition to the Republic of Capital.[65]

This perhaps explains why radical historians of labor have gravitated toward the Gilded Age as an important moment in the making of the American working class. They are right to do so, and the accomplishments of the late-nineteenth-century workers' movement were considerable. But in all too often refusing to enter into a critical dialogue with that moment of class formation, many historians have by default given too much analytic ground and abandoned the difficult task of judgment concerning that important but difficult-to-discern and rarely realized politics, class consciousness. Indeed, it is not unfair to suggest that many supposedly radical historians of the American working class have literally jettisoned class consciousness as a meaningful historical process and presence, arguing that to even suggest scrutinizing workers' organizations, ideas, and experiences for the existence of class consciousness is to construct an idealized category that not only never existed in the United States but that never developed anywhere. American workers, in this view, are just like workers everywhere else: they labor, and struggle, and draw on their own unique resources to fashion their opposition to capital.[66] This refusal of serious scrutiny of class consciousness has the curious consequence of diluting the meaning of class consciousness to suggest that virtually all opposition by workers constitutes its realization, whatever one calls it. Class consciousness by any other name apparently smells just as radical. Labor republicanism relates directly to this conceptual blurring.

Herbert Gutman and Ira Berlin, among the most insightful of American historians to write on subordinate classes, suggest the all-too-easy adoption of a particular perspective on republican ideology when they write:

> As preindustrial workers became a wage-earning class, republicanism neither disappeared nor remained a set of stale patriotic pieties. Instead, wage earners in Jacksonian America remade it into a distinctive and radical—but nonsocialist—argument against the pervasive inequalities associated with nineteenth-century capitalism. They identified republicanism with social equality, not with open competition in the race for wealth. . . . Their beliefs went beyond the redefinition of eighteenth-century republicanism, and sparked and sustained recurrent collective efforts—in the form of trade unions, strikes, cooperatives, a tart labor press, and local politics— to check the increase of power of the industrial capitalist. . . . In sum, prior to 1840, American wage earners had developed an indigenous ideology independent of and opposed to capitalism.[67]

Empirically this is indeed a statement of what happened, up to an interpretive point. And that point, about how republicanism was used and what its impact was on the consciousness of workers, is central. Could an ideology actually develop indigenously that was independent of capitalism and opposed to it, at the same time that it embraced a political creed born of and congruent with the development of that very same capitalism? Could an ideology actually be oppositional and independent when it accepted so much of the hegemonic fog of that capitalist republic that it supposedly pitted itself against? By not asking such questions, Berlin and Gutman pave the way to a particular interpretive end in which it becomes possible to imply a kind of universalistic class consciousness out of workers' struggles to forge trade unions and integrate themselves into the established body politic of capitalist society.[68]

The relevance of this analytic development to this book's concern with the reification of language in social history is the extent to which the rhetoric of republicanism has become a substitute for a discerning appreciation of the strengths and weaknesses of nineteenth-century workers' oppositional culture. A debate has developed around precisely this issue, and it was in the midst of this debate that Leon Fink, defending the practice of a labor history given to acceptance of republican rhetoric, acknowledged his retroactive assimilation to the interpretive dynamic of poststructuralism. That debate was kicked off by a somewhat ineffective assault on the Gutmanesque labor history of the last two decades, a polemical swipe contained within a larger critical commentary. In "Comrades and Citizens: New Mythologies in American Historiography," John Patrick Diggins took aim at the shared attractions of "Marxist" labor historians and what he called "republicanists" (those drawing on Pocock's proposition that America absorbed Old World classical republicanism and its dichotomization of "virtue" and "commerce"). Diggins argued that these strange bedfellows

> both assume that ideas and culture are more important than interests and power as determinants of action. They both think, moreover, that such ideas can best be appreciated by understanding what the subjects of their studies were protesting. Marxists emphasize protests against economic exploitation, republicanists the protests against political corruption. Marxists and republicanists have similarly joined together in arguing that the new way to write social and intellectual history is to pay close attention to "language," whether it be the language of labor or the language of politics. Finally, Marxists and republicanists have both been pleased to discover in early American history a moral culture of wholesome comrades and active citizens whose sense of solidarity and community helped resist the supposedly corrosive effects of liberal capitalism.[69]

In spite of himself, for the depiction of the social history of labor and other subordinate groups was nothing more than a caricature drawn from a cursory examination of the writing on American workers and slaves, Diggins scored a hit. Paralleling Diggins's invective was a more sophisticated go at the same problem, T. J. Jackson Lears's attempt to read American history in the light of Gramsci's theory of cultural hegemony.[70]

Leon Fink responded with a spirited rejection of Diggins's "insistence on the universal saturation of American culture in a dreary liberalism of private accumulation" and a questioning of Lears's "overvaluation of intellectual coherence as a test of political and cultural authenticity." It is an invaluable response on many levels, but disappointing in its defensive insistence on the class validity of the working-class language of republicanism. And it is also caught in a massive contradiction, at least in terms of language. For by the 1880s the universalism of labor's language of republicanism, which acquiesced in the impartiality of the state and its legislative tradition of "equal rights," was beginning to break down. McNeill could declare an inevitable and irresistible conflict between "wage slavery" and republican government, and from a militant anarcho-communist minority to his left came demands for "destruction of the existing class rule, by all means, i.e., by energetic, relentless, revolutionary and international action." Among the German and Bohemian immigrant quarters of cities like Chicago, Detroit, New York, Pittsburgh, and Milwaukee the language of revolution was spoken as well as the language of republicanism.[71] The point is not that the United States was on the verge of a socialist insurrection pitted consciously against the Republic, just as it is not that American workers were immune to the attractions of republicanism. Rather, the Great Upheaval can be seen as a moment of class agitation representing the culmination of the late-nineteenth-century experience; one part of it drew on tradition, one part on a forward-looking opposition to the consolidation of economic and political power.[72]

It is not necessary to embrace labor republicanism in this context as a class virtue, and it is surprising the extent to which Fink does just this, arguing that "labor's appropriation of the very 'vital center' of American political discourse, rather than a denial of alternative social ends, was a testament to the still undetermined character of that political discussion, a sign of latent possibilities yet unrealized." He champions a popular frontist notion of historic blocs (which, as Diggins later argues, misconstrues Gramsci's use of the term), praising the Knights of Labor capacity—one part of which was undoubtedly forged in the employment of "a moralistic, republican message"—"to tap 'bourgeois' as well as 'proletarian' segments of society and thus to constitute themselves as a potential sociopolitical alternative to the mass political parties and the corporations." Finally, Fink suggests that those who question the validity of his interpretation and have the temerity to raise the whole matter of class consciousness are no doubt seeking refuge in an idealized "model of a class conscious and revolutionary working class, equipped with a rigorous class ideology and theoretical understanding of the capitalist economy." That, he says, is a rare beast, and one he does not want to waste time tracking down. Instead, he poses a question that he regards as "more interesting and important": "What would it have taken for America to be different by 1900—or by extension—today?"[73] There is an answer, of course, but not one he will enjoy hearing. If the language of labor had been more class conscious and less republican—a big *if*, for the rhetoric, like the program of the Knights of Labor, was a product of a specific conjuncture of political economy, class formation, and labor organization—things might very well have ended up much different.

But they did not. One reason they did not was because of the materially embedded language of labor republicanism. I do not think that acknowledgment of this belittles the tremendous accomplishments of Gilded Age labor. Yet others obviously do. In his involvement in the Fink-Diggins-Lears debate, George Lipsitz, for instance, wants to go further than Fink in his identification with the struggles of the 1880s. He opts, tellingly, for a privileging of struggle for struggle's sake, a sympathetic reading of failure that goes so far as to actually question the possibility of realizing working-class power:

> Long traditions of working-class self-activity have properly focused on concrete material gains or desired structures of social organization, but only as instruments for ending alienation and for promoting democracy and justice. We have learned from hard and bitter experience that even the seizure of state power by oppositional movements does not necessarily entail victory for aggrieved populations. No single material or structural improvement has meaning in itself, only as a means toward building a world without exploitation and hierarchy. And building that world is a political process in which people change themselves and others at the same time that they change the social distribution of wealth and power. . . . Even failure has its uses; it brings to the surface necessary information about the shortcomings and contradictions of oppositional movements. . . . Even in failure, social contestation changes the material and ideological balance of power in society. Conversely, even when social contestation succeeds, it is only setting the stage for future changes.

Small wonder that the author of this kind of pessimistic relativism, in which failure is just as good as victory and material meaning is so nebulous, should close with a statement that forces us back into the domain of literary theory:

> The literary critic Mikhail Bakhtin tells us that there is no such thing as a pure monologue, that every utterance is part of a dialogue already in progress. As much as anyone historians know the wisdom of that formulation. . . . But the habit of dialogue is not the property of historians alone, or of traditional intellectuals who write books and articles; it is an essential way of understanding the world for historical actors as well. The organic intellectuals engaged in past and present social contestation can never be static entities embodying a pure consciousness. Rather, they are participants in a dialogue, authors of an ongoing narrative whose final chapter is never written.[74]

American workers, their history and their historians, have now been deconstructed.

Fink, too, ends with language, suggesting that historians need to pursue the decline of the language of labor republicanism.[75] Did immigration, changing labor processes, state reform, or state repression "weaken its intrinsic explanatory powers?" How was it "effectively marginalized in public discourse" and "what streams of thought displaced it?" The last sentence of Fink's essay states bluntly, "By focusing less on changing basic values than on the very processes by which meanings were organized and empowered in American life, a cultural history of labor movements will no doubt continue to have plenty to teach us."[76] Yes, it will, and Fink's essay suggests how much. But in the unconscious drift into discourse characteristic of sectors of the so-called new labor history, much has also been lost, including an almost elementary appreciation of material life and its structures, where all meaning is mediated.

It is significant that in the years since the publication of Fink's book on the Knights of Labor and American politics, *Workingmen's Democracy*, the major theoretical ground he has chosen to stake out with more clarity and rigor is that of the language of republicanism. His book can be read as touching down on this subject only gingerly, although of course his argument and evidence can be interpreted within its frame of reference.[77] Later articles, however, paid more homage to the "republican heritage that linked the welfare of the nation to the economic and political independence of the citizenry."[78] And now, with the publication of "The New Labor History and the Powers of Historical Pessimism," the language of labor republicanism assumes an unambiguous importance. Fink's article has the tremendous virtue of posing explicitly what has become, cavalierly and implicitly, convention.[79]

The language of labor republicanism existed; this is not at issue. What matters is how historians read a language of this sort; or, to put the same matter differently: what labor republicanism meant in its own times. For the most part it has been read at its word, accepted as a positive force mobilizing American labor on its own cultural terms. And in this kind of reading the politics of pragmatism are all too evident: because labor reformers in the nineteenth century were able to galvanize masses of workers, indeed because they could at particular times sustain a movement culture of opposition, they must have been on the right track. And one rail of that track was their thoroughly American language.

It is possible to "read" this language differently. To do so let me reach back to Rhys Isaac's "Discourse on Method" in his book *The Transformation of Virginia, 1740–1790*. The language of labor republicanism was, in Isaac's terms, one of the great metaphors of nineteenth-century American political culture. As such it was indeed a factor that entered into the process of how subordinate groups interpreted the meaning of social relations, governing in part their style of self-presentation and setting limits within which the drama of politics was played out. This metaphor was, as Isaac suggests of other metaphors, a container that was handled according to its contents. Labor reformers struggled to pour as much oppositional and critical matter into it as they could, and they succeeded to an unprecedented degree. But that oppositional content was nevertheless then contained, reconstructed by the extent to which it was bottled up within distinct sets of possibilities. The language of labor republicanism thus unleashed radicalism, but it did so within boundaries of limitation/determination: there was a limited field within which that radicalism could range. My elementary point is that the language of labor republicanism—and indeed the symbolism surrounding it, which was a ubiquitous presence highlighted on days like the Fourth of July—was two-sided and contradictory and, as a controlling metaphor within American politics, simultaneously encouraged and contained resistance to authority.[80]

Consider, for instance, the building of "Little Jim Park" on a tiny plot of U.S. Steel property in Pittsburgh in 1909. A worker was asked, "Who gave this park?" He replied, "We took it." That defiant statement, and that act of appropriation, are instances of class struggle. Those who participated in that mundane movement of resistance created space for themselves. Out of remnants of a church once occupying the site they built flower beds, a canopy, an arch, and a gate. And then, to legitimize this class-motivated seizure and impulse of self-creation, they built a flagpole and flew the colors of twentieth-century capitalism—the American flag—planted in soil brutally expropriated, dripping with the blood of imperialist adventure, soaked in the surplus value extracted from native and immigrant American workers. The metaphor of the Republic and its symbol brought an act of resistance back into line, possibly securing the park in defiance of property, but also insuring that a single, isolated act of rebellion did not generalize and spread. Resistance, opposition, defiance, on the one hand, accommodation and legitimation on the other.[81] The language of labor republicanism spoke in many voices.

▶   Language's analytic presence is felt differently in these two historiographic moments. In the reinterpretation of the French Revolution it rears its proud head aggressively and polemically, looking defiantly into the face of Marxist analysis. It shouts the need to make the linguistic turn and makes the descent into discourse consciously and purposively, informed by if not espousing openly the guidance offered in the texts of critical theory. The case of American republicanism, and the reading of its longevity among contemporary historians of the working class, is an entirely different matter. There no explicit confrontation with Marxist class analysis has broken out, although some subtle distancing from particular Marxisms—especially anything smacking of Leninism—has been evident. Neither has there been any open identification with the discourse orientation of poststructuralist thought. Instead, assimilation to the implosion of theory takes place almost by default and not without contradiction.

There is nevertheless a point where the stress on language—in the one case militant and reified, in the other almost unconscious—channels these quite different readings of politics on to similiar ground. The reinterpretation of the French Revolution is nothing if it is not a repudiation of class; the language of labor republicanism is taken so seriously only by denying that class consciousness is an identifiable and important phenomenon, blurring its meaning in an indiscriminate eclecticism. It seems appropriate to turn, then, to recent discussions of the language of class, which inevitably assume a particular reading of class consciousness.

4 *Class*

*The bourgeoisie has more in common with every
other nation of the earth than with the workers in
whose midst it lives. The workers speak other
dialects, have other thoughts and ideals, other
customs and moral principles, a different religion and
other politics than those of the bourgeoisie.*

—Frederick Engels, The Condition of the Working-
Class in England in 1844 *(1845)*

AS IS OBVIOUS FROM A READING OF THE LAST CHAPTER,
class, a fundamental concept within historical materialism, has fallen
on rough times of late. Few terms elicit the skepticism and condescension reserved for *class* in the 1980s. Those who remain convinced of its
analytic power and historical presence, and write histories premised on
this, are now depicted routinely as rather confused and antiquated.
Reviews take on the tone of obituaries.[1] Norman McCord has castigated those "for whom the concept of class forms the adored central
mystery of a quasi-religious cult," finding in the recent works of Eric
Hobsbawm, Dorothy Thompson, and Gareth Stedman Jones "an uncritical devotion to the concept of class . . . an immutable foundation to
which everything else must be accommodated."[2]

Much "criticism" of this sort is ill informed, amounting to little more
than an ideologically mounted charge against the materialist view that
how people are placed within the socioeconomic structure is, ultimately, of fundamental importance in understanding both individual
lives and society as a whole. When specific people earn more than
others, vote for parties that do not appeal to a sharply demarcated class
constituency, and dispose of their wages in ways that result in different
patterns of consumption, all of this is seen as repudiation of class. This,
of course, is a very old argument, the status versus class analytic dichot-

120

omy having separated Weberian and Marxist interpretations of social structure from the beginnings of sociological inquiry in the nineteenth century.

What is new in the 1980s is the wholesale retreat from class among those ostensibly linked to the socialist project. As Ellen Meiksins Wood has argued forcefully, this development shares a certain intellectual and political space with the "true" socialists of the 1840s, against whom Marx and Engels polemicized.[3] This "true" socialism of almost 150 years ago championed "not the interests of the proletariat, but the interests of Human Nature, of Man in general, who belongs to no class, has no reality, who exists only in the misty realm of philosophical fantasy," adopting a vocabulary and orientation that bore a striking resemblance to much that is now routine within the "innovative breakthroughs" of critical theory. Marx and Engels saw this movement of the 1840s as a rearguard action of the German petty bourgeoisie, threatened by the concentration of capital and the rise of a revolutionary proletariat. "True" socialism, they argued, "appeared to kill these two birds with one stone." Spreading like "an epidemic," "true" socialism wrapped itself in "the robe of speculative cobwebs, embroidered with flowers of rhetoric, steeped in the dew of sickly sentiment," all the while "directly opposing the 'brutally destructive' tendency of Communism, and of proclaiming its supreme and impartial contempt of all class struggles."[4]

It is not difficult to see this process reproduced in the flight from class politics evident in the personal histories of so many repentant socialists of our time, for whom the failures of "actually existing socialism" in the east and of class struggle in the west are sufficient to condition a stampede into the camp of reaction. André Gorz's "farewell to the working class," Laclau's and Mouffe's rejection of proletarian politics in favor of a "socialism" paced by popular social movements, Gavin Kitching's notion of socialism as the outcome of capitalist prosperity and the "intellectual sophistication" of mental, as opposed to manual, workers, and Gareth Stedman Jones's attempt to revive the fortunes of the Labour Party with a plea to junk its long-standing reliance on "a homogeneous proletarian estate whose sectional political interest is encompassed by trade unions"—these and many, many more examples could be cited to establish the current "socialist" disdain for labor and the politics of class struggle.[5]

It is tempting, and in certain circumstances and circles it would be entirely appropriate, to see this denigration of class as nothing more than the renewal, in the face of class defeats at the hands of capital and continued degenerations and deformations of existing workers' states, of popular frontism, with its suppression of class and elevation of the politics of pragmatic alliance. This is all too evident in the historiography of American communism, where a New Left scholarship has burgeoned on the basis of attraction to Browderism and elevation of local struggles above the politics of the Comintern and Stalinist containment.[6] Here, however, another factor in the retreat from class is the descent into discourse. For as class fades from predominance, the reification of language soon seems to follow.[7] Indeed, language often seems to be used to exorcise class, an odd process of interpretive dichotomization that flies directly in the face of older linguistic demonstrations of the reciprocities of speech, dialect, and socioeconomic place.[8]

A recent essay ostensibly concerned with the political language of the American labor movement exposes the crude purpose of a great deal of this writing, opening with an apostatic insistence on facing the hard realities of a classless United States. "It is time for the US left to shed a grand and fond illusion," declares Michael Kazin, adding that the working class in American history has "seldom been more than a structural and rhetorical abstraction, employed primarily by socialist activists and intellectuals who hoped wage-earners would someday share their socialist analysis and vision of a better society." Kazin "reads" the political language of labor to reflect this absence of class, arguing that it has spoken to a majority of American wage earners either indifferent or hostile to the consciousness and institutions of class. Within the labor movement, then, it was understandable that "an essentially homegrown political language developed," taken up by "discontented worker activists who thought of themselves more as virtuous representatives of the American 'people' than as members of a class." An old story has been given a new twist: out of the language of a classless people comes pluralistic America.[9]

Kazin's argument actually has little to do with language, on any serious plane. For all his gestures toward what he constantly calls language, his article is nothing more than a highly selective, one-sided reading of the episodic contours of American labor politics. Since he eschews any engagement with critical theory or poststructuralist thought, his interpretive stand is little more than an indication of the fashion of discourse, rather than a substantive elaboration of "readings" dependent on an understanding of the importance of language. It is actually the undisguised effort to recast class struggle in America according to the dictates of what Kazin trendily appropriates as "discourse" that makes the position he adopts worth mention.

According to his assessment of the language of American labor, there is little class presence in the history of the United States. The Knights of Labor were racist "saviors of an embattled middle class." Nineteenth-century trade unionists were little more than proponents of Americanism. Gompers's ideology of business unionism was "essentially middle class." When the Industrial Workers of the World declared that in the future society run by the One Big Union "Every one of [the capitalists] would have to go to work," they were merely revolutionizing an old republican producerism, but this was enough to insure their outlaw status in a society that could romanticize Billy the Kid but would never follow him politically. Socialist party activists spoke "in a vernacular filled with references to citizenship, the producer ethic, and evangelical religion . . . more racist than those of their 'bourgeois' opponents . . . but could not put class power itself on the agenda." The Congress of Industrial Organizations is reduced to the rhetoric of Lewis and Murray, just as the history of the amalgamated AFL-CIO boils down to a few statements drawn from the easily collected banalities of Meaney and Reuther. As the Communist party shifted slogans between 1932 and 1938, changing the banners of the Third Period to those of the Popular Front, exchanging "Towards a Soviet America" for "Communism is Twentieth-Century Americanism," they were apparently realigning themselves with classless reality rather than marching to the Stalinized tune of "Socialism in One Country." Even the League of Revolutionary Black Workers is not spared: its "most glaring weakness was its inability to speak a language which either Black *or* white auto workers could accept without a sudden (and therefore superficial) ideological conversion."[10] That there are other "readings" of this history, that other traditions existed or even could have existed, is not acknowledged.

This is such a blatantly distorted sweep across the history of one hundred years of class struggle, such a shameless pillaging of the written record (and of historians that Kazin ungraciously draws upon without the slightest recognition of their profound disagreements with his position), that its stature as propaganda is actually a little too transparent. Like others whom we will meet in this chapter, Kazin simultaneously embraces an idealized, essentialist notion of class as *the* expression of an unmediated revolutionary class consciousness and, judging the American working class to come up short against this measurement, dismisses the very existence of class and the potential of a politics rooted in a class perspective.[11] The anti-working-class content of Kazin's own brand of "true" socialism emerges on the last pages of his text:

> What creativity and dynamism exist in the labor movement today emanate mainly from activists from a variety of social backgrounds who had their political training elsewhere. The anti-war New Left and radical feminist movements spoke about class with an anguished self-consciousness larded thickly with guilt. But they and

the Black liberation movement also educated organizers to recognize and speak movingly about oppression in all its forms. The current drive to gain for workers some control over how new technologies are used stems, in part, from that sensitivity and that skill. At the same time, labor has become only one of several movements struggling, in an uncoordinated and politically-muddled way, for a truly democratic society. The language of class divisions has little role to play in that effort and may, as the eco-anarchist Murray Bookchin has argued, even be a barrier to "the ability to voice broadly human concerns," to speak "for the general interest of society."[12]

Kazin's proclamation of the death of class is little more than an advertisement for himself, an intellectually dishonest misrepresentation of the history of the working class aimed at promoting a politics of classlessness orchestrated by the new social movements and their often university-ensconced proponents. It is also obvious that present political disillusionment and arrogant dismissal of a long-standing, albeit small and all too uninfluential, working-class left of which Kazin is undoubtedly unaware, has conditioned a generalized historical denial of the possibility of class politics. The present "reads" the past in a pernicious way.

Kazin is not without company. Chantal Mouffe arrives at the same end via a different route, asserting bluntly, "It is actually an illusion of language that lies behind the belief that the 'class struggle' can only be the work of determined political agents—the 'social classes.'"[13] In the context of the 1984–1985 miners' strike in Britain, Michael Ignatieff revealed how attraction to language could strike a concrete blow against class struggle and ingratiate its advocates with the structures of "progressive" authority. Ignatieff's "Strangers and Comrades" launched him out of the confines of the scholastically enclosed "socialist feminism" of the *History Workshop Journal* and into the mainstream of the British media. It was a timely, refined, caring blow against class and its politics, a selfless strike for advancement:

> There are those on the Left who maintain that the miners' strike is a vindication of a class-based politics after decades in which the agenda of the Left was defined by cross-class campaigns like feminism and CND. Yet the strike demonstrates the reverse: a labour movement which is incapable of presenting a class claim as a national claim, which can only pose its demands in the language of total victory, which takes on the State and ends up on the wrong side of the law cannot hope to conserve its support and legitimacy among the working class public. The miners' strike is not the vindication of class politics but its death throes. . . . The trouble with Arthur Scargill's politics is not that it doesn't have justice on

its side, but that it utterly lacks a conception of how competing classes, regions, races, and religions can be reconciled with each other in a national community.

What the Left needs is a language of national unity expressed as commitment to fellowship among strangers. We need a language of trust built upon a practice of social comradeship.[14]

A year later, the logic of Ignatieff's linguistic turn had led him sufficiently far from class that his *Needs of Strangers* did not need to touch on issues like the miners' strike. Instead, in the manner of the "true" socialism of the 1840s, it agonized over the conceptualization of liberty, finding a predictable resolution of the dilemmas of the modern market world in words:

> We need words to keep us human. Being human is an accomplishment like playing an instrument. It takes practice. . . . Our needs are made of words: they come to us in speech, and can die for lack of expression. Without a public language to help us find our own words, our needs will dry up in silence. It is words only, the common meanings they bear, which give me the right to speak in the name of the strangers at my door. Without a language adequate to this moment we risk losing ourselves in resignation towards the portion of life which has been allotted to us.[15]

As Marx and Engels concluded in their attack on the German "true socialism" of the 1840s: "After these samples of . . . Holy Scripture one cannot wonder at the applause it has met with among certain drowsy and easy-going readers."[16]

▶   *Rancière's Long Night of Class Formation*

Ignatieff began his journey toward such a scriptural end with a Foucauldian history of the prison,[17] but for class to be read as a text in a post-structural manner demanded French input. That development would be launched by Jacques Rancière, a former Althusserian, lapsed Maoist, and *gauchiste philosophe* who could not quite stomach the ugly drift to the right of a confident "new philosophy" that saw Marxism as the first step on the road to the Gulag. Associated since 1975 with the freewheeling journal of ideas and social history *Revoltes logiques*, Rancière and others declared their difference from, if not opposition to, traditional depictions of labor in French society. Instead of knowing more about what was already conceived, they wanted to strike out in new analytic directions altogether. "What interests us," they stated in a 1977 centennial issue of *Mouvement social*, is "that archives be discourses, that ideas be events, that history be at all times a break, to be interrogated (*questionnable*) only *here*, only politically." By the opening years of the

1980s *Revoltes logiques* had ceased to publish, but the same year of its demise saw the appearance of Rancière's *La nuit des proletaires, Archives du rêve ouvrier*, arguably the single most poststructuralist, discourse-oriented reconsideration of class to have appeared in this decade.[18]

Rancière's book, which explored the thought of a few hundred French worker intellectuals from 1830 to the 1850s, as well as a number of articles that preceded it, insisted that the working class as an historical subject could not be known with the certainty and "scientific" pretensions of the Marxist tradition or the ideology of the organized labor movement. Against long-standing notions of the importance of skill and workplace in the making of class identity and militancy, Rancière claimed that it was marginalization that most often was associated with activism, and that "the organic cohesion of the trade, the strength of the organization, and the ideology of the group" were impediments to mobilization.[19] He rejected long-standing conceptions of a causal relationship between economic deprivation and awareness of class place, claiming that Thompson's *Making of the English Working Class* had shown that "the notion of class is only ever the product of a bundle of identifications. . . . the formation of the working class in England was the product of a certain number of representations, recognitions, discourses. As to the material reality that supports these identifications, it rightly differs from the usual sociological and ethnological objectifications."[20]

Exploitation and class struggle, the wage and forms of organization and resistance—the very stuff of traditional treatments of labor—were thus of little interest to Rancière. Instead, class is understood in *La nuit des proletaires* as a philosophical reflection that breaks decisively with experience. Rancière's study of working-class thought in nineteenth-century France lays great stress on the encounter with an "other"—a poet, a peripheral intellectual, a Saint-Simonian savior—that widens the gap between workers and their conditions. "The revolution begins at that moment when most workers should be enjoying the peaceful sleep of those whose labor does not require them to think," argued Rancière in introducing *La nuit des proletaires*.[21] It was then that they moved toward the "other," writing poetry, founding a newspaper, assimilating an aesthetic drawn from bourgeois culture:

> The poetry of the workers was not at first the echo of popular speech but the imitation of the sacred language, the forbidden and fascinating language of others.

> The worker who, without knowing how to spell, attempts to make rhymes according to the fashion of the day is perhaps more dan-

gerous to the existing ideological order than one who recites revolutionary songs. . . . With the introduction—however limited—however ambiguous—of the aesthetic sentiment in the workers' universe, the very foundation of the whole political order is placed in question.

On the supposed direct path from exploitation to class speech and from workers' identity to collective expression, one must pass by this detour, this mixed scene where, with the complicity of intellectuals gone to meet them and desirous sometimes of taking their role, the proletarians try their skill in the words and theories from above, replay and displace the old myth defining who has the right to speak for the others. Through a few singular passions, a few fortuitous meetings, some discussions on the sex of God and the origins of the world, perhaps we will see the image take shape and the voice establish itself of the great collectivity of workers.[22]

Language, broadly conceived, was thus the anvil on which class and class consciousness were forged, the meeting ground where in the freedoms of the evening workers made their contact with the dominant culture, a connection that exposed them to a Derridean *différance* that separated the speech, writing, and thinking of bourgeois and proletarian like night and day.[23]

Rancière does not cite Derrida and makes no attempt to situate his text or approach within literary theory in general or deconstruction in particular. Yet as Donald Reid has suggested, Rancière's long night of class formation is a world in which class is regarded as a set of texts, each productive of discourses that demand decoding, and each heavy with the contradictory traces of needs and aspirations that interrupt the received wisdom of what constitutes class and class consciousness. Evidence such as that published on the industries of Paris by the Chamber of Commerce during the Revolution of 1848, or "workers' discourse" itself are often the beginning point of such received wisdom, themselves pointed interventions in the attempt to shape reality in particular ways. They move historians, according to Rancière, "back to a *habitus*, to a workers' ethos, confirming, in the last analysis, that things could not have been otherwise, therefore cancelling out that which is singular in that production of meaning, in that expression which captures the encounter with the impossible."[24]

In such a *habitus*, suggests Rancière, lies the pernicious notion of class authenticity, embedded in an atavistic insistence on the linkage of the "identifications and symbolizations of the workingman with the practices of his work and his material conditions as a worker."[25] Long ago Kenneth Burke gestured toward the same insight, commenting that "we find the *differences* between 'bourgeois' and 'proletarian' treated, under dialectical pressure, as an *absolute antithesis,* until critics, accustomed to thinking by this pat schematization, become almost demoralized at the suggestion that there may be a 'margin of overlap' held in common between different classes."[26] But as is typical of poststructuralism's capacity to overreach itself, this is not sufficient for Rancière. Discourse has taught him that this intellectual fossil of class as differentiation rooted in labor petrifies the living complexity and contradiction of working-class life, in which the historical formation of the proletariat is far less significant than the history of the analytic category of the working class. After the long night of class formation it is interpretation of class as a conceptualization, not analysis of class as an historical process, that is on the historiographic agenda.[27] However creatively Rancière has interrogated the texts of working-class Saint-Simonians, Republicans, Icarians, Buchezians, and Fourierists, and whatever advances are registered by his own unmasking of the ways in which actual workers interrupted class convention to strive for and dream of a world in which they would not be bound by one *travail* after another, one is reminded, yet again, of Marx and Engels and the "true" socialism of the 1840s: "It is difficult to see why these true socialists mention society at all if they believe with the philosophers that all real cleavages are evoked by the cleavage of concepts. On the basis of the philosophical belief in the power of concepts to make or destroy the world, they can perfectly well imagine that some individual 'disposed of the cleavage of life' by 'disposing' in some way or other of concepts. . . . true socialists continually mix up literary history and real history as equally effective."[28]

▶   ### Stedman Jones and the Language of Chartism
The separation of "literary" and "real" history, of course, is more than a little strained, especially in the case of Rancière, who could quite rightly reply that his whole historical discussion in *La nuit des proletaires* is an attempt to bridge such a division. Yet in Gareth Stedman Jones's reinterpretation of Chartism, which focuses exclusively on the public language of mobilization as reported in the press, the focus on the literary history of the movement does indeed obscure the real history of this important moment of class formation.[29] "Rethinking Chartism" is noteworthy for it represents one of the most appreciated and challenged attempts to elevate language above class in the history of modern labor and its movements.[30]

Stedman Jones draws a rather hard and dichotomous line of interpretation, separating out the analysis of Chartism as a political movement and the conception of Chartism as a social phenomenon flowing out of the anger, distress, and breakdown of social relationships associated with the Industrial Revolution. He stresses that virtually all writing on Chartism, except that of the Chartists themselves, emphasizes the movement's class character and, implicitly, understates the extent to which the campaigns of the 1830s and 1840s were about precisely what the movement claimed they were about: the Charter. Political power was what Chartism was about; economic power had, apparently, little to do with the program or practice of the Chartists.

That division of political and economic separated to his satisfaction, Stedman Jones then moves on to consider the specific form in which the political aspirations of Chartism were articulated, arguing for the necessity of scrutinizing the language of Chartism as a way of establishing the relationship between the vocabulary of demand and consciousness of particular class, social, or occupational groupings. He argues that "the ideology of Chartism cannot be constructed in abstraction from its linguistic form" and that "it was not simply experience, but rather a particular linguistic ordering of experience which could lead the masses to believe that "their exclusion from political power is the cause of our social anomalies' and that 'political power' was the cause of 'opulence.' " The result was that Chartism as a movement of working-class people spoke a language of class that was "constructed and inscribed within a complex rhetoric of metaphorical association, causal inference and imaginative construction." This process owed less to the material underpinnings of class than it did to the assumptions of eighteenth-century radicalism, "a vision and analysis of social and political evils which certainly long predated the advent of class consciousness, however defined." Chartism is reinterpreted within a framework that "assigns some autonomous weight to the language within which it was conceived." Radical analysis was thus limited in terms of a particular linguistic paradigm: capitalist power was personalized in a language of parasitism and oppression, linked to a system of force and fraud rather than exploitation and accumulation; mobilization was orchestrated by a language of "natural rights" laden with "individualist presuppositions."[31]

This is an important attempt to reread the language of Chartist radicalism in ways that allow us entry into the mass appeal the Charter obviously exercised within working-class communities and among some reform-minded constituencies of the petty bourgeoisie. In hammering home the political content of Chartism, Stedman Jones forces us to deal with the nonclass character of popular radicalism, an important feature that both extended the reform cause and limited it. More social interpretations of the 1790–1850 years are by no means as inattentive to this process as Stedman Jones implies, however, and writings on other national contexts in later periods allude to much the same kind of historical developments.[32] There is no doubt, nevertheless, that Stedman Jones provides insight—if not the whole story—into why Chartism foundered in the 1840s and 1850s, as the language of radicalism increasingly found the liberalized state of Sir Robert Peel undercutting popular antagonism by removing some of the more blatant material foundations of widespread discontent.

Nevertheless, for all of its contributions, the Stedman Jones piece is flawed deeply. Its reinterpretation of Chartism ultimately takes us backward analytically, a consequence of Stedman Jones's willingness to privilege language and retreat from class and the material context of a particular social formation.

We can begin with theory. For all of Stedman Jones's attention to language, which has even led one reviewer to address "Rethinking Chartism" under the title "The Deconstructing of the English Working Class," this linguistic reinterpretation rests on a conceptual foundation of naïveté. Stedman Jones gestures constantly to the "non-referential conception of language" in the introduction to *Languages of Class*, where we are told of the broad significance of Saussure, but any substantial engagement with critical theory is absent. In its place there are persistent declarative injunctions:

> Language disrupts any simple notion of the determination of consciousness by social being because it is itself part of social being. We cannot therefore decode political language to reach a primal and material expression of interest since it is the discursive structure of political language which conceives and defines interest in the first place. What we must therefore do is to study the production of interest, identification, grievance and aspiration within political languages themselves. We need to map out these successive languages of radicalism, liberalism, socialism, etc., both in relation to the political languages they replace and laterally in relation to rival political languages with which they are in conflict. . . . To peer straight through these languages into the structural changes to which they may be notionally referred is no substitute for such an investigation, not because there is not a relationship of some kind, but because such connections can never be established with any satisfying degree of finality.[33]

As Dorothy Thompson has pointed out, these kinds of assertions represent little in the way of theoretical fine tuning. "What is being discussed in the Chartist essay," she correctly points out, "is something much like the old—and now regrettably old-fashioned—discipline of Political Thought."[34] Yet it is being dressed up as Theory, writ large. "If history is to renew itself, and in particular, in this context, social and labour history, it cannot be by the defensive reiteration of well tried and by now well worn formulae," concludes Stedman Jones, adding, "It can only be by an engagement with the contemporary intellectual terrain—not to counter a threat, but to discover an opportunity."[35]

This is, unfortunately, precisely what is lacking in "Rethinking Chartism." The point is not that Stedman Jones has been theoretically lazy, which he has been, but that his failure to enter into the labyrinth where language and theory intersect in the 1980s allows him to overemphasize the coherence of political discourse. The words speak too unequivocally; the tradition of eighteenth-century radicalism is too fixed and preconstituted.[36]

On one level this is determined "technically," through Stedman Jones's reduction of language to the published vocabulary of political radicalism. This containment of the discourse of Chartism, recognized theoretically by Joan Scott and challenged by the empirical studies of the symbolism of working-class mobilization by James Epstein and Paul A. Pickering, forces Stedman Jones's analysis toward privileging the rhetoric of eighteenth-century radicalism. What gets left out are precisely those forms of discourse—from the cap of liberty and the fustian jacket to the torchlit processions descending on mills, where pistol volleys were fired and demands for universal arming voiced—that might reveal a class dimension to Chartism standing outside and beyond the possibilities of a public language of reform rooted in an earlier age.[37] Neville Kirk, drawing on the Chartist language of class in the factory districts of Lancashire, has located just such a class presence, while N. W. Thompson's study of popular political economy in the nineteenth-century pre-Chartist years develops a picture of a materialist analysis of poverty and exploitation that flies in the face of Stedman Jones's insistence that radicalism's language had little place for anticapitalist economics.[38]

From theory we can move to evidence. For Stedman Jones fails to interrogate the language of radicalism as a produced discourse. As so many of the critiques of his "Rethinking Chartism" note, his flimsy theory is actually exacerbated by a highly selective and questionable handling of sources. Some seventy-odd footnotes (out of a total of approximately two hundred thirty) in the "Rethinking Chartism" essay refer to either the *Northern Star* or the *Poor Man's Guardian*, and the overwhelming bulk of the remaining citations draw upon secondary sources (whose authors, while providing a host of texts to be strip-mined by Stedman Jones, would seldom agree with his conclusions) or accessible printed tracts. This ends up constructing a particular language of Chartism, one not without its internal dilemmas. As Dorothy Thompson has noted perceptively, the language of the press cannot just be appropriated uncritically and nominated as *the* language of Chartism:

> for the style and within certain limits the subject matter of mid-century journalism had largely been set by the time the *Northern Star* was started in 1837, by an existing tradition of upper-class newspaper production. The radical journals made innovations in style and content, but they rewrote speeches and contributions from demotic into standard English, for example, and for reasons of style or to avoid persecution, ironed out militant, local, blasphemous and overly idiomatic references—as can occasionally be seen by comparing police reports of speeches with those printed in Chartist journals.[39]

Thompson's point is all the more important when one tries to balance the levels of differentiation separating regions and locales, with their mixtures of constituencies, occupations, incomes, and dependencies, levels that a national movement stepped over consciously in order to maximize unity. Stedman Jones takes the construction of that national movement as his terrain, but in specific locales the language of Chartism may well have had inflections, undiplomatic outbursts, or puzzled silences that never made their way into the public proclamations of the edited press.[40]

Capitalism's uneven development, moreover, insured that in various locales the experience of exploitation and class differentiation was lived, not as a simplistic unitary process, but as a confusing piling up of dissimiliar forms of economic and political subordination. Stedman Jones stresses the extent to which the language of popular radicalism was incapable of attending to the character of wage relations, seeing access to the state as a guarantee of equality and rooting privilege in the inequities of exchange rather than the extraction of surplus value. His inattention to the structurally rooted political economies of highly differentiated regions and locales necessarily bypasses those regions where the factory system was most developed. Focusing on the national public discourse of Chartism narrowly and with resolute scholasticism, Stedman Jones elevates the language of radicalism and depresses the language of class.

"Rethinking Chartism" thus rethinks what it wants to. It is understandable that given the continuing, if deteriorating, hold of merchant capital, outwork, and sweated metropolitan and country forms of petty production, many segments of the laboring poor would see their plight not in terms of a Marxist grasp of the way surplus value was extracted from them, but as the inadequacy of the price their product commanded. A Marxist analysis of the economic context, acknowledging national patterns and local divergences, might well suggest, ironically, the lack of materialist justification for insisting that an incompletely formed working class speak in the words and meaning of a Marxist political economy that was yet to be elaborated.[41] This does not mean, as Stedman Jones seems to imply, that language determines political being, but that material life sets the boundaries within which language and politics develop.

The materially erected boundaries of the second quarter of the nineteenth century were not yet unambiguously in place. This was a moment when the political economy of the world's first industrial-capitalist nation was congealing. Different orientations and specific kinds of classes and consciousnesses were in the making; social, economic, and political relations balanced on the experience of the past and the threatening possibilities of the future.[42]

Language reflected this, opening out into ambiguities and ambivalences. Stedman Jones cannot accept this. He quotes a correspondent to the *Poor Man's Guardian* in 1834: "The capitalists will never increase wages except through fear of the physical force of the labourers, let there be a universal strike for some minimum of wages in every trade." What does Stedman Jones make of this formulation? Without providing the reader with any further language of this correspondent, he tells us, categorically, that "The rationale for this position . . . was not the destruction of the class power of the employers, but rather to strike a blow against the propertied idlers and their state."[43] When words that seem to say something that speaks to class antagonism and an emerging consciousness of the potency of class power can be so easily slipped into a particular kind of interpretive containment, we know that we are descending, quickly, into discourse. And it should come as no surprise that class is the ostentatiously discarded historical process.

As Neville Kirk has argued, Stedman Jones's "Rethinking Chartism" abandons class at considerable cost. It suppresses actively what was new and class-based in the discourse of Chartism, ignores the developing class antagonisms of capitalist social relations of production and reproduction, and covers state activity in an all-too-benevolent patina, in which the glare of liberal reform obscures the more persistent undercoat of coercion and repression. He quite rightly concludes that this linguistically ordered reinterpretation of Chartism, aimed at overcoming the deficiencies of economic reductionism associated with class analysis, fails to culminate in anything more than "an unconvincing idealism."[44]

▶   ## Class, Struggle, and Consciousness:
A Reiteration of Orthodoxy

This penchant for idealism, or the elevation of concepts above material life, runs rampant through those texts that repudiate class. Among those that have made the linguistic turn most decisively, that idealism is fostered, as in the case of Stedman Jones, by a willingness to twist words into whatever misshapen meaning is required to undercut analysis premised on the existence of classes.

Consider this confident interpretive assertion from William M. Reddy's *Money and Liberty in Modern Europe,* a sustained discussion of "the crisis of the class concept in historical research" that grows out of the discourse-influenced new revisionism of European—particulary French—historiography:

> It has long been recognized that one cannot call Chartism a working-class movement in the sense that its supporters were all proletarians strictly defined. That is, a very large percentage of Chartism's supporters were depressed outworkers; skilled millwrights and shipwrights who worked on a subcontracting basis; mule spinners paid by the pound who were employers in their own right of piecers and bobbin boys; and numerous small-scale shop operators, such as tailors and shoemakers, who dealt directly with the public. The journalists and barkeepers who came to lead the movement, in addition, found within the warm atmosphere of popular patronage welcome refuge from the chill winds on the laissez-faire tundra. . . . Chartism thus united people who were not a working class behind a program of radical reform not formulated to express working-class interests; their grievances concerned the programs of an activist state, and they correctly saw control of the state as a critical step toward reining in the unbounded pretensions of large property owners. Chartism was a movement of the "class" of the unjustly disciplined, of the unfree, both male and female. . . . It is thus quite possible to account for the whole of English social history down through 1850 without evoking class interest to explain events either on the local or on the national level.[45]

Note what is being said here. First, it is argued that since Chartism's constituency embraced a highly differentiated population, some of whom could be "strictly defined" as proletarian inasmuch as they worked for wages in the most impersonalized factory-like settings imaginable, while others only approached this ideal type in their incomplete forms of degradation and dependency, then the movement was not working class. Second, it is implied that the journalists and barkeepers who led the movement—and no actual evidence is provided to establish that the leadership was in fact uniformly drawn from such social strata—also compromised its class essence. Third, from these simplistic truths, the proposition is put forward that Chartism was not really about "class," but about unjust discipline, which was supposedly more inclusive and historically demonstrable than class, to which it was also apparently unrelated. Finally, all of this said, the rather large inferential leap is then made to entirely new and more generalized ground: the whole of English social history down through 1850 has nothing to do with class.

There are two points that need to be made in response to such argument. First is the reliance upon ahistorical, idealized typologies. A class movement is a class movement *only* if each and every individual in its ranks conforms to a conceptual categorization that encompasses every feature of an idealized proletarian essence, regardless of the stage of economic development and the maturity of the productive forces. This is nonsense, as a reading of Bolshevism, working-class organization and consciousness, and the fall of the Old Regime in Russia would suggest.[46] A class movement knows no factions, no differentiations, and allows entry only to leaders that are themselves pristine in their class place. As Marx and Engels were well aware through their work in the Chartist movement, this is not the way the workers' movement develops. They knew the problematic consequences of a vacillating leadership and a movement internally divided, but they also knew that ideal types and definitions of social essences would not overcome the contradictions and ambiguities in actually existing working-class consciousness. And they perceived that, in general (with all the limitations that this acknowledged), Chartism signified a mounting opposition to laissez-faire capitalism and a growing solidarity among workers opposed to the bourgeoisie.[47] Finally, a class program is a class program only if it poses ultimate class interests, as if transitional demands are somehow a repudiation of class. In the case of Chartism, Engels knew different, writing that "the 'Six Points' which for the Radical bourgeois are the beginning and end of the matter . . . are for the proletarian a mere means to further ends."[48] Reddy is but one of a host of social historians who pride themselves in rejecting "interpretations of social class . . . that are utterly mythical in form."[49] What is curious is their own reliance on another mythology of class, an idealized conception that no one who has actually embraced class within an interpretive framework of historical materialism has ever espoused.

The second point that needs to be made against Reddy's view of Chartism relates to how he comes to his conclusion. In repudiating the class nature of Chartism and arguing that this has "long been recognized," Reddy cites four texts: Asa Briggs's edited collection, *Chartist Studies* (1959); Epstein and Thompson's much later comparable volume of articles, *The Chartist Experience* (1982); a monograph on Feargus O'Connor by Epstein, *The Lion of Freedom* (1982); and Dorothy Thompson's recent history of the movement, *The Chartists: Popular Politics in the Industrial Revolution* (1984).[50] Of course interpretation is always open to different readings, but this list of Chartist studies is a surprising one to turn to if one wants to repudiate class and deny the "social" content of the mass mobilization around the Six Points. My reading of these sources is exactly opposite that of Reddy, and although all of the authors cited might acknowledge that Stedman Jones and Reddy have forced reconsideration of the nature of Chartist ideology and suggested important new ways of reading the language of class and radicalism in the 1830s and 1840s, none, I daresay, would stand unequivocally with the new revisionism; most have actually issued counterstatements of one sort or another.

Dorothy Thompson's *The Chartists* can hardly be read as a denial of the importance of class, as almost any sampling of her pages will confirm:

> The events of 1842 sharply underlined the rift which existed between the classes in Britain.

> Class domination was not confined to the work-place. All aspects of social life—dwelling places, shops, drinking-places, recreational and instructional institutions, churches and chapel seating—were segregated on class lines.

> If the consciousness of these workers did not always conform to what the theoreticians consider should have been correct for their stage of industrialisation, it may help to stand back a bit from theoretical preconceptions, and see what the people actually were demanding, what they were defending, and why they took certain forms of action. Women, labourers, Irish workers, artisans, alehouse keepers and itinerant dissenting clergymen took part in the Chartist movement as well as factory workers, miners and keelmen. These people shared a common sense of class, based on the feeling of exclusion from the political system, and of exploitation by the new merchant and industrial powers which were growing up in the country.

> Even when bereft of most of their other senses, citizens were held to retain the quintessential awareness of class.[51]

Thompson's study is in fact a statement on the importance of class in the Chartist upheaval, albeit one that recognizes the role of middle-class reform and identifies the importance of the political form of the struggle and the language with which it was waged.[52] Lest there be any misconception here, she has made the point bluntly in a review of Stedman Jones's *Languages of Class*: "None of this, however, alters the fact that, if the concept of class means anything, Chartism was a working-class movement. Its language at all levels was class language, the concepts of universal suffrage, the rights of man and of equality of citizenship were only held by the lower orders, the working class or classes. The sense of class solidarity for a time overrode regional, occupational, ethnic and gender divisions in ways that were not to recur for generations."[53]

Reddy's *Money and Liberty* contains a concluding "Note on Language," in which he declares, "I hope at least to open up some breathing space for fresh thought on the crucial importance of choice of words and of their theoretical context. Doing social history without being constantly aware of this problem is like navigating the seas without instruments: It is possible with great skill and luck, but it is unnecessarily difficult and risky."[54] There is nothing to disagree with here. But there is something to add. Reddy's statement smacks loudly of sanctimoniousness when it is apparent how willfully he misreads others' words. He has obviously taken a leaf from the book of hedonistic literary theory, when meaning can so easily be adapted and molded to fit the contours of its own antitheses. We are left with the impression that those who reify language hold words in some contempt.[55]

This is evident in the misappropriation of E. P. Thompson by Reddy. Thompson's *Making of the English Working Class*, like the literature on Chartism, is read in a perverse way, mined against itself to prove its opposite. In the process, Thompson is forced into the camp of virtually every kind of anti-Marxist revisionism, including the work on the French Revolution discussed in the last chapter. Once again, with class as ideal type emblazoned on his crusading pages, Reddy reads Thompson as proving that "there was no uniform class of wage laborers behind the stormy protest movements of the period." He concludes that "whenever it becomes a question of linking political comportment with social or economic status, endless subtleties and the constant discovery of new exceptions and subgroups have taken the place of the simple schemas of class conflict." Thompson's 1978 essay on eighteenth-century England, "Class Struggle without Class?" merely confirms the case in Reddy's view. Class needs to be jettisoned, argues Reddy, for "human identity is not constructed this way."[56]

Yet this is exactly not what Thompson argues. His "Class Struggle without Class?" contains a brief, accessible, and difficult-to-misconstrue statement on class as an historical process. Whatever its problematic emphases and order of analytic priorities, it is not a confirmation of Reddy's rejection of class. Thompson recognizes that class is born of industrial-capitalist society and as such is a nineteenth-century phenomenon marked by its presence in class institutions, class parties, and class cultures. Prior to the Industrial Revolution, class can nevertheless be employed by historians heuristically, to convey, in particular, a sense of struggle in ancient, feudal, and early modern societies. This makes the link for Thompson between class and class struggle, and he argues that class struggle as a long-standing historical process, rather than class as an objective category, is thus the prior and influential development. Class is a special case of the historical formations that arise out of class struggle. Finally, none of this implies, for Thompson, that class is independent of objective, economic determinations. When mature class relations, struggles, and consciousness appear, Thompson argues, this "does not mean that whatever happens less decisively is not class."[57] Class, in short, is a persistent and vital presence in history according to Thompson. Reddy reads him to deny this: "A class in the making is not a class; a class that is fully made, in this world of becoming, this vale of tears that is history, is dead."[58]

We may be allowed to espouse a more orthodox view. Class *is*, in the first instance and at its most basic, an objective, structurally determined relationship to the means of production. By no means always easily locatable, class defies simplistic, straightforward identification precisely because productive life develops unevenly and never quite homogenizes the human material at its core to a congealed, undifferentiated mass. Nevertheless, class relations are, in origin, economic relations, rooted in the capitalist process of accumulation, whereby one social stratum expropriates surplus from another. Through this process of exploitation, concentrating ownership of productive property in the hands of the few, profit accrues to one group, wages to another. To be sure, intermediate groups subsist on the margins of this essential relationship, and within its boundaries profit takers and wage earners are by no means uniformly rewarded: the pettiest of capitalists can, conceivably, take less in profit than the most privileged aristocrat of labor, whose wage can be considerable. Status differences and self-identification, however contradictory, are nevertheless irrelevant in this generalized class system, determined first and foremost by the homogenizing tendencies (never absolute) of modern industry and its master, capital.

It follows that class takes on its most clear-cut objective presence in the epoch of classical industrial capitalism, stretching from the triumph of the Industrial Revolution in the mid-nineteenth century to the high-water mark of monopoly capitalism just prior to World War II.[59] Before and after these rough benchmarks, the lines of class demarcation are blurred by, first, the incomplete impersonalization and rationalization of productive life, and, second, the decay of industrial capitalism in a First World economy transformed by the dizzying pace and overconsumptionist logic of an aggressively imperialistic Fordism. In this contemporary political economy the place of class is often obscured by a series of complex developments, among them the capacities of the service sector to seemingly override the primacy of heavy industry and traditional proletarian communities, the ways in which deficit-funded militarism displaces productive capital, and the dwarfing of First World output in the context of the global reach of the low wage and the super-exploitation of the Third World.[60]

In analysis of precapitalist epochs, therefore, class is less of a presence, socially and economically, and more of a metaphor encompassing a range of tensions, antagonisms, and conflicts.[61] Thus even if class as an objectively determined economic reality is not present before the arrival of industrial capitalism, classlike struggles pitting plebeians against patricians, slaves against masters, serfs and peasants against lords have been usefully explored by historians.[62] This was what Marx and Engels, who were of course aware of the non-class-based organization of precapitalist societies and who argued that class was born with bourgeois society, meant when they proclaimed, "The history of all hitherto existing society is the history of class struggles."[63] With the Industrial Revolution, class struggle assumed a new clarity, diversity, and pervasiveness.[64]

That struggle was not necessarily and inevitably informed by an ultimate class consciousness, although rudimentary awareness of class differentiation was more often than not present. The distinction is an important one, for it allows entry into the domain of historical intention. The working class, as an objective, structurally determined entity, does of course have motivation, but that motivation is often bounded by capital's needs, not its own: survival and reproduction are at the core of this inert motivation. Class struggle expands the horizon of motivation infinitely, but no inevitable generalization of motivation to embrace the needs of the entire working class takes place: class struggles can be brought into being by demands small and large, mundane and historic; they can espouse the interests of the many or the few, just as they can confine themselves to sectional or economistic matters or proclaim more universal politico-economic ends. The presence of class consciousness, regardless of whether one accepts the Leninist-Kautsky-ian proposition that it can be brought to the working class only from the outside, denotes an understanding of the irreconcilable antagonism of the objectively situated contending classes of bourgeois and proletarian. It promotes a consequent appreciation of the importance and inevitability of class struggle, and strives to overcome the possible parochialisms of such struggle in constant reiteration of the interests of all labor and its need to overthrow ruling authority and establish a society governed by and for the working class.[65]

What I am suggesting is that if we could (which we cannot) stop the clock of history at some point in the mid-nineteenth century and take an aerial photograph of an entire nation's social relations, we would see many things, some of them quite unfocused. But dotting the landscape would be the inert presence of class, measured out in concentrations in factories, mills, mines, docks, fields, and construction sites, visible to the trained eye in neighborhoods, families, and taverns, drawn most heavily in the urban centers, but spreading throughout the countryside as well. Swirling around this presence of class would be a myriad of struggles, in which contending voices shouted and whispered for improved work conditions, higher wages, familial needs, political rights, social recognition, a grog allowance, or a piece of park. Barely heard and visible in only a few locales would be class consciousness itself, and there would be some moments in time when it would be silenced and obliterated altogether. But it would be back.

That, of course, is the interpretive count of only some of the players. I have focused on the working class precisely because the efforts to "deconstruct" class have, for the most part, been aimed at the labor side of the class equation. With the exception of the critical-theory-inspired critique of the French Revolution as a bourgeois revolution, little effort has been expended on a discourse-directed examination of the bourgeoisie. Yet here, as many works suggest, *is* fertile ground for an exploration of signification.[66] Indeed, the last century closed with publication of one of the most insightful commentaries on the discourse of the ruling class, Thorstein Veblen's *Theory of the Leisure Class* (1899). Its subject matter prefiguring concerns of Barthes and Foucault, this text is nothing if it is not an elaboration of the symbolic and substantive content of class distinction, with due consideration of the ways in which hegemony is perpetuated via the diffusion and transfer of the "language" of the ruling order throughout the society as a whole. To be sure, Veblen hardly endorses the kind of class analysis outlined above, but in his attempt to probe the discourse of class power and authority he searches for meaning in corners of everyday life where critical theory seldom deigns to venture: "The walking stick serves the purpose of an advertisement that the bearer's hands are employed otherwise than in useful effort, and it therefore has utility as an evidence of leisure. But it is also a weapon, and it meets a felt need of barbarian man on that ground."[67]

Veblen is not now much in fashion. Neither is the reiteration of the categories and conceptualizations of orthodox historical materialism. Dismissed by those who have made the linguistic turn, historical materialism is castigated for its insistence on the primacy of a determining economy, refusal to consign class to the status of mythology, and belief that not all struggles and all consciousness are equally valid (though it does not suggest that certain struggles and certain consciousness are unworthy of study and examination). There will be many, including a goodly number who have resisted the descent into discourse, who will dismiss all of this as platonic and "essentialist." That cannot be avoided. But let me suggest, with reference to some texts that link the discussion of this chapter to the writing on labor republicanism that was examined previously, that this kind of conception of class, struggle, and consciousness is the only way to make sense of what has become an interpretive quagmire.

Those social historians who champion the positive contribution of a language of labor republicanism almost universally deny the validity of an interpretive stress on class consciousness. Thus Leon Fink quotes favorably Robert Gray's rejection of "the straw person model of a class conscious and revolutionary working class, equipped with a rigorous class ideology and theoretical understanding of the capitalist economy." Gray's argument that such cases are rare was waged against Stedman Jones's "Rethinking Chartism," where Gray discerned an underlying conception of class consciousness that Stedman Jones sees Chartism not living up to. Yet Fink ackowledges the influence of Stedman Jones's treatment of Chartism in his own thinking. Similarly, Sean Wilentz, who champions the labor republicanism of the 1830s and rails against the attempt to measure American workers against some essentialist notion of class consciousness, is also drawn uncritically to Stedman Jones's depiction of Chartism, which, if Gray and others are right, is as essentialist in its conception of class consciousness as one would want.[68] What is involved in this contradictory confusion?

On one level, it is a function of the internal inconsistencies of "Rethinking Chartism," which is pulled in one direction by Stedman Jones's new-found attraction to popular frontist cross-class alliances, most evident in his essay "Why is the Labour Party in a Mess?" This is the Stedman Jones of the 1980s, a reconstructed "true" socialist disillusioned with class and its long-standing political failures at home and abroad, willing to rest his argument on the determinations of discourse and to interpret historical experience on the ground of reified language. But there lies between the lines of "Rethinking Chartism," not unlike a Derridean trace, the high structuralism of the Stedman Jones of the 1960s and 1970s, pulling the essay clandestinely in another direction. *That* Stedman Jones knew the poverty of empiricism and how to measure class consciousness with the refined idealism of an Althusserian gage block. (This past/present dualism is reproduced, shorn of any attempt to situate it theoretically, in Michael Kazin's analysis of the political language of the American labor movement. There, too, we see an implicit model of revolutionary class consciousness determining the historical conception of class, alongside a current refusal of class as a force in American politics.)[69] Critics of Stedman Jones are right to suggest that the "Rethinking Chartism" essay seems to imply a model of mature class consciousness against which Chartism is found wanting. But they have sidestepped the questions that should then follow: why does Stedman Jones so resolutely avoid evidence of transitional consciousness, why does he pay so little attention to the bedrock of class consciousness, the level of development of production itself, and why, finally, does he conclude his reinterpretation with a statement that, on the surface, denies any place to class consciousness's role in the rise and fall of Chartism?

> Attention to the language of Chartism suggests that its rise and fall is to be related in the first instance not to movements in the economy, divisions in the movement or an immature class consciousness, but to the changing policies of the state—the principal enemy upon whose actions radicals had always found their credibility depended.[70]

The answer lies in the changed politics of Stedman Jones. He has moved away from the scholasticism of a Marxism fixated on an idealized class consciousness toward a reformist popular frontism in which class consciousness is immaterial. His "Reinterpreting Chartism" has narrowed the language of mobilization to a radicalism fixated on state power, a focus that Stedman Jones reads as an explanation of the mass character of protest in the 1830s and 1840s. What more, then, is needed in the 1980s, with the retreat from class in full flight and the enemy so clearly and precisely identified as the Thatcherite state? If Stedman Jones fails in his movement to shake entirely his intellectual past, he nevertheless ends up sufficiently clear in his espousal of a politics of broad classless opposition to the state—which is what Chartism's success was about, he argues, and what the Labour Party needs to cultivate now—that he finds support in many quarters.

One of those quarters happens to be, not surprisingly, among American historians of labor republicanism who, like Stedman Jones, are attracted in their studies of the past to a politics of the masses rather than a politics of class precisely because in their present they are overwhelmed by disillusionment and cynicism regarding the possibilities of class. The point is not that both Chartism and the Great Upheaval associated with the Knights of Labor in the United States of the 1880s were not class movements and did not articulate an unprecedented level of class struggle. They were class movements and they were most emphatically about class struggle. Their discourses were not uniformly cut from the same cloth (either in comparison with one another, or internally), however, and although they were undoubtedly languages of class and struggle, they were not always—understandably so—unadulterated voices of class consciousness. Stedman Jones makes too much of this, the advocates of labor republicanism too little. If Chartism can be forced into the loose container of eclectic radicalism with the lever of language, so be it. And if, by the denial of the importance of class consciousness and neglect of languages of (anarcho-communist/socialist) hostility to republicanism, the eclectic radicalism of labor republicanism looks less accommodated and more acceptable in the process, all the better. History read wrongly and politics conceived poorly are but two sides of the same coin. Against this reading of the past and this politics of the present, there remains no better antidote than adherence to the tenets of historical materialism, where class, struggle, and consciousness remain vital points of entry.

▶   The study of language can tell us much about class. That much is not questioned. As Peter Burke has suggested, the medium is a message and social historians cannot afford to be deaf or blind to it.[71] But it is not *the* message. Studies of the language of patriotism and the languages of factory reform, for instance, tell us much about class, but they do not, as their authors remind us, displace class. Nor do they vanquish from the historical scene and interpretive agenda the difficult matter of class consciousness and how it is situated within the periodization of class formation and struggle. Robert Gray, in a recent discussion of the languages through which mid-nineteenth-century factory reform was negotiated, concludes by saying as much:

> Factory reform was . . . an important site for renegotiating some of the inherent contradictions of liberal ideology. The market of liberal economics—as the economists themselves realised—existed in a legal and moral framework. But the setting of that framework, and the drawing of boundaries around it was a matter of continuing contention. . . . Whatever social harmony prevailed in the mid-Victorian decade has to be seen as a fragile construct rather than an achieved and stable state. A fuller history of factory reform will have to investigate the subterranean currents below the smooth flow of consensual rhetoric.[72]

Even Reddy's recent exploration of dialect and *patois* literature among Lille factory laborers in the mid-nineteenth century can be read this way, not as a repudiation of class but as an expression of it in a particular political and economic context.[73] Indeed, such particular studies of everyday speech underscore the general point in Ivan Illich's discussion of how Elio Antonio de Nebrija proposed to the Queen of Spain that she suppress her subjects' vernacular tongues through the imposition of an official grammarian's language that would consolidate royal authority, power, and economic pursuits. Language, in late fifteenth-century Spain, was conceived as a tool in the creation of the nation-state, a means to secure the political economy of ends so single-mindedly sought by the absolutist monarch. Illich sees this aggressive grammarian attack on the vernacular as "the most significant . . . event in the coming of a commodity-intensive society," an undertaking that restructured everyday life.[74] Whatever his insight into the connection between language, power, and political economy, Illich understates the continuities and resiliency of vernacular speech, rooted in class difference. This is why the language of insult in both the Old World and the New took the forms that it did: the rhetoric and show of abuse was rooted "in the particular social and economic context in which people found themselves."[75]

Yet it is nevertheless the case that among those social historians most drawn to language and its rarefied importance, fundamental aspects of class experience are either being denied an historical presence or, in extreme cases, written out of the record of the past altogether. For Rancière, *a* language of encounter with bourgeois culture is reified, in the process wiping the historical slate clean of a great deal of struggle and important forms of revolutionary consciousness, which are castigated as mythological. In Stedman Jones's rereading of Chartism, *a* narrow, specifically situated and constructed language of public radicalism is privileged to the point of obliterating more class-constituted symbolic and verbal discourses, writing the history of class out of a movement in which material circumstances and political demands are held to be in a state of persistent noncorrespondence. Finally, drawing on these and other texts, many of them read quite perversely against their own grains, William Reddy has called for the abandonment of class as an analytic category, arguing that it has never been a presence within which actual men and women lived. Language's supposed capacity to constitute being, in this reading of the past, rides roughshod over the conditions and ideas of labor as an historically situated force. In recent arguments about the social history of gender, language is also drawn upon to invalidate materialist analysis and elevate a problematic reading of the past.

5 *Gender*

*In forging a concept of women as unity, we promoted
a situation in which old class antagonisms would
shift through a period of chaos into something new. In
recognizing on paper the class and race distinctions of
women but being unable, by definition, to make them
the focal thrust of our movement, we contributed to
an ideology that temporarily homogenized classes
and created a polarity that disguised other
distinctions by the comprehensive, all-embracing
opposition—men/women.*

*—Juliet Mitchell, "Reflections on Twenty Years of
Feminism" (1986)*

IN 1895 ELIZABETH CADY STANTON REWROTE THE BIBLE, ELIM-
inating all unjust ways of writing about and referring to women.[1] A
half-century later Mary Beard's *Women as Force in History* continued
the complaint, opposing the universalism of language that effectively
suppresses women's experience. "Freedom of speech allows for large
liberties," she commented, "but speech so free as to be inexact and
unintelligible is markedly licentious—and dangerous—when such subjects as human nature, the emotions, education, science, art, democracy, government, society, literary values, history, progress, retro-
gression, barbarism, and civilization are brought under a discussion
intended to be serious and informed."[2] Decades later, writing out of the
so-called second wave of feminism (by which Stanton is perceived as of
the first wave and Beard is somehow unintelligible), Sheila Rowbotham
addressed the same issue, her tone understandably more forceful. "Language conveys a certain power," she argued. "It is one of the instruments of domination . . . , carefully guarded by the superior people
because it is one of the means through which they conserve their

145

supremacy." For Rowbotham, "language is part of the political and ideological power of the rulers."[3]

This history of explicit confrontation with language as one site of the construction of gender as, first, a perceived set of differences between the sexes and among sociosexual orientations, and, second, a vital process in signifying relations of power is thus a long and protracted one.[4] It predates Stanton, of course, and reaches past Rowbotham. Indeed, the past two decades have seen a proliferation of texts, primarily anthropological, linguistic, and philosophical, that address language and gender, albeit in ways that often collapse gender into a reductionist essentialism that poses the issue only in terms of the binary oppositions of biological sex: male/female.[5]

Gerda Lerner provides a useful summing up of what gender is often taken to be and of some problems in contemporary usage of the term:

> Gender is the cultural definition of behavior defined as appropriate to the sexes in a given society at a given time. Gender is a set of cultural roles. It is a costume, a mask, a straightjacket in which men and women dance their unequal dance. Unfortunately, the term is used both in academic discourse and in the media as interchangeable with "sex." In fact, its widespread public use probably is due to it sounding a bit more "refined" than the plain word "sex" with its "nasty" connotations. Such usage is unfortunate because it hides and mystifies the difference between the biological given—sex—and the culturally created—gender.[6]

Lerner, as the discussion below will indicate, too easily locates sex as a biological "given" and assumes gender as a cultural construction, resolving with facile assertion much of the analytic difficulty of sociohistorical relations associated with masculinity, femininity, and other identities.

The relation of language and gender, complex enough on its own terms, is ironically made all the more opaque because of the tremendous output of a scholarship that can be called "feminist" at the same time that it encompasses different trajectories and orientations. A deterministic essentialism[7] associated with Shulamith Firestone's early statement of female biology as destiny lives on in another body, displaced to the realm of signification in works by Dale Spender and others, where language, rather than reproduction, tyrannizes women.[8] Though such work has exposed relentlessly the ways in which women are silenced by language,[9] it has increasingly come under critical scrutiny by a plethora of differentiated feminisms. Feminist philosophers concerned with reason, nature, and Western thought have launched explicit and implicit challenges to the essentialist argument,[10] as have psychologists.[11]

This contested terrain is also littered with the awkward differences of national idioms, French and Anglo-American feminist theory being characterized by fundamental divergences of approach. In the former an emphasis on symbolic process attunes the discourse of French feminism to poststructuralism; the latter's more pragmatic and ethical stand has, for a few years at least, insulated it from the theoretical writings of the advocates of "language." Yet as Alice A. Jardine's *Gynesis* (1985), as well as much that will be discussed below, reveals, these national divides are disintegrating. In Jardine's words, the challenge of "woman" to discourse is intrinsic to the recent destabilization of Western thought. "The object produced by this process," argues Jardine, "is neither a person nor a thing, but a horizon, that toward which the process is tending: a *gynema*. This gynema is a reading effect, a woman-in-effect that is never stable and has no identity."[12]

Nor is national location itself sufficient to insure agreement and common ground. Polemical exchanges within the French women's movement often pit the Psychanalyse et Politique camp associated with Antoinette Fouque and Hélène Cixous, premised on a feminist reworking of Lacanian fixations on language, against the materialism of a feminism suspicious of this descent into discourse.[13] As spheres of feminist theory increasingly appropriate the vocabulary of poststructuralism, with discourse and difference taking places of prominence, other feminisms stake out their own ground of emphasis. Radical feminist Catharine MacKinnon wants the feminist course steered away from such diversions, directed back to the blunt realities of power:

> Gender is an inequality of power, a social status based on who is permitted to do what to whom. Only derivatively is it a difference. . . . Inequality comes first; differences come after. . . . Difference is the velvet glove on the iron fist of domination. This is as true when differences are affirmed as when they are denied, when their substance is applauded or when it is disparaged, when women are punished or when they are protected in their name. A sex inequality is not a difference gone wrong, a lesson the law of sex discrimination has yet to learn. One of the most deceptive antifeminisms in society, scholarship, politics, and law is the persistent treatment of gender as if it truly is a question of difference, rather than treating the gender difference as a construct of the difference gender makes.[14]

To survey contemporary feminist thought on language and gender is to enter into a minefield of conflicting stresses and strains. One heuristic way through this interpretive terrain is to pause and assess specific locales.

▶   *Feminism and Linguistic Theory*

As Ivan Illich notes, "The gender-distinctive grasp of reality finds its expression in language."[15] It has long been known that men and women can, in certain cultures, speak differently from one another, although this is never a simple, universal phenomenon. A part of this potential differentiation no doubt relates directly to the material circumstances of the sexes, although this by no means resolves the maze of meanings associated with language as both a site of gender construction and a process grounded in gender-determined possibilities. Studying women and words in a Spanish village, Susan Harding concluded:

> If a man's world of words revolves more around objects and his own concerns, a woman's revolves more around subjects, around persons and their concerns. The divison of men and women in their language use is, however, even deeper. Oroel men and women not only have distinct behavioral roles that structure their use of language and assign to them distinct verbal skills and speech genres. The division of labor, in effect, ascribes to men and women different mental tasks and obligations, in terms of internal and external discourse, as well as different physical tasks and obligations in village life.[16]

Within the superficial universalism of this phenomenon, demonstrable in the gender-subordinated societies stretching from the underdeveloped Third World through "peasant" Spain to capitalistic middle America, there remain, however, diverse particularities of form. Phonology, intonation, syntax, vocabulary, and pronominal and nominal references mark out, in many cultures, the masculine and the feminine, but they do so in decidedly different ways. Men in Madagascar adopt an allusive, formal style, men's language being considered prestigious to the degree that it is indirect and avoids confrontation. Women, in comparison, argue, haggle, and barter aggressively, it being their "place" to attend to the marketing. They gain prestige through use of a language as blunt and contentious as the men's is subdued and conciliatory.[17] This is not the way things work in Scarsdale, at least not on the level of generalities.

These linguistic complexities and differences have long been recognized. But it was not until the early 1970s, with the development of women's studies, that they became the subject of scholarly scrutiny. The book generally recognized to have opened up serious discussion of the area was Robin Lakoff's *Language and Woman's Place* (1975).[18] More of a prod to further research and theoretical refinement, Lakoff's study seems strangely commonplace, politically tame, and conceptually underdeveloped in the context of the late 1980s, a reflection of how much has changed in this field in little more than a decade. Popularly written, consciously stepping outside of the specialized jargon of linguistics, *Language and Women's Place* was introspective and intuitive rather than methodologically rigorous and scientific. It made small claims and avoided treading on the sensitive toes of a tradition known to insist on the acceptability of the generic *he*.[19] All that Lakoff claimed was that women's actual language *was* different than that of men and that such differences demonstrated and reinforced their subordination in society: women's words related to their special interests in the domestic realm, they used "empty" adjectives more often than men, were more prone to questioning and rising intonations, hedged their sentences in ways that could give an impression of tentativeness even when authority was not lacking, and utilized hypercorrect grammar, excessively polite forms, and emphatic voices to compensate for the perception of women as weak and inconsequential.

This was hardly startling news, although the undertheorized manner in which it was presented, the empirical looseness of the data, and the implicit essentialism of the universalizing depiction of women's words called into question some of its findings and interpretations. On one level it was the linguistic equivalent of the attempts within social history to introduce women into the picture, a "her-story" to counter the male focus of "*his*tory." Its effort, like that of "her-story," could thus hardly help but contribute to stereotyping/caricaturing (the heroic presence and importance of "influential" women versus the absence of one sex; women's language as qualified and subservient versus the denial of a gendered language). By the 1980s "her-stories" had served their introductory and legitimating purposes and feminist historians had moved on to a series of new agendas.[20] Lakoff, too, was soon superseded.

Dale Spender's *Man Made Language* (1980) has now replaced Lakoff as the best-known text on women and language, and it has upped the political ante considerably. Insistent that it is through their control over meaning that men are able to impose their world view on women, Spender sees women's linguistic options as slim or none: they can internalize male reality, accepting their inability to articulate their experience within the limitations of language's maleness and thus live out a life of profound linguistic alienation, or they can be silent. Far too purposively popular a writer to encase herself within the "scientism" of linguistics or the obscurantism of poststructuralism, and far more prone to turn to women for inspiration than men, Spender quotes none of the pillars of critical theory, being at home with a reference to Lakoff, Adrienne Rich, Betty Friedan, or, most prominently, Mary Daly,[21] rather than Saussure, Barthes, Foucault, Lacan, or Derrida. But her conceptualization of language, patriarchy, and the power of definition is cast in the mold of poststructuralist thought:

> Language is our means of classifying and ordering the world: our means of manipulating reality. In its structure and in its use we bring our world into realisation, and if it is inherently inaccurate, then we are misled. If the rules which underlie our language system, our symbolic order, are invalid, then we are daily deceived. . . . While at one level we may support or refute the myth of male superiority—it being a matter of political choice—at another level we are unaware of the way in which it structures our behaviour and forms some of the limits of our world. With the crucial underlying rule that the world can be divided into plus male and minus male categories we have seen the construction of a *patriarchal order*. It is a symbolic order into which we are born, and as we become members of society and begin to enter the meanings which the symbols represent, we also begin to structure the world so that those symbols are seen to be applicable: we enter into the meaning of patriarchal order and we then help to give it substance, we help it come true.[22]

That this is a rather ahistorical, loosely theorized notion of patriarchy is obvious;[23] that it embraces a forceful linguistic determinism within which Spender's ideas about language unfold is a point scrutinized in Deborah Cameron's important *Feminism and Linguistic Theory* (1985).[24]

The determinism of Spender's man-made language is easily translatable into a politics of linguistic liberation. The promotional blurb on the inside cover of *Man Made Language* declares that "once women expose the falseness of male meanings and encode their own, language and society can assume new forms, and women can move towards autonomy and self determination." In the new beginning for womankind, Spender's analysis does indeed suggest the primacy of the word. Other feminists disagree, among them the more poststructurally inclined Maria Black and Rosalind Coward, who take Spender to task for assuming that "meaning" derives from clear-cut groups generated by different social experiences. They suggest that not all men are implicated in the construction of linguistic and patriarchal control, and insist that men do not uniformly share some essentialist exercise of gender power.[25]

More sympathetic to "experience," but equally antagonistic to Spender's esentialism, is Cameron, who rejects the radical feminist assertion that women are entirely silenced by man-made language and thus lack their own arenas of discourse, traditions, and meanings. Her text is unambiguously feminist, but it refuses to collapse meaning and causality into a linguistic determinism and idealism. As a linguistic materialist she calls for appreciation of "the historical moment and circumstances in which a particular practice arose and the specific group who initiated it or whose authority and interests maintain it." She suggests that "we rarely find that a practice is initiated/maintained by all men [although she does acknowledge rare exceptions] . . . or that it extends into every linguistic register." Her conception of language is thus open to difference and dominance but denies vigorously the totalizing tendencies evident in the writings of radical feminists such as Spender and Daly, whose work Cameron sees as descriptively useful but limited in its capacity to explain the relation of language and gender. Attentive to language and its important connections to oppression and subordination, Cameron is nevertheless soberingly remindful of the determining capacities of other spheres:

> I do not believe that language is the first cause, and I see nothing wrong with asserting that meaning derives from something we might call experience, as well as from immediate context. . . . I agree with the semiologists and with all anti-humanists that our "personalities," our desires, our needs, our ways of behaving, are constructed in our interactions with the world. . . . What I cannot accept, however, is the privileged status accorded language in this process of construction. . . . other things are important too: perhaps even more important, for they happen earlier in our lives and are less able than language to become objects of reflection and interpretation in their own right. I am thinking of socio-familial relations; of the division of labour and economic organization that regulates societies; of the physical environment; of individual genetic make-up.

And from this materialist vantage point, it is apparent that the language people use is not the cause of their social place, and changes in language (or, by extension, in the entire symbolic repertoire of the society) are, while important, by no means a shortcut to social transformation. "The use of linguistic and metalinguistic resources to oppress others should not be ignored," Cameron concludes, "but we must acknowledge the limitation of theories of oppression that do not go beyond the linguistic."[26]

What is curious is how rare this kind of perspective seems to be in contemporary feminist circles. Cameron confesses in the introduction to her book that she has "never encountered opinions similar to mine in feminist writings on language." She adds a note of political sorrow: "I am an active feminist who also happens to be a linguist . . . it has been exciting for me to see the growth of interest in language that has recently occurred in the women's movement: but I am sorry the movement seems to be adopting an orthodoxy on the subject which is rarely challenged, and with which I disagree."[27] What explains the perceived, if perhaps overstated, isolation of Cameron's kind of linguistic materialism? One force obscuring it is the poststructuralist descent into discourse so evident in the French feminist engagement with psychoanalysis.

▶   ***The French Connection***
Fifteen years ago Juliet Mitchell opened her book *Psychoanalysis and Feminism* with the declarative statement, "The greater part of the feminist movement has identified Freud as the enemy." This was a time when popular feminist texts such as Firestone's *The Dialectic of Sex* and Kate Millett's *Sexual Politics* routinely castigated Freud. Her book was meant to undo this repudiation, a salutory statement that psychoanalysis was not an endorsement of gender inequality and subordination but potentially an analysis of such potent social forces, an exploration of the material reality of ideas and the unconscious. Insistent that the radicalism of Freudian theory has more potential for women's liberation than the more fashionable, rhetorical, and transitory postulates of Laing or Reich, Mitchell advocated Freud when many other feminists had little time for psychoanalysis.[28]

She also acknowledged the exemplary role of the Paris-based Psychanalyse et Politique, a "Marxist" component of the Mouvement de Liberation des Femmes that was struggling to combine dialectical materialism and the psychoanalytic conceptualization of the unconscious in an understanding of sexuality, gender difference, and the lived experience of contemporary men and women.[29] What appeared novel and progressive in the early 1970s, however, was destined to take a turn for the worse.

Psych et Po drew on the Lacanian suggestion that woman/femininity is in contradiction to the Symbolic Order, the signs, codes, rituals, and language that orchestrate interaction in any social formation. Woman was thus historically suppressed:

> From the moment that she begins to speak, to exist, she has to face problems which are all masculine and this is what puts her in mortal danger—if she doesn't use them, she doesn't exist, if she does use them, she kills herself with them. This is the fringe area where we are, and this is where we will lead the struggle. I think that historically women have never existed. The movement's goal is to bring them to existence as a differentiated space, a space for difference. Alterity is woman.[30]

As a tendency of the French women's liberation movement rigorous in its theoretical alignment, Psych et Po defined its primary purpose as battling the masculinity in women's heads. Hostile to the attempt to secure legislative protections for women, which were regarded as but another act of seeking "recognition by the Father," the group called for a Revolution of the Symbolic, in which dependence on men was broken and woman-ness and its body was celebrated. Ways of thinking, conceiving, and speaking/writing were to be assessed and altered. Material conditions of women were, if not irrelevant, absent from the program of concern.

Psych et Po was nothing less than the feminist variant of the implosion of theory, a post-1968, poststructuralist freefall that soon lost any moorings in the absolutist pseudo-Marxism of Parisian Maoism evident in its early manifesto ("In the political, ideological and social struggle the only theoretical discourse that exists these days about class struggle and proletarian and cultural revolutions, is to be found in the texts on historical and dialectical materialism [Marx, Lenin, Mao]").[31] It soon found itself on a collision course with other French feminisms, and in its push to decenter (which took the form of this resolutely feminist contingent's carrying banners proclaiming "Down with feminism") employed a language that women's activists found threatening (some claimed it was an "intellectual terrorism"):

> we insisted on stating that we were not feminists, which meant, which means, that feminism is not the goal of our revolution. We are neither pre- nor anti-feminist but post-feminist; we work for heterosexuality, to bring about the other . . . it is to project, to programme here, now, the beyond of the reality principle. Because we have to go beyond it, this reality to which we women have been subjected, up to feminist emancipation—which is as much of a travesty as femininity. We have to transform this reality, if it is based on the principle of the oppression by one class, race, sex over the others.[32]

The wars were not long in coming; and they were fought in the old-fashioned male ways. Ironically enough, Psych et Po, dedicated to the principled rejection of seeking "recognition by the Father," moved in October 1979 to register the name and logo of the Mouvement de liberation des femmes, or MLF, as its own company title. After launching a magazine, opening bookshops, and starting up a publishing company, Psych et Po initiated a number of court suits against authors, employees, and another feminist publisher, Tierce (for "unfair competition" in trading practices). They apparently don't like their writings translated. Bad signs, again.[33]

Psych et Po appears, at a glance, as nothing more than the tragicomedy of a particularly contentious entrepreneurial strand within French feminism. As an organized tendency it has no doubt lost much of its appeal and spent its political force in an orgy of litigation and proprietorial coups. But it nevertheless articulated the trajectory of an influential strand of French feminism. In the works of Julia Kristeva and Luce Irigaray, discourse, subjectivity, and psychoanalysis met in ways that would internationalize a peculiarly French reading of gender.[34]

Kristeva arrived in Paris from Bulgaria in 1966, integrating herself into the structuralist milieu at the very moment of its breakup.[35] Trained in linguistics, she took the Left Bank by storm with her semiological studies, drawing on Marxism, Russian formalism, Hegelian dialectics, and Bakhtinian insights in ways that Barthes and others found impressively subversive. She herself explained the force of her work as a consequence of being an intellectual exile and a woman, the marginality of her place infusing her work on language and signification with a push that carried it to the borders of analytic venturesomeness.[36] The semiotic is conceived by Kristeva as the pre-Oedipal, gender-free language that stands as Other in clandestine opposition to and subversion of the Lacanian Symbolic Order. By no means definable as male or female, the Kristevan semiotic, which she locates in a series of "revolutionary" literary texts, is nevertheless related to gender:

> One might see the semiotic as a kind of internal limit or borderline of the symbolic order; and in this sense the "feminine" could equally be seen as existing on such a border. For the feminine is at once constructed within the symbolic order, like any gender, and yet is relegated to its margins, judged inferior to masculine power. The woman is both "inside" and "outside" male society, both a romantically idealized member of it and a victimized outcast. . . . This is why she troubles the neat categories of such a regime, blurring its well-defined boundaries. Women are represented within male-governed society, fixed by sign, image, meaning, yet because they are also the "negative" of that social order there is always in them something which is left over, superfluous, unrepresentable, which refuses to be figured there.[37]

Subjectivity, so often evaded in structuralist canons, is thus central to Kristeva's project. In *Desire in Language* (1977) she summed up her semiological approach, constructed of a wedding of "two radical instrumentalities," discourse and the unconscious, situating her own perspective within the entire historical making and unmaking of structuralist thought:

> Following upon the phenomenological and existentialist shock of the postwar period, the sixties witnessed a theoretical ebullience that could roughly be summarized as leading to the discovery of the

determinative role of *language* in all human sciences. . . . one did nevertheless, from then on . . . question the metaphysical premises on which rest not only the sciences of language but their exportation to other domains. Then, next to structuralism, a critique of Hegelian, Heideggerian, Marxian, or Freudian derivation jolted its occasionally simplistic elegance and carried theoretical thought to an intensity of white heat that set categories and concepts ablaze—sparing not even discourse itself. *Semanalysis,* as I tried to define it and put it to work . . . meets that requirement to describe the signifying phenomena, while analyzing, criticizing, and dissolving "phenomenon," "meaning," and "signifier." . . . an insertion of subjectivity into matters of language and meaning unfailingly led one to confront a semiology stemming from Saussure or Peirce with Hegelian logic and with Husserl's phenomenology as well; in a more specifically linguistic fashion, it resumed Benveniste's masterly undertaking and necessarily led to a linguistics of enunciation. Finally, mindful of the splitting of subjectivity implied by the discovery of the unconscious, and taking advantage of the breakthrough accomplished by Lacan in French psychoanalysis, semanalysis attempted to draw out its consequences with respect to the different practices of discourse.

Kristeva's *ouevre* was born poststructuralist.[38]

And it quickly traveled an apostatic route, moving, if not from "left" to right, at least away from Marxism. Early associated with the *Tel Quel* group, where she remained until its liquidation in 1983, Kristeva, like others in this circle, identified with Maoism and the disillusionments and regroupings associated with May 1968. By the early-to-mid 1970s the collective solidarities of this moment—domestic and international—were shattering under a series of pressures, and Kristeva was gravitating toward feminism, psychoanalysis, and gendered subjectivity and moving away from Marxism and the collective politics of public dissidence. "I am not interested in groups," she has recently declared, in what was probably a purposeful distancing from both socioeconomic entities and left organizations; "I am interested in individuals."[39]

Her book *About Chinese Women,* drawing on a three-week visit to China in 1974, signaled this shift, and Kristeva later recalled that by this time she had decided that it "would be more honest for me not to engage politically but to try to be helpful or useful in a narrow field, where the individual life is concerned, and where I can do something more objective and maybe more sharp, and more independent of different political pressures."[40] Her semiological gaze increasingly fell on gender, more particularly on "woman" as something "that cannot be represented, something that is not said, something above and beyond nomenclatures and ideologies."[41] This was not, it needs to be stressed, a biological essentialism, inasmuch as Kristeva's theory of the subject as unstable, constituted in language, and constantly in motion was used to scrutinize feminine and masculine modes of discourse rather than the physiology of sex differentiation.[42]

Paralleled by her psychoanalytic training, the birth of a son in 1976, and her establishment of a practice in 1979, this development culminated in her *Histoires d'amour* (1983).[43] In "Women's Time" Kristeva articulates a Psych et Po–like concern with feminism as Symbolic Revolution: "The sharpest and most subtle point of feminist subversion bought about by the new generation will henceforth be situated on the terrain of the inseparable conjunction of the sexual and the symbolic, in order to try to discover, first, the specificity of the female, and then, in the end, that of each individual woman."[44] To carry through to this end Kristeva argues that the exhaustion of socialism/Marxism must be acknowledged and the radical potential of a vision of women that stretches beyond Freud be recognized in the psychoanalytic breakthroughs of the recent past.[45] Pleading for love, bemoaning our lack of an "amatory code"—while recognizing the impossibility of proposing one—Kristeva moves toward a reappropriation of essentialism in suggesting that the specifically female access to love in motherhood holds out the promise of a new psychoanalytic understanding of the *herethics of love*.[46] Given that Kristeva has been judged a major figure in spelling out "the radical rejection of anatomy as destiny entailed by Lacanian linguistics," her later work suggests the need for new evaluations, if not of an epistemological break, then at least of shifts in emphasis.[47]

All of this is not unrelated to Kristeva's increasing denial of the politics of the left, for which she expresses a marked lack of patience and understanding, nor is it perhaps separable from her attraction to the culture of postmodernistic familialism. In well-known conversations under the title "Why the United States?" Kristeva caricatures Marxism and espouses a sort of love-hate relationship with the American Empire that is a little long on love for the tastes of some.[48] The views of America espoused by Kristeva are truly remarkable, if not at times absurd. American thought and culture is said to be "contaminated by European culture and, in particular, by Marxism." Ideas are politicized only "under the auspices of Marxism, which is a recent trend, a return of everything McCarthyism repressed." At the same time, the culture as a whole is supposedly *nonverbal*, excelling in the pursuit of gesture, color, and sound. It is tempting to think that in her visits to the United States Kristeva has imbibed too intoxicatingly from the well of "Miami Vice" and taken a small, marginalized academic community of Marxologists too much at their self-congratulatory word.[49]

It is surprising the contortions that some Kristeva supporters will go through to excuse such nonsense.[50] What these comments reveal is nothing less than a profound ignorance of the American political scene and a capacity to totalize a cultural characterization out of the most marginal acquaintance with the diversities of the social order. That Kristeva considers herself some kind of leftist is indisputable, but her political trajectory is a reminder of where the descent into discourse, unmindful of any material moorings and historical context, leads:

> I am an exile from socialism and Marxist rationality, but far from seeing socialism as an impossible hypothesis for the West, as those from the Gulag think, I believe on the contrary that it is inevitable and consequently something that one can speak to. We must therefore attack the very premises of this rationality and this society, as well as the notion of a complete historical cycle, and dismantle them patiently and meticulously, starting with language and working right up to culture and institutions. This ruthless and irreverent dismantling of the workings of discourse, thought, and existence, is therefore the work of a dissident. Such dissidence requires ceaseless analysis, vigilance and will to subversion, and therefore necessarily enters into complicity with other dissident practices in the modern Western world.

True dissidence for Kristeva is what it has always been: *thought*. The efforts of that thought, in language and its excesses, "can attempt to bring about multiple sublations of the unnameable, the unrepresentable, the void."[51] Those may encompass many experiences, not the least of which is gender, but it is questionable, as Terry Eagleton has pointed out, how far such a libertarian celebration of decentering will *necessarily* go in actually overturning power relations and the manifold forms of subordination they insure and perpetuate.[52]

The centrality of woman as subject, present but obscured in Kristeva, is unambiguous in Luce Irigaray. Trained in Lacanian psychoanalysis, Irigaray was promptly expelled from his school upon the publication of her *Speculum of the Other Woman* (1974). Lacan was capable of doing unto others what had been done unto him. Insistent that it is woman's difference that is central and actively suppressed, Irigaray challenged the Lacanian premise of gender as a set of oppositions. To his famous pronouncement "the unconscious is structured like a language," Irigaray offers, not a denial, but a question, "which language?" Whereas both Lacan and Kristeva conceive of only one language, in which woman is negative, Irigaray recognizes a suppressed language of woman, differing from that of man in its persistent refusal of the logocentrism of Western thought and in its plurality of meanings. Irigaray thus rejects the Saussurean apparatus of Lacanian theory, which demands that there be a fixed order of meanings, linguistically determined, into which the sub-

ject enters. But she does recognize that language is currently the preserve of males and that it is used, in her terms, to secure the patriarchal
domination of one sex over another:

> The question of language is closely allied to that of feminine sex-
> uality. For I do not believe that language is universal, or neutral with
> regard to the difference of the sexes. In the face of language, con-
> structed and maintained by men only, I raise the question of the
> specificity of a feminine language; of a language which would be
> adequate for the body, sex and the imagination . . . of the woman. A
> language which presents itself as universal, and which is in fact
> produced by men only, is this not what maintains the alienation and
> exploitation of women in and by society?

From this determinism it follows that Irigaray is in some ways the
psychoanalytic counterpart of Spender, claiming for woman's language
a critical place in overturning the power relations of "patriarchy":
"Women are not allowed to speak, otherwise they challenge the monopoly of discourse and of theory exerted by men."[53]

In order for this language to surface against the coercive silencing of
maleness, however, women must, in Irigarian terms, "write their
bodies."[54] Literally nothing is more important than breaking the alien-
ating captivity of a language that perpetually denies the rhythms of
femininity and imprisons the female unconscious:

> Woman's improper access to representation, her entry into a specu-
> lar and speculative economy that affords her instincts no signs, no
> symbols, or emblems, or methods of writing that could figure her
> instincts, make it impossible for her to work out or transpose spe-
> cific representatives of her instinctual object goals. The latter are in
> fact subjected to a particularly preemptory repression and will only
> be translated into a *script of body language.* Silent and cryptic.
> Replacing the fantasies she cannot have—or can have only when
> her amputated desires turn back on her masochistically or when she
> is obliged to lend a hand with "penis-envy." There is no longer any
> question, even at this stage, of a system of fantasies that would
> correspond to her own instincts, particularly her primary instincts.
> Nothing will be known about those, except, perhaps, in *dream.*
> Woman's desire can find expression only in dreams. It can never,
> under any circumstances, take on a "conscious" shape.

For Irigaray, then, the politics of the hour demand a colonization of the
field of discourse, an insistence that the "barbarous" language of so-
called patriarchy, which is never anything more than a monologue, be
undermined and forced to engage in a dialogue premised on hetero-
geneity/otherness.[55]

In *This Sex Which Is Not One* (1977) this point was made relentlessly, the text structured around a constant reiteration of women's difference, sexual and biological, and the powerful ways discourse subordinates this difference. Out of "women's autoerotism," in which women, unlike men, are capable of a constant self-stimulation "without mediation, and before any distinction between activity and passivity is possible," women must find their counterdiscourse.[56] In "When Our Lips Speak Together" Irigaray lays stress on the political imperative of constructing a language of woman-ness:

> If we don't invent a language, if we don't find our body's language, its gestures will be too few to accompany our story. When we become tired of the same ones, we'll keep our desires secret, unrealized. Asleep again, dissatisfied, we will be turned over to the words of men—who have claimed to "know" for a long time. But *not our body*. Thus seduced, allured, fascinated, ecstatic over our becoming, we will be paralyzed. Deprived of *our movements*. Frozen, although we are made for endless change. With leaps or falls, and without repetition.[57]

Rooted in a radical feminist deconstruction of Freud,[58] this discourse is regarded by some feminists with reverential awe, an opening out into discovery and exploration of the relation of language, sexuality, and meaning that is wide enough to embrace all women: " 'When Our Lips Speak Together' knows all along that it is only an essay, an attempt, a beginning. Refuting closure and espousing the openness of the female bodies that it celebrates, her text ends with the words: *'nous/toute(s).'* The conclusion of this love poem opens itself to all women (e)merging from the old order."[59]

There are nevertheless some troubling features of Irigaray's psychoanalytic reading of gender. Some feminists have understandably seen it as a dangerous biologism, so essentialist as to misconstrue and obscure the origin of gendered power. In the first issue of a French woman's publication, *Questions feministes*, Irigaray's emphasis was criticized as misplaced:

> To advocate a "woman's language" . . . seems to us . . . illusory. . . . It is at times said that women's language is closer to the body, to sexual pleasure, to direct sensations and so on, which means that the body could express itself directly without special mediation and that, moreover this closeness to the body and to nature would be subversive. In our opinion, there is no such thing as a direct relation to the body. To advocate a direct relation to the body is therefore not subversive because it is equivalent to denying the reality and the strength of social mediations, the very same ones that oppress us in our bodies. At most, one would advocate a different socialisation of the body, but without searching for a true and eternal nature, for this

search takes us away from the most effective struggle against the socio-historical contexts in which human beings are and will always be trapped.[60]

Irigaray's appreciation of subjecthood leads her to a literal endorsement of mysticism, which she regards as the one spiritual endeavor under "patriarchy" within which women have been allowed to excel, an arena particularly open to the confused consciousness and loss of subjecthood she associates with the "feminine."[61] Many French feminists have little time for the resulting ahistorical, idealist meanderings of an Irigarayan essentialism constantly proclaiming itself to be something else. Monique Plaza strikes hard at Irigaray's construction of gendered subjectivity: "All that is woman comes to her in the last instances from her anatomical sex, which touches itself all the time."[62]

Irigaray's reification of "woman" as subject also articulates a worrisome concept of this subjectivity's "morphology" as that which is unthinkable, unfathomable within and through the confining repressions of "patriarchal," "specular" logic. Woman's body/pleasure defies the unitary conventionality of masculine thought, a discursive denial of traditional parameters of thinking/being: "But *woman has sex organs more or less everywhere. She finds pleasure almost anywhere.* Even if we refrain from invoking the hystericization of her entire body, the geography of her pleasure is far more diversified, more multiple in its differences, more complex, more subtle, than is commonly imagined— in an imaginary rather too narrowly focused on sameness."[63] From this pluralism and expansive geographic pleasure is constructed a subjectivity and a language that knows little order or coherence:

> Woman never speaks the same way. What she emits is flowing, fluctuating. *Blurring.*
>
> Q. What method have you adopted for this research? A. A delicate question. For isn't it the method, the path to knowledge, that has always also led us away, led us astray, by fraud and artifice, from woman's path, and to the point of consecrating its oblivion? This second interpretation of the term method—as detour, fraud, artifice—is moreover its second possible translation.
>
> Don't fret about the "right" word. There is none. No truth between our lips. Everything has the right to be. Everything is worth exchanging, without privileges or refusals. Everything can be exchanged when nothing is bought. Between us, there are no owners and no purchasers, no determinable objects and no prices. Our bodies are enriched by our mutual pleasure. Our abundance is inexhaustible: it knows neither want nor plenty. When we give ourselves "all" without holding back or hoarding, our exchanges have no terms.

This licenses a lot.[64]

For one thing it means that Irigaray can contradict herself from one page to the next and it is nothing more than the processual fluidity of nonspecular thought. Consider the issue of class and woman, a theme of some importance in contemporary critical analysis, and one that lends itself to the preoccupations, conceptualizations, and vocabulary of Marxism. Irigaray does not shy away from this realm of specular thought[65] but appropriates it when it suits her purposes. At one point she is capable of asserting that "women do not constitute, strictly speaking, a class, and their dispersion among several classes makes their political struggle complex, their demands sometimes contradictory." But she later elaborates an opposing theoretical position:

> To be sure, the means of production have evolved, new techniques have been developed, but it does seem that as soon as the father-man was assured of his reproductive power and had marked his products with his name, that is, from the very origin of private property and the patriarchal family, social exploitation occurred. In other words, all the social regimes of "History" are based upon the exploitation of one "class" of producers, namely women.[66]

When this kind of universalism rears its head, it is time to consider how past and present are differentiated through historical scrutiny of context.

▶ *Discourse and the History of the "Other"*

The history of gender remains to be written. Many bold steps have, of course, been taken, but for the most part concern with gender is new, and the theoretical signs that can point us in the direction of a history reconceived through attention to gender are in fact quite rare. Gender is still being written about as if it was a virtual synonym for "woman,"[67] and even some of the most heralded "theoretical" statements of feminist historians move only gingerly beyond this powerful field-of-force.[68] From the ranks of sociology, law, and the early women's movement itself essentialist quests for the origin of patriarchy emerged. Such writing, from Firestone through O'Brien and MacKinnon, concerned itself primarily with the subordination of women within a virtually unchanging set of patriarchal social formations stretching from the medieval to the modern.[69] This work has had a tendency to structure even opposing scholarship into its frame of reference, with the consequence that whole realms of gender experience remain obscure and understudied. This unfortunate containment of gender is slowly being broken down as sexuality—heterosexual and homosexual—is reconstructed historically to reveal the complexities and powers of desires and needs that encompass femininity, masculinity, and same-sex relations.[70] Feminist theoreticians such as Cora Kaplan have begun to address the forms of struggle and contestation around sexual difference that have a chance "of reinventing masculinity and femininity as things both 'rich and strange.' "[71] Studies of the sexual division of labor, from the macro to the micro, are beginning to reinvest the political economy of everyday life with significance for the comprehension of politics and power, not only in specific communities, the home, and the corridors of state power, but in the accumulation process on a world scale.[72] Much of this work has an intensely destabilizing quality, breaking down wisdoms, shattering long-cherished "truisms," and striking out at the concepts and categories that have played important roles in constructing gender as biological and sexual essentialism.

This work proceeds and will continue to do so. Some of it has been guided by identifiable fragments of the implosion of theory, but little of this writing, until quite recently, actually grasped discourse theory in any sustained, sophisticated way. Instead, the original attraction was to the terminology of critical theory, which served as something of a semantic adornment to texts of social history that remained, at the methodological level, quite conventional. The result is that in a range of texts discourse and language have ingratiated themselves as increasingly *popular* words, and *deconstruct* is used routinely as a verb, if not as a methodological imperative. Thus Christine Stansell, in her recent study of sex and class in antebellum New York City, refers to factory girls as creations "of a discourse, a representation of experience refracted through political concerns," and of employers writing "a language of women's sphere—working-class version—into industrial capitalism."[73] In an influential study of patriarchy, class, and gender during industrialization, Judy Lown addresses the need to "deconstruct" familiar concepts.[74] Like most studies of the sexual, John D'Emilio's and Estelle B. Freedman's *Intimate Matters* (1988) contains the obligatory nod in the direction of Foucault and addresses language and metaphor. This synthetic treatment of sexuality in America, however, rests on an unambiguous methodological and conceptual traditionalism that rocks few disciplinary conventions or understandings of relations of causality. They argue, though they often do not demonstrate, that "sexuality has been continually reshaped by the changing nature of the economy, the family, and politics."[75] Few of the studies championing some of the language and conceptualization of critical theory that have appeared in the past few years are thus unambiguously *of* this theoretical moment of poststructuralism.

Judith R. Walkowitz's *Prostitution and Victorian Society: Women,*

Class, and the State (1980) is representative of much of this kind of
work done in the last decade. It commences with a gesture in the
direction of Foucault, citing the first introductory volume of his *History
of Sexuality*. But Walkowitz is clearly no captive of discourse theory,
and for her Foucault presents only a loose indication of a subject. Moreover, she refuses, implicitly, much of poststructuralism with her conception of ideology:

> The study of the [Contagious Diseases] acts that follows begins
> where Foucault's schematization leaves off; it will examine how
> sexual and social ideology became embedded in laws, institutions,
> and social policy. This study treats ideology as a "child of social
> experience"; not as an abstract, static system, but something more
> fluid, reflective of the power dynamics of Victorian society and
> responsive to changing historical circumstances.[76]

Few historical studies of gender or gender-related subjects that have
appeared in the proliferation of writing on women's history, outside of
the kind of speculative "histories/sociologies" common in France, actually take their cues any more directly from poststructuralist thought
than does Walkowitz.[77] When they have, it is most often a narrow,
Lacanian slice of the discourse pie that is offered up for consumption.[78]
But the times, and their writings, *are* changing.

The movement toward poststructuralism and the centrality of discourse emerges vividly in the Winter 1989 issue of the *Radical History
Review*, devoted to "feminst challenges to the traditions of analysis and
narrative that have been regarded as the stuff of history writing."[79] In an
exchange among Walkowitz, Myra Jehlen, and Bell Chevigny, the borders where historical writing and literary theory meet are scrutinized,
with Walkowitz's comments an indication of how much she has moved
into the field-of-force structured by discourse since the publication of
her study of the Contagious Diseases Act. Concerned with the melo-
dramatic and stereotypical construction of sexual danger (explored
through the sensationalized publication of and response to W. T. Stead's
London-based exposé of the procurement of young virgins by corrupt
aristocratic males), Walkowitz is cognizant of the extent to which her
concerns with material context and its capacities to influence the social
and political networks within which processes of representation take
place remove her somewhat from discourse theory. Within her new
research, tentatively entitled *City of Dreadful Delight*, she finds herself
engaged in what she calls a "productive dialogue with post-structuralist
critics, reformulating their insights to address analytic categories conventionally of interest to the historian." Drawing on Foucault, she is
nevertheless aware of some of the difficulties of his stress on the discur-

siveness of power: "There is a danger in representing power as so diffuse and decentered that there is no agency, and there are no oppressors." Walkowitz in effect straddles the conceptual fence separating discourse and materialism, drawing from the vocabulary and premises of post-structuralism to frame the entirety of her comments, but closing with acknowledgment of just how much "material reality" exists as a "certain pressure," insisting that power's historical use can be addressed only as "an empirical question!"[80]

What separates the Walkowitz of *Prostitution and Victorian Society* from the Walkowitz of *City of Dreadful Delight* is a level of theoretical self-consciousness. Drawn upon loosely and selectively in 1980, the poststructuralist presence is far more explicit and forceful in 1989: discourse and its determinations have moved from the obscured side-lines of rather cavalier conceptual adornment to the unmistakable analytic foundations of a new project. Unable to embrace discourse theory unambiguously, Walkowitz nevertheless grasps it far more purposely in the present than she ever did in the past. She is something of a sign of the times.[81]

There are feminist writings and feminist positions that highlight the divergences that can be drawn between histories paced by discourses and those determined by the ways in which material life acts upon systems of meaning. This emerges clearly in the *Radical History Review* attempt to "resolve the tension between a post-structuralist and a materialist theory." Judith Newton, for instance, reviews Leonore Davidoff and Catherine Hall's *Family Fortunes: Men and Women of the English Middle Class, 1780–1850* (1987) to point out how the discourse-oriented feminist literary criticism known as "new historicism" relates "systems of meaning to the material in interesting and provocative ways," as do Davidoff and Hall. But she also stresses the differences in the two undertakings, with the emphasis of Davidoff and Hall (historians) being on "the way the material acts upon systems of meaning," whereas feminist deconstructionists working through historical themes inevitably elaborate on how "systems of meaning inform and construct the material." Whereas one tradition is marked by a textual analysis that subverts "the real" in the multiplicity of writing's displacements, condensations, repressions, and symbolism, skirting social practices and institutions, the other is more concerned with structures of being and is "less strict in its modes of reference to 'the real.'" Newton regards these approaches as complementary and overlapping, two sides of the reexamination of meaning and experience.[82]

More skeptical is Myra Jehlen. She distrusts the invocation of discourse, suggesting that the reification of language has come to occupy a space once reserved for an older, pejoratively conceived, deterministic "historicism." Whereas literary criticism once dismissed the reductionism of empirical historical research, with its simple-minded notions of causality and meaning and its lack of theoretical direction, the newer literary historicism ironically reproduces the problem with what Jehlen dubs "vulgar linguicism" or "vulgar representationism":

> That is, what is historicist about doing historical research, from the point of view of the new historicist, is that we find ourselves within language, and there is nothing we can do about the limits this imposes on us. Language operates the way in which historical institutions might have been thought to operate at an earlier period: immutably, and in a way that, ironically, we cannot even interpret. Without imposing our views on it, least of all our political views, we report the way in which language has constituted a historicist historical reality.

It follows that Jehlen is more sympathetic to class as a feature of historical relations and developments, and less enamored of the collapse of history "into the common denominator of language," than many drawn to critical theory. She also notes that causality and agency, traditional concerns of historical investigation, have become "the token of the historical naif." Finally, Jehlen's abbreviated comment points to the problematic consequences of reducing everything to homogenized representation and rivets attention on the poststructuralist inability to grapple with change: "conflict and contradiction shape the world more fundamentally than convergence and agreement . . . the homogeneity of representative systems in a culture of society has to be *dis*assembled, because the disassembling will open a way to the conflictual levels of that culture or society where change can be imagined, let alone brought about." In the process, Jehlen adopts an orthodox Marxist view of representation as ideology: "historians who have been classically and essentially concerned with exploring change, whose narrative is necessarily about change, can make very good use of the idea of representation, but only if it's treated not as a truth . . . but on the contrary, always a lie. One among many possible lies, all of them posing problems and hopefully projecting, exposing, revealing their own limits."[83]

The special issue of the *Radical History Review* containing these and other commentaries makes it apparent that the history of gender is drawn powerfully in the direction of discourse. As this has been happening, the tacit theoretical inhibitions of the past fade and poststructuralism's influence within the writing of social history increases: the history of gender is now the site where discourse theory is currently exercising its greatest impact. Some recent studies distinguish themselves from the apparent hesitancy of earlier writing to embrace discourse rigorously. They also reveal the ways in which new developments in critical theory can be employed within historical writing.

Dorinda Outram provides a suggestive reading of the pivotal importance of a gender-laden concept of virtue in the language of the French Revolution, developing a fruitful analysis of the bipolarism of the revolutionary frame of reference, in which "Woman" was a sign of corruption associated with the Old Regime. Women as subjective human agents within the unfolding of revolutionary events were therefore circumscribed severely in terms of what it was possible for them to do. Those women who struggled to combat this context of a defined discourse of denigration were forced into a contorted encounter with the revolution and its language, but for the most part, Outram argues, women rejected "the Revolution itself, and . . . the discourse that went with it." She claims that this feminine distance from the revolution and its discourse is virtually unrecognized in the women's history of 1789, in which an image of woman as activist has been perpetuated. Yet she sees the revolution's discourse as an entrapment with consequences reaching across the nineteenth century:

> The series of deceptions and catch-22 positions in which the discourse of the Revolution ensnared [women] contributed enormously to their lack of long-term public authority. The failure of a "women's movement" using a male-oriented political discourse was not only, however, completely foreseeable: it had the converse consequences, that those women who campaigned against the Revolution, using another universalistic discourse, far more adapted for women's needs as public persons, that provided by the Church, were those who were going to set the trend of women's political role, for all except a minority, for the next century in France. That role would be founded on a total separation of the political ideologies of men and of women, leaving men to reject the programmes and language of the Church and women to reject the programmes and language of secular republicanism. Arguably, therefore, the discourse of the Revolution succeeded perfectly in carrying out its "hidden agenda" of the exclusion of women from a public role, leaving for them recourse to the surviving universalistic language of the Church.

Outram's account is a rare statement within the history of gender that attends to both historical context and discourse seriously.[84]

At the opposite end of the spectrum is Denise Riley's exploration of feminism and the category of "women" in history. Riley shatters historical time, ranging across centuries, to echo Lacanian notions of "women's" fictive status and a Derridean grasp of the "undecidability" of "woman." She replaces Sojourner Truth's 1851 refrain "Ain't I a woman?" with the rather more cumbersome "Ain't I a fluctuating identity?" There is no historically continuous "woman" or "women"; rather, "woman" is "discursively constructed, and always relatively to other categories which themselves change." "History" itself is not an unproblematic category—this stands as nothing less than a foundation of much poststructuralist thought[85]—and Riley's positioning vis-à-vis history is appropriately ambivalent, marked by the ubiquitous single quotation marks of the cognoscente: "It is the misleading familiarity of 'history' which can break open the daily naturalism of what surrounds us."[86]

Riley marches through the seventeenth, eighteenth, and nineteenth centuries, claiming that each period is marked by a different construction of "woman," in which the category was embedded in relations of the soul, the natural, and the social. It is heady stuff, but it is itself constructed out of the rather thin air of highly selective sources. (Two pages of footnotes contain more than fifty ibids.) So fixated on this narrow and narrowly chosen body of writing is Riley that she effectively denies a dialogue between the category as written and the process of a lived experience on the part of human beings—women—who were never constructed only categorically. When Riley states that "the history of women's suffrage gives rise to the less than celebratory reflection that categories often achieve their desired ends by subdued routes—not gloriously and triumphantly, as if at the end of an exhaustive rewarded struggle to speak themselves, but almost as by-products in the interstices of other discourses," it is all too apparent that, whatever her insights into the historically shifting and transitory character of "woman," she suffocates the very possibility of "women's" constructing a part of their being with the weight of the categorical imperative. In the words of Christine Stansell, commenting on this issue in another context, "What has dropped out of the theoretical discussion is historical subjectivity, the conscious activity of people in making and remaking the world." As Thompson noted in his assault on Althusserian structuralism, "The category has attained to a primacy over its material referent; the conceptual structure hangs above and dominates social being."[87]

Useful as an uncompromising polemical slash directed at essentialist positions and politics, Riley's text is an attempt to redirect history by redirecting feminism, urging it to be, not fixed, rigid, and "woman" bound, but moving, supple, versatile. Just what the politics of this would look like, and how effective they could be against the strong and persistent forces of an opposition that, whatever *its* fluctuations and instabilities, has a visible continuity and powerful, identifiable presences, remains to be seen; they are certainly not spelled out with any precision or clarity. Equally in need of illumination is the history of gender that, however much it was "socially constructed," was not simply "made" in Foucauldian discourse. For, Riley notwithstanding, gender was lived in ways that categories alone—"man" and "woman"— never totally determined.[88]

Of those writers who have tackled the difficult area of gender in ways that draw most explicitly upon poststructuralism, Jeffrey Weeks's books on sexuality are marked by a particular indebtedness to theoretical developments of recent decades. Like much feminist engagement with this writing,[89] Weeks draws directly from Foucault to argue that it is discourses on sexuality, not sexual acts and their histories, that are central in any understanding of power in Western society. "Sexuality is as much about words, images, ritual and fantasy as it is about the body," notes Weeks in the first sentence of his *Sexuality and Its Discontents* (1985), and he goes on to claim that "politics operate through metaphors." Another text, *Sexuality* (1986), opens with a chapter on "The Languages of Sex." His exploration of the history of sexuality follows Foucault in its insistence that sexualities are constructed and invented, a changing set of articulations that have nothing to do with nature and everything to do with power, its consolidation, and the ways in which it makes meanings and regulations pivotal in its project. Weeks takes as his starting point Foucault's blunt statement that sex is "the truth of our being" and then turns it deftly on its head, propelling us into what he calls a "whirlwind of deconstruction." What is this truth, he asks? On what basis is something natural or unnatural? Who "laws" what is sexually acceptable?[90]

Weeks has received little in the way of critical commentary. Precisely because he has pioneered the development of a new area of historical and sociological inquiry, an accomplishment enhanced by his sensible refusals of some of the outlandish positions espoused by radical (separatist/lesbian) feminists on matters such as heterosexuality as *the* enemy or a politics of antipornography that unites Moral Majority and segments of the women's movement, Weeks is rightly championed among many leftists. His commitment to and engagement with the movement for gay rights, which extends in his writing into an unwillingness to sidestep difficult questions such as intergenerational sex (paedophilia) and the meaning of "consent," insures that Weeks is warmly received in certain circles. There are, however, signs that his advocacy of a radical sexual pluralism sidesteps matters of importance, some in the gay milieu arguing that it submerges the specificities of homosexuality in a reformist sea of any and all sexualities.[91] There is also no doubt that his focus on contemporary gay identity, a "homosexual" community, and the political movements associated with these developments collapses into the very essentialism Weeks has long been at pains to challenge, an irony that does not escape the attention of Weeks himself.[92]

These emerging areas of interpretive contestation are not unrelated to Weeks's fixation on sexuality *as* discourse. Among gay rights activists Weeks's embrace of radical pluralism and his Foucauldian insistence on the constructedness—and hence historically transitory/ mobile meaning—of "the homosexual" appears as a liberal evasion of both the particularities of oppression and the positive features of sexual-cultural life that both stigmatize homosexuality and allow for some small spaces of celebration and creativity, carved out of the dominant culture with much pain and effort. When Weeks, like Denise Riley, argues that because "homosexuality" is a fragmented, volatile, constantly moving discourse and thus the category does not "exist," some gay writers react with hostility: at bottom their skepticism is rooted in a knowledge of how homophobic power is *lived* and *used* against them as something more than discourse/representation.

Weeks himself is caught on the horns of this dilemma, for in spite of his theoretical dependency on this kind of Foucauldian scaffolding he is sufficiently embedded in the politics of gay activism to privilege the "gay community," *the* gay identity. He does this by understating, and monumentally so, the class-ridden character of this "community." When it was apparent at the beginnings of the AIDS crisis that a horrible disease was in fact ravaging gays and that its spread was somehow related to the commercialized commodification of sex concentrated in specific North American urban centers, it was the powerful, literally monopolistic, bathhouse and bar owners who blocked attempts on the part of gay activists to stop the drift to epidemic. Too much money was being made off of the back of gay sexuality for this capitalistic component of "the community" to act against its class, as opposed to cultural, interests.[93] In effect, the "gay community," long enclosed within the boundaries of capitalist America, succumbed to its own vision of itself as "one," as the "Other," and a tragic internalized popular frontism ran its course in the spread of a disease that ended up exacerbating homophobia, killing off whole realms of gay culture and sexuality, and decimating "communities" of sexual identity in San Francisco, Toronto, New York, and elsewhere.[94]

Weeks's writing oscillates uneasily between its theoretical fixation and fixedness on sexuality as discourse, and all of the ramifications that this positioning entails, and its political acknowledgment that "sex does not unproblematically speak its own truth," and that those subjected to the categories and definitions of discourses of sexuality "have taken and used the definitions for their own purposes."[95] Where this ambivalence manifests itself most pointedly is in Weeks's failure to actually probe this history of human agency and his willingness to analytically lapse all too easily into the more accessible "texts" of sexology, psychoanalysis, and other writings concerned with sex. Like Foucault, Weeks has his surrogates, which become *the* history of sexuality.

Within this substitutionism, recognition of the importance of class sometimes appears, but partially and often with vital qualifications.[96] Weeks is quick to pillory "class reductionism," but he is slow to address the material embeddedness of sexuality, save for the extent to which it relates to the proliferation of commodified sexuality in the post–World War II epoch. Class does not even enter into Weeks's list of "the really fundamental issues around sexuality today: the social nature of identity, the criteria for sexual choice, the meaning of pleasure and consent, and the relations between sexuality and power," just as it is often ignored among feminists drawn to Foucault. Almost as a matter of faith Weeks proclaims that "the living history of desire disappears when grasped too firmly either to a transhistorical biology or to a class-reductionist view of social regulation." Attentive to the unconscious to the extent that it is the site of desire *and* repression, Weeks cannot bring himself to see this realm as constructed, in part, out of the material world of actual, economically determined social relations. The hidden injuries of class are somehow all too peripheral in the making of sexualities and their many meanings.[97]

To say all of this is not to suggest that the sexual can be reduced to the economic. It is to claim that the two cannot be cavalierly divorced and their relationship tossed off with a slap in the face of crude reductionism and determinism. Yet this is what Weeks's Foucauldian framework allows him to do. Power is never locatable but is relentlessly complex and overlapping, residing always in the determinations of discourse, which spins itself in a never-ending and analytically and politically impenetrable Lacanian circularity: "Society does not influence an autonomous individual; on the contrary the individual is constituted in the world of language and symbols, which come to dwell in, and constitute, the individual." With this kind of theoretical focus, it is not surprising that Weeks can politically gravitate to what he calls a radical sexual pluralism; nor is it inconsistent for him to embrace what can only be regarded as a naive voluntarism. "We have the chance to regain control of our bodies," he ends a recent book, "to recognise their potentialities to the full, to take ourselves beyond the boundaries of sexuality as we know it. All we need is the political commitment, imagination and vision. The future now, as ever, is in our hands."[98] Yet if sex does indeed not speak its own truth, the potentialities and control Weeks and others seek will never be attained by a focus on it, and its discourses,

alone. In doing just that Weeks avoids the relationships—among sex/
not sex, discourse/not discourse—that are central to the possibilities of
a human condition that reaches beyond many boundaries, those of
sexuality among them.

The history of the "Other" *is* being written, and advances in our
understandings *are* being registered. Not as much of this writing is as
unambiguously *of* poststructuralism as some would now claim. But the
signs are clearly there for all to see. These texts, with their varying
stresses and strains, are indications of a theoretical calling to order;
more and more feminist historical research, gay discussion of sexuality,
and theoretically informed writing on the past of gender will undoubtedly move in poststructuralist directions. Quantifying such a trend is
an impossibility, but conferences and reviews speak to the trajectory
now in the making.

The 1988 American Studies Conference, held in that enclave of postmodernism Miami Beach,[99] addressed the theme of "Creativity in Difference: The Cultures of Gender, Race, Ethnicity, and Class." Many of
the sessions were predictably traditionalist, but others bore titles such
as "Constructing the Other in American Inventions of Tradition,"
"From Demystification to Deconstruction and Beyond: The Challenge
of the New Scholarship to American Studies," and "Working From the
Margin: Displacing the Center: The Politics of Our Scholarship." Sessions like these apparently drew large numbers, whereas other panels,
structured around more historical and conventionally political topics,
languished.[100]

When Dorothy Smith, an internationally renowned sociologist, reviewed Deborah Gorham's book *The Victorian Girl and the Feminine
Ideal* (1982), her critical response seemed rooted in poststructuralist
premises and language:

> There are methods of thinking which will both make texts them-
> selves visible and at the same time recognize the activity of individ-
> uals in the making of consciousness as textual discourse. . . . we
> should understand the emergence of a public textually-mediated
> discourse as a new form of social relation transcending and organiz-
> ing local settings and bringing about relations among them of a
> wholly different order. . . . It seems probable that "femininity" is
> from the outset an accomplishment of textual discourse. . . . The
> books of advice and counsel not only supplied standards and prac-
> tices, they also created a common code among readers vested in
> languages and images which could be referenced in conversation
> and in interpreting behaviour and events; they also standarized
> household and family health and socialization practices, hence pro-
> gressively articulating household and family to changing retail,

> medical, and educational practices. . . . I do not think we can understand femininity as ideal or as practice unless we understand it as a discourse in which women were active as writers and as readers and were joined to and conscious of one another in new ways, unless we understand the complexity of themes, and intertextuality, and the character of the relation between text and she who read it for whatever relevance it had to her everyday world.[101]

How did Professor Gorham "read" this countertext? With wonderment? With exasperation? With a sinking feeling that she was being sucked into the descent into discourse, where all of gender is to be related to reading/writing woman?[102]

▶ ***The Scott Files***

This is perhaps not quite a theoretical coup d'état, especially when a good deal of this scholarship appears outside the boundaries of the disciplinary nation-state. But it is an unambiguous calling to a particular kind of theoretical order. Moreover, as the new stock of discourse rises, its promoters are inevitably more visible and confident. More than any other single social historian of gender, Joan Wallach Scott is advocating the value and importance of borrowing from poststructuralist thought to develop the history of gender and reorder our understanding of a past governed by relations of subordination, a present that continues to live within those confinements, and a future freed from them.[103] Her gravitation toward the implosion of theory, in both its acceleration over the last few years and in its rather cavalier grasp of what is at stake in the—for her—mainly French fragments of critical theory, is instructive in exposing the promise and problem of reinterpreting gender through the lens of poststructuralism.[104] Even highly sympathetic feminist colleagues have pointed out that this unapologetic partisanship "mysteriously exempts [poststructuralism] from critical dissection, employing it instead as a toolbox from which theories can be picked up and applied to historical problems."[105]

As Scott has herself acknowledged, her early work, including discussions that addressed matters of gender, was innocent of any insights drawn from critical theory. In a 1984 publication on men and women in the Parisian garment trades she toyed with some of the vocabulary of poststructuralism, but aside from a passing reference to Donzelot's *The Policing of Families* (1979) there was little hint of any serious commitment to a new theoretical agenda. But in the concern with images and language lay a suggestion of what was to come:

> As tailors and seamstresses read working-class newspapers, debated plans for reform and (especially in the revolutionary days of 1848)

joined political organizations, their craft concerns merged into and drew upon a larger discourse which had at its centre a critique of capitalism formulated in terms of common images. Those images recurred and resonated and perhaps even shaped the trade strategies. . . . Woman was synonymous with love and with the emotional bond of the family. What she actually did with her time was less important than what she represented. Women represented human feeling. The destruction of that feeling was depicted by the downfall of a young girl. . . . The choice of a female to represent capitalism's victim resonated with cultural images for virginity and purity and for women's subordination and subjection to domination. Workers were to capitalists what women were to men. . . . the family metaphors used in the 1890s were not the result of the inherent logic either of traditional or bourgeois ideas about women and the family employed in the 1830s and 1840s. Indeed, it is the *differences* in usage and meaning that demand explanation. . . . Gender relationships and family structures were as "economic" and "political" as were relations of production and the organization of work.

If this discussion of the gender relations of Parisian tailors and seamstresses in the 1830s and 1840s was developed out of a perceived need to rewrite women back into history, it is apparent that Scott's "discovery" of gender was "conceived" of formulations and orientations congruent loosely with the premises of a differentiated but discernible theoretical milieu.[106] Indeed, in the rewritten version of this essay published in Scott's *Gender and the Politics of History* (1988), the focus on discourse has been sharpened to expose the extent to which a series of gender-related oppositions—work and family, producer and childbearer, economic and domestic, public and private, husband and wife, factory and home—constructed working-class identities and political appeals, though hardly in the dichotomized ways one might expect from a reliance on bourgeois notions of inevitable separations.[107]

Only the faintest outlines of this approach appeared in Scott's 1983 review essay on women in modern history, confined to a few gestures toward the importance of sexual difference.[108] Three years later there was no mistaking the new-found emphasis, as articles commenced with quotations from Foucault and acknowledgments to LaCapra, were peppered with assertions of the constructing capacities of *discourse*, and, in their focus on gender, adopted a set of interpretive stances and forms of presentation that left no doubt as to the theoretical grounding of the new project. In her analysis of the statistical representation of work in Paris in 1847–1848, Scott explored the making of the sexual and class representations of the time, which forged an ideological context conducive to the established relations of power:

The prostitute represented sexuality—male as well as female—corrupted, inverted, or simply unregulated, out of control. Women, in their "natural" subordination and dependency, metaphorically represented the working class in relation to capital. In the text, representations of class and sexuality were displaced onto one another; the figure of the single working woman carried both references. Thus, in the *Statistique's* obsessive preoccupation with women of "doubtful conduct" one finds encoded a set of observations and warnings about another "reality"—the dark and dangerous side of the working class (indeed of the human personality), which must be known if only to be contained. Indeed, this "reality" always lurked below the surface; it was the underside of the busy, artistic, prosperous world of work the authors had proudly extolled in the introduction to the volume. It was, as the insurrection of June 1848 had shown, a dangerous and chaotic universe in which ordinary rules of conduct and natural hierarchies were overturned, in which the fatherly surveillance of employers could no longer contain the "turbulence" of their sons. The only corrective to this situation, the only way to prevent its reemergence, was to reimpose the terms of patriarchal law.[109]

This fascinating reading of class and gender contains considerable insight, as well as a dual problem.

For all the advances in interpretation Scott offers, her grasp of poststructuralist thought seems too partial and convenient. She concludes her discussion of the statistical representation of work with a dichotomized statement on historical method. Her source, the *Statistique de l'Industrie à Paris*, could be "read" two ways, she claimed: either at face value, incorporating its documentation without questioning its categories and interpretations; or critically, through situating it within a context in which its presentation is scrutinized "not as a reflection of some external reality, but as an integral part of that reality, as a contribution to the definition or elaboration of meaning, to the creation of social relationships, economic institutions, and political structures."[110] This amounts to little more than a traditional leftist call for attention to the determining nature of power. It hardly takes us much beyond Marx:

> The ideas of the ruling class are in every epoch the ruling ideas: i.e. the class, which is the ruling material force of society, is at the same time its ruling intellectual force. The class which has the means of material production at its disposal, has control at the same time over the means of mental production, so that thereby, generally speaking, the ideas of those who lack the means of mental production are subject to it. The ruling ideas are nothing more than the ideal expression of the dominant material relationships, the domi-

nant material relationsips grasped as ideas; hence of the relationships which make the one class the ruling one, therefore the ideas of
dominance.[111]

This is a point that has been made directly about the *Statistique de
l'industrie à Paris* by Jacques Rancière, whose comments on the ideological construction of skill and labor in this source in his discussion of
the "myth of the artisan" remain curiously unacknowledged by Scott.
Instead, she attributes the stimulus behind her essay to a lecture by
Dominick LaCapra on "documentary history."[112]

Scott's presentations of meaning, reality, authorial intention, and
textual discourse in this binary opposition of the choice of historical
methods—critical/uncritical—and of how to "read" documents—
"internalist" (face value)/"externalist" (in context)—are thus, at the
least, neglectful of some of the fundamental issues raised for historians
by the very poststructuralism she champions. Admittedly highly differentiated, the implosion of theory has produced many fragments that
would refuse outright the oppositions Scott posits. In avoiding this
theoretical complexity in what seems an instinctual reach into the
traditional—and not to be maligned—familiar historian's insistence on
contextuality, Scott coats her commitment to innovative discourse
theory in a layer of disciplinary orthodoxy. There is no crime in this,
provided that it is clearly recognized and justified. But this is not done,
perhaps because to engage in this kind of self-conscious scrutiny and
adjustment of the theoretical scaffolding that more and more of her
work is mounted on exposes too many instabilities. The consequence,
however, is an undertheorized project draped in theoretical pretense.

This is also the case in another study, "Women Workers in the Discourse of French Political Economy, 1840–1860." An exciting and illuminating explication of the process whereby French political economy merged considerations of economy and morality through an
idealized and ideological appropriation of a set of oppositions originating in the reproductive/sexual realms, Scott's article exposes the
important image of women's disordered sexuality as a metaphor for the
chaotic, often catastrophic consequences of urban/industrial capitalist
development. Like the essay on the statistical representations of work
in Paris at mid-century, this writing takes us in new directions in which
gender figures prominently. Its insights are important, and its ramifications will be many. But in its undertheorized state, which both allows
discourse too easily to subsume material conditions and halts the analytic project at the level of the literary, Scott's presentation of female
marginality and political economy suggests the need to take interpretation farther.[113]

This problem also appears in her approach to gender: "The references to sexuality seem to be part of a more complicated process of 'class construction' in which definitions of the middle class involve notions of sexual self-control and those definitions depend on negative examples, or social 'others.' In this case the social 'other' is the working class; its 'otherness' is indicated by representing it as woman."[114] A reading of this passage suggests three responses: the extent, again, to which whole realms of poststructuralist thought—such as that of Kristeva—could be marshaled against it; the blunt recognition that no matter how many times we are *told* that class is constructed as image, with gendered content, it is still critical to comprehend that class is also constructed materially; and, finally, the all-too-easy slippage of a discussion of gender into a discussion of "woman." For all of Scott's recent assault on the traditionalist assumption that "categories like man and woman are transparent" and her implicit call to deconstruct the opposition masculine/feminine, she is content to rest a critique of Thompson's *Making of the English Working Class* on a rather essentialist, universalizing understanding of gender: "So although 'man' may stand for a neutral or universal human subject, the question of 'woman' is hard to articulate or represent, for her difference implies disunity and challenges coherence."[115] Putting *woman* in quotation marks and asserting that *her* difference implies a set of consequences hardly alerts us to how, as Scott notes in another context, the category woman is at once an empty and an overflowing category: empty inasmuch as it has no ultimate, transcendant meaning; overflowing because it contains within it denied, suppressed, and alternative possibilities.[116]

Scott is of course aware that gender is not synonymous with woman, but it is striking how little she moves beyond this equation in her article "Gender: A Useful Category of Historical Analysis." The opposition, man/woman, far more complex and differentiated than that mere duality suggests, is collapsed in the essay even further inward. It is almost as though homosexuality is introduced in a concluding aside to deflect criticism that Scott has reduced the history of gender to the by now rather old-fashioned project of making women visible.[117] Even Luce Irigaray, in her essentialist texts, provides more in the way of thoughtful provocation:

> The exchanges upon which patriarchal societies are based take place exclusively among men. Women, signs, commodities, and currency always pass from one man to another; if it were otherwise, we are told, the social order would fall back upon incestuous and exclusively endogamous ties that would paralyze all commerce. Thus the labor force and its products, including those of mother earth, are the object of transactions among men and women alone.

This means that the *very possibility of a sociocultural order re-quires homosexuality* as its organizing principle. . . . Why is mascu-line homosexuality considered exceptional, then, when in fact the economy as a whole is based upon it? Why are homosexuals os-tracized, when society postulates homosexuality? . . . they chal-lenge the nature, status, and "exogamic" necessity of the product of exchange. By short-circuiting the mechanisms of commerce, might they also expose what is really at stake? Furthermore, they might lower the sublime value of the standard, the yard-stick. . . . Sexual pleasure, we are told, is best left to those creatures who are ill-suited for the seriousness of symbolic rules, namely, women. Exchanges and relationships, always among men, would thus be *both required and forbidden by law.* There is a price to pay for being agents of exchange: male subjects have to give up the possibility of serving as commodities themselves. Thus all economic organization is homosexual. That of desire as well, even the desire for women. Woman exists only as an occasion for mediation, transaction, tran-sition, transference, between man and his fellow man, indeed be-tween man and himself.[118]

The point is not whether Irigaray is right or wrong (she is both, but ultimately the latter), but that there are aspects of gender's history intimately enmeshed with the experience of woman that also extend beyond it. Scott's articulation of gender misses this, just as, for all of her conclusion's gratuitous gesture toward class and race—"gender must be redefined and restructured in conjunction with a vision of political and social equality that includes not only sex, but class and race"[119]—her essay bypasses these important realms.[120]

In making the case for gender as a useful category of historical anal-ysis, Scott, dissatisfied with feminism's inability to theorize gender adequately, reaches explicitly for the first time for the pillars of post-structuralist theory. She not surprisingly prefaces such a move with a critique of "Marxist feminism,"[121] asserting that "the self-imposed requirement that there be a 'material' explanation for gender has lim-ited or at least slowed the development of new lines of analysis," and deploring what she perhaps mistakenly perceives as the drift of femi-nists such as Juliet Mitchell away from the reconciliation of Marxist materialism and psychoanalysis.[122] What is avoided here is perhaps as important as what is asserted, for Scott manages to skirt engagement with the relevant chapters of Michèle Barrett's *Women's Oppression Today* (1980), an early text that took direct Marxist-feminist aim at much of discourse theory's reification of language and texts.[123]

The way out of the impasse created by the inadequacies of radical essentialism and Marxist economism lie, for Scott, in a "genuine histor-icizaton and deconstruction of the terms of sexual difference."[124] Derrida provides the inspiration for the necessary subjection of all categories to criticism and analyses to self-criticism. But what deconstruction means to Scott is a little too simplistic:

> analyzing in context the way any binary opposition operates, reversing and displacing its hierarchical construction, rather than accepting it as real or self-evident in the nature of things. In a sense, of course, feminists have been doing this for years. The history of feminist thought is a history of the refusal of the hierarchical construction of the relationship between male and female in its specific contexts and an attempt to reverse or displace its operations. Feminist historians are now in a position to theorize their practice and to develop gender as an analytic category.[125]

What contexts? What feminisms? What is real? Do not feminist thought's refusals often reproduce binary oppositions? These, surely, are questions high on any deconstructionist agenda. When Scott elaborates, there remain as many questions, from within poststructuralism as from outside of it:

> To pursue meaning, we need to deal with the individual subject as well as social organization and to articulate the nature of their interrelationships, for both are crucial to understanding how gender works, how change occurs. Finally, we need to replace the notion that social power is unified, coherent, and centralized with something like Foucault's concept of power as dispersed constellations of unequal relationships, discursively constituted in social "fields of force." Within these processes and structures, there is room for a concept of human agency as the attempt (at least partially rational) to construct an identity, a life, a set of relationships, a society with certain limits and with language—conceptual language that at once sets boundaries and contains the possibility for negation, resistance, reinterpretation, the play of metaphoric invention and imagination.[126]

There is nothing necessarily wrong with a good deal of this passage. But it is hard to see how such a formulation is any more indebted to Derridean deconstruction than it is to so-called culturalist Marxism, in which human agency is often regarded similiarly. And, as Geoffrey Kay and James Mott have recognized, this appropriation of a Foucauldian concept of power as dispersed and discursive exacts a particular cost, analytically and politically, inasmuch as it shields immense and massive structural locales of power from the concentrated, focused scrutiny and opposition demanded to overthrow them.[127]

Scott has further attempted to popularize the potential of discourse theory for the study of gender in two recent articles. In a discussion piece in *International Labor and Working-Class History* she criticizes the cavalier appropriation of the terms and gaze of poststructuralism by male labor historians such as Gareth Stedman Jones and rightly insists on the importance of gender, too long marginalized in historical writing on class:

> It is in analyzing the process of making meaning that gender becomes important because it so often serves as a source of organization, analogy, metaphor or legitimation for other relationships. Sexual difference is simultaneously a signifying system of differentiation *and* a historically specific system of gendered differences. Although the meanings of masculine/feminine and the roles of male/female vary historically and culturally, in specific situations they are presented as natural, rooted in biology, self-evidently different. Gender serves as a way not only to distinguish men from women, but also to identify (and contrast) abstract qualities and characteristics (strong/weak, public/private, rational/expressive, material/spiritual are some of the frequent associations in Western culture since the Enlightenment). These qualities and characteristics are encoded as masculine or feminine, and they do not correlate exactly with what real men and women can do.
>
> Yet they are not entirely unrelated to social roles either, because they provide some of the concepts that set rules, that articulate limits and possibilities for the behavior of women and men. Gender thus provides conceptual language and is created by and through that language. The allusions to masculine/feminine in Chartism, for example, not only offer insight into how politics, class, and other relationships were conceived, but also into the ways women would be able to relate to and identify with the movement.[128]

As useful and as uncontestable as is this formulation, it provides the push to a specific drift, as Scott's essay (and a consequent reply to criticism) follows the logic of poststructuralism in a one-sided reification of language and stubborn refusal of the multitude of structurally embedded historical factors that, while related to discourse, are indeed separable.[129] In the introduction to her 1988 collection of essays, she stakes out her position clearly. Knowledge, in the Foucauldian sense, is how power is constructed, and gender is one vital component in this making of power. More than mere ideas, knowledge is in fact *everything*: institutions, structures, everyday practices, rituals, a way of ordering the world and constituting social relationships.[130]

Consider, for instance, Scott's comments on discourse, Chartism, and the working-class family: "The version of class that Chartists espoused established a working-class family structure resembling middle-class ideals and susceptible to middle-class pressures; a family organization that no later radical theories of economics managed entirely to displace. From this perspective the working-class family was created within working-class political discourse, by the particular gendered conception of class evident in (though not invented by) the Chartist program." When Scott adds, almost as an afterthought, that "the family then cannot be studied as a structure apart from work processes or contemporaries' theories of social change," it is too little recognition of the material substance of life beyond discourse, and it comes too late. Moreover, it is quickly displaced anyway, with the phrase that this material realm is also "integral to the process by which language constructs social meaning." Scott later adds that to say that "the working-class family was created within working-class discourse is not to say that 'words' alone brought families into being. It is to indicate the inseparability of concepts of the family (and of class) from relationships actually established."[131] Yes, of course. But to unpack the "meaning" of this position is to grasp that language, which admittedly is not reducible to words as Scott is so insistent on repeating, *is* a totalizing process that encompasses all that exists. This is a reification that displaces too much, an ultimatism that obscures rather than clarifies.[132]

This problematic reading of power *as* language collapses in upon itself in a reduction of historical process to the perception of meaning. In what is at once a problematic statement within both poststructuralism and a more traditional materialism, Scott states bluntly, "There is no social experience apart from people's perception of it."[133] Derrida would distance himself from such a formulation as would Marx.[134] So, too, should historians.

Scott's most recent plug for critical theory appears in a two-pronged statement in the pages of *Feminist Studies*. There she presents a glossary of poststructuralist terminology—language, discourse, difference, deconstruction—with a brief, but forceful, advocacy of their utility for feminist scholarship.[135] She then applies the theory concretely in a discussion of a feminist debate that pits "equality" against "difference" in the conceptual ordering of women's experience, drawing an argument out of a reading of the legal unfolding of the sex discrimination suit brought against the Sears retailing giant by the Equal Employment Opportunities Commission (EEOC) in 1979, and in which historians Alice Kessler-Harris and Rosalind Rosenberg testified. The case turned on whether Sears could be legally held accountable for its failure to effectively implement an affirmative action program aimed at integrating female and nonwhite employees into nontraditional jobs. After six years this program was judged an abject failure by the EEOC, and women remained underrepresented in the better-paying commission sales jobs and managerial posts within the Sears empire. The company challenged the federal government's right to propose and enforce hiring guidelines in the courts, and when it lost, the EEOC filed a discrimination suit against the firm, charging that women were being excluded from high-paying commission sales jobs and that they were paid less than men in administrative/managerial posts. Sears rationalized its sexual discrimination on the grounds that men's and women's needs, material circumstances, and cultures are different, and their interest in different kinds of jobs therefore varies accordingly. Women at Sears were underrepresented in commission sales and well-paid supervisory positions because they chose, on the basis of female difference, other kinds of jobs. The issue was posed as one of culture rather than sexism.

Kessler-Harris took the stand for the EEOC, while Rosenberg effectively testified in the interests of Sears. The former acknowledged difference but argued in vain for the equal interest of men and women in the employment market; the latter put forward a more rigid argument that stressed to the point of closure male/female difference. It was Rosenberg's testimony, praised by the judge as coherent and lucid, that helped to carry the day for corporate capital. In a February 1986 ruling, the hiring practices of Sears were given an implicit legalistic seal of approval, the EEOC suit was dismissed, and discriminatory activity was renamed recognition and adaptation to natural difference. As Scott rightly concludes, "Difference was substituted for inequality, the appropriate antithesis of equality, becoming inequality's explanation and legitimation. The judge's decision illustrates a process literary scholar Naomi Schor has described in another context: it 'essentializes difference and naturalizes social inequality.' "[136]

In her reading of the Sears case, Scott correctly refuses the binary opposition difference/equality, drawing on the insights she has gained from critical theory:

> When equality and difference are paired dichotomously, they structure an impossible choice. If one opts for equality, one is forced to accept the notion that difference is antithetical to it. If one opts for difference, one admits that equality is unattainable. . . . Feminists cannot give up "difference"; it has been our most creative analytic tool. We cannot give up equality, at least as long as we want to speak to the principles and values of our political system.

The point is that difference *is* there as a bedrock of gender relations, a basic part of the geology of the personal and public realms of life under capitalism. Opting for it may not in fact be the issue, since it is a structural component of human and market relations. But it can and must be recognized that such difference is not natural or inevitable. Whether one chooses to celebrate such difference—as many feminists and feminisms have done uncritically—depends upon where one wants to get to politically.[137]

Scott's choice of interpreting the disappointing outcome of the Sears case through the poststructuralist medium of the binary opposition equality/difference yields some important and suggestive guidelines for the creation of a history of gender:

> The alternatives to the binary construction of sexual difference is not sameness, identity, or androgyny. By subsuming women into a general "human" identity, we lose the specificity of female diversity and women's experiences; we are back, in other words, to the days when "Man's" story was supposed to be everyone's story, when women were "hidden from history," when the feminine served as the negative counterpoint, the "Other," for the construction of positive masculine identity.

But it also tends to close off other readings in a rather one-sided elevation of the discourse of oppositions as both *the* problem and *the* solution:

> The resolution of the "difference dilemma" comes neither from ignoring or embracing difference as it is normatively constituted. Instead, it seems to me that the critical feminist position must always involve *two* moves. The first is the systematic criticism of the operations of categorical difference, the exposure of the kinds of exclusions and inclusions—the hierarchies—it constructs, and a refusal of their ultimate "truth." A refusal, however, not in the name of an equality that implies sameness or identity, but rather (and this is the second move) in the name of an equality that rests on differences—differences that confound, disrupt, and render ambiguous the meaning of any fixed binary opposition. To do anything else is to buy into the political argument that sameness is a requirement for equality, an untenable position for feminists (and historians) who know that power is constructed on and so must be challenged from the ground of difference.[138]

As a program for liberation this seems too enclosed, just as, in the end, for all of its insights, Scott's discussion of the Sears case is so resolutely structured around the equality-versus-difference opposition that it understates the context of the court, where law's limitations demand consideration.[139] As Claudia Koonz comments bluntly, "It defies common sense to think that a fully articulated deconstructive position, presented in the language of academic theory, would ever persuade a reactionary judge to rule in favor of women claiming discrimination."[140]

Within Scott's new collection of essays, where politics are constantly alluded to, no space is actually more vacant and vacuously underdeveloped than the *political*. Scott seems a particular case of a general problem located by the literary critic Barbara Foley: "there is an urgent necessity for literary critics to examine more closely the concept of the 'political' as it applies to our investigations. We are quite willing these days to admit that all discursive activity is in some sense political, but we are ordinarily quite imprecise, even naive, when actual political questions arise."[141]

Historically Scott asks us to interrogate Thompson's *Making of the English Working Class* in order to politically resurrect the deluded Joanna Southcott because she embodied a gendered difference that supposedly universalistic, masculinist conceptions of class have denigrated, at the same time that we are nudged subtly to reconsider if not reject the likes of Mary Wollstonecraft and others whose rationalist radical individualism suited them up to be "fitting partners for Radical men." It is as though Lacan's Symbolic Order has surpassed the order of politics and economics, and those whose language and activity strike out at the order of the unconscious attain a primacy above those whose political project remains trapped within the confinements of worldly institutions and repressions. At the cutting edge of contemporary politics, if we read this text seriously, is the need to deconstruct equality and difference so that court cases such as the Sears-EEOC legal case can be won, or the gender imbalance of history departments be redressed.[142] My point is not that Scott does not have some insightful things to say about the historical linkage of gender and class within representations, identities, and political practices of the past and present, for she most emphatically does address these issues in fascinating ways. Nor is it my argument that the Sears case is unimportant, or that the issue of women's underrepresentation—and all that that entails—in the historical profession is of little significance. Rather, politically I am suggesting that discourse theory, whatever its analytic potential, will not resolve these political matters, which are linked to larger and more potent structures of oppression. But this context of discourse and not-discourse is actually obscured by Scott's view of politics as "the process by which plays of power and knowledge constitute identity and experience," a rather circular conception given her previous insistence on knowledge's all-encompassing and determining capacities.[143]

This making of the poststructuralist case is thus two-sided. Joan Scott has goaded many historians out of their atheoretical lairs, where they have lounged contentedly in the empiricism of *the* archives and *the* documents.[144] She has been suggestive at the same time as she has underdeveloped theory by collapsing it inward on what often seems to be its own lowest common denominators. In overstating language's importance she has left aside too much, spiraling downward in the descent into discourse. Keen to bring to the history of gender an understanding of poststructuralism's potential to illuminate the history of the "Other," she actually backs away from a deconstruction of feminist thought to champion a universalistic feminist accomplishment:

> It is surely not easy to formulate a "deconstructive" political strategy in the face of powerful tendencies that construct the world in binary terms. Yet there seems to me no other choice. Perhaps as we learn to think this way solutions will become more readily apparent. Perhaps the theoretical and historical work we do can prepare the ground. Certainly we can take heart from the history of feminism, which is full of illustrations of refusals of simple dichotomies and attempts instead to demonstrate that equality requires the recogniton and inclusion of differences.[145]

This uncritical applause for an undifferentiated feminist project in fact stops any deconstructive strategy dead in its tracks, contributing to what Catharine R. Stimpson has called feminism's cultural consensus.[146] As Koonz comments: "The message seems clear: *Cherchez la femme* and leave real women on the side."[147]

This message also refuses considerations Juliet Mitchell forces into our understanding of gender and its history of rootedness in class relations and large-scale social change. In an important reflection on twenty years of feminism, Mitchell actually puts forward a "deconstructive" reading of feminism that is at odds with the congratulatory and rather complacent tone of Scott's assessment:

> Feminism does emanate from the bourgeoisie or the petit-bourgeoisie, the social class which, in capitalist society, where it is dominant, gives its values to the society as a whole. It represents its particular interest as universal interest, its women as "woman." To see this is not to turn aside from feminism, but to note that as yet it has not transcended the limitations of its origins. We should use any radical movement or thought as an early warning system to make us aware of changes already in process. . . . If women are the vanguard troops of change, it is not only because the whole society is becoming feminized or androgynized—though that is partly true. It is also because, as women, we occupy a socially marginal and hence shiftable position. At each crisis of change, I believe, we imagine this androgyne and this endless circulation and free play of multifarious differences; with each period of stabilization, something has to occupy the new point of opposition. . . . For the time being, we should note that, between the sexes, this new point of difference is called "woman." . . . There was nothing wrong with our visions; they just reflected a shift already in process—as indeed they must, but we should have been conscious of this and (a matter for self-criticism) we were not. . . . As feminists we conceived yesterday's future.[148]

This all fits well with Jane Flax's definition of "postmodern discourses" as "deconstructive" inasmuch as they seek to create distance from and skepticism about "beliefs concerning truth, knowledge, power, the self, and language that are taken for granted within and serve as legitimation for contemporary Western culture."[149]

Feminism, in its differentiated forms, is most emphatically *of* this culture, its premises demanding the same deconstructive attention as other modes of thought.[150] As Flax argues:

> the notion of *a* feminist standpoint that is truer than previous (male) ones seems to rest upon many problematic and unexamined assumptions. These include an optimistic belief that people act rationally in their own interests and that reality has a structure that perfect reasons (once perfected) can dissolve. Both of these assumptions in turn depend upon an uncritical appropriation of . . . Enlightenment ideas. . . . Furthermore, the notion of such a standpoint also assumes that the oppressed are not in fundamental ways damaged by their social experience. On the contrary, this position assumes that the oppressed have a privileged (and not just different) relation and ability to comprehend reality that is "out there" waiting for our representation. It also presupposes gendered social relations in which there is a category of beings who are fundamentally like each other by virtue of their sex—that is, it assumes the otherness men assign to women. Such a standpoint also assumes that women, unlike men, can be free of determination from their own participation in relations of domination such as those rooted in the social relations of race, class, or homophobia.

Flax believes, on the contrary, that there is no force outside of social relations capable of rescuing humanity from partiality and difference. She argues that language alone "is merely the medium in and through which . . . representation occurs." Against the poststructuralist project and much of feminist scholarship she questions the extent to which objects and, implicitly, social relations are linguistically or socially constructed.[151] Flax strikes a much needed critical note:

> The emphasis that (especially) French feminists place on the centrality of language (i.e. chains of signification, signs, and symbols) to the construction of gender . . . seems problematic. A problem with thinking about (or only in terms of), texts, signs or signification is that they tend to take on a life of their own or become the world, as in the claim that nothing exists outside of the text; everything is a comment upon or a displacement of another text, as if the modal human activity is literary criticism (or writing).

For Flax, there is no need to descend into discourse to understand gender. There are ways of combining the role of signification and a grasp of material social relations so that ambivalence, ambiguity, and multiplicity are given their due. As a feminist she argues that such a project, done well, will reveal a "reality" "even more unstable, complex and disorderly" than it appears now. "In this sense," she suggests, "Freud was right when he declared that women are the enemies of civilization." Or perhaps we can change this formulation slightly to posit that a decoding and demystification of gender will be a blow against the current regime of "civilization."[152]

Discourse is central to that undertaking, both because it does play a role in constructing gender and because its contemporary theorization provides us with ways of appreciating gender's centrality in the making of culture, thought, and the material structures of everyday life and political economy. Power *is* in some ways constituted as that which is not the "Other." Discourse figures in this process. But so also do other phenomena that must be differentiated from signification, representation, and language if these forces are to mean anything. The problem with the current elevation of discourse interpretively is that it blurs all of this and, consequently, reifies one component in the making of social relations and their histories. Consider the following:

> In the nineteenth century . . . certain concepts of male skill rested on a contrast with female labor (by definition unskilled). The organization and reorganization of work processes was accomplished by reference to gender attributes of workers, rather than to issues of training, education, or social class. And wage differentials between the sexes were attributed to fundamentally different family roles that preceded (rather than followed from) employment arrangements. In all these processes the meaning of "worker" was established through a contrast between the presumably natural qualities of women and men.[153]

That this passage pushes us forward in new interpretive directions is undeniable. That it proceeds unconcerned with areas that are absolutely vital to the understanding of the issues of class formation and gender construction and their "meanings" is equally apparent. The reification of language thus has the ironic and unfortunate effect of obscuring the importance of the chain of signification in overstatement/understatement.[154] Gender, like politics and class and their respective, related relations to discourse, demands a different interpretive agenda.

6 Conclusion: Theory and the Politics of Historical Interpretation

There are many tongues speaking differently in one
   man's head.
They speak little bits of each other
And are united without knowing it
When a man thinks alone with himself,
And wants to invent production useful to all.

—Mutimati Barnabé João, "Languages"

words   oh words
that us poets avidly searched for
among the rarest in the trunks of our memories
to say what we weren't able to say
in those old days

oh words   words
and over everything the chastity belt of silence
tearing us to pieces the founts of inspiration
chaining us one by one
in an infinite metaphor
from the most secret synonyms
the most illusive and inaccessible
to the appetizing pidescas

that was our way of struggle
in those old days

—Rui Nogar, "Words of the Old Days"

"AS IN JUDO, THE BEST ANSWER TO AN ADVERSARY MANEU-
ver is not to retreat," Foucault is reported to have said, adding that the
better course is "to go along with it, turning it to one's own advantage,
as a resting point for the next phase."[1] The poets of Mozambique's
guerrilla war, two of whom are quoted above, would probably agree.[2]
Yet there are times when such a response—militarily, politically, and
intellectually—would be foolhardy.

Is the theoretical implosion associated with the coming to prominence of discourse to be turned to the advantage of those social historians who want to come to grips with the past? Or is it a barrier to such a
project, an obfuscating aestheticism that clouds understanding, displaces appropriate emphases, and obscures essential relationships and
reciprocities? There can be no doubt that this moment of theory is often
mobilized consciously against the conceptual order and concrete practice of historical materialism, lending itself to the privileging of signification and detracting from appreciation of a set of processes—capital,
labor, exploitation, accumulation, class formation, revolution—of
long-standing centrality to Marxist interpretation. It is unmistakably
an adversary maneuver, in this sense, as a close reading of any of the
historians advocating discourse/language as a theoretical key capable
of unlocking the analytic dilemmas posed by such much-studied phenomena as politics, class, and gender will easily show.

Social historians will gain nothing by retreating in the face of this
challenge. But neither is uncritical adaptation a productive response.
These are in fact the kind of oppositions that critical theory would lead
us to be suspicious of, just as they are also the dichotomized responses
that the "culture" of historical practice conditions. They can be refused.
As a former member of Socialisme ou Barbarie, Jean-Francois Lyotard,
declared in 1971, "one does not at all break with metaphysics by putting
language everywhere."[3]

This refusal will be adamant in its resistance to the ultimatism of
critical theory's worst elements, in which discourse is made to stand as
the text among a world ordered by texts, just as it will reject a hedonistic descent into a plurality of discourses that decenter the world in a
chaotic denial of any acknowledgment of tangible structures of power
and comprehensions of meaning. It will exhibit a justifiable lack of
patience with the reduction of analysis and theory to the puns and word
games of scholastic pretension. And it will have little time for the
messianic faddism of social historians who, with the most elementary
reading of mere fragments of the implosion of theory, turn their analytic
backs on the accomplishments of historical materialism to proclaim
the new conceptual light of discourse. These are refusals that must be
made, and made clearly.

But in and of themselves these refusals are inadequate. While it is true that the implosion of theory has generated and continues to produce many fragments, all of which share something in the rather nebulous space of poststructuralism (complicated by the intrusion of its relative, postmodernism), it is equally apparent that among the differentiated segments of this theoretical rupture lie important messages for social historians. For before critical theory reaches the point of the reification of language, it contains insights and guides capable of opening new doors of understanding to historians committed to a materialism that recognizes the need for a rigorous reading of documents and texts/contexts.

To probe critical theory at its best, to grasp its potential for historical analysis as well as to comprehend the point beyond which it cannot go, we can turn to Derrida's most lucid, most explicitly contextualized, and most emphatically political deconstructive reading/writing. In his response to Paul de Man's "war," Derrida exposes the potential and problem of critical theory.

▶ *Derrida/de Man: Reading/Writing:*
   Theory/Politics

As already noted at the end of the first chapter, the revelation that Paul de Man, one of the leading lights of contemporary literary theory and an influential Yale deconstructionist, albeit lately arrived, had authored articles that appeared in Belgian newspapers published under German occupation fell like a bombshell on the critical theory community. Ortwin de Graef, a Belgian researcher sympathetic to and respectful of de Man, uncovered well over one hundred newspaper essays, many undertaken for the French-language *Le Soir,* which ran a literary and cultural column authored by de Man. These "discoveries," supplemented by minor findings of other scholars, came to the attention of the critical theory community and the wider public in 1986–1987. Not all of these (now numbered at over 180) articles have yet been examined thoroughly, but enough has surfaced to make some elementary statements.[4]

First, as to timing: the articles appeared in print between December 1940 and November 1942. De Man also published seven short essays and ninety-three one-paragraph reviews in the *Bibliographie Dechenne,* a monthly bulletin of a Brussels publishing firm that was appropriated and controlled by German forces during the occupation. These pieces appeared from February 1942 through March 1943, and de Man may possibly have been an editor of the publication. This writing thus coincides with the period during which the Nazis occupied Belgium and, indeed, exercised censorship over "important" political articles in all newspapers. Reports of contemporaries suggest that this kind of censorship was later, in August 1942, extended to all writings, including literary columns such as that of de Man. That same month Jews, recently forced to wear a yellow star, were first evacuated to Auschwitz in a Belgian transport, although it would be months before the horror of the Nazi's "final solution" would be known in de Man's homeland. Writing for a newspaper "occupied" by fascist forces, in this context, could be politically perceived as collaboration, which is why *Le Soir*'s other main literary critic was assassinated by the Resistance two months after de Man left the paper in November 1942. De Man himself was, along with the editors and staff writers of *Le Soir*, summoned before a military tribunal upon Belgium's liberation from the Nazis in September 1944, but no charges were in the end brought against him.[5]

Second, as to de Man: his history in this cauldron of journalism and politics remains obscure, if not deliberately obscured. De Man repressed, consciously certainly, unconsciously almost certainly, this involvement that he understood well could cause him shame. In 1955 he was forced to address the matter because an anonymous denunciation of his wartime activity threatened his admission to the Harvard Society of Fellows. De Man wrote in explanation that "in 1940 and 1941 I wrote some literary articles in the newspaper 'Le Soir' and, I like most of the other contributors, stopped doing so when nazi thought-control did no longer allow freedom of statement. During the rest of the occupation I did what was the duty of any decent person."[6] Whether de Man deliberately distorted the dating of his writing, knowing that to admit to contributing to *Le Soir* well into the late months of 1942 had an entirely different political meaning than a vague reference to 1940 and 1941, is impossible to prove. So, too, is his statement that he resigned for reasons of conscience, when a friend from college recalls his leaving "mainly for financial reasons: he wished to secure a more stable and better-paid job." This "reading" is shored up by the circumstances of de Man's immediate post–*Le Soir* years, consumed in a business failure that ate away family funds in a disastrous publishing house investment. Whatever de Man's cloudy history between 1940 and 1947 entailed, however, it was not a story he offered up for public consumption. Indeed, he lied about his past: when Juliet Flower MacCannell, a former student of de Man's, asked him how he had spent the war, he replied, "I went to England and worked as a translator."[7]

Third, as to the politics of de Man and the writing of these articles: little evidence exists that de Man was personally given to anti-Semitic acts in the course of his everyday life or that he embraced all of fascism's tenets enthusiastically. Derrida provides statements from de Man's

Belgian contemporaries, one of whom was active in the Resistance, adamant in their insistence that the young de Man was neither anti-Semitic nor pro-Nazi. Esther Sluszny, wife of a Jewish pianist whose concerts de Man attended and reviewed, recalls de Man's taking her and her husband into his Brussels home late one evening as they found themselves locked out of the apartment they were hiding in. With the deportations then in full gear, they faced possible death had de Man not acted. Derrida emphasizes, furthermore, that the de Man who so influenced American literary criticism in the post-1955 years was uncontaminated by racist/fascist thought or practice.[8]

This is a beginning and a differentiation. But as the journalistic furor that has swirled around such beginnings/differentiations indicates, it is not enough. Derrida takes us into a reading of these writings in which the personal relationship of Derrida and de Man is never left behind and in which deconstruction's sensitivities to the two-sidedness of writing articulates a theory's analytic edge as well as its political boundaries.

Derrida's reading of de Man's war, a close reading of some of the texts of his journalism from the 1940–1942 years, is noteworthy because it places in sharp relief how unambiguously historical, as opposed to canonical, texts can be interrogated deconstructively. The accomplishment, on one level, is impressive. Derrida probes each line, insisting that this kind of close reading is absolutely essential, suggesting that until all of the articles are cross-examined in this way, the story of de Man and *the* war(s) of 1940–1942 will never be known.[9] He implies straightforwardly as well that to actually excavate the full meaning of this episode from a buried past, inasmuch as it turns on the individual life of de Man, also demands a scrutiny of de Man's entire corpus of writing. This, predictably, is what has been avoided in the journalistic rush to condemnation.

No such massive reading is provided by Derrida. What he does do, relentlessly so, is expose the obvious content of de Man's articles and then, without denigrating that obviousness, reach beyond it to suggest a more obscure content moving around its outer edges. He does this through positing persistently the existence of *a* content here, on the one hand, and then developing the possibility of *another* content, there, on the other hand. This allows Derrida to recognize, simultaneously, de Man's captivity within the conventions of the epoch and his subtle (indeed, often all too subtle) distancing of himself from (Derrida would say subverting, but I take that as too strong a term to apply to the de Man pieces) these conventions in questions, critiques, and nuanced differentiations: "Paul de Man's discourse appeared to me right off to be clearly more engaged than I had hoped, but also more differentiated and no doubt more heterogeneous."[10]

Well before his involvement with *Le Soir*, de Man was locked into the deeply problematic acceptance of Western civilization and its ubiquitous struggle against internal decay, decadence and barbarism that Derrida is capable of decoding as an opposition of particular use in the general history of repression and coercion and the specific rise of Nazism. De Man thus easily places his wartime writing within an acceptance of the German (the word *Nazi* is, significantly, almost never used in these writings, indicating a repression of politics in the euphemism of nation) "victory," the necessity of a European "reconstruction" attentive to the national question (particularly, in de Man's case, as it relates to Belgium and the Flemish-speaking population), the potential promise of the "revolution" of occupation, and, most hurtfully for Derrida, the linkage of race and art in the single, but singular, article of de Man's anti-Semitism. In that essay, "Les Juifs dans la litterature actuelle" (Jews in present-day literature), which appeared in *Le Soir* in March 1941, the page marked by abundant signs of the most grotesque racism, de Man concluded that Jewish writers have always been of the second rank and have historically exercised little influence on the literary genres of European excellence. He then ended the article on a particularly ugly note:

> The observation is, moreover, comforting for Western intellectuals. That they have been able to safeguard themselves from Jewish influence in a domain as representative of culture as literature proves their vitality. If our civilization had let itself be invaded by a foreign force, then we would have to give up much hope for its future. By keeping, in spite of semitic interference in all aspects of European life, an intact originality and character, it has shown that its basic nature is healthy. What is more, one sees that a solution of the Jewish problem that would aim at the creation of a Jewish colony isolated from Europe would not entail, for the literary life of the west, deplorable consequences. The latter would lose, in all, a few personalities of mediocre value and would continue, as in the past, to develop according to its great evolutive laws.

All of this Derrida attends to, at times with considerable anguish: "the *massive, immediate, and dominant* effect of all these texts is that of a *relatively* coherent ideological ensemble which, *most often and in a preponderant fashion*, conforms to official rhetoric, that of the occupation forces or of the milieux that, in Belgium, had accepted the defeat and, if not state and governmental collaboration as in France, then at least the perspective of a European unity under German hegemony." This is on the one hand.

But on the other he finds an implicit counter to this "logic." Those "writers" who echo the German "victory" and "revolution," precisely those who can be reviewed under the censorship of occupation because they "give lessons," are held up to de Manian denigration as "conventional," "insipid," "uninteresting," swelling "the ranks of those who talk to no useful purpose." De Man occasionally breaks through legitimation to warn against those who would "adopt the mystical beliefs from which the victors have drawn their strength and power." The contradiction at the heart of "reconstruction" is constantly posed in terms of nationalistic tensions that Derrida perceives must have torn at German hegemony: "We can only be worthy members of a Germanic State as long as the State allows us to be worthy Netherlanders," wrote de Man in 1941. And, most startlingly, de Man's article on Jews and literature is "read" not just as an unpardonably confused piece of anti-Semitism but as a condemnation of vulgar anti-Semitism. A times, in Derrida's words, the de Man article describes "the Jewish spirit" in "unquestioningly positive terms": "Their cerebralness, their capacity to assimilate doctrines while maintaining a certain coldness in the face of them, would seem to be very precious qualities for the work of lucid analysis that the novel demands."[11] It is almost surprising that Derrida does not reach farther to suggest that the disturbing commentary at the end of the article on Jews and literature is not, in fact, about Jews at all, but a metaphor, in which the Jews are actually the Nazis, a coded reversal that could perhaps be stretched to make some sense given a language, in 1941, that asserted, "If our civilization had let itself be invaded by a foreign force, then we would have to give up much hope for its future." But this is not what Derrida says; even he can grasp that in this context such a metaphor would border on the obscene, would push the heterogeneity of a text too far, would stretch meaning to points where even poststructuralism cannot legitimately go.[12]

What *is* Derrida saying? What does his deconstructive reading tell us, not about de Man, but about historical interpretation? Deconstruction is premised on a blunt refusal of the binary oppositions so much of Western culture revolves around. In the particularities of this historically embedded set of writings, in a context of war and fascism, the principal opposition rears its head all too easily: collaboration versus resistance. This opposition has consumed the journalistic coverage of the de Man involvement in literary production for *Le Soir*. It is what Derrida rejects.

On one level, this rejection is central to historical understanding, although, as I will stress, it is never an entirely effective substitute for *interpretation*. Derrida's reading of de Man is insightful because it suggests how those who lived through the Nazi years encompassed men and women who did not necessarily and unambivalently fit into these clear-cut ranks of collaboration and resistance. Some, of course, lived these oppositions, conscious of the stand they chose to make; others were offered no choice, their sign—the pink, the yellow, the red—marking them out as "others" by definition against the Nazi project. But for the de Mans of Europe, few of whom left their literary trace in the evidence of the past, an adaptation that was *perceived* as something short of collaboration and that never ventured into the realm of "criminal" activity, collaborationist or resistant, was often taken, not necessarily even consciously. A series of events would have led them to where they found themselves. Lacking political commitments of the organized, institutional sort, they had, in their view, their lives to live. For de Man, it was a literary life; for others it was family, or business, or love, or perhaps sport—the options are and were endless. In adapting in this way, their lives, like de Man's writings, would have contained an infinite mixture of positions, postures, and nonorganizational politics composed of on the one hand and . . . on the other. They would live within, even articulate some aspects of, the dominant subordination of occupation and defeat, but other possibilities were always present. "There are many tongues speaking differently in one man's head," wrote the Mozambique poet João. In the absence of historic confrontations on the scale of those that convulsed Europe between 1939 and 1945, lives are led as a series of "wars" within and against dominant cultures: individuals embrace, accept, fragment, and oppose bits and pieces of what any social formation and culture offers them as a carrot or beats into them with a stick. This is how hegemony is made and then lived. Some try to continue in the face of the world's being turned upside down. Derrida's reading of de Man's writings is an exemplary exploration of this process, an entry into a text extending well beyond literary and cultural commentary. For in refusing an easy reading of this set of writings, in which only the deafening sound of the collaborative hand clapping could possibly be heard, Derrida opens our ears to the tensions, contradictions, and muffled refusals of those who considered themselves somewhat apart from war and fascism at the same time as they were very much within these material and ideological realities. His deconstructive sensitivity allows a theoretical reading that opens out into a set of wider political questions that historians need to explore: how men and women not entirely of historical transformation live through it.[13] On one level, then, critical theory proves, ironically enough at the very point that it faces a considerable public challenge, that it holds forth the possibilities of advancing historical understanding.[14]

It is central to grasp how Derrida's reading of de Man constructs this possibility. For his intense account of "Paul de Man's War" does not follow paths usually trod by critical theory. There is of course the usual attention to language, and an understandable concern with de Man's early journalistic commentary on language, in which the politics of language figure in a forceful Flemish nationalism: "language before all else and of that form of freedom that permits creators to work in accordance with their impulses and not as imitators of a neighbor whose spirit is dissimilar."[15] Derrida, interestingly enough, never attempts to deconstruct this politics of nationalism which, in an extreme variant, fueled the Nazi drive across Europe just as it was marhsaled indiscriminately to justify resistance and collaboration. Derrida's commentary is, superficially at least, rigidly attentive to the texts themselves: its intertextuality seems cut from the cloth of discourse theory. But it is not. Derrida puts great emphasis, contrary to the usual practices of critical theory, on contextualizing this writing, and in the process he is forced into some unfamiliar corners.[16]

This contextualization is evident throughout. He begins with a pertinent question about the journalistic attraction to the de Man case, asking why it is that the anti-Semitism of an individual Yale professor during the war is newsworthy, but the long-standing history of anti-Semitism at Ivy League institutions, detailed in accessible academic studies, has attracted no comparable attention in the press. That aside, Derrida addresses the writings from *Le Soir* and elsewhere. He insists that de Man "knew what he was doing" but is also careful to return repeatedly to de Man's youth at the time of writing (between twenty-one and twenty-three years old), the influence of his "socialist" uncle, Henri de Man (who flirted briefly with the German occupation),[17] and, above all else, the movement of a history that quite definitely set determining limits within which discourse unfolded. Derrida lays great stress on the mobility of the European situation at the beginning of the German occupation of Belgium: "The diachronic overdetermination of the context demanded that one proceed carefully in the reading of this series of articles." Once this reading commenced, it was also essential to locate them within "the equivocal structure of all the politico-philosophical discourses at play in this story, the discourses from all sides. Today, yesterday, and tomorrow. . . ."[18] In this assertion of context and insistence on its significance, Derrida acknowledges determination, "explaining" de Man and his writings as a product of what was possible, going so far as to suggest editorial tampering with the article on Jews and literature, implying that for de Man to have quit the paper in protest would have necessitated an essentially political decision about the certainty "that this rupture was a better idea than his ambiguous and sometimes anticonformist continuation on the job."[19]

It is on this level, the ultimate level of political responsibility, that Derrida's deconstructive reading of de Man breaks down. For however sensitively one contextualizes human accommodation to power and coercion, there are moments when all of the blurred needs and ambivalences get put under a political microscope, forced into focus. Many will live their lives blind to this, but ultimately history will not forget that focus, however much individuals such as de Man try to continue their lives as before and, having accomplished that to some limited extent, repress that past in escape into a "new" future. In such contexts, blunt unequivocal oppositions are often the only choice. Derrida himself is aware of this, structuring his entire reading of de Man around what he confesses, "out of concern for clarity, I will be obliged to harden into an *opposition* through the rhetoric of an 'on the one hand, on the other hand.'"[20] But for all its insights, all of its layered reading of these articles, Derrida's account of "Paul de Man's War" retreats too easily and too uncritically in the face of de Man's blatantly evident failure to confront the need for unambiguous opposition. Adept at deconstructing the obvious, uncovering the subtle and suggestive ways in which someone not of an unreconstructed Nazism but definitely caught up in its wake undercut that project at some distant margins, Derrida proves incapable of going to a center he cannot acknowledge. His reading of de Man depends finally on ahistorical fantasizing of what de Man may have meant but did not say and apolitical, if not antipolitical, questioning of any individual's right to judge another.

"Unable to respond to the questions, to all the questions, I will ask myself instead *whether responding is possible* and what that would mean in such a situation," is the opening statement in Derrida's treatment of the de Man articles. "Who has the right to judge . . . , to condemn or to absolve?" he asks. We are all captives of a certain discourse, he implies later, adding, "let the dispensers of justice not forget that!" Having suggestively developed the view that de Man's anti-Semitic article on Jews and literature was also a muffled response to vulgar anti-Semitism, Derrida "reads" the article in what can only be conceived as a willfully evasive and wistful manner:

> To condemn vulgar antisemitism may leave one to understand that there is a distinguished antisemitism in whose name the vulgar variety is put down. De Man never says such a thing, even though one may condemn his silence. But the phrase can also mean something else, and this reading can always contaminate the other in a clandestine fashion: to condemn "vulgar antisemitism," *especially if one makes no mention of the other kind*, is to condemn antisemitism itself *inasmuch as* it is vulgar, always and essentially vulgar. De Man does not say that either. If that is what he thought, a possibility I will never exclude, he could not say so clearly in this context. One will say at this point: his fault was to have accepted the context. Certainly, but what is that, to accept a context?

To read this is to cringe in the presence of scholastic apologetics, for there are times when accepting or rejecting a context is, all subtleties aside, *everything*. It is not out of line to suggest that in occupied Belgium in 1941, writing for a newspaper that contained stereotypical racism, contributing articles that were at best ambiguously situated in their relationship to fascism and uncritical national parochialism, and at worst themselves at times a voice of Nazi "reconstruction" and culturalist anti-Semitism, was an unsavory context.[21]

Derrida has written on "Paul de Man's War" precisely because he knows this to be the case. But he cannot accept it. Derrida's theoretical limitations are evident in their refusal of any center, their denial that difference, always to be respected, has politically constituted limits, that texts, however heterogeneous in their many-sided contents, do occasionally come down to a hardened core demanding a for/against opposition. To say this is not to argue that all differences need be accorded this "reading" and that all texts always boil down to an unambiguous content that will inevitably demarcate specific oppositions. But it is to claim, without reservation, that there are specific interpretive moments that cannot be "handled," intellectually and politically, by a disclosure of what exists on one hand, and a gesture toward what resides on the other. However much Derrida is right to reject the simplistic attacks on deconstruction in the aftermath of the de Man revelations, his suggestion that such journalism reproduces the logic of totalitarianism is overstated, just as his defense of deconstruction(s) as "the tireless analysis (both theoretical and practical) of . . . residual adherences to the discourse one is claiming to combat" rings a little hollow in an article devoted to a close, highly sympathetic, often insightful reading of texts authored by a figure who, in 1940–1942, can hardly be considered to have been engaged in exposing the residual adherences of a discourse of totalitarianism very much in the making. The issue is not, as Derrida seems to think defensively, the uninformed, cynical utilization of de Man's youthful journalism against deconstruction, the figurative closing of a theoretical project in "censuring or burning his books," although there will be the few who opt for this response.[22] Rather more important is the general question. Can deconstruction, and critical theory broadly conceived in terms of its focus on discourse, transcend its limitation as a project destined by its defining premises to turn ever inward and refuse the final difficult demands of an interpretive imperative that, at specific historic conjunctures, lies outside of texts, discourses, languages, signification?

As Derrida's reading of "Paul de Man's War" suggests, the likelihood of this happening is small indeed. Consider what is at stake for Derrida in the history of Paul de Man:

He must have lived this war, in himself, according to two temporalities or two histories that were at the same time disjoined and inextricably associated. On the one hand, youth and the years of Occupation appeared there as a sort of prehistoric prelude: more and more distant, derealized, abstract, foreign. The "real" history, the effective and fruitful history, was constituted slowly, laboriously, painfully after this rupture that was also a second birth. But, on the other hand and inversely, the "real" events (public and private), the grave, traumatic events, the effective and indelible history had already taken place, over there, during those terrible years. What happened next in America . . . would have been nothing more than a posthistoric afterlife, lighter, less serious, a day after with which one can play more easily, more ironically, without owing any explanations. These two lives, these two "histories" (prehistory and posthistory) are not totalizable. In that infinitely rapid oscillation he often spoke of in reference to irony and allegory, the one is as absolute, "absolved" as the other. Naturally these two nontotalizable dimensions are also equally true or illusory, equally aberrant, but the true and the false do not go together. His "living present," as someone might put it, was the crossroads of these two incompatible and disjunctive temporalities, temporalities that nevertheless went together, articulated in history, in what was *his history,* the only one.[23]

As much as we can bow to subjectivity, this is a bow too long and too low, collapsing a decisive turn in the history of humanity into a text read and reread within the individualized consciousness of one troubled figure. What Derrida's deconstruction of Paul de Man's war exposes, ultimately, is that, *as method,* discourse theory is capable only of standing aloof from the historical moment. When the meanings of human behavior and experience are most compelling, when human agency is most urgently called on to the historical stage, deconstruction takes its leave of large explanation and ultimate moral and political authority, retreating, figuratively and literally, into the smaller worlds of its own refusals.[24]

▶   ***Writing History/Reifying Language:***
or Why the Descent into Discourse Is
Happening Now

The temptation to end this discourse now, with my own statement of on the one hand and . . . on the other, is great. But some nagging questions remain. Why has this happened at this time, in a particular context, both historiographical and political? Why are social historians, many of whom divorce themselves consciously from the mainstream, identifying themselves as dissidents, a number of them retaining allegiance to historical materialism, albeit a historical materialism in need of revision and refinement, jumping so haphazardly on this bandwagon of discourse? Why are they conducting seminars, advising students, encouraging the writing of dissertations, conceiving their own research projects, and suggesting reading lists in ways that demand historiographic engagement with language and the theoretical implosions that revolve around it in a much-proclaimed age of poststructuralism/postmodernism? There is no question that this *is* happening. To be sure, as I think I have made apparent, there are reasons why language must be attended to, and there are potential theoretical gains to be registered in the critical engagement with critical theory. But the rush to descend into discourse in some quarters exceeds this reasoned response.

It is not necessary to accept all of Edward Thompson's views on the threat posed by what he referred to as the theoreticist, structuralist Althusserianism of the late 1970s to grasp that what he feared then, and thus polemicized against, has returned in a more diversified form in the late 1980s.

> This campaign had almost overwhelmed the older Marxist tradition in sociology, rooted itself deeply in the criticisms of film, art, and literature, and was massing on the borders of history. What seemed to be at risk, then, was not this or that book . . . but a whole tradition of Marxist historical practice, which had never been theoretically vacant, and whose very continuity seemed to be under threat.[25]

Althusserianism, if not quite dead, is certainly subdued; discourse rages on, and in many historical circles is, as they say, all the rage. Within the deconstructive community the disdain for "history" bears a remarkable similarity to the contemptuous dismissals—from Hindess and Hirst, Balibar, and others—associated with the structural Marxism of Althusser.[26]

This moment of discourse has sufficient troubling signification to alert historians to the need to be cautious. Much writing that appears under the designer label of poststructuralism/postmodernism is, quite bluntly, *crap,* a kind of academic wordplaying with no possible link to anything but the pseudo-intellectualized ghettoes of the most self-promotionally avant-garde enclaves of that bastion of protectionism, the University.[27] I have avoided making any kind of case *against* discourse on the basis of this writing, although it is certainly common enough, precisely because it is more important to draw out what is useful than to expose how that useful theory can and does sanction nonsense. Nevertheless, historians who champion discourse need to be aware of the direction of some of the fragments of a theoretical implosion they all too indiscriminately embrace.

To make this point I pick a volume from my shelf and open it randomly. There I read:

> Everywhere today the aestheticization of the body and its dissolution into a semiury of floating body parts reveals that *we* are being processed through a media scene consisting of our own (exteriorized) body organs in the form of second-order simulcra. And subordinations of the body to the apparatus of (dead) power are multiple. *Ideologically*, the body is inscribed by the mutating signs of the fashion industry as skin itself is transformed into a screen-effect for a last, decadent and desperate, search for desire after desire. *Epistemologically*, the body is at the center of a grisly and false sense of subjectivity, as knowledge of the body (what Californians like to call "heightened body consciousness") is made a basic condition of possibility for the operation of postmodern power: the "cynical body" for a culture of cynical power. *Semiotically*, the body is tattooed, a floating sign, processed through the double imperatives of the cultural politics of advanced capitalism: the *exteriorization* of all the body organs as the key telemetry of a system that depends on the *outering* of the body functions (computers as the externalization of memory; *in vitro* fertilization as the alienation of the womb; Sony Walkmans as ablated ears; computer generated imagery as *virtual perspective* of the hyper-modern kind; body scanners as the intensive care unit of the exteriorization of the central nervous system); and the *interiorization* of ersatz subjectivity as a prepackaged ideological receptor for the pulsations of the desiring-machine of the fashion scene. *Technologically*, the body is subordinated to the twofold hypothesis of hyper-functionality and ultra refuse: never has the body (as a floating sign-system at the intersection of the conflation of power and life) been so necessary for the teleonomic functioning of the system; and yet never has the body (as a prime failure from the perspective of a technological society that has solved the problem of mortality in the form of technique as species-being) been so superflous to the operation of advanced capitalist culture. In technological society, the body has achieved a purely *rhetorical* existence: its reality is that of refuse expelled as surplus-matter no longer necessary for the autonomous functioning of the technoscape. Ironically, though, just when the body has been transformed in practice into the missing matter of technological society, it is finally free to be emancipated as the rhetorical centre of the lost subject of desire after desire. . . .

And what is the conclusion of this extraordinary paragraph? That "the *body as metaphor*" now stands as signification "for a culture where power is always only fictional." Whatever there is of interest here is overwhelmed by what we can only politely refer to, borrowing the authors' vocabulary, as refuse. Still, my curiosity has been aroused, and I flip some pages. There I read that Gary Hart's presidential aspirations were doomed "when he said that Kierkegaard was his favourite philosopher. A presidential candidate of the cynical, neo-liberal kind should have been reading Derrida, Bataille, Baudrillard, and Nietzsche as keys to understanding the post-modern politics of the USA today, that is, the poststructuralist politics of *all text, no sex.*"[28] I have had enough. And this is all more than a little beside the point.

Assuming that this kind of crap has no connection to what is positive and potentially invigorating in the best of critical theory (an assumption I do not necessarily share, but . . .), why then are social historians turning to it so unquestioningly? It is possible to offer, first, some easy generalizations, all of which have some substantive explanatory power, however empirically unprovable they remain.

We find ourselves in a period hardly conducive to the left, which in an organizational sense has been in a state of disarray and dissolution for a number of years. Not all of this has been bad, since it has cleared the table of some unpalpable deformations. But on balance this collapse, occasioned by new aggressions and agendas on the part of capital and a reinvigorated right as well as internal political instabilities, must be understood as defeat. No championing of the new social movements, acclaim for the advances of peace, ecology, and women's liberation, can mask the harsh realities of a political economy of the 1980s, in global terms, that is in the midst of an ascendant and triumphant march that threatens working-class interests and broad progressive gains of the past. Much has already been lost.

One casualty of this context has been, not only the essential institutions and basic material well-being of labor, but also the politics and perspective of a left that defined itself in class terms. Class politics are "out" and the working class is often regarded as some atavistic entity capable of contributing little, except barriers and inhibitions, to a new politics of "left" renewal. This is not the place to argue seriously whether this is a good or a bad development, although I will state unambiguously that I look on it as a retrogressive, indeed disastrous, process. The point is that it has happened.[29]

Given this "happening," the intellectual climate within an admittedly variegated social history has shifted as well. There is much hostility to economism, but very little critical evaluation of voluntarism and idealism. This coincides with a distinct lack of interest in differentiating economism from materialism. Ideology is granted increasing weightiness and determinative capacities, while the severe limitations imposed by mundane, material reality are often skirted if not ignored outright. Much more is being written about the "social" or subjective construction of virtually everything—skill, gender, documentary reality—than there are studies about the way particular processes are grounded within boundaries set by the economy and its relations.

Feminist scholarship in general and feminist historical writing in particular, for all the differentiations of varied "feminisms," has occupied a central place in this general process. "Second wave" feminism was in part mobilized around the premise that the personal is political, and many feminists have pointed out how this perspective in fact anticipated many of the positions about the discursiveness of power associated with a Foucauldian reading of institutions, knowledges, and historical discourses. Under feminist scrutiny the explanatory authority of orthodox historical materialism, with its concerns located in economic and class structures, often appeared inadequate, as did the strategic weight placed on a vanguard party that was increasingly dismissed as a male form. The pervasive power of masculinist perspectives and constructions took on new and enhanced meaning, simultaneously destabilizing and decentering the conception of power and adding new interpretive weight to the ubiquitous realm of the ideological.[30]

Where class and gender habitually now meet, for instance, is along the *ideological* axis of skill as the constructed site of difference and male dominance, in which skill is often depicted as little more than the capacity of powerful male workers to define their jobs as the preserve of men against women. In the words of two feminist theorists: "Skill definitions are saturated with sexual bias. The work of women is often deemed inferior simply because it is women who do it."[31] The point is not to rebut the undeniable reality of labor market segmentation in which gender figures forcefully, nor is it to deny the ways in which skill is defined within gender relations. As far as this recent feminist sensibility to skill's construction has taken us in new and critically important directions, it has also skewed the treatment of skill, pressuring its conceptualization ideologically to the detriment of a more nuanced materialist reading cognizant of the two-sidedness of skill's making within the processes of production/reproduction and its consequences—often ambiguous—for class and gender relations. It has also tended toward an ahistorical assessment, the much-studied cauldron of sexual antagonism pitting skilled male labor against an "intruding" lot of unskilled women being the tailoring/seamstress trade of the pre-1850 years.[32] Yet to generalize from this experience across time, as is often done, understates the highly differentiated histories of context-bound skills, drawing too selectively on relations in a particular trade that was closely associated with the domestic realm—thus perhaps forced into a defensiveness around questions of intraclass, gender-defined relations of subordination—and acutely aware of the perilous incursions of petty technologies and debasing reorganizations of work.

This historically contextualized two-sidedness was grasped much more forcefully by Marx than is currently readily acknowledged. Marx anticipated the argument of some contemporary feminists when he noted in Volume I of *Capital:*

> The distinction between skilled and unskilled labour rests in part on pure illusion, or, to say the least, on distinctions that have long since ceased to be real, and that survive only by virtue of a traditional convention; in part on the helpless condition of some groups of the working-class, a condition that prevents them from exacting equally with the rest the value of their labour-power.[33]

Yet he was also capable of understanding that skill is only in part illusory, that its reality is constructed, not only ideologically, but also in the material realm of historically changing production, representing, again, in part, a substantive side of the never-ceasing process of accumulation:

> The accumulation of the skill and knowledge (scientific power) of the workers themselves is the chief form of accumulation, and infinitely more important than the accumulation—which goes hand in hand with it and merely represents it—of the *existing objective* conditions of this accumulated activity. These objective conditions are only nominally accumulated and must be constantly produced and consumed anew.[34]

And in this ongoing production, consumption, and renewal of skill lay much of the history of class struggle and class/gender fragmentation.[35] To slide past this history of skill on a skidding discourse-like theory of a timeless social construction of absolutely everything is to insure that you find yourself at a particular end.

Social history is perilously close to arriving there. The privileged terrain of social history is no longer economically generated and politically situated relations and struggles, but the expression those struggles and relations take in culture, ideas, sexuality—in *discourses*. All of this is, of course, overgeneralized,[36] but the trends are unmistakable. It is not all a step backward, with some studies providing stimulating and innovative discussions of the interpenetration and interdependency of the economic and noneconomic realms, exposing to our view how determination is complex and not simply and simplistically a mechanical edifice arising out of *the* economic.[37] But on the whole the interpretive and political costs now outweigh the advancing analytic prices this trend has established.

One measure of this problematic realignment of the balance sheet associated with the appropriation of poststructuralism within social history is related to the larger issue addressed in Russell Jacoby's controversial *The Last Intellectuals: American Culture in the Age of Academe* (1987). Jacoby argues that left intellectuals in the United States have abandoned influence with a larger public for the spoils of office. Speaking only to themselves, left intellectuals are the prisoners of their own esoteric language and narrow specializations. Concerned less with their capacity to engage the interest of a mass audience, the left intellectuals cavort at international conferences, publish in journals that no one outside of their small circle of intellectual friends reads, and languish over their word processors, paid for by the last grant. The writing that emerges out of this context, Jacoby argues, is opaque and garrulous, an expression of how much "form passes into content."[38]

Jacoby offers a range of explanations for why this has happened, drawing on structural and intellectual developments as varied as the decline of bohemia and the redrawing of the urban landscape or the suffocating conformities of the universities, where so many leftists sought their ultimate sustenance—material and cerebral. However partial his explanations and problematic his assessments, there is no doubt that Jacoby has captured something of what has happened to those who set out, after the 1960s, to write and think in ways that would influence public life. Yet his book has been met with a set of denials and challenges, some of them quite vicious and self-important.[39] It is all too apparent that many on the academic left refuse to see the extent to which they have been marginalized and removed from effective influence, allowed their spaces within a specific milieu whose every opening and leeway tames them with a seductive and comforting illusion.

Those who opt for poststructural thought and privilege discourse bear no special blame for this academic drift. But they are a part of the general process. Inasmuch as their writing and its conceptual ordering make few concessions to the needs and character of a reading public, indeed often revel in its aestheticized bombast, the claims made for a *politics* informed by language usually remain isolated within a narrow academic discourse itself. Those social historians championing the political potential of discourse theory and specific methods such as deconstruction will soon have to address the quite pointed assessments of the political limitations of poststructuralism that have been posed by critics such as Peter Dews and Barbara Foley.[40] Those drawn to Foucault will need to grapple with the extent to which his thought gravitated toward a rapprochement with classical liberalism and its "freedoms."[41] Finally, if the poststructuralist promise is ultimately political, as so many of its advocates claim, then just how the politics of a discourse-led historiography get translated to audiences that have little patience for many of the decentered meanderings of critical theory or the density of its language needs to be considered.

Textually, the issue is obvious. Who and how many read Sheila Row-botham's *Hidden From History* (1973)?[42] Who and how many will read Joan Scott's *History and the Politics of Gender* (1988)? Who and how many read Thompson's *Making of the English Working Class* (1963)? Who and how many will read the the proliferation of poststructurally inclined books repudiating class? This is not to suggest that what is easily read and confirms a set of prejudices is therefore what is needed and wanted. It is to confirm Jacoby's general argument that left academia is enclosed within its own referentiality, a process strikingly obvious in the case of those drawn uncritically in the direction of discourse.

Earlier texts of historical materialism such as Rowbotham's account of women in history or Thompson's discussion of the making of a class combined a set of intellectual concerns and a political project with a respect for an audience. They were also produced, for the most part, outside of the university, although it needs to be stressed that much of value was also generated within the confines of that institution.[43] The political and academic context of the mid-to-late 1980s has jettisoned much of this in a new set of intellectual and theoretical self-indulgences in which recognition of the needs of and respect for an audience has dissipated.

The contemporary intellectual scene, in which poststructuralism figures as a not inconsequential player, has thus shifted a series of relationships, altering not only the conception of meaning but the understanding of how one develops a politics of involvement. Within this transformation historical materialism, class politics, and appeal to an audience located in a particular political space have all succumbed to a dizzying process of decentering that has disrupted both the content and the form of writing. Intellectually and politically, the drift away from interpretation as rooted in material moorings often takes the form of a gravitation toward discourse, in all its poststructuralist richness, a trajectory that, in certain circles, denies material forms of determination in the assertion of the autonomy and nonreferentiality of language, broadly defined.[44] For professors now suspicious of historical materialism as a perspective and class as a heuristic device, adamant in their denial of Marxism as method or class as the site of political transformation, discourse provides a comfortable niche. It also allows certain conveniences, practical and political.

If discourse is indeed the new interpretive key, all of that mucking around in original sources is hardly necessary. A few key "texts" will suffice, and their creative "reading" will offer up a history untainted by costly, often uncomfortable, research trips, years in front of the microfilm reader, or months breathing the dust off of old archival documents.

Couple this with the analytic possibilities of a discourse-centered history, where the much-proclaimed heterogeneity of texts and the refusal of *any* center allows considerable interpretive latitude, giving free rein to the "social construction of historical argument," and the conclusion that historical writing that takes its cues from discourse is a more convenient endeavor than many other kinds of production is hard to avoid. Finally, the politics of this historical practice are equally attractive to some: if discourse is what matters, then intellectuals, who trade as a matter of course in language and texts, stand to be elevated considerably in the current political struggles. They are the identifiable interpreters of the code.[45] Add to all of this the high fashion of the moment of discourse, its Parisian chic, and the package as a whole is compelling in its drawing power.

Many will rightly suggest that this apocalyptic scenario of the current milieu in which much social history is forged is unduly pessimistic and overly inattentive to the many positive developments of the recent past. Moreover, this depiction will be rightly castigated as impressionistic assessment with little in the way of rigorous sociological or historical scrutiny of the actual writings and preoccupations of social historians. True, but that project is another book. What I will do to round out this all too cavalier judgment about the state of current historical practice is suggest that a theoretical development of the past has played some role in paving the way to this end. My final point will be that a conceptual reordering associated with historical materialism's finest texts of social history/cultural studies has, ironically enough, facilitated this drift into discourse.

▶   ### Base and Superstructure in Marxist Theory and Historical Practice

If there is a single, most highly contested terrain within the Marxist conceptualization of historical development and social practice, it is undoubtedly the metaphorical allusion, present throughout the works of Marx and Engels, to a determining economic base and a consequently derived superstructure.[46] Any number of citations could be provided, the following from Volume III of *Capital* serving as well as any:

> It is always the direct relationship of the owners of the conditions of production to the direct producers—a relation always naturally corresponding to a definite stage in the development of the methods of labour and thereby its social productivity—which reveals the innermost secret, the hidden basis of the entire social structure, and with it the political form of the relation of sovereignty and dependence, in short, the corresponding specific form of the state. This

does not prevent the same economic basis—the same from the standpoint of its main conditions—due to innumerable different empirical circumstances, natural environment, racial relations, external historical influences, etc., from showing infinite variations and gradations in appearance, which can be ascertained only by analysis of the empirically given circumstances.[47]

As indicated here, the notion of determination is by no means rigidly economistic, but rather materialistically open to historical complexity.

Yet the actual scrutiny of historical process, subject as it always is to an infinitely obscured set of causalities and always contextualized within periods of discrete confinement, never yields easily and without contradiction and complexity some direct base-superstructure relation. Marxist social histories and cultural studies have developed, over the last three decades, very much within this *problematique*.[48] Edward Thompson's break from Stalinism and the Communist party in 1956 was theoretically posed as a rejection of what he identified as "a make-believe 'model,' the 'basis' of social relations (in production) and the 'superstructure' of various branches of thought, institutions, etc., arising from it and reacting upon it." His conclusion was blunt and uncompromising: "In fact, no such basis and superstructure ever existed; it is a metaphor to help us to understand what does exist—men, who act, experience, think, and act again." On the political plane it took on even more sinister trappings: "It turns out that it is a bad and dangerous model, since Stalin used it not as an image of men changing in society but as a mechanical model, operating semi-automatically and independently of conscious human agency."

From this Thompson drew the conclusion that "because Marx reduced his concept of *process* to a clumsy static model, Stalinism evolved this mystique wherein blind, non-human, material forces are endowed with volition—even consciousness—of their own," reducing "human consciousness to a form of erratic, involuntary response to steel-mills and brickyards, which are in a spontaneous process of looming and becoming." The consequences of such theory are politically disastrous: "We learn to our cost that ideas are indeed real and material forces within society," Thompson pointed out, arguing that "false, warped, fragmentary ideas can leave their evidence in the thronged corpses, the barbed-wire encampments, economic dislocation and international conflict." In Thompson's view it was necessary to relearn what Marx and Engels understood well, "that man is human by virtue of his culture, the transmission of experience from generation to generation; that his history is the record of his struggle truly to apprehend his own social existence," a contest of liberation "from false, partial, class consciousness," thereby freeing humanity "from victimhood to blind economic causation, and extending immeasurably the region of . . . choice and conscious agency."[49]

As Thompson worked this theoretical resistance to the metaphorical notion of *a* base and its reflective superstructure(s) into writings of unrivaled historical richness, he never abandoned his distrust of this original Marxist "sin," closing his impeccably researched examination of the coercive history of the eighteenth-century Black Act, *Whigs and Hunters*, with words like these:

> I sit here in my study, at the age of fifty, the desk and the floor piled high with five years of notes, xeroxes, rejected drafts, the clock once again moving into the small hours, and see myself, in a lucid instant, as an anachronism. Why have I spent these years trying to find out what could, in its essential structures, have been known without any investigation at all? And does it matter a damn who gave Parson Power his instructions; which forms brought "Vulcan" Gates to the gallows; or how an obscure Richmond publican managed to evade a death sentence already determined upon by the Law Officers, the First Minister and the King? I am disposed to think that it does matter; I have a vested interest (in five years of labour) to think it may. But to show this must involve evacuating received assumptions . . . and moving out onto an even narrower theoretical ledge. This would accept, as it must, some part of the Marxist-structural critique; indeed, some parts of this study have confirmed the class-bound and mystifying functions of the law. But it would reject its ulterior reductionism and would modify its typology of superior and inferior (but determining) structures. . . . analysis of the eighteenth century (and perhaps of other centuries) calls in question the validity of separating off the law as a whole and placing it in some typological superstructure. The law when considered as institution (the courts, with their class theatre and class procedures) or as personnel (the judges, the lawyers, the Justices of the Peace) may very easily be assimilated to those of the ruling class. But all that is entailed in the "law" is not subsumed in these institutions. The law may also be seen as ideology, or as particular rules and sanctions which stand in a definite and active relationship (often a field of conflict) to social norms; and, finally, it may be seen simply in terms of its own logic, rules and procedures—that is, simply *as law*.[50]

This wrestling with determination in ways that could step outside of the rigidities of base/superstructure is the theoretical context of all of Thompson's writing, from *The Making of the English Working Class* (1963) through the *Poverty of Theory* (1978) and into the yet-to-be published studies of eighteenth-century society gathered together in the forthcoming *Customs in Common*, and presented as a series of six lectures at Queen's University, Canada, in 1988. Yet none of this argument was ever meant to imply that critical processes of historical formation, such as class, exercised an independence of "objective determinations" or could be "defined simply as cultural formation."[51]

As Thompson's critical engagement with the inadequacies of the base-superstructure metaphor unfolded within histories and polemics, Raymond Williams was staking out different, but complementary, ground in his theoretical elaborations on "cultural materialism." Less prone to reject the language of orthodox Marxism, Williams nevertheless paralleled Thompson in his relentless pursuit of the limitations of orthodoxy and, in particular, in his insistence that the base be conceived in such a way as to allow entry to the materiality of areas presumably once relegated irrevocably to the superstructure. With his writing addressing literature and culture, rather than history and politics, Williams's rethinking of the categories/processes of Marxist analysis always took a form more congruent with literary criticism and structuralism/poststructuralism than that adopted by Thompson. But, in the end, their positions shared significant refusals and points of departure. In describing his theoretical purpose, Williams states:

> I was trying to say something very much against the grain of two traditions, one which has totally spiritualized cultural production, the other which has relegated it to secondary status. My aim was to emphasize that cultural practices are forms of material production, and that until this is understood it is impossible to think about them in their real social relations—there can only ever be a second order of correlation. But, of course, it is true that there are forms of material production which always and everywhere precede all other forms. . . . The enormous theoretical shift introduced by classical Marxism—in saying *these* are the primary productive activities—was of the most fundamental importance.[52]

This kind of point, certainly congruent with Thompson's understanding of how history works, is the core of a wide range of Williams's writing and has, like Thompson's influence within social history and other disciplines, exercised an at times overwhelming influence.[53]

This Thompson-Williams influence has informed so much positive and exciting work within social history and Marxist theory that it will seem ungenerous to suggest that it has also forced a certain price to be paid. But that is what I will maintain. For as much as was gained in the necessary confrontation with the mechanical consequences of an undialectical and rigidly structuralist implementation of the one-sidedness of vulgarly conceived notions of base and superstructure, so too was something lost in the assimilation of agency and structure, culture and materiality. Through no fault of their own, for they had charted much-needed and creative advances in the development of historical materialism, the theoretical claims of Thompson and Williams were all too easily incorporated into an emerging orthodoxy (no less orthodox because of its lack of self-consciousness and careful elaboration) that closed its nostrils to the foul smell of economism without reflecting on the extent to which it was also, simultaneously, shutting its eyes to materialism. The cultural became the material; the ideological became *the* real. What Thompson and Williams argued with a strong sense of the need to grasp determination, what in Thompson was always subordinate to a tough-minded insistence on an exacting confrontation with historical sources and what in Williams was always developed with a sense of theoretical complexity, others took up far more indiscriminately. When structuralism gave way to poststructuralism, the way was thus unconsciously prepared for the reification of discourse, even within those very sectors of intellectual life supposedly most committed to historical materialism.

One critic of Williams, too given to slighting his contributions, captures something of this drift in his identification of the kinds of spaces where he conceives Williams moving away from historical materialism:

> What are required are analyses and descriptions of modes of production which can show how the residual, the emergent and the biological continuities, as they are manifested in specific social and cultural forms, may be related to what may well be a complex articulation of modes of production. . . . Such analyses and descriptions of the articulation of modes of production would be able to incorporate cultural production in all its forms—architecture to literary production—as creative responses to the tensions and conflicts in *class* societies, as dialectical images. These are images which bring certain relationships within any social formation or articulation of modes of production into sharper focus, or into the forefront of human consciousness, not as reflections of "reality" but as multiple-faceted (at least two-sided) images. As products of human experience and consciousness these images are also elements in "reality." But they should not be mistaken for it. . . . Accordingly, it may not be claimed that these images are determining in a strong sense because, as Williams rightly observes, they are material productions. They enter "the indissoluble process" as images reinforcing or enhancing determinations located elsewhere in the articulation of modes of production or, sometimes, appear as challenging and critical appraisals of dominant *classes* and of ideology, as in the materialist conception of history itself. But they are always subject to alternative readings and to incorporation into an already determined hegemonic ideology. Because cultural materialism, through the significance it attribues to the evident materiality of cultural

practice, threatens to prise loose determinate relationships between modes of production and cultural production, cultural materialism is itself on the way to such incorporation.[54]

This is unduly harsh. But as a rejection of Williams penned without any explicit attention to poststructuralist thought, it is suggestive how easily uncritical acceptance of the historical materialist rejection of the base/superstructure opposition could slide into discourse as determination. As Thompson would surely appreciate, the consequences of consequences are what history is often about, just as they are profoundly unpredictable.[55]

The point needs to be made unambiguously. I am not, of course, suggesting an unthinking return to mechanical Marxism. Rather, my argument is that with the contribution of Thompson, Williams, and others working in many diverse fields, it is now imperative to begin to reconsider the now somewhat neglected importance of determination, a process that seems to be slipping all too casually out of intellectual fashion, a movement accelerated by the current attraction to poststructuralism.[56]

▶   *The Intergalactic Travels of the Poet Oi Paz*

It is almost as if Thompson recognizes this ironic twist. He would certainly deny any responsibility for the current analytic fashion. He is no friend of poststructuralist theory, which he would no doubt "read" as a politically denuded theoreticist idealism, a 1980s extension of the Althusserianism he pilloried in *The Poverty of Theory*. Yet for all of this, his most recent writing, departing from the form of his previous publications, is a Swiftian futuristic satire that fuses his long-standing concerns with history and nuclear disarmament in an account of the voyage to Earth (Sykaos) of Oi Paz, a poet-explorer dispatched from Oitar, a perfectly programmed computer-like social formation threatened with environmental collapse, to determine the suitability of colonizing the alien globe. Oi Paz is quickly made into an international celebrity, "exploited" by a promotional huckster and painfully but brusquely introduced to the capitalist essentials of Western existence: commodification and alienation.

After this first public captivity has run its course in chaotic commercialism and the pacification of Oi Paz with liquor, he is incarcerated by contending components of the Anglo-American-NATO military-industrial complex, with the KGB not uninterested in him. In order to decode Oi Paz's language and culture, academics are imported into this confinement complex, one of whom is an anthropologist, Helena Sage.

Eventually Oi Paz and Sage connect, spiritually and physically, and conceive a child, with the none-too-subtle handle of Adam. Since the Oitarians are growing restless all this while, sending down search and reconnaisance missionaries to do the job Oi Paz is obviously botching, and the superpowers and their allies are responding with aggressive retaliation, the end is easily envisioned. Oi Paz and Helena Sage and Adam are dispatched to the moon, where Oitarians have established an environment simulating their own planet, in a last-ditch effort to avoid global destruction. But the bureaucracies of the superpowers win the day (they each offer to trade the other's territories to the Oitarians for a pact of separate-but-equal peaceful coexistence), and insure a cata-strophic resolution to the crisis.

Oi Paz and Helena Sage do not survive, but Adam, "rechristened" (again, a bit too cutely) Ho Mo, does, to become the first Rebel of a new intergalactic order. Inciting his peers to riot against Oitarian authority, known as the Wheel, Ho Mo proclaims his dissidence in a language of futuristic protest:

> The Wheel is a lie. There is nothing in the universe, from the pole of Oitar to the Milky Way to my ancient home of Earth, which is not cross-grained, contradictory, divided against itself, awkward, and at odds. . . . Our ratios must always be in flux. We must search always for the perfect ratio: but even as we reach out to grasp it, we have become changed through searching, and the ratio is no longer ours but it has become our own alienation, and we must begin the search again. My species destroyed itself in the search, but they might have reached out to new ratios far beyond your circinate programmes. They failed because they became too much like you. They fell into your binary logic-paths and feedback-loops.

This inspirational call to revolt wins to Ho Mo's cause the aesthetically deviant but, again, all too appropriately named Vev. After the required act of disobediance to authority, they blast off to recommence the project of life.[57] All very biblical.

My concern here is not with plot and character, but with the per-sistent importance of language, a not surprising feature of Thompson's fiction given the extent to which, as argued in an earlier chapter, his historical writing attends so assiduously to this realm. A sensitively ethnocentric intelligence officer in *The Sykaos Papers* situates lan-guage's contemporary debasement, a process paralleled by the elevation of *discourse* within academic circles: "In those, poor, simple societies language leapt and sang. Language constituted their consciousness, grief, terror and joy. I think that language is dying now, all over the world. It's being cured and modernised. It's like a deciduous forest, poisoned in mid-summer, shedding its leaves, so that only the skeletal structures of the trees are left. Then they will cut it all down and feed the wood into computers." Oitarian language is regarded by this same earthly figure as "a sort of cobweb trapping their minds," a conceptualization not far from that offered by many poststructuralist thinkers. Indeed, the book is peppered with passages that, in classic Thompson fashion, mock the pretensions of interpretive discourse-ordered faddishness in their own assault on postmodernism:

> Sapio the Spaceman is now in orbit: Moscow—Beijing—Sydney—LA, with maybe a break in Manhattan as he passes through next week. We have now had, thanks to NBC, four of his British series on East Coast TV. What is this thing? It is a new number: that's certain. It's addictive. The audience doesn't *enjoy* Sapio. It is mesmerized, like a mouse in the eye of a rattlesnake. How does one deconstruct a Sapio show? It is, already, a deconstruction. And one by one, the fellow panelists are deconstructed. This is entertainment for the age of semiotics. It is about signals and the crossing of signals—gender, race, ethnic. Sapio looks like Chief Sitting Bull and sounds like Marlene Dietrich. At one moment, s/he (and they won't say which) talks like an Old Testament Patriarch and at another like a victim of penis-envy. Some of the lines are pure Zen, but some are as old-timey as Emerson. The genius of the program is, in some ways, a turn-off rather than a turn-on. It raises a sado-masochistic itch and the viewers want to go on scratching. Like comedy *noire*, people come back, again and again, to be publicly deconstructed. But maybe the computer should shed some of the Revelation bit? There is a kind of Apocalypse ground-base which is getting heavier each time and drowning out the wit. Maybe a hangover from the boring Eighties, when the anti-nuclear trip became a culture trap? Surely if Sapio really came from another galaxy, s/he wouldn't go on about something so provincial and boring as the deconstruction of the planet?

But behind this poke at poststructuralism lie Oi Paz's "readings" of earthly realities: "Be it known that the entire society of Sykaans is controlled within a code whose name is 'property.' . . . property governs all their intercourse from birth to dead-line, and, were property to be removed no one would know how to come or how to go. . . . If property is the Rule, then 'money' is its Messenger. It is money which commands obedience."[58]

Thompson offers some curiously Oi Pazian formulations that, for all their embeddedness in a programmed culture, remind us that determination is very much a part of his conceptual making:

> Sage, for many months you have talked about your freedoms and your choice. You mortals are very important about your little bits of freewheel. . . . You suppose that you are a very special species, each

one of you a special, and your little freewheel you call a freewill. . . .
On Oitar there is ordering of all. It is clear. . . . Yet on Earth there is
programming also. But the programmers are hidden and the pro-
grammes are secret. Your lives are a great play in which you pretend
there are none. . . . On Earth the great programme is Property and
Money. . . . Are you, Sage, free to have all the property and money
you want. . . ? . . . No, it is programmed. . . . What is beastly history?
It is war after war, millions upon millions of deadlines. Did the dead
choose this? How were they free? It is the same with your blocks
and your nukes. Your species will end itself in nuclear war. Soon. It
will not be your choice.

Sage, frustrated at her inability to respond adequately, feels as if "tangled in one of those hopeless, recessive arguments about determinism
with a post-Marxist French structuralist," but Oi Paz is relentless:

> And what is your "culture" but your programme? What can you
> change it with, except your programme? Your uncured language
> closes your mind like a room without windows. You suppose your
> culture to be full of choices and of frees. . . . most of it is Sykotic
> bosh. You live inside your little darkroom of Sykotic words and
> pretend your thoughts are limitless.

Misreading these passages can be easily done. But they restate the
complexity and difficulty of determination, reasserting, in one form at
least, the problematic swirl of tough questions that encase the controversial notions of base and superstructure.[59]

The intergalactic travels of the poet Oi Paz thus bring us back to the
relationship of language and social being, situating us in a politicized,
interpretive space attentive to language's importance as well as its
limitations. In *The Sykaos Papers* we encounter a quest for language
surrounded by its many material referents. Unlike the headlong descent
into discourse taking place in some circles of social history, this satir-
ical work of fiction draws us out of the theoretical implosion of poststructuralism toward a more historically materialistic reading of experience.

▶   ## Discourse and/versus Materialism

I do not want these conclusions to be misunderstood. Some may read
them as a plague cast on two interpretive houses, my opposition directed equally at the practitioners of histories and criticisms that understate the determinations of the economic base and discourse theorists
who reify language and challenge or reject historical materialism in its
entirety. Such a reading could be attributed to my words, attentive as
they attempt to be to irony, explanation, causal origins, and the unin-

tended consequences of consequences. But it would not be true to the spirit of this text or to my intentions. So-called culturalist, Thompsonian histories and the materialism of a Williams-like criticism may have prepared the way for the reification of language, but in and of themselves they never succumbed to such an end. They were two-sided in their richness, their theoretical engagements, their concrete contributions, *and* their ambivalences. With this tradition, and these texts, it is possible to engage in a dialogue about discourse *and* materialism, however many refinements and qualifications, along with the occasional rejections and refusals, one wants to register.

This is because ultimately the writers and writings located within this body of theory and specific studies never jettisoned the notion of determination, abandoned meaning to the vagaries of a tyrannical discursiveness that effectively inhibits analysis and action from locating influential centers of power, or backed away from the importance of matters of interpretive and political responsibility. Critical or discourse theory, whatever the verbal and written gymnastics of its claimants, tends in precisely this direction. And because it proceeds along these paths, discourse inevitably poses itself *against* historical materialism, denying its interpretive capacities and asserting the superiority of discourse's own project, in which language is reified, texts decontextualized, and politics and understanding textualized. It is discourse, within contemporary theory, not materialism, that time and time again refuses a relationship between these interpretive directions, setting up a connection of opposition.

Historical materialism has no difficulty accommodating an appreciation of the materiality of texts and the importance of discourse.[60] To the extent that it has always embraced a tension-ridden duality in which human agency and structural determination rub up against each other creatively, historical materialism is rooted in appreciation of the extents to which men and women make history and are made within it. It can accept that discourse plays a role in constructing social being, just as it can appreciate the importance language plays in the politics of labor and the process of revolutionary transformation.[61] The opposition between discourse and materialism hardens into a this versus that countering of interpretive choice at the very point where discourse demands recognition of the totalizing and discursive determinations of language, writing, and texts, elevating itself to an all-encompassing authority that is both everywhere and nowhere. To be sure, in this process the "text" is often conceived so broadly as to include virtually everything, from words, to institutions, to social relations of authority. But that is precisely the problem. In refusing interpretive differentiation theoretically and avoiding the "texts" beyond *the* texts (literally) with which they are most comfortable in practice, the advocates of discourse almost universally stop their analytic and political projects short of a consideration of precisely those primarily economic realms that historical materialism considers, in the last instance (a phrase that critical theory cannot countenance), to set the limits within which determination unfolds.

It is because the insights and interpretive possibilities unleashed by discourse can enrich historical understanding *up to a point* that I have bothered to write this book. That statement has two sides. First, historians *do* need to deal with and assimilate *some* of what discourse theory has been claiming. Second, they also need to comprehend and challenge its containments, limitations, and refusals, many of which are now making their way via a contingent of true believers into historical argument that, ironically, slights the ways in which works of historical materialism have attended to language and betrays an incomplete appreciation of the origins and perspectives of discourse theory. It is not so much that I am urging those who are promoting language to do a better job in their campaign and so more effectively turn historical materialism aside, if not on its head. Rather, in scrutinizing the undertheorized and often incomplete grasp of discourse theory among those social historians gravitating to language, I am exposing the theoretically problematic and overtly idealist nature of much of this writing. It is also apparent how much of the discourse-inspired critique of specific texts of historical materialism is dependent, not on theoretical advances, but on flawed methods and troubling use of evidence, not to mention incomplete, contentious, and one-sided "readings." There are thus two problems in the discourse and materialism equation within the writing of social history: the nature and meaning of discourse theory itself, and the ways in which that nature and meaning are translated into writing by particular historians.

Social historians taking the linguistic turn have devoted little attention to such matters, nor have advocates of historical materialism yet responded fully to this challenge posed by discourse, many acquiescing to the new theoretical imperatives in their silence or accommodations. Both the implosion of theory and its consequent reification of language, as well as the impact of these developments within a social history once generally congruent with the tenets of historical materialism, relate to the contemporary social, political, and economic context of late capitalism.[62] This protracted moment is a disabling one for many left intellectuals. The socioeconomic formation of Western capitalism reconstitutes itself in ways that seemingly destabilize the values and perspectives of Marxism and historical materialism and supposedly undercut and displace the mobilizations and politics of a "progressive" past orchestrated by class as both an historical presence and a preeminent category of analysis. While this is a period of intense restructuring, both the shifting structural content and much-discussed new political meaning of what has happened of late is more apparent than real. In spite of the absolute failure of a plethora of new theorists and theories to come up with an appropriate politics of resistance in this much-proclaimed crucible of change, the exodus from the theory and practice of orthodox Marxism is pronounced.[63] Many have found their way to discourse.

Once there, they often refuse what Elizabeth Fox Genovese and Eugene D. Genovese, starting with Marx, have recently chosen to emphasize:

> "Men," and women, we should add, "make their history, but not under conditions of their own choosing." So, also do they live their politics. The languages in which they express their political convictions and in which they mobilize their fellows, like the forms through whch they enact their political passions and the political goals they seek to secure, are all hostage to the social relations in which they are reared and live. . . . the language of politics articulates social relations and, in so doing, can reformulate their representation; but it is never severed from its social moorings.[64]

Those who, in their descent into discourse, exhibit little concern with this historically materialist form of reasoning are also unusually unconcerned with the tensions that encase a politics articulated within the reification of language. Pierre Bourdieu's implicit warning to those captivated by discourse falls too often on deaf ears:

> The dominant language discredits and destroys the spontaneous political discourse of the dominated. It leaves them only silence or a borrowed language, whose logic departs from that of popular usage but without becoming that of erudite usage, a deranged language, in which the "fine words" are only there to mark the dignity of the expressive intention, and which, unable to express anything true, real, or "felt" dispossesses the speaker of the very experience it is supposed to express. . . . This suspicion of the political "stage," a "theatre" whose rules are not understood and which leaves ordinary taste with a sense of helplessness, is often the source of "apathy" and of a generalized distrust of all forms of speech and spokesmen. And often the only escape from ambivalence or indeterminacy towards language is to fall back on what one *can* appreciate, the body rather than words, substance rather than form, an honest face rather than a smooth tongue.[65]

Those championing a new interpretive politics for social history, in which language is elevated to unprecedented heights of influence and authority, seldom pause to consider such thoughts. Instead they offer social history their own program: simplistic denial of the base/super-structure distinction; unproblematic reification of language as non-referential and autonomous; refusal of any center that might, in however nuanced a manner, draw lines of separation between substance and form. This program has a smooth tongue, too smooth.

Notes

Preface

1. See Peter Novick, *That Noble Dream: The "Objectivity Question" and the American Historical Profession* (New York: Cambridge University Press, 1988), pp. 178–180, 440–445. For one assault on social history see Gertrude Himmelfarb, *The New History and the Old: Critical Essays and Reappraisals* (Cambridge: Harvard University Press, 1987).

2. See Lawrence Stone, "Whigs, Marxists, and Poachers," *New York Review of Books* 23 (5 February 1976); Stone, "The Revival of the Narrative: Reflections on a New Old History,: *Past & Present* 85 (November 1979).

3. Lawrence Stone, letter to *Harper's* 268 (June 1984): 4–5, responding to Gertrude Himmelfarb, "Denigrating the Rule of Reason: The 'New History' Goes Bottom-Up," *Harper's* 268 (April 1984): 88, and quoted in Novick, *That Noble Dream*, p. 610.

4. Peter Dews, *The Logics of Disintegration: Post-structuralist Thought and the Claims of Critical Theory* (London: Verso, 1987).

5. See Arthur Kroker and David Cook, *The Postmodern Scene: Excremental Culture and Hyper-Aesthetics* (Montreal: New World Perspectives, 1987). This book is not concerned with postmodernism, as a *condition* of contemporary history, except insofar as the ostensibly postmodern scene is paralleled in the realm of "theory" by poststructuralism. I take poststructuralism to be the ideology of postmodernism, and it is the impact of this theoretical implosion on the writing of social history that is addressed in what follows.

Chapter 1

1. Edward W. Said, *Beginnings: Intention and Method* (New York: Basic Books, 1975), p. xiii.

2. Gareth Stedman Jones, *Languages of Class: Studies in English Working-Class History, 1832–1982* (Cambridge: Cambridge University Press, 1983), p. 20.

3. See Richard Rorty, ed., *The Linguistic Turn: Recent Essays in Philosophical Method* (Chicago: University of Chicago Press, 1967).

4. Roland Barthes, "Why I Love Benveniste," in Roland Barthes, *The Rustle of Language*, trans. by Richard Howard (New York: Hill & Wang, 1986), p. 162.

5. Malcolm Bradbury, *Mensonge: Structuralism's Hidden Hero* (London: Andre Deutsch, 1987), pp. 1, 5, 21–22.

6. Stedman Jones, *Languages of Class*, pp. 22, 24.

7. Patrick Joyce, "The Historical Meanings of Work: An Introduction," in Joyce, ed., *The Historical Meanings of Work* (Cambridge: Cambridge University Press, 1987), p. 13. Note the special issue of the *Radical History Review* 34 (January 1986), entitled "Language, Work and Ideology."

8. As a term *discourse* has long been used by historians in a descriptive way and will continue to be so used. See, for instance, E. P. Thompson, "The Poverty of Theory: or an Orrery of Errors," in Thompson, *The Poverty of Theory and Other Essays* (London: Merlin, 1978); and Thompson, "The Politics of Theory," in Raphael Samuel, ed., *People's History and Socialist Theory* (London: Routledge & Kegan Paul, 1981), pp. 403, 406–407.

9. See, among many others: Peter Wagner, "The Discourse on Sex—or Sex as Discourse: Eighteenth-Century Medical and Paramedical Erotica," in G. S. Rousseau and Roy Porter, eds., *Sexual Underworlds of the Enlightenment* (Chapel Hill: University of North Carolina Press, 1988), pp. 46–68; Roy Porter, "The Language of Quackery in England, 1660–1800," in Peter Burke and Roy Porter, eds., *The Social History of Language* (Cambridge: Cambridge University Press, 1987), pp. 73–103; Robert Gray, "The Languages of Factory Reform in Britain, c. 1830–1860," in Joyce, ed., *Historical Meanings of Work*, pp. 143–179; John Dwyer, *Virtuous Discourse: Sensibility and Community in Late Eighteenth-Century Scotland* (Edinburgh: John Donald, 1987); Donald Reid, "Industrial Paternalism: Discourse and Practice in Nineteenth-Century French Mining and Metallurgy," *Comparative Studies in Society and History* 27 (1985): 579–607; Christopher Lloyd, "The Discourse of Social History," in Lloyd, *Explanation in Social History* (Oxford: Basil Blackwell, 1986), pp. 3–5.

10. For another comment on this process see Jean Baudrillard, *Forget Foucault* (New York: Foreign Agents/Semiotext[e], 1987), pp. 126–129.

11. Karl Marx and Frederick Engels, "Manifesto of the Communist Party," *Selected Works* (Moscow: Progress, 1968), p. 38.

12. See Robert Paul Wolff, *Moneybags Must Be So Lucky: On the Literary Structure of Capital* (Amherst: University of Massachusetts Press, 1988), pp. 52–53.

13. Quoted in Marshall Berman, *All That Is Solid Melts into Air: The Experience of Modernity* (New York: Simon and Schuster, 1982), p. 22.

14. Allan Megill, *Prophets of Extremity: Nietzsche, Heidegger, Foucault, Derrida* (Berkeley: University of California Press, 1985), pp. 2–3; Raman Selden, *A Reader's Guide to Contemporary Literary Theory* (Lexington: University Press of Kentucky, 1985), pp. 91, 98, 100; Said, *Beginnings*, p. 66; Michael Sprinker, *Imaginary Relations: Aesthetics and Ideology in the Theory of Historical Materialism* (London: Verso, 1987), pp. 72–92.

15. Note especially Tracy B. Strong, "Language and Nihilism: Nietzsche's Critique of Epistemology," in Michael Shapiro, ed., *Language and Politics: Readings in Social and Political Theory* (Oxford: Basil Blackwell, 1984), p. 83

16. J. G. Merquior, *From Prague to Paris: A Critique of Structuralist and Post-Structuralist Thought* (London: Verso, 1986), pp. 258–259.

17. Saussure is discussed in virtually every text dealing with the development of linguistics, literary theory, and structuralism/poststructuralism. The following draws upon Ferdinand de Saussure, *Course in General Linguistics* (Toronto: McGraw-Hill, 1966); Jonathan Culler, *Ferdinand de Saussure* (Ithaca, N.Y.: Cornell University Press, 1986); Selden, *Contemporary Literary Theory,* pp. 53–57; Kaja Silverman, *The Subject of Semiotics* (New York: Oxford University Press, 1983), pp. 4–14; Robert Scholes, *Structuralism in Literature: An Introduction* (New Haven, Conn.: Yale University Press, 1974), pp. 9–18; James A. Boon, "Saussure/Pierce à propos Language, Society, and Culture," in Irene Portis Winner and Jean Umiker-Sebeok, eds., *Semiotics of Culture* (New York: Mouton, 1979), pp. 83–102; and Michael Lane, ed., *Structuralism: A Reader* (London: Jonathan Cape, 1970), pp. 43–56, 85–123. Saussure's major writings, rarely read, included his 1881 doctoral dissertation, *On the Use of the Genitive Absolute in Sanskrit,* a rigorously synchronic study, and a more diachronic work, still referred to today, *Mémoire sur le système primitif des voyelles en indo-européen* (1878), published when Saussure was twenty-one. For these texts, their relation and importance, see Calvert Watkins, "Language and Its History," in Einar Haugen and Morton Bloomfield, eds., *Language as a Human Problem* (New York: Norton, 1974), pp. 89–90.

18. See, for instance, Hans Aarsleff, *The Study of Language in England, 1780–1860* (Princeton, N.J.: Princeton University Press, 1967), p. 127; Culler, *Saussure,* pp. 70–71; Holger Pedersen, *The Discovery of Language: Linguistic Science in the Nineteenth Century* (Bloomington: Indiana University Press, 1962).

19. Perry Anderson, *In the Tracks of Historical Materialism* (Chicago: University of Chicago Press, 1984), p. 45, is one of the few texts to make this point.

20. Fredric Jameson, *The Prison-House of Language: A Critical Account of Structuralism and Russian Formalism* (Princeton, N.J.: Princeton University Press, 1972), pp. 5–6, 18; Culler, *Saussure,* pp. 45–46.

21. Sebastiano Timpanaro, *On Materialism* (London: Verso, 1976), pp. 135–158; Anderson, *Tracks of Historical Materialism,* pp. 40–45.

22. Raymond Williams, *Keywords: A Vocabulary of Culture and Society* (London: Fontana, 1988), pp. 138–139. More generally see Kenneth Burke, "Formalist Criticism: Its Principles and Limits," in *Language as Symbolic Action: Essays on Life, Literature and Method* (Berkeley: University of California Press, 1966), pp. 408–506.

23. Leon Trotsky, *Literature and Revolution* (New York: Russell & Russell, n.d., original 1924); Robert A. Maguire, *Red Virgin Soil: Soviet Literature in the 1920s* (Princeton, N.J.: Princeton University Press, 1968). For background cf. Jameson, *Prison-House of Language;* and, on the openness of the early Bolshevik tradition on matters of art/literature, Terry Eagleton, *Marxism and Literary Criticism* (Berkeley: University of California Press, 1976).

24. Trotsky, *Literature and Revolution,* p. 180. A useful overview of Russian formalism is found in John Frow, *Marxism and Literary History* (Cambridge: Harvard University Press, 1986), pp. 83–102. Cf. Christopher Pike, ed., *The Futurists, the Formalists, and the Marxist Critique* (London: Ink Links, 1979).

25. For a right-wing discussion of the importance of language in consolidat-

ing a "totalitarian" state in the Soviet Union see Mikhail Heller, *Cogs in the Soviet Wheel: The Formation of Soviet Man* (London: Collins Harvill, 1988), pp. 266–297.

26. Robert H. Stacy, *Russian Literary Criticism: A Short History* (Syracuse, N.Y.: Syracuse University Press, 1974), presents a view of the formalists (pp. 163–184) and of Marxist and Soviet criticism (pp. 185–230).

27. Leon Trotsky, *My Life: An Attempt at an Autobiography* (New York: Pathfinder, 1970), p. 564. For a useful discussion of Trotsky and Voronskii, which stresses their parallel histories rather than any overt political links, see Maguire, *Red Virgin Soil*, pp. 417–445.

28. See P. N. Medvedev and M. M. Bakhtin, *The Formal Method in Literary Scholarship* (Baltimore: Johns Hopkins University Press, 1978, original 1928); Pike, ed., *The Futurists, the Formalists, and the Marxist Critique*; Dominick LaCapra, "Bakhtin, Marxism, and the Carnivalesque," in LaCapra, *Rethinking Intellectual History: Texts, Contexts, Language* (Ithaca, N.Y.: Cornell University Press, 1983), esp. pp. 306–309.

29. For brief and useful introductions to the Bakhtin circle's critique of Saussure see Terry Eagleton, *Literary Theory: An Introduction* (Minneapolis: University of Minnesota Press, 1983), pp. 116–118; John Foster, "The Declassing of Language," *New Left Review*, 150 (March/April 1985): 38–40; Selden, *Contemporary Literary Theory*, pp. 16–17.

30. V. N. Volosinov, *Marxism and the Philosophy of Language* (Cambridge: Harvard University Press, 1973), p. 23. Volosinov and the contribution of this text, supposedly at least partly authored by Bakhtin, are discussed in Raymond Williams, *Marxism and Literature* (Oxford: Oxford University Press, 1977), pp. 35–43. At least one contemporary non-Marxist literary critic distances himself from the entire trajectory of linguistic/discourse theory in the twentieth century in ways that are reminiscent of Volosinov-Bakhtin. See Philip Hobsbaum, *Theory of Criticism* (Bloomington: Indiana University Press, 1970), p. 194: "It must now be apparent that what I am objecting to is not a theory of language alone, but a whole mode of discussion of language. There is a basic and ill-concealed assumption in linguistic studies that language operates homogeneously."

31. See Joseph Stalin, *Marxism and Linguistics* (New York: International, 1951), a text "in the making" in the discussions of linguistics in the late 1920s and 1930s. It would betray a theological approach to language, articulated in Genesis 11:6: "And the Lord said, Behold, the people is one, and they have all one language; and this they begin to do: and now nothing will be restrained from them, which they have imagined to do." Quoted in David Sless, *In Search of Semiotics* (London: Croom Helm, 1986), p. 1. As LaCapra argues, Bakhtin grew increasingly estranged from the Stalinist regime and his *Rabelais and His World*, submitted as a dissertation in 1940 and published only in 1965, can be read as a hidden polemic against the degeneration of revolutionary Marxism within the Soviet Union. What LaCapra bypasses is the relatively late date at which the Bakhtin circle "arrived," insuring that it remained isolated from the politics of a Trotskyist left opposition and structuring the Bakhtinian project toward what LaCapra rightly labels a "strategic populism." See "Bakhtin, Marx-

ism, and the Carnivalesque," in LaCapra, *Rethinking Intellectual History*, pp. 319–323. On Bakhtin's western rehabilitation see, as well as LaCapra: Ken Hirschkop, "Bakhtin, Discourse, and Democracy," *New Left Review* 160 (November–December 1986): 92–113; Tzvetan Todorov, *The Dialogic Imagination* (Austin: University of Texas Press, 1981); Natalie Zemon Davis, "The Reasons of Misrule," in Davis, *Society and Culture in Early Modern France* (Stanford, Calif.: Stanford University Press, 1975), pp. 97–123. Given the non-Marxist use of Bakhtin in most of this work, there are some interesting comments in Terry Eagleton, *Walter Benjamin; or Towards a Revolutionary Criticism* (London: Verso, 1981), esp. pp. 141–151. Volosinov's fate is mentioned in passing in Williams, *Marxism and Literature*, p. 35.

32. It is surprising how little is actually known of Jakobson's coming to Prague, but there is little doubt that his decision to relinquish involvement in the revolutionary project was made quite early. Professor Lubomir Dolezel of the University of Toronto's Centre for Comparative Literature, now working on a chapter on the Prague school for the Cambridge history of literary criticism, notes: "To my knowledge, Jakobson came to Prague as interpreter of the first Soviet trade mission to Czechoslovakia. I assume that he was qualified for this function by his studies of Slavic philology in Moscow. Shortly after his arrival Jakobson decided not to return to Soviet Russia and was ultimately appointed professor at the University of Brno." Dolezel to Palmer, 28 November 1988.

33. I use this term rather loosely, but also advisedly. Jakobson was apparently denounced as a Trotskyist by a Czech Stalinist in the 1950s, a charge without political substance.

34. On Jakobson and phonology see Ronald Schleifer, *A. J. Greimas and the Nature of Meaning: Linguistics, Semiotics, and Discourse Theory* (Lincoln: University of Nebraska Press, 1987), pp. 23–26, 48–50; Watkins, "Language and Its History," p. 90, the latter stressing Jakobson's phonological revision of Saussure's antinomy between synchrony and diachrony in a way that lent new rigidity to linguistic structuralism. This point is also developed in Simon Clarke, *The Foundations of Structuralism: A Critique of Lévi-Strauss and the Structuralism Movement* (Sussex: Harvester Press, 1981), pp. 145–156.

35. The above paragraphs draw on the insights and arguments of Merquior, *From Prague to Paris*, pp. 19–33. For other accounts, which treat Jakobson and Mukarovsky differently, see Eagleton, *Literary Theory*, pp. 98–100; Selden, *Contemporary Literary Theory*, pp. 14–16; Frow, *Marxism and Literary History*, pp. 94–96; F. W. Galan, *Historic Structures: The Prague School Project, 1928–1946* (Austin: University of Texas Press, 1985).

36. All of this has led Raman Selden to argue that Mukarovsky "marks a decisive shift towards a sociological explanation of the literary system," and J. G. Merquior to claim that Mukarovsky's mature suppression of formalism constituted a "socio-semantics." See Selden, *Criticism and Objectivity* (London: Allen & Unwin, 1984), pp. 61–62; Merquior, *From Prague to Paris*, p. 27.

37. Merquior, *From Prague to Paris*, p. 29.

38. The linguistic and anthropological coupling that produced structuralism is universally acknowledged. See Clarke, *The Foundations of Structuralism*, esp. pp. 117–183; Merquior, *From Prague to Paris*, pp. 35–106; Anderson, *Tracks*

of Historical Materialism, pp. 40–53; and the explicit reprintings of some early key texts in Claude Lévi-Strauss, *Structural Anthropology* (New York: Basic books, 1963), pp. 31–97.

39. G. Charbonnier, *Conversations with Claude Lévi-Strauss* (London: Jonathan Cape, 1973), p. 154.

40. Saussure, *Course in General Linguistics*, p. 80.

41. Cited in Peter Caws, "What is Structuralism?" in E. Nelson Hayes and Tanya Hayes, eds., *Claude Lévi-Strauss: The Anthropologist as Hero* (Cambridge: The MIT Press, 1970), pp. 199–200. Note, as well, the statement in Claude Lévi-Strauss, *Totemism* (Boston: Beacon Press, 1963), p. 100: "The advent of culture thus coincides with the birth of the intellect."

42. See esp., Merquior, *From Prague to Paris*, pp. 40–44.

43. Claude Lévi-Strauss, *The Savage Mind* (Chicago: University of Chicago Press, 1973), p. 252. Cf. Wesley Morris, *Friday's Footprint: Structuralism and the Articulated Text* (Columbus: Ohio State University Press, 1979), p. 217.

44. Lévi-Strauss, *Totemism*, p. 91.

45. Claude Lévi-Strauss, *The Raw and the Cooked: Introduction to a Science of Mythology*, vol. 1 (New York: Harper & Row, 1975), pp. 10, 13.

46. Claude Lévi-Strauss, *From Honey to Ashes: Introduction to a Science of Mythology*, vol. 2 (New York: Harper & Row, 1973), p. 475; Lévi-Strauss, *Savage Mind*, p. 262. Cf. Lévi-Strauss, *The Scope of Anthropology* (London: Jonathan Cape, 1971), esp. pp. 24–25; Anderson, *Tracks of Historical Materialism*, pp. 45–51; Merquior, *From Prague to Paris*, pp. 68–74, 88–106.

47. Claude Lévi-Strauss, "Language and the Analysis of Social Laws," in *Structural Anthropology*, pp. 57, 61.

48. The quote from Said is taken from *Beginnings*, p. 315.

49. See Umberto Eco, *A Theory of Semiotics* (Bloomington: Indiana University Press, 1976); Silverman, *The Subject of Semiotics*, esp. pp. 14–25; Eagleton, *Literary Theory*, pp. 100–104; Irene Portis Winner and Jean Umiker-Sebeok, eds., *Semiotics of Culture* (New York: Mouton, 1979), esp. pp. 75–82; David Sless, *In Search of Semiotics* (London: Croom Helm, 1986); Robert Scholes, *Semiotics and Interpretation* (New Haven, Conn.: Yale University Press, 1982); Stuart Hall, Dorothy Hobson, Andrew Lowe, and Paul Willis, eds., *Culture, Media, Language* (London: Hutchinson, 1982).

50. See, for instance, Anderson, *Tracks of Historical Materialism*, p. 57; Tony Judt, *Marxism and the French Left: Studies on Labour and Politics in France, 1830–1981* (Oxford: Oxford University Press, 1986), p. 189.

51. Quoted in Stuart Hall, "Notes on Deconstructing 'the Popular,'" in Samuel, ed., *People's History and Socialist Theory*, p. 236.

52. Jonathan Culler, *Structuralist Poetics: Structuralism, Linguistics, and the Study of Literature* (Ithaca, N.Y.: Cornell University Press, 1975), p. 4.

53. See Merquior, *From Prague to Paris*, pp. 107–120; Frank Lentricchia, *After the New Criticism* (Chicago: University of Chicago Press, 1980), pp. 132–141.

54. Roland Barthes, *Mythologies* (London: Jonathan Cape, 1972), pp. 143, 147, 151.

55. See, for instance, Bryan D. Palmer, "Reform Thought and the Producer

Ideology," in *A Culture in Conflict: Skilled Workers and Industrial Capitalism in Hamilton, Ontario, 1860–1914* (Montreal: McGill-Queen's University Press, 1979), pp. 97–122.

56. Merquoir, *From Prague to Paris*, p. 117.

57. Lentricchia, *After the New Criticism*, p. 132. Note, as well, Edward Said, *The World, the Text, and the Critic* (Cambridge: Cambridge University Press, 1983), pp. 23–25; Said, "Opponents, Audiences, Constituencies, and Community," *Critical Inquiry*, 9 (September 1982): 1–26.

58. Note Barthes, *Mythologies*, pp. 109, 110–111, 112, and the passage quoted, on p. 135.

59. Roland Barthes, "Myth Today," originally in *Mythologies*, but reprinted in Susan Sontag, ed., *A Barthes Reader* (New York: Hill & Wang, 1982), pp. 93–157, with the quote appearing on pp. 96–97 and the *Paris-Match* analysis on pp. 101–114.

60. Merquior, *From Prague to Paris*, pp. 124–125; Georges Mounin, *Introduction à la Semiologie* (Paris: Minuit, 1970), pp. 194–195. For other general treatments of Barthes that do not necessarily raise this kind of issue see Silverman, *The Subject of Semiotics*, pp. 25–32; Jonathan Culler, *Barthes* (London: Fontana, 1983; John Sturrock, ed., *Structuralism and Since: From Lévi-Strauss to Derrida* (New York: Oxford University Press), pp. 52–80. Merquior concludes, with characteristic uncharitability: "Instead of taking language as the richest province in the land of signs, he mistook all the other provinces for what they are not: languages, that is, territories of coded sign units dominated by manifest conventional meaning. When all is said and done, Barthes was a very gifted semiologist who had no clear idea of what he was doing." More charitable is Jameson, *Prison-House of Language*, pp. 147, 159.

61. Samples of Barthes's writing from this period are found in Sontag, ed., *A Barthes Reader*, pp. 169–313; and scattered throughout Roland Barthes, *The Rustle of Language* (New York: Hill & Wang, 1986).

62. Quoted in Lentricchia, *After the New Criticism*, p. 141. Note, as well, Culler, *Structuralist Poetics*, pp. 264–265.

63. Roland Barthes, "Authors and Writers," in Sontag, ed., *A Barthes Reader*, pp. 185–193; Barthes, "The Death of the Author," *The Rustle of Language*, pp. 49–55.

64. I am unrepentantly unconcerned with a "deep" reading of *S/Z* here, leaving that for others. Merquoir, *From Prague to Paris*, pp. 128–147, offers a merciless demolition; and the comments of Barbara Johnson, *The Critical Difference: Essays in the Contemorary Rhetoric of Reading* (Baltimore: Johns Hopkins University Press, 1980), pp. 9–11, are notable. More deferential and descriptive of Barthes's scrutiny of Balzac is Silverman, *The Subject of Semiotics*, pp. 237–283. My own tastes, not surprisingly, run toward the more orthodox. See George Lukacs, *Studies in European Realism* (New York: Grossett and Dunlap, 1964), pp. 1–96.

65. Roland Barthes, *S/Z* (London: Jonathan Cape, 1975); Merquoir, *From Prague to Paris*, pp. 129, 131.

66. *Roland Barthes par Roland Barthes* (Paris: Seuil, 1975); Barthes, *The Pleasure of the Text* (London: Jonathan Cape, 1976); Merquior, *From Prague to*

Paris, pp. 148–162. Cf. Roland Champagne, *Literary History in the Wake of Roland Barthes: Re-defining the Myths of Reading* (Birmingham, Ala.: Summa Publications, 1984).

67. Merquior, *From Prague to Paris*, esp. pp. 175, 188. Cf. Philip Thody, *Roland Barthes: A Conservative Estimate* (London: Macmillan, 1977), p. 132; Culler, *Structuralist Poetics*, pp. 39–40, 264–265; Eagleton, *Literary Theory*, pp. 141–142. For a more sympathetic assessment see Annette Lavers, *Roland Barthes: Structuralism and After* (Cambridge: Harvard University Press, 1982).

68. I pay less attention to Althusserian Marxism here than some would like because (a) it has less direct relevance to the linguistic turn than other theoretical developments and (b) it has already been thoroughly debated and counterdebated. The obvious texts are Thompson, "The Poverty of Theory"; and, for rejoinders: Paul Q. Hirst, "The Necessity of Theory—A Critique of E. P. Thompson's *The Poverty of Theory*," in Hirst, *Marxism and Historical Writing* (London: Routledge & Kegan Paul, 1985), pp. 57–90; Perry Anderson, *Arguments Within English Marxism* (London: Verso, 1980); the contributions of Eagleton and others in *Literature and History* 5 (Autumn 1979): 139–164, which represent the tip of the iceberg. Regarding Althusser's difference from those whose descent into discourse is outlined below, note the views of Judt, *Marxism and the French Left*, pp. 191–192, which correspond with my own. For an introduction to the Parisian milieu of this moment see H. Stuart Hughes, *Sophisticated Rebels: The Political Culture of European Dissent, 1968–1987* (Cambridge: Harvard University Press, 1988), pp. 15–33.

69. For a succinct introduction to this Marx-Lenin differentiation see "Ideology," in Tom Bottomore, ed., *A Dictionary of Marxist Thought* (Cambridge: Harvard University Press, 1983), pp. 219–223.

70. See, among many other studies, Harold Mah, *The End of Philosophy, the Origin of "Ideology": Karl Marx and the Crisis of the Young Hegelians* (Berkeley: University of California Press, 1987).

71. See, for instance, Louis Althusser, *For Marx* (London: Verso, 1979); and the much heralded Althusser, "Ideology and Ideological State Apparatuses," in *Lenin and Philosophy* (New York: Monthly Review, 1971).

72. Althusser, *Lenin and Philosophy*, p. 162; and quoted in Frow, *Marxism and Literary History*, p. 57. See, as well, Alice A. Jardine, *Gynesis: Configurations of Woman and Modernity* (Ithaca, N.Y.: Cornell University Press, 1985), p. 125.

73. See Thompson, "The Poverty of Theory: or an Orrery of Errors"; Norman Geras, "Althusser's Marxism: An Assessment," in New Left Review, ed., *Western Marxism: A Critical Reader* (London: Verso, 1978), pp. 232–272.

74. Geras, "Althusser's Marxism," p. 266, 268.

75. See Althusser, *Reading Capital* (London: Verso, 1979), pp. 45, 103.

76. Michel Foucault, *The Order of Things: An Archaeology of the Human Sciences* (New York: Pantheon, 1970), p. xiv. Althusser offered up the same kind of denial. See "Foreword to the Italian Edition," *Reading Capital*, pp. 7–8.

77. This is argued clearly in Megill, *Prophets of Extremity*, pp. 190–192, but it also forms the substance of his entire useful discussion of Foucault, pp. 181–256.

78. Merquior, *From Prague to Paris*, p. 199. An insightful account of Foucault came to my attention after the completion of this manuscript: Peter Dews, *Logics of Disintegration: Post-structuralist Thought and the Claims of Critical Theory* (London: Verso, 1987), pp. 144–219.

79. Michel Foucault, *The Archaeology of Knowledge and the Discourse on Language* (New York: Pantheon, 1972), pp. 47–49. For a critical yet supportive reading of this text note Frow, *Marxism and Literary History*, pp. 72–82.

80. Foucault quoted in Richard Harland, *Superstructuralism: The Philosophy of Structuralism and Post-Structuralism* (London: Methuen, 1987), p. 112.

81. Merquior, *From Prague to Paris*, p. 196.

82. Michel Foucault, *The Birth of the Clinic: An Archaeology of Medical Perception* (London: Tavistock, 1973), p. xix.

83. Said, *The World, the Text, and the Critic*, p. 219, quoting Foucault. On Said and Foucault see Selden, *Contemporary Literary Theory*, pp. 98–102. For a gesture toward Barthes's anticipation of Foucault see Lentricchia, *After the New Criticism*, p. 196.

84. Michel Foucault, *Power/Knowledge: Selected Interviews and Other Writings*, ed. by Colin Gordon (New York: Pantheon, 1980), p. 193, quoted in Megill, *Prophets of Extremity*, p. 234.

85. Michel Foucault, *Discipline and Punish: The Birth of the Prison* (New York: Pantheon, 1977), p. 23.

86. Megill, *Prophets of Extremity*, pp. 240–241.

87. Foucault, *Archaeology of Knowledge*, p. 76; Foucault, ed., *I, Pierre Rivière, having slaughtered my mother, my sister, and my brother . . . : A Case of Parricide in the 19th Century* (New York: Pantheon, 1975), p. 10; Megill, *Prophets of Extremity*, pp. 231, 238.

88. The Chomsky-Foucault exchange took place on Dutch television and is briefly alluded to in Said, *The World, the Text, and the Critic*, pp. 245–247. Chomsky criticizes Foucault in *Language and Responsibility: Based on Conversations with Mitsou Ronat* (New York: Pantheon, 1979), pp. 74–80.

89. Michel Foucault, *Language, Counter-Memory, Practice: Selected Essays and Interviews*, ed., by Donald F. Bouchard (Ithaca, N.Y.: Cornell University Press, 1977), p. 231, quoted in Megill, *Prophets of Extremity*, p. 195.

90. Said, *The World, the Text, and the Critic*, pp. 219–220; Merquior, *From Prague to Paris*, p. 208.

91. See John Sturrock, ed., *Structuralism and Since: From Lévi-Strauss to Derrida* (New York: Oxford University Press, 1979), p. 91.

92. Terry Eagleton, *Against the Grain: Selected Essays* (London: Verso, 1986), p. 116.

93. For introductions see Silverman, *The Subject of Semiotics*, pp. 149–193; John Sturrock, ed., *Structuralism and Since*, pp. 116–153; Stuart Schneiderman, *Jacques Lacan: The Death of an Intellectual Hero* (Cambridge: Harvard University Press, 1983); Catherine Clément, *The Lives and Legends of Jacques Lacan* (New York: Columbia University Press, 1983); Catherine Belsey, *Critical Practice* (London: Methuen, 1980); Deborah Cameron, *Feminism and Linguistic Theory* (London: Macmillan Press, 1985), esp. pp. 95–96, 119–121. Again, although it came to my attention too late to influence these pages, the discussion

of Lacan in Dews, *Logics of Disintegration*, pp. 45–108, while difficult, is illuminating.

94. Juliet Flower MacCannell, *Figuring Lacan: Criticism and the Cultural Unconscious* (London: Croom Helm, 1986), p. 2.

95. Jacques Lacan, *Speech and Language in Psychoanalysis*, trans. by Anthony Wilden (Baltimore: Johns Hopkins University Press, 1968), pp. 7–8, 27, 32. Cf. Paul Ricoeur, *Freud and Philosophy: An Essay on Interpretation* (New Haven, Conn.: Yale University Press, 1970), pp. 395–396.

96. Jacques Lacan, "Function and Field of Speech and Language," quoted in Silverman, *The Subject of Semiotics*, p. 165. Note, as well, Clément, *Lives and Legends of Lacan*, p. 40.

97. Eagleton, *Literary Theory*, pp. 168–169; MacCannell, *Figuring Lacan*, pp. 123–126; J. Laplance and J. B. Pontalis, *The Language of Psycho-Analysis* (London: Hogarth Press, 1973), pp. 439–431.

98. Quoted in Dews, *Logics of Disintegration*, pp. 80–81.

99. Jacques Lacan, *Écrits: A Selection* (London: Tavistock, 1977), p. 154.

100. See, for instance, Eagleton, *Literary Theory*, pp. 168–69; Wesley Morris, *Friday's Footprint*, pp. 135–136; Merquior, *From Prague to Paris*, p. 150, drawing on Emile Benveniste, *Problems in General Linguistics* (Coral Gables, Fla.: University of Miami Press, 1971); and Anderson, *Tracks of Historical Materialism*, pp. 44–47.

101. Merquior, *From Paris to Prague*, p. 151.

102. Quoted in Dews, *Logics of Disintegration*, p. 63.

103. Clément, *Lives and Legends of Lacan*, pp. 32, 34, 44. Cf. Merquior, *From Prague to Paris*, p. 151, which stresses Lacan's early connection with surrealism. Note the more general statement in Clément, *The Weary Sons of Freud* (London: Verso, 1987).

104. Note the discussion in Louis Althusser, "Freud and Lacan," in *Lenin and Philosophy and Other Essays* (London: New Left Books, 1971), pp. 177–202.

105. See Clément, "The Ladies Way," *Lives and Legends of Lacan*, pp. 53–101, for an account of how some feminists read Lacan as misogynist and why this is mistaken. MacCannell provides a lucid and convincing reading of Lacan's contributions, especially as they relate to sexuality and the gender order in *Figuring Lacan*, esp. pp. 22–115. Kristeva is the site of some controversy. Her advocates seldom address the matter of her political degeneration. For a sympathetic placing of Kristeva see Jacqueline Rose, "Julia Kristeva—Take Two," in *Sexuality in the Field of Vision* (London: Verso, 1986), pp. 141–164, a text that also offers a positive view of Lacan in "Feminine Sexuality—Jacques Lacan and the *école freudienne*," pp. 49–82. There are brief and useful statements on Lacan in Jeffrey Weeks, *Sexuality and Its Discontents: Meanings, Myths, and Modern Sexualities* (London: Routledge & Kegan Paul, 1985), pp. 170–175; Rosemarie Tong, *Feminist Thought: A Comprehensive Introduction* (Boulder and San Francisco: Westview Press, 1989), pp. 220–222.

106. Lacan, *Speech and Language in Psychoanalysis*, pp. 57, 64.

107. Clément, *Lives and Legends of Lacan*, p. 204.

108. Clément, *Weary Sons of Freud*, p. 53.

109. This is not the place for an extended consideration. For one outsider's

view see Tariq Ali, *Street Fighting Years: An Autobiography of the Sixties* (Glasgow: Fontana, 1987), pp. 163–230. Note, as well, Joseph Hue, ed., *Mai 68: Les mouvements étudiants en France et dans le monde* (Paris: Bibliothèque de Documentation Internationale Contemporaine, 1988).

110. For Foucault, esp., note Megill, *Prophets of Extremity*, pp. 233–235.

111. Eagleton, *Literary Theory*, p. 142.

112. Anderson, *Tracks of Historical Materialism*, pp. 29, 57; Merquior, *From Prague to Paris*, pp. 192–194; Judt, *Marxism and the French Left*, pp. 195–198; Clement, *Lives and Legends of Lacan*, p. 16; Michel Foucault, "On Popular Justice: A Discussion with Maoists," in Foucault, *Power/Knowledge: Selected Interviews and Other Writings 1971–1977*, trans. by Colin Gordon (New York: Pantheon, 1980).

113. Quoted in Merquior, *From Prague to Paris*, p. 193.

114. I am stretching metaphor here. I obviously do not mean that Derrida "mastered" the personnel and politics of 1968. This matter has been addressed in Eagleton's review of Anderson's *Tracks of Historical Materialism*, reprinted in Eagleton, *Against the Grain*, pp. 89–98; and in Michael Sprinker, *Imaginary Relations: Aesthetics and Ideology in the Theory of Historical Materialism* (London: Verso, 1987), pp. 211–213. I simply mean to suggest that Derrida would take Parisian thought, so obviously decomposing by 1968, in new directions. This does *not* imply that Derrida would prove important to the politics of the Parisian left, which would find its own, more sordid, exits from the aftermath of 1968. Only that he would prove critical in the intellectual descent into discourse.

115. See Lentricchia, *After the New Criticism*, pp. 157–210; Christopher Norris, *Derrida* (London: Fontana, 1987), pp. 194–237; Edward Said, "The Problem of Textuality: Two Exemplary Positons," *Critical Inquiry* 4 (1978): 673–714.

116. See Dews, *Logics of Disintegration*, esp. pp. 11–19, and, for a more wide-ranging commentary on Derrida, pp. 1–44, 87–108.

117. All quotes from Jacques Derrida, "Structure, Sign, and Play in the Discourse of the Human Sciences," in Derrida, *Writing and Difference* (Chicago: University of Chicago Press, 1978), pp. 279–280, 291, 292.

118. Anderson, *Tracks of Historical Materialism*, p. 54. Derrida's biographer and erstwhile defender, Christopher Norris, *Derrida* (London: Fontana, 1987), pp. 139–141, points to the importance of these passages to Derrida's critical reception but chooses to argue that they fall "below the highest standards of Derridean rigour."

119. All quotes from Jacques Derrida, *On Grammatology*, trans. by Gayatria Chakrovorty Spivak (Baltimore: Johns Hopkins University Press, 1976), pp. 6, 8, 35, 93. Megill, *Prophets of Extremity*, pp. 285–290, suggests that in these texts Derrida comes as close as he ever does to elaborating a "thesis."

120. Note the comments in Lentricchia, *After the New Criticism*, pp. 174–176.

121. Derrida, *Of Grammatology*, esp. pp. 35, 41. The whole Derrida-Saussure confrontation is outlined nicely in Norris, *Derrida*, pp. 87–96.

122. Dews, *Logics of Disintegration*, pp. 10, 19. More sympathetic is Michael

Ryan, *Marxism and Deconstruction: A Critical Articulation* (Baltimore: Johns Hopkins University Press, 1982), esp. pp. 9–42.

123. Jonathan Culler, *The Pursuit of Signs: Semiotics, Literature, Deconstruction* (Ithaca, N.Y.: Cornell University Press, 1981), pp. 14–15; Geoffrey Thurley, *Counter Modernism in Current Critical Theory* (London: Macmillan, 1983), pp. 176, 200; Merquior, *From Prague to Paris*, pp. 211, 219.

124. See G. Douglas Atkins, *Reading Deconsruction: Deconstructive Reading* (Lexington: University of Kentucky Press, 1983), esp. pp. 20–21; T. K. Seung, *Structuralism and Hermeneutics* (New York: Columbia University Press, 1982), p. 130; Jim Merod, *The Political Responsibility of the Critic* (Ithaca, N.Y.: Cornell University Press, 1987), p. 31; Richard Harland, *Superstructuralism: The Philosophy of Structuralism and Post-Structuralism* (London: Methuen, 1987), pp. 146–147.

125. The major statement is Michael Ryan, *Marxism and Deconstruction: A Critical Articulation* (Baltimore: Johns Hopkins University Press, 1982). Note, as well, Gayatria Chakrovorty Spivak, *In Other Worlds: Essays in Cultural Politics* (New York: Methuen, 1987), esp. pp. 77–92, 118–133, 154–175. A forceful and thoroughly convincing response appears in Barbara Foley, "The Politics of Deconstruction," in Robert Con Davis and Ronald Schleifer, eds., *Rhetoric and Form: Deconstruction at Yale* (Norman: University of Oklahoma Press, 1985), pp. 113–134. Note as well the symposium on Marxism and deconstruction, which exposes the ideological anti-Marxism of some Yale deconstructionists, in *Rhetoric and Form*, pp. 75–100. Ryan's book is the subject of Eagleton's "Frère Jacques: The Politics of Deconstruction," in *Against the Grain*, pp. 79–88.

126. Foley, "The Politics of Deconstruction," pp. 122–133. Reinforcing Foley's point are the feminist deconstructionist comments on Marx and Derrida in Jardine, *Gynesis*, pp. 129–132. It is worth noting that French Derrideans are not drawn to the Ryan-Spivak position. See Nancy Fraser, "The French Derrideans: Politicizing Deconstruction or Deconstructing Politics," *New German Critique* 33 (Fall 1984): esp. 129.

127. Spivak, "Scattered Speculations on the Question of Value," and "Subaltern Studies: Deconstructing Historiography," in *In Other Worlds*, pp. 154–175, 205.

128. Ryan, *Marxism and Deconstruction*, esp. p. 197.

129. Foley, "The Politics of Deconstruction," esp. pp. 131–133. Note that Ryan's concluding chapters in *Marxism and Deconstruction* take up positions entirely congruent with the arguments in Ernesto Laclau and Chantal Mouffe, *Hegemony and Socialist Strategy: Towards a Radical Democratic Politics* (London: Verso, 1985), a text that espouses left pluralism openly and breaks with Marx.

130. Derrida has many influences, including Heidegger, but the Nietzschean legacy is striking. It is pilloried in Merquior, *From Prague to Paris*, pp. 189–260, and handled more sympathetically in Megill, *Prophets of Extremity*, pp. 257–338; Christopher Norris, *Deconstruction: Theory and Practice* (London: Methuen, 1982), pp. 56–72.

131. Note Lentricchia, *After the New Criticism*, pp. 157–177; Imre Salusins-zky, ed., "Interview with Edward Said" and "Interview with Frank Lentricchia," *Criticism in Society* (New York: Methuen, 1987), pp. 138–139, 206; Said, *The World, the Text, and the Critic*, pp. 178–225; Jameson, *Prison House of Language*, p. 186; Merod, *Political Responsibility of the Critic*, pp. 35–36; and Barbara Johnson's comments in Davis and Schleifer, eds., *Rhetoric and Form*, p. 78.

132. Jacques Derrida, *Positions* (Chicago: University of Chicago Press, 1981), pp. 74–75; Merod, *Political Responsibility of the Critic*, pp. 25–36. Ryan, *Marxism and Deconstruction*, pp. 43–46, cites approvingly instances of the Derrida-Marx relation.

133. Note Barbara Johnson, "Gender Theory and the Yale School," in Davis and Schleifer, eds., *Rhetoric and Form*, pp. 101–112; Gayatri Chakrovorty Spivak, "Displacement and the Discourse of Woman," in Mark Kruptnick, ed., *Displacement: Derrida and After* (Bloomington: Indiana University Press, 1987), pp. 169–195; Spivak, "Can the Subaltern Speak?" in Cary Nelson and Lawrence Grossberg, eds., *Marxism and the Interpretation of Culture* (Urbana and Chicago: University of Illinois Press, 1988), pp. 271–313; Spivak, "Love Me, Love My Ombre, Elle: Derrida's "La Carte Postale,'" *Diacritics* 14 (1984): 19–36. An entire double issue of the *Oxford Literary Review* 8 (Nos. 1–2, 1986) is given over to the theme of "Sexual Difference."

134. Harland, *Superstructuralism*, p. 136; Merquior, *From Prague to Paris*, pp. 219, 222.

135. Dews, *Logics of Disintegration*, p. 30. Even as sympathetic a reader of Derrida as Ryan, *Marxism and Deconstruction*, p. xiv, notes that since 1975 Derrida's writing has become "increasingly difficult, self-referential, and esoteric."

136. Derrida quoted in Richard Macksey and Eugenio Donato, eds., *Structuralist Controversy: The Languages of Criticism and the Sciences of Man* (Baltimore: Johns Hopkins University Press, 1972), p. 271.

137. Derrida quoted in Macksey and Donato, eds., *Structuralist Controversy*, p. 267.

138. Jacques Derrida, *The Archeology of the Frivolous: Reading Condillac*, trans. by John P. Leavey, Jr. (Lincoln: University of Nebraska Press, 1980), pp. 78, 110; Derrida, *Glas*, trans. by John P. Leavey, Jr., and Richard Rand (Lincoln: University of Nebraska Press, 1986); Derrida, *La carte postale de Socrate à Freud et au-dela* (Paris: Aubier-Flammarion, 1980); Derrida, *Of Grammatology*, p. 35.

139. This is not the place and I am not the person to take on this development. It is substantively dealt with in Lentricchia, *After the New Criticism*, esp. pp. 177–190, as an introduction, and in more detail in "Part Two—The American Scene: Four Exemplary Careers." Lentricchia's book is discussed in Eagleton, "The Idealism of American Criticism," *New Left Review* 127 (May–June 1981): 53–65. For mainstream criticism of the deconstructive turn note H. M. Abrams, "The Deconstructive Angel," *Critical Inquiry* 3 (Spring 1977): 425–438. For Stanley Fish see Fish, "Is There a Text in This Class?" in Hazard Adams and

Leroy Searle, *Critical Theory Since 1965* (Tallahassee: Florida State University Press, 1986), pp. 525–535, a useful collection of articles and extracts from a wide variety of discourse theorists; J. Timothy Bagwell, "The Reader as Author," *American Formalism and the Problem of Interpretation* (Houston, Tex.: Rice University Press, 1986), pp. 65–89. The Yale deconstructionists speak for themselves in David and Schleifer, eds., *Rhetoric and Form.* Cf. Said, *The World, the Text, and the Critic,* pp. 158–177.

140. Derrida's interview in *The Literary Review* 14 (April–May 1980) is alluded to twice in different essays in Eagleton's *Against the Grain,* pp. 54, 79, to make this point. The quote appears on the latter page. Merod, *The Political Responsibility of the Critic,* pp. 25–36, sees Derrida's recent public statements similarly.

141. Harland, *Superstructuralism,* esp. pp. 131–132, 141, although the whole text addresses this matter.

142. Some fascinating criticism inspired by deconstruction has appeared, in spite of the Yale school's stranglehold. See Robin Lydenberg, *Word Cultures: Radical Theory and Practice in William S. Burroughs' Fiction* (Urbana and Chicago: University of Illinois Press, 1987).

143. I do not agree with Dews's judgment that Derrida's influence was waning by the mid-1970s, although he is undoubtedly correct in seeing Derrida's work as increasingly routinized. See Dews, *Logics of Disintegration,* p. 93.

144. Paul de Man, *Blindness and Insight: Essays in the Rhetoric of Contemporary Criticism* (London: Methuen, 1983), p. 165; Lentricchia, *After the New Criticism,* p. 186; Lentricchia, *Criticism and Social Change* (Chicago: University of Chicago Press, 1983), p. 51; Gerald Graff, *Literature Against Itself: Literary Ideas in Modern Society* (Chicago: University of Chicago Press, 1979), esp. pp. 72–89; Merquior, *From Prague to Paris,* pp. 244–253; Andrew Wernick, "Structuralism and the Dislocation of the French Rationalist Project," in John Fekete, ed., *The Structual Allegory: Reconstructive Encounters with the New French Thought* (Minneapolis: University of Minnesota Press, 1984), p. 132.

145. Pierre Macherey, *A Theory of Literary Production* (London: Routledge & Kegal Paul, 1978), pp. 53, 67–68. Note "Macherey and Marxist Literary Theory," in Eagleton, *Against the Grain,* pp. 9–22.

146. Pierre Bourdieu, *Ce que parler veut dire: l'économie des échanges linguistiques* (Paris: Fayard, 1981), p. 38, translated and quoted in John B. Thompson, *Studies in the Theory of Ideology* (Berkeley: University of California Press, 1984), p. 58. Chapter 2 of this study, "Symbolic Violence: Language and Power in the Writings of Pierre Bourdieu," pp. 42–72, presents a useful discussion. See, as well, Bourdieu, *Distinction: A Social Critique of the Judgement of Taste* (Cambridge: Harvard University Press, 1984).

147. Edward Said, *Orientalism* (New York: Pantheon, 1978), pp. 23–24; Said, *The World, the Text, and the Critic,* pp. 4–5; "Interview with Edward Said," in Salusinszky, ed., *Criticism in Society,* pp. 122–149.

148. Lentricchia, *Criticism and Social Change;* Lentricchia, *After the New Criticism;* "Interview with Frank Lentricchia," in Salusinszky, ed., *Criticism in Society,* pp. 176–207, quote on p. 206. For a sample of Burke see Kenneth Burke, *The Philosophy of Literary Form: Studies in Symbolic Action* (New York:

Vintage, 1957). The Trotsky quote and the hearsay reference to a libel suit are found in Eagleton, *Against the Grain*, pp. 64, 83.

149. Merquior, *From Prague to Paris*, pp. 241, 253. For critical appreciations of Jameson see Eagleton, *Against the Grain*, pp. 49–78; Cornel West, "Ethics and Action in Fredric Jameson's Marxist Hermeneutics," in Jonathan Arac, ed., *Postmodernism and Politics* (Minneapolis: University of Minnesota Press, 1986), pp. 123–144; Merod, *Political Responsibility of the Critic*, esp. pp. 132–152; Frow, *Marxism and Literary History*, pp. 30–41; Michael Sprinker, *Imaginary Relations*, pp. 153–166.

150. Fredric Jameson, *Marxism and Form: Twentieth Century Dialectical Theories of Literature* (Princeton, N.J.: Princeton University Press, 1971), p. 415.

151. Jameson, *Prison-House of Language*, p. 216; Jameson, *The Political Unconscious: Narrative as a Socially Symbolic Act* (Ithaca, N.Y.: Cornell University Press, 1981), p. 9.

152. Note, for instance, Jameson, "Reification and Utopia in Mass Culture," *Social Text* 1 (1979): 130–148.

153. Fredric Jameson, "Cognitive Mapping," in Nelson and Grossberg, eds., *Marxism and the Interpretation of Culture*, p. 347.

154. The point is addressed in Eagleton, *Against the Grain*, pp. 49–78; West, "Ethics and Action in Fredric Jameson's Marxist Hermeneutics," pp. 123–144; and the quote is from Frow, *Marxism and Literary History*, p. 31. Note, as well, William C. Dowling, *Jameson, Althusser, Marx: An Introduction to the Political Unconscious* (Ithaca, N.Y.: Cornell University Press, 1984). The matter is also raised, more harshly and dismissively, in the ongoing work of Jerry Zaslove, currently engaged in writing a book on literacy, domination, and modernity. I have seen fragments of this work under the titles "The Production of Literate Culture: The Legacies of Formalism and the Dilemmas of Bureaucratic Literacy," in Michele Schiavione, ed., *Quaderno: Filosofia e Scienca Sociali, Nuove Perspetive* (Genoa, 1985), pp. 157–186, and "The Bureaucratization of Eros: Formalist Culture and the Spirit of Modernity—The Case of Literacy and Cultural Value," in Makota Ueda, ed., *Explorations: Essays in Comparative Literature* (New York and London: Lanham, 1986), pp. 326–379.

155. Jameson, *The Prison-House of Language*, p. vii, cited in Eagleton, *Literary Theory*, p. 97.

156. Jameson, *The Political Unconscious*, pp. 63–64, 299.

157. Ibid., p. 102.

158. Merod, *Political Responsibility of the Critic*, pp. 132–152, quote from p. 145.

159. Although not entirely in agreement with my position, see Janet Montefiore, "The Rhetoric of Experience: Eagleton's 'Literary Theory,'" *New Left Review* 145 (May–June 1984): 122–128. John Frow, *Marxism and Literary History*, pp. 31–50; West, "Jameson's Marxist Hermeneutics," in Arac, ed., *Postmodernism and Politics*, pp. 123–144. Eagleton and Jameson are of course quite different, as a reading of Eagleton's *Walter Benjamin; or Towards a Revolutionary Criticism* (London: Verso, 1981) would suggest. My point is that they share a common, if generalized, *space* that is a product of the limitations of the times,

their preoccupations, and their ambivalences regarding structuralist/poststructuralist theory. Note as well Catherine Belsey, *Critical Practice* (London: Methuen, 1980), a text more sympathetic to poststructuralist thought.

160. Compare K. S. Karol, "The Tragedy of the Althussers," *New Left Review* 124 (November–December 1980): 93–95, with the unforgivable discussion in Geraldine Finn, "Why Althusser Killed His Wife," *Canadian Forum* 61 (September–October 1981): 28–29.

161. Dews, *Logics of Disintegration*, p. xv.

162. The making of the de Man affair has seen coverage of the story in the *New York Times* and many other prominent journalistic organs, including the *Manchester Guardian* and major continental European newspapers. There have been conferences of the Deconstructionist Elect, Derrida present, that have discussed what exactly is to be done with the articles by de Man that appeared in *Le Soir*, Belgium's leading French-language newspaper under the Nazi occupation, and in the Flemish *Het Vlaamsche Land*. One article, in particular, can be read as an ugly piece of anti-Semitism. At best it is an opaque dance around the edges of overtly racist thought. De Man resigned from *Le Soir* late in 1942, but there is no question of his involvement in what can, with considerable charity, be judged a dubious, if not collaborationist project. A mere two months after de Man broke with the paper, *Le Soir*'s other main literary critic was assassinated by the Resistance, an indication that attachment to the journal was itself regarded publicly as a political act. The ultimate organ of high deconstruction, the *Oxford Literary Review*, seems to have been thrown into turmoil over the whole affair, promising publication of the articles in September 1987, failing to follow through, and now scheduling a French-only reprint. This material, along with responses to the whole affair from literary critics (most of whom are pro–de Man), is now presented in two volumes. See Werner Hamacher, Neil Hertz, and Tom Keenan, eds., *Wartime Journalism, 1939–1944*, by Paul de Man, and Hamacher, Hertz, and Keenan, eds., *Responses: On Paul de Man's Wartime Journalism* (Lincoln and London: University of Nebraska Press, 1988 and 1989, respectively). For the history of all this and its publishing, see James Atlas, "Paul De Man," *New York Times Magazine*, 28 August 1988, pp. 37, 60, 66, 68–69; "Ideas & Trends," *New York Times*, 17 July 1988, Section E, p. 6; the statements of Tzvetan Todorov and J. Hillis Miller, *Times Literary Supplement*, 17–23 June 1988, pp. 676, 685; Jon Wiener, "Deconstructing de Man," *Nation* 9 January 1988, pp. 22–24; Geoffrey Hartman, "Blindness and Insight: Paul de Man, Fascism, and Deconstruction," *New Republic*, 7 March 1988, pp. 27–31; Mark Edmundson, "A Will to Cultural Power: Deconstructing the de Man Scandal," *Harper's* 277 (July 1988): 67–71. De Man's "Literary History and Literary Modernity" appeared in his *Blindness and Insight*, pp. 142–165. For a pre-revelation treatment of de Man, Marxist and sympathetic, see Sprinker, *Imaginary Relations*, pp. 237–266. The more orthodox Marxist and radical hostility is evident in Eagleton, *Against the Grain*, pp. 137–138, 158, 160–161, 165; Lentricchia, *After the New Criticism*, pp. 310–11, 317; Lentricchia, *Criticism and Social Change*, pp. 38–52; Merquior, *From Prague to Paris*, pp. 228, 249–250, 255–256.

163. See Jacques Derrida, "Like the Sound of the Sea Deep within a Shell: Paul

de Man's War," *Critical Inquiry* 14 (Spring 1988): 590–652, which is addressed below in the conclusion.

164. Jacques Derrida, *De l'esprit: Heidegger et la question* (Paris, 1987), cited in Derrida, "Paul de Man's War," p. 600.

165. Heidegger's centrality to much of what is discussed above is argued in Megill, *Prophets of Extremity*, pp. 103–188, with the importance of Heidegger to Derrida noted on p. 269. Heidegger's collusion with the Nazis is noted on pp. 128–136, 137, 146, 174–175, 347, but the case of Heidegger's nazism has now been made with uncontestable vigor in Victor Farias's *Heidegger et le nazisme* (Lagrasse, France: Verdier, 1987), a text that is no doubt guilty of distortions but that makes it impossible to ignore Heidegger's fascism. See Thomas Sheehan, "Heidegger and the Nazis," *New York Review of Books* 35 (16 June 1988): 38–47; Michael Zimmerman, "*L'affaire* Heidegger," *Times Literary Supplement*, 7–13 October 1988, pp. 1115–1116.

166. Consider Peter Dews, "The *Nouvelle Philosophie* and Foucault," *Economy and Society* 8 (May 1979): 125–176.

167. Thompson, "The Poverty of Theory," pp. 193–397; Jameson, *The Political Unconscious*, pp. 36–37. Note Maria Antonietta Macciocchi, *Letters from Inside the Italian Communist Party to Louis Althusser* (London: New Left Books, 1973).

168. Clément, *Lives and Legends of Lacan*, p. 7.

Chapter 2

1. See, for instance, J. G. A. Pocock, *The Machiavellian Moment: Florentine Political Thought and the Atlantic Republican Tradition* (Princeton, N.J.: Princeton University Press, 1975); Nancy S. Streuver, *The Language of History in the Renaissance: Rhetoric and Historical Consciousness in Florentine Humanism* (Princeton, N.J.: Princeton University Press, 1970); Donald R. Kelley, *The Foundations of Modern Historical Scholarship: Language, Law, and History in the French Renaissance* (New York: Columbia University Press, 1970). Note, as well, John E. Toews, "Intellectual History after the Linguistic Turn: The Autonomy of Meaning and the Irreducibility of Experience," *American Historical Review* 92 (October 1987): 879–907; Martin Jay, "Should Intellectual History Take a Linguistic Turn? Reflections on the Habermas-Gadamer Debate," in Dominick LaCapra and Steven Kaplan, eds., *Modern European Intellectual History: Reappraisals and New Perspectives* (Ithaca, N.Y.: Cornell University Press, 1982), pp. 86–110.

2. For another assessment of this duo see Peter Novick, *That Noble Dream: The "Objectivity" Question and the American Historical Profession* (New York: Cambridge University Press, 1988), pp. 599–607. White and LaCapra figure centrally in Linda Hutcheon, "The Postmodern Problematizing of History," *English Studies in Canada* 14 (December 1988): 365–382.

3. Hayden White, "The Absurdist Moment in Contemporary Literary Theory," in White, *Tropics of Discourse: Essays in Cultural Criticism* (Baltimore: Johns Hopkins University Press, 1978), pp. 279–280. Note also "Foucault Decoded: Notes from Underground," in ibid., pp. 230–260.

4. See Hayden White, *The Content of the Form: Narrative Discourse and Historical Representation* (Baltimore: Johns Hopkins University Press, 1987), p. 201.

5. Dominick LaCapra, *History, Politics, and the Novel* (Ithaca, N.Y.: Cornell University Press, 1987), p. 206. It comes as no surprise to find that LaCapra's only moment of dissent concerning White's *Tropics of Discourse* is his antagonism to "The Absurdist Moment," which he labels "caricatural." See LaCapra, *Rethinking Intellectual History: Texts, Contexts, Language* (Ithaca, N.Y.: Cornell University Press, 1983), esp. pp. 78–81. This latter text is obviously an enthusiastic advocate of language in general and Derrida in particular. Note pp. 18–22, 126, 140.

6. Dominick LaCapra, *History and Criticism* (Ithaca, N.Y.: Cornell University Press, 1985), pp. 10–11.

7. LaCapra, *Rethinking Intellectual History*, pp. 18–19.

8. LaCapra, *History and Criticism*, pp. 10, 117–118, 93.

9. See, for instance, LaCapra, *Rethinking Intellectual History*, pp. 14, 18–19, 20, 34, 117.

10. LaCapra, *History and Criticism*, p. 80.

11. Ibid., p. 72, with the chapters on Ginzburg and *Mentalité* appearing on pp. 45–69 and 70–94.

12. As a mere introduction see John Clarke, Chas Critcher, and Richard Johnson, eds., *Working-Class Culture: Studies in History and Theory* (London: Hutchinson, 1979); the remarks of Raphael Samuel, Stuart Hall, Richard Johnson, and E. P. Thompson in "Culturalism: Debates around *The Poverty of Theory*," in Samuel, ed., *People's History and Socialist Theory* (London: Routledge & Kegan Paul, 1981), pp. 375–408; Richard Johnson, "Thompson, Genovese, and Socialist Humanist History," *History Workshop Journal* 6 (Autumn 1978): 79–100; Ian McKay, "History, Anthropology, and the Concept of Culture," *Labour/Le Travailleur* 8/9 (1981–82): 185–241; R. S. Neale, "Cultural Materialism: A Critique," in Neale, *Writing Marxist History: British Society, Economy & Culture since 1700* (Oxford: Basil Blackwell, 1985), pp. 255–280.

13. Note Elizabeth Fox-Genovese and Eugene D. Genovese, "The Political Crisis of Social History: A Marxian Perspective," *Journal of Social History* 10 (Winter 1976): 205–222; Tony Judt, "A Clown in Regal Purple," *History Workshop Journal* 7 (Spring 1979): 66–94; Lawrence McDonnell, " 'You are too sentimental': Suggestions for a New Labor History," *Journal of Social History* 17 (Summer 1984): 629–654.

14. For response to the Gutman volume note Michael Kazin, "The Historian as Populist," *New York Review of Books,* 12 May 1988, pp. 48–50; Melvyn Dubofsky, "Workers, Jews, and the American Past," *Tikkun* 3 (1988): 95–97.

15. Herbert G. Gutman, *Slavery and the Numbers Game: A Critique of "Time on the Cross"* (Urbana: University of Illinois Press, 1976). Cf. Pierre Vilar, "Marxist History, a History in the Making: Towards a Dialogue with Althusser," *New Left Review* 80 (1973): 101; Bryan D. Palmer, "Emperor Katz's New Clothes; or with the Wizard in Oz," *Labour/Le Travail* 13 (Spring 1984): 190–197.

16. The quotes from Marx-Engels come, respectively, from Engels to Borgius,

25 January 1894, quoted in Gerard Bekerman, *Marx and Engels: A Conceptual Concordance* (Oxford: Blackwell Reference, 1983), pp. 71–72; Marx to Annenkov, 28 December 1848, in *Marx-Engels: Selected Correspondence, 1846–1895* (New York: International Publishers, 1935), pp. 7–8; "Theses on Fuerbach," in Karl Marx and Frederick Engels, *Selected Works* (Moscow: Progress Publishers, 1968), pp. 28–29.

17. See Hayden White, *Metahistory: The Historical Imagination in Nineteenth-Century Europe* (Baltimore: Johns Hopkins University Press, 1973), pp. 320–327; White, *Tropics of Discourse*, pp. 15, 67–68; White, *The Content of the Form*, pp. 46–47, 101; LaCapra, *Rethinking Intellectual History*, pp. 268–290.

18. LaCapra, *Rethinking Intellectual History*, esp. pp. 284–285, 289–290; White, *The Content of the Form*, pp. 63–64.

19. Karl Marx, "The Eighteenth Brumaire of Louis Bonaparte," in Marx and Engels, *Selected Works*, p. 97. For but two examples of the importance of this passage see R. S. Neale, *Writing Marxist History*, p. 146; Gregory S. Kealey and Bryan D. Palmer, *"Dreaming of What Might Be": The Knights of Labor in Ontario, 1880–1900* (New York: Cambridge University Press, 1982), p. 23.

20. "It is not enough to say, as the French do, that their nation was taken unawares. A nation and a woman are not forgiven the unguarded hour in which the first adventurer that came along could violate them" and "He brought the bride home at last, but only after she had been prostituted" and "France has experienced a government of mistresses; but never before a government of *hommes entretenus*." From Marx, "Eighteenth Brumaire," pp. 101, 112, 180.

21. "As often as the confused noise of *parliament* grew silent during these recesses and its body dissolved in the nation, it became unmistakably clear that only one thing was still wanting to complete the true form of this republic: to make the *former's* recess permanent and replace the *latter's* inscription: Liberté, Égalité, Fraternité by the unambiguous words: Infantry, Cavalry, Artillery!" and "Even bourgeois liberalism is declared *socialistic*, bourgeois enlightenment socialistic, bourgeois financial reform socialistic. It was socialistic to build a railway, where a canal already existed, and it was socialistic to defend oneself with a cane when one was attacked with a rapier" and "Only theft can still save property; only perjury, religion; bastardy, the family; disorder, order!" From ibid., pp. 127, 131, 177.

22. Ibid., pp. 99, 102.

23. "The social revolution of the nineteenth century cannot draw its poetry from the past, but only from the future. It cannot begin with itself before it has stripped off all superstition in regard to the past. Earlier revolutions required recollections of past world history in order to drug themselves concerning their own content. In order to arrive at its own content, the revolution of the nineteenth century must let the dead bury their dead. There the phrase went beyond the content; here the content goes beyond the phrase." Ibid., p. 99.

24. Note Eric Williams, *Capitalism and Slavery* (New York: Capricorn Books, 1966; original, 1943); Walter Rodney, *How Europe Underdeveloped Africa* (Washington: Howard University Press, 1981; original, 1972).

25. Quoted in Ivan Illich, *Shadow Work* (Boston: Marion Boyars, 1981), p. 34. I am grateful to Colin Duncan for pointing out this account to me.

26. This is not the place for a critical appraisal of James's entire *oeuvre*, for which I have simultaneously a great deal of respect and not a little opposition. Paul Buhle is currently at work on an intellectual biography of James, and it will no doubt tell us a great deal, albeit in ways that are sympathetic to James's politics, in which a 1940s break from Trotskyism and Soviet defensism, articulated in the adoption of a view of Russia as state capitalist, figured centrally. James's major works include *The Black Jacobins: Toussaint L'Ouverture and the San Domingo Revolution* (New York: Vintage, 1963); *Mariners, Renegades, and Castaways: The Story of Herman Melville and the World We Live In* (London: Allison and Busby, 1985); *Notes on Dialectics: Hegel-Marx-Lenin* (London: Allison and Busby, 1980); and *State Capitalism and World Revolution* (Detroit: Facing Reality, 1969), all reprints. Selections from his writings also appear in *The Future as Present* (London: Allison and Busby, 1977); *Modern Politics: A Series of Lectures On the Subject Given at the Trinidad Public Library, in its Adult Education Program* (Detroit: Bewick/ed, 1973); and a special edition of *Radical America* 4 (May 1970). Commentary on James can be found in the invaluable "C. L. R. James: His Life and Work," *Urgent Tasks: Journal of the Revolutionary Left* 12 (Summer 1981); Cedric J. Robinson, *Black Marxism: The Making of the Black Radical Tradition* (London: Zed Press, 1983), esp. pp. 349–415; and in James D. Young, *Socialism Since 1889: A Biographical History* (London: Pinter, 1988), pp. 179–205. There is an important interview with James in Henry Abelove et al., eds., *Visions of History* (New York: Pantheon, 1983), pp. 263–278.

27. Note, esp., James, *Mariners, Renegades, and Castaways*, pp. 29, 35, 43, 51, 60, 86–87, 121.

28. One of the few critical commentaries on C. L. R. James, *Beyond a Boundary* (New York: Pantheon, 1983; original, 1963), is Sylvia Wynter, "In Quest of Matthew Bondsman: Some Cultural Notes on the Jamesian Journey," *Urgent Tasks: Journal of the Revolutionary Left* 12 (Summer 1981): 54–68.

29. Another leftist whose reach extends across colony and empire recalls the importance of cricket circa 1956: "A new language was entered in my tatty autograph book, which jostled uneasily with the likes of Hanif Mohammed and the three W's of West Indian cricket (Worrell, Weekes, and Walcott)." See Tariq Ali, *Street Fighting Years: An Autobiography of the Sixties* (London: Fontana, 1968), p. 14.

30. C. L. R. James, *Beyond a Boundary*, pp. 34–35, 52–53, 149–150.

31. Ibid., pp. 150–151, 168. For North American accounts see Roy Rozensweig, *Eight Hours for What We Will: Workers and Leisure in an Industrial City, 1870–1920* (New York: Cambridge University Press, 1983); Bryan D. Palmer, *A Culture in Conflict: Skilled Workers and Industrial Capitalism in Hamilton, Ontario, 1860–1914* (Montreal: McGill-Queen's University Press, 1979), esp. pp. 35–70; Alan Metcalfe, *Canada Learns to Play: The Emergence of Organized Sport, 1807–1914* (Toronto: McClelland and Stewart, 1987); Richard Gruneau, *Class, Sports, and Social Development* (Amherst: University of Massachusetts Press, 1983); Hart Cantelon and Richard Gruneau, eds., *Sport, Culture, and the Modern State* (Toronto: University of Toronto Press, 1982). James never collapses sport into some culturalist closure, a problem evident in some of this

North American work. See my review of the Rosenzweig volume and Francis G. Couvares, *The Remaking of Pittsburgh: Class and Culture in an Industrializing City, 1877–1919* (Albany: State University of New York Press, 1984), in *Social History* 10 (October 1985): 400–404.

32. James, *Beyond a Boundary*, pp. 71, xi–xiii.

33. Ibid., pp. 13–15, 49, 81–82.

34. Ibid., p. 41.

35. Ibid., pp. 241, 243.

36. Ibid. In an interview James cites the "Eighteenth Brumaire" passage: "Proletarian revolutions, like those of the nineteenth century, criticize themselves constantly, interrupt themselves continually in their own course, come back to the apparently accomplished in order to begin it afresh, deride with unmerciful thoroughness the inadequacies, weaknesses and paltriness of their first attempts, seem to throw down their adversary only in order that he may draw new strength from the earth and rise again." See "Interview," *Urgent Tasks: Journal of the Revolutionary Left* 12 (Summer 1981): 81.

37. The above two paragraphs draw on Ariel Dorfman, *The Empire's Old Clothes: What the Lone Ranger, Babar, and Other Innocent Heroes Do to Our Minds* (New York: Pantheon, 1983), pp. 3–13.

38. Ibid., quotes from pp. 63–64, 173.

39. Ibid., pp. 78–81

40. For convenience note the appropriate essays in Christopher Hill, *The Collected Essays of Christopher Hill: Volume I—Writing and Revolution in 17th Century England*, and *Volume III—People and Ideas in 17th Century England* (Amherst: University of Massachusetts Press, 1985); *The World Turned Upside Down: Radical Ideas During the English Revolution* (New York: Viking Press, 1972); *Milton and the English Revolution* (New York: Penguin, 1979).

41. They originally appeared in collections of essays but are conveniently reprinted as "The Language of 'Class' in Early Nineteenth-Century England" and "The Language of 'Mass' and 'Masses' in Nineteenth-Century England," in *The Collected Essays of Asa Briggs: Volume I—Words, Numbers, Places, People* (Urbana and Chicago: University of Illinois Press, 1985), pp. 3–33, 34–54.

42. "Preface," *ibid.*, p. xv.

43. Ibid., p. 45, quoting *Science Siftings*, 3 April 1897.

44. Raymond Williams, *The Country and the City* (Frogmore: Paladin, 1975), pp. 158–175, quote from 174. On Clare see as well Johanne Clare, *John Clare and the Bounds of Circumstance* (Montreal: McGill-Queen's University Press, 1987).

45. Raymond Williams, *Marxism and Literature* (Oxford: Oxford University Press, 1977), pp. 43–44.

46. See Terry Eagleton, "Resources for a Journey of Hope: The Significance of Raymond Williams," and Robin Blackburn, "Raymond Williams and the Politics of a New Left," in *New Left Review* 168 (March–April 1988): 3–23.

47. This occurs throughout Raymond Williams, *Politics and Letters: Interviews with New Left Review* (London: New Left Books, 1979).

48. Neale, *Writing Marxist History*, pp. 268, 279.

49. Even in terms of the relation of language and labor Neale may be overstating the case. See Len Doyal and Roger Harris, "The Practical Foundations of Human Understanding," *New Left Review* 139 (May–June 1983): 59–78.

50. For an appreciative note see Fred Inglis, *Radical Earnestness: English Social Theory, 1880–1980* (Oxford: Martin Robertson, 1982), pp. 169–184.

51. Williams, *Keywords* (London: Fontana, 1976), with the quote from Williams, *Politics and Letters*, pp. 176–177.

52. See Williams, *Problems in Materialism and Culture* (London: Verso, 1980), pp. 31–49, 121; *Marxism and Literature*, pp. 165–172, but more generally the entire book, with its discussions of basic concepts, cultural theory, and literary theory; *Culture* (Glasgow: Fontana, 1981), esp. pp. 87–118; *Writing in Society* (London: Verso, 1986).

53. What is surprising, indeed shocking, is the extent to which the contributions of Williams and Briggs have been ignored in a recent text that purports to introduce the social history of language. See Peter Burke and Roy Porter, eds., *The Social History of Language* (Cambridge: Cambridge University Press, 1987). Burke's "Introduction," pp. 1–20, fails to mention or cite either Williams or Briggs.

54. On the Thompson industry see, as a beginning only: Perry Anderson, *Arguments within English Marxism* (London: Verso, 1980); Bryan D. Palmer, *The Making of E. P. Thompson: Marxism, Humanism, and History* (Toronto: New Hogtown Press, 1981); Paul Q. Hirst, *Marxism and Historical Writing* (London: Routledge & Kegan Paul, 1985); Gregor McLennan, "E. P. Thompson and the Discipline of Historical Context," in Richard Johnson et al., eds., *Making Histories: Studies in History-Writing and Politics* (London: Hutchinson, 1982); Allan Dawley, "E. P. Thompson and the Peculiarities of the Americans," *Radical History Review* 19 (Winter 1978–1979): 33–60; F. K. Donnelly, "Ideology and Early English Working-Class History: Edward Thompson and His Critics," *Social History* 2 (May 1976): 219–238; Richard Johnson, "Thompson, Genovese, and Socialist-Humanist History," *History Workshop Journal* 6 (Autumn 1978): 79–100; Harvey J. Kaye, *The British Marxist Historians* (Cambridge: Polity Press, 1984), pp. 167–220; Craig Calhoun, *The Question of Class Struggle: Social Foundations of Popular Radicalism during the Industrial Revolution* (Chicago: University of Chicago Press, 1982).

55. Joan Scott's 1983 previously unpublished essay "Women in *The Making of the English Working Class*," has recently appeared in her *Gender and the Politics of History* (New York: Columbia University Press, 1988), pp. 68–90, and is considered below.

56. Jim Merod, *The Political Responsibility of the Critic* (Ithaca, N.Y.: Cornell University Press, 1987), pp. 117–118.

57. White, *Tropics of Discourse*, pp. 14–19.

58. One of the few commentaries that gestures toward the importance of language in Thompson in ways beyond those located by White is Fred Inglis, *Radical Earnestness*, pp. 193–204.

59. See E. P. Thompson, "Time, Work-Discipline, and Industrial Capitalism," *Past & Present* 38 (February 1967): 56–97; Thompson, "The Moral Economy of the English Crowd in the Eighteenth Century," *Past & Present* 50 (February

1971): 71–136; Thompson, "Rough Music: Le charivari anglaise," *Annales: E.S.C.* 27 (janvier–juin 1972): 285–312; Thompson, "The Crime of Anonymity," in Douglas Hay et al., eds., *Albion's Fatal Tree: Crime and Society in Eighteenth-Century England* (New York: Pantheon, 1975), pp. 255–344. The wife sale work remains unpublished but for fragmentary discussion see Thompson, "Folklore, Anthropology, and Social History," *Indian Historical Review* 3 (January 1978): 252–253; Thompson, "Anthropology and the Discipline of Historical Context," *Midland History* 1 (Spring 1972): 52, 55; Thompson, "Eighteenth-century English Society: Class Struggle without Class?" *Social History* 3 (May 1978): 156.

60. Now nearing completion, this study represents much-revised work on charivari, crowd, and wife sale, as well as newer material on custom and common right in agrarian England and its colonial outposts. Thompson delivered six lectures on these themes at Queen's University, 27 January–16 March 1988.

61. Cited in Thompson, "Patrician Society, Plebian Culture," *Journal of Social History* 7 (Summer 1974): 384.

62. Thompson, "On History, Sociology, and Historical Relevance," *British Journal of Sociology* 27 (1976): 402.

63. E. P. Thompson, *The Making of the English Working Class* (New York: Vintage, 1963), pp. 18–19.

64. Ibid., pp. 30–31, 40, 47, 49–50.

65. This forms the substance of Gareth Stedman Jones, "Rethinking Chartism," in *Languages of Class: Studies in English Working Class History, 1832–1982* (Cambridge: Cambridge University Press, 1983), pp. 90–178; Calhoun, *The Question of Class Struggle*; Anderson, *Arguments within English Marxism*, pp. 43–47.

66. Thompson, *Making of the English Working Class*, pp. 90, 95–96, 98.

67. Ibid., pp. 141, 159, 167, 183, 185, 189.

68. For a discussion of structure of feeling see Williams, *Marxism and Literature*, pp. 128–141. For use of the term in *Making of the English Working Class*, see p. 194.

69. As will be noted in the next chapter with respect to discourse-theory inspired critique of Soboul, this kind of situating of a historical problem on the ground of experience *is* a departure from mainstream scholarship's caricature of Marxist treatment of the past. There is no question that in the case of Thompson this willingness to conceive of history as it was lived and perceived by actual men and women of the past brings us face-to-face with historical development in new and invigorating ways. But in understating the way men and women were structured into their ways of perception, a process that was often only dimly perceived by subordinate groups/classes, this Thompsonian stress on agency has its limitations and problematic consequences. These will be addressed below, in the Conclusion.

70. Thompson, *Making of the English Working Class*, esp. pp. 203, 205.

71. Ibid., pp. 192–195.

72. Ibid., pp. 268, 318, 349.

73. Ibid., pp. 357, 368, 392–393.

74. Ibid., pp. 401, 422–424. Cf. Alfred F. Young, "English Plebeian Culture and Eighteenth-Century American Radicalism," in Margaret Jacob and James Jacob, eds., *The Origins of Anglo-American Radicalism* (London: George Allen and Unwin, 1984), pp. 185–213.

75. Thompson, *Making of the English Working Class*, pp. 492–493.

76. Ibid., pp. 625, 677, 686, 692. On the cap of liberty see James Epstein, "Understanding the Cap of Liberty: Symbolic Practice and Social Conflict in Early Nineteenth-Century England," *Past & Present* 122 (February 1989), pp. 75–118.

77. Thompson, *Making of the English Working Class*, pp. 748–749, 755, 762.

78. Ibid., pp. 831–832.

79. Scott, "Women in *The Making of the English Working Class*," in *Gender and the Politics of History*, pp. 68–90, with reference to Marxism on p. 69 and women artisans on p. 74. For Scott's earlier writing see Joan Wallach Scott, *The Glassworkers of Carmaux: French Craftsmen and Political Action in a Nineteenth-Century City* (Cambridge: Harvard University Press, 1974); Eric Hobsbawm and Joan W. Scott, "Political Shoemakers," in Hobsbawm, *Workers: Worlds of Labor* (New York: Pantheon, 1984), pp. 103–130. Feminist potshotting of an unfair sort has long been directed at Thompson. I once heard Laura Strumingher, delivering a lecture at the State University of New York at Binghamton, dismiss Thompson's *Making of the English Working Class* for its inattention to women and gender-specific conception of class and add, for good measure, that Thompson had never really "worked" and that his wife Dorothy had been the member of the household to hold down a regular, paying university post. That this was untrue historically and that it seemed an oddly unthinking criticism for someone who likely rejected the notion of *a* male breadwinner did not register with much of the crowd, which seemed to appreciate this kind of gender bashing. This is *not* to say that there cannot be feminist criticism of books like *The Making of the English Working Class*. It is to urge that such criticism be intellectually rigorous and not ad hominem.

80. A recent text, presenting itself as a "modified version of deconstruction theory," tackles Thompson's "The Poverty of Theory: or an Orrery of Errors," in *The Poverty of Theory & Other Essays* (London: Merlin, 1978), pp. 193–397, but entirely avoids dirtying its hands with the immense literature around this subject. See Sande Cohen, "Leftist Historical Narration: On the Academization of Class Conflict," in *Historical Culture: On the Recoding of an Academic Discipline* (Berkeley: University of California Press, 1986), pp. 174–229. I recommend this "exercise" in criticism as an exemplary case of the worst that critical theory can produce. Scott cites it with apparent favor.

81. On Taylor see *Eve and the New Jerusalem: Socialism and Feminism in the Nineteenth Century* (London: Virago, 1983); "Socialist Feminism: Utopian or Scientific?" in Raphael Samuel, ed., *People's History and Socialist Theory* (London: Routledge & Kegan Paul, 1981), pp. 158–163. For a brief critique of this work, which has been overwhelmingly endorsed within the academic and feminist communities, see Angela Weir and Elizabeth Wilson, "The British

Women's Movement," *New Left Review* 148 (November–December 1984): 85–88.

82. Scott, *Gender and the Politics of History*, p. 77; Thompson, *Making of the English Working Class*, p. 391.

83. Scott, *Gender and the Politics of History*, pp. 71, 90.

84. Ibid., pp. 73–74.

85. See, for instance, Louise A. Tilly and Joan Scott, *Women, Work & Family* (New York: Holt, Rinehart, and Winston, 1978), esp. pp. 61–146.

86. Thompson, *Making of the English Working Class*, pp. 416–417, 730. Note Gayatri Chakravorty Spivak, "Feminism and Critical Theory," in *In Other Worlds: Essays in Cultural Politics* (New York: Methuen, 1987), p. 79, for some pertinent comments on this matter. For a critique of Thompson's assessment of women see James Epstein, "Understanding the Cap of Liberty: Symbolic Practice and Social Conflict in Early Nineteenth-Century England," *Past & Present* 122 (February 1989): 75–118.

87. Scott, *Gender and the Politics of History*, pp. 78–79; Thompson, *Making of the English Working Class*, esp. p. 706.

88. Scott, *Gender and the Politics of History*, p. 72.

89. For Scott's development of this position, which takes an interesting direction regarding Thompson's attachment to poetry, see *Gender and the Politics of History*, pp. 79–83. She relies heavily on Henry Abelove's review essay on Thompson's *Poverty of Theory* in *History and Theory* 21 (1982): 132–142, but virtually ignores *The Making of the English Working Class*.

90. Perhaps Scott recognizes that a politics of "sincere attachment to the Throne" is not one to defend too vigorously. For comment on this episode, directed against Thompson's understanding of class formation and radicalism, see Calhoun, *The Question of Class Struggle*, pp. 105–115. For the most recent discussion of Queen Caroline see Iain McCalman, *Radical Underworld: Prophets, Revolutionaries, and Pornographers in London, 1795–1840* (New York: Cambridge University Press, 1988), esp. pp. 162–177. McCalman draws suggestive links between the radical pressmen, their embrace of Queen Caroline, and the drift of many radicals into the pornography trade in the 1830s. Unconcerned with critical theory or the issues of the gendered construction of class central to Scott's critique of Thompson, McCalman nevertheless provides a more historically grounded foundation for a theoretically informed analysis of gender and representation.

91. Note, as well, Weir and Wilson, "British Women's Movement," pp. 82–85.

92. These themes will be readdressed in Chapter 5, the chapter on gender. A case could be made that Scott is arguing for a politics of femininity that bears some resemblance to Irigaray's conception of women and writing, which is premised on expressivity and defiance of so-called masculinist rationality.

93. Cohen, *Historical Culture*, p. 1.

94. In the case of gender it will be necessary to detail specifically feminist theoretical developments within poststructuralism as an introduction to the actual discussion of the promotion of discourse as an interpretive advance in the historical understanding of gender.

Chapter 3

1. A recent study takes its cues from some of the literature discussed below, especially those studies of American republicanism and the French Revolution that stress the ideological origins rather than the social/class content of the late eighteenth-century transatlantic upheavals. Nevertheless, the book is uninformed by discourse theory and is especially weak in its treatment of the consequences of American republicanism, being little more than a synthesis of the anti-Marxism of recent writing on 1789 and a restatement of conventional wisdoms on the pluralism of American civil society. See Patrice Higonnet, *Sister Republics: The Origins of French and American Republicanism* (Cambridge: Harvard University Press, 1988).

2. See, among many other studies, William Doyle, *Origins of the French Revolution* (Oxford: Oxford University Press, 1980), pp. 7–40; G. Ellis, "The 'Marxist Interpretation' of the French Revolution," *English Historical Review* 90 (1978): 353–376; François Furet, *Interpreting the French Revolution* (Cambridge: Cambridge University Press, 1981).

3. Marx and Engels, *Collected Works*, "Bourgeoisie and Counter-Revolution," cited in Gerard Bekerman, *Marx and Engels: A Conceptual Concordance* (Oxford: Blackwell Reference, 1983), p. 153. The importance of this passage is noted in Michael Lowy, *The Politics of Combined and Uneven Development: The Theory of Permanent Revolution* (London: Verso, 1981), p. 3.

4. Lefebvre's most influential book is undoubtedly *The Coming of the French Revolution* (Princeton, N.J.: Princeton University Press, 1947), although it could be argued that his most impressive writing focused on the peasantry and rural panic on the eve of 1789. See Lefebvre, *The Great Fear of 1789: Rural Panic in Revolutionary France* (London: New Left Books, 1973). Note, as well, Lefebvre, *The Directory* (New York: Vintage, 1967); Lefebvre, *Napoleon: From Eighteen Brumaire to Tilsit, 1799–1807* (New York: Columbia University Press, 1969). Soboul is justifiably known as the historian of the Parisian sans-culottes on the basis of *The Parisian Sans-Culottes and the French Revolution, 1793–1794* (Oxford: Clarendon Press, 1964), but see, as well, his two-volume history of the revolution, *The French Revolution, 1789–1799* (London: New Left Books, 1974). For portraits of Lefebvre and Soboul from their closest non-Marxist collaborator, Richard Cobb, see "Georges Lefebvre," in Cobb, *A Second Identity: Essays on France and French History* (London: Oxford University Press, 1969), pp. 84–100; "Albert-Marius Soboul: A Tribute," in Cobb, *People and Places* (New York: Oxford University Press, 1986), pp. 46–92.

5. Alfred Cobban, *Aspects of the French Revolution* (London: Paladin, 1971), pp. 95, 105.

6. William M. Reddy, *Money and Liberty in Modern Europe: A Critique of Historical Understanding* (Cambridge: Cambridge University Press, 1987), pp. 4–6.

7. Reddy is given to this kind of idealized creation of a strawman that is then knocked down with much fanfare. Note his discussion of entrepreneurs and markets in William M. Reddy, *The Rise of Market Culture: The Textile Trade and French Society, 1750–1900* (Cambridge: Cambridge University Press, 1984).

8. Karl Marx, "Preface to the Critique of Political Economy," in Karl Marx and Frederick Engels, *Selected Works* (Moscow: Progress, 1968), p. 183.

9. Karl Marx, *The Holy Family* (London: Lawrence and Wishart, 1956), pp. 160–167; and *Deutsche Brusseler Zeitung* 11 (November 1847), quoted in Shlomo Avineri, *The Social and Political Thought of Karl Marx* (Cambridge: Cambridge University Press, 1968), p. 191. On Jacobinism see, as well, Ferene Fehér, *The Frozen Revolution: An Essay on Jacobinism* (New York: Cambridge University Press, 1987).

10. Trotsky's discussion of "Jacobinism and Social Democracy" forms the final chapter of *Our Political Tasks* (1904), written as a Menshevik polemic against Lenin. See Baruch Knei-Paz, *The Social and Politial Thought of Leon Trotsky* (Oxford: Clarendon Press, 1978), pp. 199–206.

11. Antonio Gramsci, *Selections from the Prison Notebooks* (New York: International, 1971), pp. 77–79. Cf. Walter L. Adamson, *Hegemony and Revolution: Antonio Gramsci's Political and Cultural Theory* (Berkeley: University of California Press, 1980), pp. 184–188.

12. Trotsky quoted in Knei-Paz, *Social and Political Thought of Trotsky*, p. 200. Cf. Marx, *The Holy Family*, pp. 164–165.

13. Note the forceful discussion in Elizabeth Fox-Genovese and Eugene D. Genovese, "On the Social History of the French Revolution," in *Fruits of Merchant Capital: Slavery and Bourgeois Property in the Rise and Expansion of Capitalism* (Oxford: Oxford University Press, 1983), pp. 213–248.

14. For a treatment of one aspect of language and the French Revolution that remains committed to the importance of class forces see Patrice L.-R. Higonnet, "The Politics of Linguistic Terrorism and Grammatical Hegemony during the French Revolution," *Social History* 5 (1980): 41–69.

15. All drawn from Lynn Hunt, *Politics, Culture, and Class in the French Revolution* (London: Methuen, 1986), pp. 19, 77–78, 187.

16. Quoted in Janis Langins, "Words and Institutions during the French Revolution: The Case of 'Revolutionary' Scientific and Technical Education," in Peter Burke and Roy Porter, eds., *The Social History of Language* (Cambridge: Cambridge University Press, 1987), pp. 136–137. For a traditional discussion of the importance of language in the revolution and of the attempt to replace the "underlanguage" of *patois* with a modernized single French language see Jean-Yves Lartichaux, "Linguistic Politics during the French Revolution," *Diogenes* 97 (1977): 65–84.

17. See, for instance, James A. Leith, *The Idea of Art as Propaganda in France, 1750–1799: A Study in the History of Ideas* (Toronto: University of Toronto Press, 1965); James A. Leith, "Symbols in the French Revolution: The Strange Metamorphoses of the Triangle," in Leith, ed., *Symbols in Life and Art: The Royal Society of Canada* (Montreal: McGill-Queen's University Press, 1987), pp. 105–117; Maurice Agulhon, *Marianne into Battle; Republican Imagery and Symbolism in France, 1789–1880* (Cambridge: Cambridge University Press, 1979); Agulhon, "Politics, Images, and Symbols in Post-Revolutionary France," in Sean Wilentz, ed., *Rites of Power: Symbolism, Ritual, and Politics since the Middle Ages* (Philadelphia: University of Pennsylvania Press, 1985), pp. 177–205; Mona Ozouf, *Festivals and the French Revolution* (Cambridge: Harvard

University Press, 1988); Michel Vovelle, *The Fall of the French Monarchy,
1787–1792* (New York: Cambridge University Press, 1984), pp. 192–199. For a
general discussion of the importance of symbolism, politics, and history see
Sean Wilentz, "Introduction: Teufelsdrockh's Dilemma: On Symbolism, Politics and History," in Wilentz, ed., *Rites of Power*, pp. 1–10, a statement that
notes the spreading use of the term *discourse* within historical studies and that
suggests that although social historians have not yet expressed much interest in
literary textual analysis and Derrida, this may change.

18. Though the latter two essays in the collection do not break interpretively
from the preceding chapters, Furet's discussions of Tocqueville and Cochin as a
theorist of Jacobinism add little to an understanding of the concepts of the new
revisionism, and my discussion thus focuses on the first two essays. Furet,
Interpreting the French Revolution, pp. 1–131. For recent acknowledgment of
the importance of Furet in a history of the French Revolution that lays increasing stress on language note Dorinda Outram, *"Le langage male de la vertu*:
Women and the Discourse of the French Revolution," and Janis Langins, "Words
and Institutions during the French Revolution: The Case of 'Revolutionary'
Scientific and Technical Education," in Burke and Porter, eds., *The Social
History of Language*, esp. pp. 120–121, 136–137. For an abbreviated statement
by Soboul on this area see his "Equality: On the Power and Danger of Words,"
Proceedings of the Consortium on Revolutionary Europe, vol. 1 (1974), pp. 13–
21.

19. Furet, *Interpreting the French Revolution*, esp. pp. 85–89.

20. Ibid., p. 91.

21. Ibid., pp. 90–91.

22. Kautsky is quoted in ibid., p. 103. For Soboul and the sans-culottes see, as
an example only, Albert Soboul, *The Sans-Culottes: The Popular Movement
and Revolutionary Government, 1793–1794* (Garden City, N.Y.: Doubleday,
1972), pp. 251–264.

23. Furet, *Interpreting the French Revolution*, esp. pp. 118, 130–131.

24. Lynn Hunt, "Review of *Penser La Revolution Française*," *History &
Theory* 20 (1981): 313–323, esp. 313.

25. This is precisely the point made in Fox-Genovese and Genovese, "On the
Social History of the French Revolution," pp. 217–218.

26. Furet, *Interpreting the French Revolution*, esp. pp. 77–78; Hunt, "Review," pp. 319–320.

27. Furet, *Interpreting the French Revolution*, p. 27.

28. Ibid., p. 54.

29. Ibid., p. 63.

30. Hunt, *Politics, Culture, and Class in the French Revolution*, pp. 12–13,
23–26.

31. Ibid., pp. 35–51. Hunt is obviously drawing on E. P. Thompson, "Eighteenth-Century English Society: Class Struggle without Class," *Social History*
3 (May 1978): 133–165, but she does not cite the article, and her use of the
Thompsonian vocabulary bears little relation to how it was employed in the
original essay.

32. Crane Brinton's *Anatomy of Revolution* (New York: Prentice-Hall, 1938),

is cited in Hunt, *Politics, Culture, and Class in the French Revolution*, p. 47, but only in passing, and subsequent references to his study hardly convey the extent to which Hunt's drawing on "literary theory" represents new wine in rather old interpretive bottles.

33. Hunt, *Politics, Culture, and Class in the French Revolution*, pp. 54, 58–59, 67, 72, 86, 119.

34. S. B. Liljegren, *A French Draft Constitution of 1792 Modelled on James Harrington's Oceana . . . edited with an Introduction on Harrington's Influence in France, and Notes* (Lund and London: C. W. K. Gleerup and Oxford University Press, 1932). There is a gesture toward the depth of revolutionary republicanism in Keith Michael Baker, "On the Problem of the Ideological Origins of the French Revolution," in Dominick LaCapra and Steven Kaplan, eds., *Modern European Intellectual History: Reappraisals and New Perspectives* (Ithaca, N.Y.: Cornell University Press, 1982), pp. 197–219.

35. Hunt, *Politics, Culture and Class in the French Revolution*, p. 54.

36. Sonenscher's important article "The *Sans-Culottes* of the Year II: Rethinking the Language of Labour in Revolutionary France," *Social History* 9 (October 1984): 301–328, will be discussed below. See as well his "Work and Wages in Paris in the Eighteenth Century," in Maxine Berg, Pat Hudson, and Michael Sonenscher, eds., *Manufacture in Town and Country before the Factory* (Cambridge: Cambridge University Press, 1983), pp. 147–172; "Mythical Work: Workshop Production and the *Compagnonnages* of Eighteenth-Century France," in Patrick Joyce, ed., *The Historical Meanings of Work* (Cambridge: Cambridge University Press, 1987), pp. 31–63; "Journeymen's Migrations and Workshop Organization in Eighteenth-Century France," in Steven Laurence Kaplan and Cynthia J. Koepp, eds., *Work in France: Representations, Meaning, Organization, and Practice* (Ithaca, N.Y.: Cornell University Press, 1986), pp. 74–96.

37. Hunt, *Politics, Culture, and Class in the French Revolution*, p. 177.

38. Ibid., p. 147.

39. William H. Sewell, Jr., *Work and Revolution in France: The Language of Labor from the Old Regime to 1848* (Cambridge: Cambridge University Press, 1980), esp. pp. 10–12, 281–284.

40. Sonenscher, "The *Sans-Culottes* of the Year II," p. 302. The following is based on this article, but note the sources cited in note 35 above. Note as well John Smail, "New Languages for Labour and Capital: The Transformation of the Discourse in the Early Years of the Industrial Revolution," *Social History* 12 (January 1987): 49–72.

41. Sonenscher, "The *Sans-Culottes* of the Year II," pp. 312–313. Note as well Robert Darnton, "Workers Revolt: The Great Cat Massacre of the Rue Saint-Severin," in Darnton, *The Great Cat Massacre and Other Episodes in French Cultural History* (New York: Basic Books, 1984), pp. 75–106; Peter Linebaugh, "Laboring People in Eighteenth-Century England," *International Labor and Working Class History* 213 (1983): 1–8.

42. Sonenscher, "The *Sans-Culottes* of the Year II," pp. 314, 317.

43. Ibid., p. 324.

44. Note the little-appreciated Louis M. Hacker, *The Triumph of American*

Capitalism: The Development of Forces in American History to the Beginning of the Twentieth Century (New York: Columbia University Press, 1940), Part II, "The Victory of American Mercantile Capitalism in the Revolution," pp. 93–195.

45. Charles A. Beard, *An Economic Interpretation of the Constitution of the United States* (New York: Macmillan, 1913), pp. 324–325.

46. See, among other sources, Alfred F. Young, *The Democratic Republicans of New York: The Origins, 1763–1797* (Chapel Hill: University of North Carolina Press, 1967); Young, "The Mechanics and the Jeffersonians: New York, 1789–1801," *Labor History* 5 (Fall 1964): 247–276; Young, "George Robert Twelves Hewes (1742–1840): A Boston Shoemaker and the Memory of the American Revolution," *William and Mary Quarterly* 38 (October 1981): 561–623; Young, ed., *The American Revolution: Explorations in the History of American Radicalism* (DeKalb, Ill.: Northern Illinois University Press, 1976); Gary B. Nash, *The Urban Crucible: Social Change, Political Consciousness, and the Origins of the American Revolution* (Cambridge: Harvard University Press, 1979); Nash, "Artisans and Politics in Eighteenth-Century Philadelphia," in Margaret Jacob and James Jacob, eds., *The Origins of Anglo-American Radicalism* (London: George Allen & Unwin, 1984), pp. 162–182; Roger Champagne, "Liberty Boys and Mechanics in New York City Politics, 1764–1774," *Labor History* 8 (1967): 115–135; Staughton Lynd, "The Mechanics in New York City Politics, 1774–1785," *Labor History* 5 (Fall 1964): 225–246; Lynd, *Class Conflict, Slavery, and the United States Constitution* (New York: Bobbs-Merrill, 1967); Charles Shaw Olton, "Philadelphia Artisans and the American Revolution," (Ph.D. diss., University of California at Berkeley, 1967); Edward Countryman, *A People in Revolution: The American Revolution and Political Society in New York, 1760–1790* (Baltimore: Johns Hopkins University Press, 1981); Jesse Lemisch, "The American Revolution Seen from the Bottom Up," in Barton J. Bernstein, ed., *Towards a New Past: Dissenting Essays in American History* (New York: Vintage, 1968), pp. 3–45; Lemisch, "Jack Tar in the Streets: Merchant Seamen in the Politics of Revolutionary America," *William and Mary Quarterly* 25 (July 1968): 317–407.

47. Philip S. Foner, ed., *The Democratic-Republican Societies, 1790–1800* (Westport, Conn.: Greenwood Press, 1976), p. vi.

48. See, most especially, Bernard Bailyn, *The Origins of American Politics* (New York: Vintage, 1970); Bailyn, *The Ideological Origins of the American Revolution* (Cambridge: Harvard University Press, 1967). For critiques of Bailyn see Jesse Lemisch, "Bailyn Besieged in His Bunker," *Radical History Review* 4 (Winter 1977): 72–83; Joseph Ernst, " 'Ideology' and an Economic Interpretation of the Revolution," in Young, ed., *The American Revolution*, pp. 159–185; John Patrick Diggins, *The Lost Soul of American Politics: Virtue, Self-Interest, and the Foundations of Liberalism* (New York: Basic Books, 1984), pp. 347–352.

49. Mari Jo Buhle and Paul Buhle, "The New Labor History at the Cultural Crossroads," and Leon Fink, "Relocating the Vital Center," both in *Journal of American History* 75 (June 1988): 156, 160; Michael Kazin, "The New Historians Recapture the Flag," *New York Times Book Review*, 2 July 1989.

50. Rhys Isaac, "Discourse on Method," in *The Transformation of Virginia,*

1740–1790 (Chapel Hill: University of North Carolina Press, 1982), esp. pp. 324–325, 347, 349, 350–351, 413. Cf. Isaac, "Communication and Control: Authority Metaphors and Power Contests on Colonel Landon Carter's Virginia Plantation, 1752–1778," in Wilentz, ed., *Rites of Power*, pp. 275–302.

51. Alfred F. Young, "Pope's Day, Tar and Feathers, and Cornet Joyce, Jun.: From Ritual to Rebellion in Boston, 1745–1775," paper presented to the Anglo-American Labor Historians' Conference, Rutgers University, 1973; Young, "English Plebeian Culture and Eighteenth-Century American Radicalism," in Jacob and Jacob, eds., *The Origins of Anglo-American Radicalism*, pp. 185–213; Peter Shaw, *American Patriots and the Rituals of Revolution* (Cambridge: Harvard University Press, 1981).

52. See John Brewer, *Party Ideology and Popular Politics at the Accession of George III* (Cambridge: Cambridge University Press, 1976), esp. pp. 163–200; Brewer, "The No. 45: A Wilkite Political Symbol," in Stephen Baxter, ed., *England from the Restoration to the American War* (Berkeley: University of California Press, 1980); Brewer, "Theater and Counter-Theater in Georgian Politics: The Mock Elections at Garrat," *Radical History Review* 22 (1979–1980): 7–40.

53. See J. G. A. Pocock, *The Machiavellian Moment: Florentine Political Thought and the Atlantic Republican Tradition* (Princeton, N.J.: Princeton University Press, 1975), esp. Part III, pp. 353–552.

54. For the general view see Pauline Maier, *From Resistance to Revolution: Colonial Radicals and the Development of American Opposition to Britain, 1765–1776* (New York: Vintage, 1972). The characterizations cited above are present in Bailyn, *The Ordeal of Thomas Hutchinson* (Cambridge: Harvard University Press, 1974), esp. pp. ix, 37, 38, 2, 126, 127, 32, 34; and in Bailyn, "Common Sense," *American Heritage* (December 1973), pp. 36–37, 92, as cited in Lemisch, "Bailyn Besieged in His Bunker," p. 72.

55. Joyce Appleby, *Capitalism and a New Social Order: The Republican Vision of the 1790s* (New York: New York University Press, 1984), pp. 99–100. Cf. Appleby, "What is Still American in the Political Philosophy of Thomas Jefferson?" *William and Mary Quarterly* 19 (April 1982): 287–309.

56. Eric Foner, *Tom Paine and Revolutionary America* (New York: Oxford University Press, 1976), p. 263; Richard J. Twomey, "Jacobins and Jeffersonians: Anglo-American Radical Ideology, 1790–1810," in Jacob and Jacob, ed., *The Origins of Anglo-American Radicalism*, pp. 284–299; Howard Rock, *Artisans of the New Republic: The Tradesmen of New York City in the Age of Jefferson* (New York: New York University Press, 1979).

57. Note Isaac Kramnick, "Republican Revisionism Revisited," *American Historical Review* 87 (1982): 629–664, with a quote from p. 662; John Patrick Diggins, *The Lost Soul of American Politics: Virtue, Self-Interest and the Foundations of Liberalism* (New York: Basic Books, 1984), esp. pp. 86, 96; and the general argument in Edmund S. Morgan, "Government by Fiction: the Idea of Representation," *Yale Review* 72 (April 1983): 321–339.

58. See Sean Wilentz, *Chants Democratic: New York City and the Rise of the American Working Class, 1788–1850* (New York: Oxford University Press, 1984), esp. pp. 23–103.

59. Susan G. Davis, *Parades and Power: Street Theatre in Nineteenth-Century Philadelphia* (Philadelphia: Temple University Press, 1986), p. 158.

60. Engels to Sorge, 31 December 1892, in Karl Marx and Frederick Engels, *Correspondence, 1846–1895: A Selection with Commentary and Notes* (New York: International, 1935), pp. 501–502.

61. See, for exceptions, Alan Dawley, *Class and Community: The Industrial Revolution in Lynn* (Cambridge: Harvard University Press, 1976), especially the concluding discussion "Equal Rights and Beyond," pp. 220–241; and David Montgomery, *Beyond Equality: Labor and the Radical Republicans, 1862–1872* (New York: Alfred A. Knopf, 1967).

62. Although he would by no means agree with my views, note the discussion of such developments in Wilentz, *Chants Democratic;* Wilentz, "Artisan Republican Festivals and the Rise of Class Confict in New York City, 1788–1837," in Michael H. Frisch and Daniel J. Walkowitz, eds., *Working-Class America: Essays on Labor, Community, and American Society* (Urbana: University of Illinois Press, 1983), pp. 37–77. Cf. Steven J. Ross, *Workers on the Edge: Work, Leisure and Politics in Industrializing Cincinnati, 1788–1890* (New York: Columbia University Press, 1985).

63. Montgomery, *Beyond Equality*, esp. p. x.

64. George E. McNeill, ed., *The Labor Movement: The Problem of Today* (Boston, 1887), p. 459, cited in Leon Fink, "The New Labor History and the Powers of Historical Pessimism: Consensus, Hegemony, and the Case of the Knights of Labor," *Journal of American History* 75 (June 1988): 116.

65. David Montgomery, "Labor and the Republic in Industrial America: 1860–1920," *Mouvement social* 111 (avril–juin 1980): 201–215. Though Herbert G. Gutman often espouses a rather uncritical belief in the staying power and potential of labor republicanism, a belief that I will discuss briefly below, he also provides copious anecdotal evidence of the divide separating labor radicalism and republicanism in Gilded Age America. See Herbert G. Gutman, "Work, Culture, and Society in Industrializing America, 1815–1919," in Gutman, *Work, Culture, and Society in Industrializing America* (New York: Knopf, 1976), esp. pp. 50–54.

66. See, for instance, Sean Wilentz, "Against Exceptionalism: Class Consciousness and the American Labor Movement, 1790–1920," *International Labor and Working Class History* 26 (1984): 1–24. This issue is central in "Interview with Hebert Gutman," in Henry Abelove et al., eds., *Visions of History* (New York: Pantheon, 1983), pp. 185–216, and Gutman's too easy acceptance of the labor rhetoric of republicanism is criticized in an essay that combines admiration for his accomplishments with recognition of his difficulties. See David Roediger, "What Was So Great About Herbert Gutman?" forthcoming *Labour/Le Travail* (1989). For an implicit voice of dissent on this whole question of labor republicanism see Mike Davis, *Prisoners of the American Dream: Politics and Economy in the History of the US Working Class* (London: Verso, 1986).

67. Ira Berlin and Herbert G. Gutman, "Class Composition and the Development of the American Working Class, 1840–1890," in Herbert G. Gutman,

Power and Culture: Essays on the American Working Class (New York: Pantheon, 1987), pp. 381–382.

68. See Wilentz, "Class Consciousness and the Republic of Labor," in *Chants Democratic*, pp. 237–248.

69. John Patrick Diggins, "Comrades and Citizens: New Mythologies in American Historiography," *American Historical Review* 90 (1985): 616. The critique of the reification of language is made far more effectively in Diggins, *Lost Soul of American Politics*, esp. pp. 18–99, 359–365.

70. Lears, "The Concept of Cultural Hegemony: Problems and Possibilities," *American Historical Review* 90 (1985): 567–593.

71. For the most accessible treatment of the immigrant revolutionaries and their American-born comrades see Paul Avrich, *The Haymarket Tragedy* (Princeton, N.Y.: Princeton University Press, 1984), with quote from p. 75. Cf. Montgomery, "Labor and the Republic in America," pp. 207–208; Hartmut Keil and John B. Jentz, eds., *German Workers in Industrial Chicago, 1850–1910: A Comparative Perspective* (DeKalb, Ill.: Northern Illinois University Press, 1983).

72. My own views on this are spelled out in more detail in Gregory S. Kealey and Bryan D. Palmer, *Dreaming of What Might Be: The Knights of Labor in Ontario, 1880–1900* (New York: Cambridge University Press, 1982).

73. Fink, "Labor History and Historical Pessimism," esp. pp. 118–119, 121, 123, 124. For Diggins's response, which ends with discussion of what historic blocs are, see John Patrick Diggins, "The Misuses of Gramsci," *Journal of American History* 75 (June 1988): 145.

74. George Lipsitz, "The Struggle for Hegemony," *Journal of American History* 75 (June 1988): 148, 150.

75. Montgomery does precisely this with a materially grounded suggestion in "Labor and the Republic in America."

76. Fink, "Labor History and Historical Pessimism," p. 136.

77. Leon Fink, *Workingmen's Democracy: The Knights of Labor and American Politics* (Urbana: University of Illinois Press, 1983).

78. Leon Fink, "Politics as Social History: A Case Study of Class Conflict and Political Development in Nineteenth-Century New England," in Herbert G. Gutman and Donald H. Bell, eds., *The New England Working Class and the New Labor History* (Urbana: University of Illinois Press, 1987), p. 254.

79. Note, for instance, Francis G. Couvares, *The Remaking of Pittsburgh: Class and Culture in an Industrializing City, 1877–1919* (Albany: State University of New York Press, 1984), esp. pp. 23–30; Paul Krause, "Labor Republicanism and 'Za Chlebom': Anglo-Americans and Slavic Solidarity in Homestead," in Dirk Hoerder, ed., *"Struggle a Hard Battle": Essays on Working-Class Immigrants* (DeKalb: Northern Illinois University Press, 1986), pp. 143–169; David Bensman, *The Practice of Solidarity: American Hat Finishers in the Nineteenth Century* (Urbana: University of Illinois Press, 1985), p. 56; Steven J. Ross, "The Politicization of the Working Class: Production, Ideology, Culture, and Politics in Late Nineteenth-Century Cincinnati," *Social History* 11 (May 1986): 171–195.

80. Consider Paul Schmidt, "Mark Twain's Satire on Republicanism," *American Quarterly* 5 (1953): 344–356.

81. The incident is discussed in Couvares, *Remaking of Pittsburgh*, p. 119, though the interpretation is my own.

Chapter 4

1. See the treatment of Gutman's essays, *Power and Culture*, and Montgomery's *The Fall of the House of Labor* in Alan Brinkley, "The World of Workers," *New Republic*, 8 February 1988, pp. 35–38. Montgomery's study was the subject of a *Labor History* symposium in which much of the comment was carping and petty. Note especially Michael Kazin, "The Limits of the Workplace," in "A Symposium on *The Fall of the House of Labor*," *Labor History* 30 (1989): 110–113, a curt statement that blames the decline of labor in the 1920s on "the hostility and misunderstanding of the native-born majority" and suggests that "white wage-earners found more to celebrate than to curse in the achievements of a liberal state." As a new pragmatist intent upon establishing himself as the Arthur Koestler of the New Left labor historians, Kazin is now convinced, after making his scholarly reputation on the basis of an exciting study of San Francisco building trandesmen, that class is not now and never has been a point of identification for American workers. We will meet him in a few pages.

2. Norman McCord, "A Touch of Class," *History* 70 (1985): 412, 419.

3. Ellen Meiksins Wood, *The Retreat from Class: A New "True" Socialism* (London: Verso, 1986).

4. Karl Marx and Frederick Engels, "Manifesto of the Communist Party," in *Selected Works* (Moscow: Progress, 1968), pp. 57–58. Cf. Karl Marx and Frederick Engels, *The German Ideology* (New York: International, 1947), esp. pp. 79–194.

5. André Gorz, *Farewell to the Working Class: An Essay on Post-Industrial Socialism* (London: Pluto Press, 1982); Ernesto Laclau and Chantal Mouffe, *Hegemony and Socialist Strategy: Towards a Radical Democratic Politics* (London: Verso, 1985); Gavin Kitching, *Rethinking Socialism: A Theory for a Better Practice* (London: Methuen, 1983); Gareth Stedman Jones, "Why is the Labour Party in a Mess?" in Jones, *Languages of Class: Studies in English Working-Class History, 1832–1982* (Cambridge: Cambridge University Press, 1983), esp. p. 256. Theoretically this writing signals fundamental departures from Marxism. See Gavin Kitching, *Karl Marx and the Philosophy of Praxis* (London: Routledge, 1988). Wood, *The Retreat from Class*, represents a frontal assault on these works, as does Ralph Miliband, "The New Revisionism in Britain," *New Left Review* 150 (March–April 1985): 5–28. More oblique, but also important, is the critique in Michael Burawoy, *The Politics of Production: Factory Regimes under Capitalism and Socialism* (London: Verso, 1985).

6. See, for instance, Maurice Isserman, *Which Side Were You On? The American Communist Party During the Second World War* (Middletown, Conn.: Wesleyan University Press, 1982); Isserman, *If I Had A Hammer . . . : The Death of the Old Left and the Birth of the New Left* (New York: Basic Books, 1987); Mark Naison, *Communists in Harlem During the Depression*

(Urbana: University of Illinois Press, 1983). This has drawn a critical response from the right and the left. See Theodore Draper, "American Communism Revisited," *New York Review of Books*, 9 May 1985, pp. 32–37; Draper, "The Popular Front Revisited," *New York Review of Books*, 30 May 1985: 44–50; Michael Goldfield, "Recent Historiography of the Communist Party, U.S.A.," in Mike Davis, Fred Pfeil, and Michael Sprinker, eds., *The Year Left: An American Socialist Yearbook, 1985* (London: Verso, 1985), pp. 315–356.

7. Often, of course, the phrase "language of class" is used in an entirely descriptive way, devoid of any critical theory content. See David Crew, "Class and Community: Local Research on Working-Class History in Four Countries," in Lothar Gall, ed., *Arbeiter und Arbeiterbewegung im Vergleich: Historische Zeitschrift—Sonderhelfte, Band 15* (Munchen: Oldenbourg, 1986), esp. pp. 279–284; Bernard Waites, *A Class Society at War: England, 1914–1918* (New York: St. Martin's Press, 1987), esp. pp. 34–75.

8. The classic statement is probably A. S. C. Ross, "Linguistic Class-indicators in Present-day English," *Neuphilologische Mitteilungen* 55 (1974): 20–56, but note the more recent discussion, uninformed by critical theory, in K. C. Phillipps, *Language and Class in Victorian England* (Oxford: Basil Blackwell, 1984). This point about the reciprocities of class and language is also developed in Peter Burke, "Introduction," in Peter Burke and Roy Porter, eds., *The Social History of Language* (Cambridge: Cambridge University Press, 1987), pp. 1–20.

9. Michael Kazin, "A People Not a Class: Rethinking the Political Language of the Modern US Labor Movement," in Mike Davis and Michael Sprinker, eds., *Reshaping the US Left: Popular Struggles in the 1980s* (London: Verso, 1988), pp. 257–286, esp. pp. 257–259.

10. Ibid., pp. 263, 266, 267–268, 273, 280.

11. A word on the vocabulary of this and remaining chapters is in order. *Essentialism* is a term much employed; it has also taken on various meanings. In my use of the term in conjunction with the analysis of class, *essentialism* is taken to mean the insistence that class exists only when class forces are *uniformly* conscious of their *unproblematic* class place in the society and act *unambiguously* and *persistently* on the basis of that consciousness. Those holding to this Weberian-type idealized essentialism have no problem in pointing out that such unmediated class consciousness, structural class clarity, and forceful activism have rarely occurred throughout the modern history of the working class, and they therefore reject class as either an important historical process or adequate analytic concept. More correctly, they deny that for workers class has been a point of identification. The ruling class, its consciousness, structural place, and activity, is seldom scrutinized with the skepticism that is increasingly reserved for labor, at least in terms of the period following the consolidation of bourgeois power in the nineteenth and twentieth centuries. (As the preceding chapter would indicate, the assault on the Jacobin interpretation of the French Revolution draws some of its superficial strength from the immaturity of class forces in 1789.) Essentialist views of class, and the consequent rejection of class, have thus long been a part of the one-sidedness of conservative historiography and political comment. What is more recent is the inroads essentialist views of class have made within ostensibly "left" or pro-

gressive milieux, and the extent to which this still remains, for the most part, confined to scrutiny of the working class. If, for instance, the questions currently being asked of the working class were also asked of the ruling class, what would the historical record reveal? Surely it would expose a ruling class as fractured and at odds with itself as the working class is depicted as being. Would the implication be that since class does therefore not exist, its consequences—power and control—are nonexistent? In my own field of Canadian working-class history the empiricist and conservative (although often emanating from ostensibly social-democratic quarters) attack on the so-called new labor history has often been embedded in essentialist premises. A case in point is David Bercuson, who first presented "Through the Looking Glass of Culture: An Essay on the New Labour History and Working-Class Culture in Recent Canadian Historical Writing," *Labour/Le Travailleur* 7 (Spring 1981): 95–112, at a conference on class and culture at McGill University. When asked from the floor what exactly he would consider a historical indication of the existence of class, he replied, "The Winnipeg General Strike. That was class." In the absence of such events, apparently, class does not exist. All of this said, my own views, elaborated later in this chapter, will probably be dismissed by some as essentialist, inasmuch as they adhere to orthodox Marxist interpretations of class and insist on the determining capacities of the economy. Essentialism and the analysis of gender imply slightly different interpretive emphases, and I will note these in the next chapter. I am grateful to Bob Shenton for pushing me to clarify matters discussed in this note.

12. Kazin, "People Not Class," pp. 281–282.

13. Chantal Mouffe, "Working Class Hegemony and the Struggle for Socialism," *Studies in Political Economy* 12 (Fall 1983): 23.

14. Michael Ignatieff, "Strangers and Comrades," *New Statesman*, 14 December 1984, cited in Wood, *Retreat from Class*, p. 181. For another view see Huw Benyon, ed., *Digging Deeper: Issues in the Miners' Strike* (London: Verso, 1985); and Raphael Samuel's reply to Ignatieff in *New Statesman*, 11 January 1985.

15. Michael Ignatieff, *The Needs of Strangers: An Essay on Privacy, Solidarity, and the Politics of Being Human* (New York: Viking, 1984), pp. 141–142.

16. Marx and Engels, *The German Ideology*, p. 193.

17. Michael Ignatieff, *A Just Measure of Pain: The Penitentiary in the Industrial Revolution* (New York: Pantheon, 1978).

18. An accessible introduction to Rancière for a North American audience is Donald Reid, "The Night of the Proletarians: Deconstruction and Social History," *Radical History Review* 28–30 (1984): 445–463, a review essay on Jacques Rancière, *La nuit des proletaires. Archives du rêve ouvrier* (Paris: Fayard, 1981). For abbreviated statements of the Rancière position see Jacques Rancière, "The Myth of the Artisan: Critical Reflections on a Category of Social History," in Steven Laurence Kaplan and Cynthia J. Koepp, eds., *Work in France: Representations, Meaning, Organization, and Practice* (Ithaca, N.Y.: Cornell University Press, 1986), pp. 317–334, which also appeared in *International Labor and Working-Class History* 24 (Fall 1983): 1–16; and Rancière, " 'Le social': The Lost Tradition in French Labour History," in Raphael Samuel, ed.,

People's History and Socialist Theory (London: Routledge & Kegan Paul, 1981), pp. 267–272.

19. Rancière, "The Myth of the Artisan," esp. p. 321.

20. Francois Ewald, "Qu'est-ce que la classe ouvriere?" [interview with Rancière], *Magazine litteraire* 175 (July–August 1981): 64, quoted in Reid, "The Night of the Proletarians," p. 452.

21. See the review of Rancière's book by Patrick Cingolani in *International Labor and Working Class History* 26 (Fall 1984): 136. Note, as well, Rancière, ed., *Louis Gabriel Gauny: Le philosophe plebeien* (Paris: Le Decouverte, 1983); Alain Faure and Jacques Rancière, eds., *La parole ouvriere, 1830–1851* (Paris: Union Generale, 1976).

22. These quotes are taken from, respectively, Rancière, "Ronds de fumée (les poetes ouvriers dans la France de Louis-Philippe)," *Revue des Sciences Humaines* 61 (April–June 1983): 33; Rancière, "Le bon temps ou la barriere des plaisirs," *Revoltes logiques* 7 (Spring–Summer 1978): 30; Rancière, *La nuit*, pp. 34–35, all quoted in Reid, "The Night of the Proletarians," pp. 451, 457.

23. In *The Holy Family* Marx wrote: "These *mass-minded* communist workers, employed, for instance, in Manchester or Lyons workshops, do not believe that by *'pure thinking'* they will be able to argue away their industrial masters and their own political debasement. They are most painfully aware of the *difference* between *being* and *thinking*, between *consciousness* and *life*. They know that property, capital, money, wage-labor and the like are no ideal figments of the brain but very practical, very objective products of their self-estrangement and that therefore they must be abolished in a practical, objective way for man to become man not only in *thinking*, in *consciousness*, but in mass *being*, in life." Quoted in Harold Mah, *The End of Philosophy, the Origin of "Ideology": Karl Marx and the Crisis of the Young Hegelians* (Berkeley: University of California Press, 1987), p. 213.

24. Reid, "The Night of the Proletarians," quote from p. 452, and for Reid's discussion of deconstruction, pp. 453–455; Rancière, "The Myth of the Artisan," esp. pp. 326–328. On Rancière's connection to the French Derrideans see Nancy Fraser, "The French Derrideans: Politicizing Deconstruction or Deconstructing Politics," *New German Critique* 33 (Fall 1984): 128.

25. Rancière, "The Myth of the Artisan," p. 334.

26. Kenneth Burke, *The Philosophy of Literary Form: Studies in Symbolic Action* (Baton Rouge: Louisiana State University Press, 1941), p. 139.

27. Critiques of Rancière have been waged by William Sewell, Christopher Johnson, and Nicholas Papayanis. Rancière has responded. See *International Labor and Working-Class History* 24 (Fall 1983): 17–25; ibid., 25 (Spring 1984), pp. 39–46.

28. Marx and Engels, *The German Ideology*, p. 95.

29. Two versions of the Stedman Jones article have appeared. The original statement was in Gareth Stedman Jones, "The Language of Chartism," in Dorothy Thompson and James Epstein, eds., *The Chartist Experience: Studies in Working Class Radicalism and Culture, 1830–1860* (London: Macmillan, 1982), pp. 3–58, while a fuller account appears in Stedman Jones, "Rethinking

Chartism," in his *Languages of Class: Studies in English Working Class History* (Cambridge: Cambridge University Press, 1983), pp. 90–178. All references here refer to this latter, lengthier statement.

30. Among the important responses to Stedman Jones's essay see Wood, *The Retreat from Class*, esp. pp. 102–115; John Foster, "The Declassing of Language," *New Left Review* 150 (March–April 1985): 29–46; Paul A. Pickering, "Class without Words: Symbolic Communication in the Chartist Movement," *Past & Present* 112 (August 1986): 144–162; Joan Scott, "On Language, Gender, and Working-Class History," *International Labor and Working Class History* 31 (Spring 1987), and the responses to Scott by Palmer, Stansell, and Rabinbach, pp. 1–36; Dorothy Thompson, "The Languages of Class," *Bulletin of the Society for the Study of Labour History* 52, no. 1 (1987): 54–57; Neville Kirk, "In Defence of Class: A Critique of Recent Revisionist Writing on the Nineteenth-Century English Working Class," *International Review of Social History* 32 (1987): 2–47; Robert Gray, "The Deconstructing of the English Working Class," *Social History* 11 (October 1986): 363–373; James Epstein, "Rethinking the Categories of Working Class History," *Labour/Le Travail* 18 (Fall 1986): 195–208; Epstein, "Understanding the Cap of Liberty: Symbolic Practice and Social Conflict in Early Nineteenth-Century England," *Past & Present* 122 (February 1989): 75–118; Nicholas Rogers, "Chartism and Class Struggle," *Labour/Le Travail* 19 (Spring 1987): 143–152; Christopher Clark, "Politics, Language, and Class," *Radical History Review* 34 (1986): 78–86.

31. Stedman Jones, "Rethinking Chartism," esp. pp. 94, 101, 102, 107, 125, 136, 156.

32. Note for instance Clive Behagg, "An Alliance with the Middle Class: The Birmingham Political Union and Early Chartism," in Thompson and Epstein, eds., *The Chartist Experience*, pp. 59–86; I. J. Prothero, "William Benbow and the Concept of the 'General Strike,' " *Past & Present* 63 (1974): 132–171; T. M. Parssinen, "Association, Convention, and Anti-Parliament in British Radical Politics, 1771–1848," *English Historical Review* 88 (1973): 504–533; Bryan D. Palmer, *A Culture in Conflict: Skilled Workers and Industrial Capitalism in Hamilton, Ontario, 1860–1914* (Montreal: McGill-Queen's University Press, 1979), pp. 97–123; Gregory S. Kealey, *Toronto Workers Respond to Industrial Capitalism, 1860–1892* (Toronto: University of Toronto Press, 1980), pp. 3–17.

33. Stedman Jones, "Introduction," *Languages of Class*, pp. 21–22. Cf. Gray, "The Deconstructing of the English Working Class."

34. Thompson, "The Languages of Class," p. 54.

35. Stedman Jones, "Introduction," *Languages of Class*, p. 24.

36. This point is made in Gray, "The Deconstructing of the English Working Class," pp. 367–368. Cf. J. G. A. Pocock, *Politics, Language, and Time* (New York: Atheneum, 1971), pp. 17–25.

37. See Joan Scott, "On Language, Gender, and Working-Class History," *International Labor and Working-Class History* 31 (Spring 1987): esp. 3–7; Pickering, "Class without Words"; Epstein, "The Cap of Liberty." Stedman Jones concedes the point in a footnote but then proceeds to ignore its implications. "Rethinking Chartism," p. 95, n. 10: "Nor is it intended to suggest that what is

being offered here is an exhaustive analysis of the language of Chartism. The language analysed here is largely taken from radical literature and speeches reported in the radical press. Quite apart from the fact that such reported speech took no account of accent or dialect, I am not arguing that this is the only language Chartists employed. What is examined here is only the public political language of the movement."

38. Kirk, "In Defence of Class"; Thompson, *The People's Science: The Popular Political Economy of Exploitation and Crisis, 1816–1834* (Cambridge: Cambridge University Press, 1984).

39. Dorothy Thompson, *The Chartists: Popular Politics in the Industrial Revolution* (New York: Pantheon, 1984), pp. 238–239.

40. For Stedman Jones's privileging of the national movement see "Rethinking Chartism," pp. 98–99. Yet much of the most advanced Chartist scholarship of the last two decades has attempted to uncover Chartism's local history. Note, for instance, the bulk of the essays in Thompson and Epstein, eds., *The Chartist Experience*.

41. On the persistence of small-scale production see Raphael Samuel, "The Workshop of the World: Steam Power and Hand Technology in Mid-Victorian Britain," *History Workshop Journal* 3 (Spring 1977): 6–72. This raises questions about the extent to which the working class was "made" before Chartism. See Eric J. Hobsbawm, "The Making of the Working Class, 1870–1914," in Hobsbawm, *Workers: Worlds of Labor* (New York: Pantheon, 1984), pp. 194–213.

42. Note the comments in Wood, *The Retreat from Class*, esp. pp. 107–112.

43. Stedman Jones, "Rethinking Chartism," p. 144.

44. Kirk, "In Defence of Class," pp. 41–47.

45. William M. Reddy, *Money and Liberty in Modern Europe: A Critique of Historical Understanding* (Cambridge: Cambridge University Press, 1987), pp. 194–195.

46. See David Mandel, *The Petrograd Workers and the Fall of the Old Regime*, vols. 1 and 2 (London: Macmillan, 1983); Victoria E. Bonnell, *Roots of Rebellion: Workers' Politics and Organizations in St. Petersburg and Moscow, 1900–1914* (Berkeley: University of California Press, 1983); Steve Smith, "Craft Consciousness, Class Consciousness: Petrograd, 1917," *History Workshop* 11 (Spring 1981): 33–58.

47. Karl Marx and Frederick Engels, *On Britain* (Moscow: Progress Publishers, 1953), pp. 249–271; Marx and Engels, *Selected Correspondence, 1846–1895* (New York: International, 1935), pp. 55, 58–59, 86–89, 100–102, 115–116.

48. Marx and Engels, *On Britain*, p. 270. In the *Communist Manifesto* Marx and Engels would stress that in the beginnings of its struggles the working-class challenge to the bourgeoisie would necessarily take place "by means of measures, therefore, which appear economically insufficient and untenable, but which, in the course of the movement, outstrip themselves, necessitate further inroads upon the old social order, and are unavoidable as a means of entirely revolutionising the means of production." See, as well, Leon Trotsky, *The Transitional Program for Socialist Revolution* (New York: Pathfinder Press, 1973).

49. William M. Reddy, *The Rise of Market Culture: The Textile Trade and French Society, 1750–1900* (Cambridge: Cambridge University Press, 1984), p. 256.

50. Reddy, *Money and Liberty*, pp. 195, 254. No actual page numbers are cited, nor are any specific quotations offered.

51. Thompson, *The Chartists*, pp. 269, 253, and preface, no pagination.

52. Ibid., p. 253: "A whole range of public activity was simply assumed to be the province of the higher orders, and the manner and langue in which it was conducted effectively excluded even such working men as might technically be entitled to take part."

53. Thompson, "The Languages of Class," p. 57.

54. Reddy, *Money and Liberty*, p. 203.

55. In *The Rise of Market Culture*, p. 288, Reddy writes: "What human beings need is not located in particular arrangements of words, in any case, but in what groups of individuals, with more or less accord, make of them." Agreed, but this hardly sanctions making of words whatever you want, denying implicitly that meaning has any identifiable presence.

56. Reddy, *Money and Liberty*, pp. 26, 28, 30, 203. For a different reading of Thompson see Bryan D. Palmer, *The Making of E. P. Thompson: Marxism, Humanism, and History* (Toronto: New Hogtown Press, 1981).

57. E. P. Thompson, "Eighteenth-Century English Society: Class Struggle without Class?" *Social History* 3 (1978): 146–150.

58. Reddy, *Money and Liberty*, p. 203.

59. See, for instance, Eric Hobsbawm, *Workers: Worlds of Labor* (New York: Pantheon, 1984), pp. 176–213; David M. Gordon, Richard Edwards, and Michael Reich, *Segmented Work, Divided Workers: The Historical Transformation of Labor in the United States* (New York: Cambridge University Press, 1982); Bryan D. Palmer, "Social Formation and Class Formation in North America, 1800–1900," in David Levine, ed., *Proletarianization and Family History* (New York: Academic Press, 1984), pp. 229–309.

60. See the argument in Mike Davis, *Prisoners of the American Dream: Politics and Economy in the History of the US Working Class* (London: Verso, 1986), Part II.

61. E. J. Hobsbawm, "Class Consciousness in History," in István Mészáros, ed., *Aspects of History and Class Consciousness* (London: Routledge & Kegan Paul, 1971), p. 8.

62. Note G. E. M. de Ste. Croix, *The Class Struggle in the Ancient Greek World* (London: Duckworth, 1981).

63. Karl Marx and Frederick Engels, "Manifesto of the Communist Party," in *Selected Works* (Moscow: Progress, 1968), p. 35.

64. I have offered a brief statement on the Canadian context in "Introduction," in Palmer, ed., *The Character of Class Struggle: Essays in Canadian Working-Class History, 1850–1985* (Toronto: McClelland and Stewart, 1986), pp. 9–14.

65. There is no necessity to cite the extensive literature that relates to this discussion of class, class struggle, and class consciousness. A brief introduction to the diversity of theoretical writing on these matters can be found in Tom

Bottomore, ed., *A Dictionary of Marxist Thought* (Cambridge: Harvard University Press, 1983), pp. 74–83. Cf. Derek Sayer, *The Violence of Abstraction: The Analytic Foundations of Historical Materialism* (Oxford: Basil Blackwell, 1987); Stephen A. Resnick and Richard D. Wolff, *Knowledge and Class: A Marxian Critique of Political Economy* (Chicago: University of Chicago Press, 1987).

66. See Bonnie G. Smith, *Ladies of the Leisure Class: The Bourgeoises of Northern France in the Nineteenth Century* (Princeton, N.J.: Princeton University Press, 1981), esp. pp. 53–92, "Domesticity: The Rhetoric of Reproduction," a chapter that makes reference to early poststructuralist and psychoanalytic concern with language. For one disbelieving review see Richard Cobb, "Bourgeois Ladies from the North-East of France," in Cobb, *People and Places* (New York: Oxford University Press, 1986), pp. 145–155.

67. Thorstein Veblen, *The Theory of the Leisure Class* (New York: New American Library, 1953), p. 176.

68. See Leon Fink, "The New Labor History and the Powers of Historical Pessimism: Consensus, Hegemony, and the Case of the Knights of Labor," *Journal of American History* 75 (June 1988): 123–124, 121; Gray, "The Deconstructing of the English Working Class," p. 373; Sean Wilentz, "Against Exceptionalism: Class Consciousness and the American Labor Movement, 1790–1920," *International Labor and Working-Class History* 26 (1984): 1–24; Wilentz, *Chants Democratic: New York City and the Rise of the American Working Class, 1788–1850* (New York: Oxford University Press, 1984), p. 16. It is of course hardly surprising that Michael Kazin embraces the Stedman Jones approach. See Kazin, "People Not Class," p. 282, n. 2.

69. Kazin, "People Not Class."

70. On Stedman Jones's 1980s popular frontism see "Why Is the Labour Party in a Mess?" in *Languages of Class*, pp. 239–256, while the quote on Chartism is from "Rethinking Chartism," in ibid., p. 178. On his earlier Althusserianism see ibid., pp. 12–13, and, on p. 18 reference to an unpublished Stedman Jones paper written in 1977 entitled "The Limits of a Proletarian Theory in England before 1850." Note, as well, Stedman Jones, "The Pathology of English History," *New Left Review* 44 (July–August 1967): 29–44; Stedman Jones, "The Marxism of the Early Lukacs," in New Left Review, ed., *Western Marxism: A Critical Reader* (London: Verso, 1978), pp. 11–60.

71. Peter Burke, "Languages and Anti-languages in Early Modern Italy," *History Workshop Journal* 11 (Spring 1981): 24.

72. Hugh Cunningham, "The Language of Patriotism, 1750–1914," *History Workshop Journal* 12 (Autumn 1981): 8–33; Robert Gray, "The Languages of Factory Reform in Britain, c. 1830–1860," in Patrick Joyce, ed., *The Historical Meanings of Work* (Cambridge: Cambridge University Press, 1987), pp. 143–179, esp. pp. 178–179.

73. William M. Reddy, "The Moral Sense of Farce: The Patois Literature of Lille Factory Laborers, 1848–1870," in Kaplan and Koepp, ed., *Work in France*, pp. 364–392; Reddy, *The Rise of Market Culture*, pp. 253–288.

74. See Ivan Illich, *Shadow Work* (Boston: Marion Boyars, 1981), pp. 29–51.

75. See David Garrioch, "Verbal Insults in Eighteenth-Century Paris," in

Burke and Porter, eds., *The Social History of Language*, pp. 104–119; Peter N. Moogk, " 'Thieving Buggers' and 'Stupid Sluts': Insults and Popular Culture in New France," *William and Mary Quarterly* 36 (1979): 524–547.

Chapter 5

1. Elizabeth Cady Stanton, ed., *The Woman's Bible* (New York: European Publishing, 1895). Cf. Mary Vetterling-Braggin, ed., *Sexist Language: A Modern Philosophical Analysis* (n.p.: Littlefield, Adams, 1981).

2. Mary R. Beard, *Woman as Force in History: A Study in Traditions and Realities* (New York: Macmillan, 1946), p. 51.

3. Sheila Rowbotham, *Woman's Consciousness, Man's World* (Harmondsworth: Penguin, 1973), pp. 32–33.

4. On the definition of gender see Joan Scott, "Gender: A Useful Category of Historical Analysis," *American Historical Review* 91 (October 1986): esp. 1067.

5. See, among many other studies, Robin Lakoff, *Language and Woman's Place* (New York: Octagon Books, 1976); Mary Ritchie Key, *Male/Female Language: With a Comprehensive Bibliography* (Metuchen, N.J.: Scarecrow Press, 1975); Alette Olin Hill, *Mother Tongue, Father Time: A Decade of Linguistic Revolt* (Bloomington: Indiana University Press, 1986); Cheris Kramarae, *Women and Men Speaking* (London: Newbury House, 1981); Philip M. Smith, *Language, the Sexes, and Society* (Oxford: Basil Blackwell, 1985); Joyce Penfield, ed., *Women and Language in Transition* (Albany: State University of New York Press, 1987); Barrie Thorne, Chris Kramarae, Nancy Henley, eds., *Language, Gender, and Society* (London: Newbury House, 1983); Carol P. MacCormack and Mailyn Strathern, eds., *Nature, Culture and Gender* (Cambridge: Cambridge University Press, 1980).

6. Gerda Lerner, *The Creation of Patriarchy* (New York: Oxford University Press, 1986), p. 238.

7. Essentialism and the analysis of gender now implies, as it does in the relation of essentialism and the interpretation of class, something quite specific. It lays stress on the links between women's lives, women's bodies, and nature, positing what Adrienne Rich calls the "cosmic essence of womanhood," a transhistoric, cross-class, instinctual sensitivity that, through women's reproductive capacities and motherhood, keep women in touch with the creative, nurturing, and positive aspects of life. For an introduction to essentialism, as well as a forceful critique, see Lynne Segal, *Is the Future Female? Troubled Thoughts on Contemporary Feminism* (London: Virago, 1987), where she points out: "What is most essentially human is precisely that our lives, women's and men's, are *not* just determined by biological necessity but crucially also by human action and vision" (p. 11).

8. Shulamith Firestone, *The Dialectic of Sex: The Case for Feminist Revolution* (New York: William Morrow, 1970); Dale Spender, *Man Made Language* (London: Routledge & Kegan Paul, 1980); Andrea E. Goldsmith, "Notes on the Tyranny of Language Usage," in Cheris Kramarae, ed., *The Voices and Words of Women and Men* (Oxford: Pergamon Press, 1980), pp. 179–191.

9. See Adrienne Rich, *On Lies, Secrets, and Silence: Selected Prose, 1966–1978* (New York: W. W. Norton, 1979), esp. pp. 9–20, for a succinct statement.

10. Most directly in Carol MacMillan, *Women, Reason, and Nature* (Princeton, N.J.: Princeton University Press, 1982), but see, as well, Genevieve Lloyd, *The Man of Reason: "Male" and "Female" in Western Philosophy* (Minneapolis: University of Minnesota Press, 1984); Susan Moller Okin, *Women in Western Political Thought* (Princeton, N.J.: Princeton University Press, 1979).

11. For an extremely useful introduction see Janet Sayers, *Sexual Contradictions: Psychology, Psychoanalysis, and Feminism* (London: Tavistock, 1986).

12. Alice A. Jardine, *Gynesis: Configurations of Woman and Modernity* (Ithaca, N.Y.: Cornell University Press, 1985), p. 25, with pp. 13–28 focusing on the differences of French and American feminisms. Note, as well, on this problem of national idiom, Rosemarie Tong, *Feminist Thought: A Comprehensive Introduction* (Boulder and San Francisco: Westview Press, 1989); Gayatri Chakravorty Spivak, "French Feminism in an International Frame," in *In Other Worlds: Essays in Cultural Politics* (New York: Methuen, 1987), pp. 134–153, although most of the essays in this collection address the matter by "entering the Third World."

13. See Christine Delphy, "Protofeminism and Antifeminism," in Christine Delphy, *Close to Home: A Materialist Analysis of Women's Oppression* (Amherst: University of Massachusetts Press, 1984), pp. 182–210; Jane Flax, "Postmodernism and Gender Relations in Feminist Theory," *Signs: Journal of Women in Culture and Society* 12 (1987): 621–643; Mary Poovey, "Feminism and Deconstruction," *Feminist Studies* 14 (Spring 1988): 51–65. For an introduction to Psychanalyse et Politique (or, as it came to be known, Psych et Po) see Claire Duchen, *French Connections: Voices from the Women's Movement in France* (Amherst: University of Massachusetts Press, 1987), pp. 45–54.

14. Catharine A. MacKinnon, *Feminism Unmodified: Discourses on Life and Law* (Cambridge: Harvard University Press, 1987), pp. 8–9. A different, but complementary, perspective appears in Michèle Barrett, *Women's Oppression Today: Problems in Marxist Feminist Analysis* (London: Verso, 1980), p. 113, where it is argued that, "contemporary capitalism is *not* simply 'difference,' but . . . division, oppression, inequality, internalized inferiority for women."

15. Ivan Illich, *Gender* (New York: Pantheon, 1982), pp. 132–139, provides a succinct introduction to the issues and literature involved in an exploration of the relationship of language and gender.

16. Susan Harding, "Women and Words in a Spanish Village," in Rayna R. Reiter, ed., *Toward an Anthropology of Women* (New York: Monthly Review Press, 1975), p. 287. Note, as well, Patricia C. Nichols, "Linguistic Options and Choices for Black Women in the Rural South," in Thorne, Kramarae, and Henley, eds., *Language, Gender, and Society*, pp. 54–68.

17. Elionor Keenan, "Norm Makers, Norm Breakers: Use of Speech by Men and Women in a Malagasy Community," in J. F. Sherzer and R. Bauman, eds., *Exploration in the Ethnograpy of Speaking* (New York: Cambridge University Press, 1975), cited in Illich, *Gender*, p. 138.

18. For a statement on the importance of Lakoff, see Hill, *Mother Tongue, Father Time*, pp. 1–19. Note, as well, Key, *Male/Female Language*.

19. Traditional linguistics remains resistant to any tampering with the masculine as unmarked gender. For an example see the preface in Roy Harris, *The Language Makers* (Ithaca, N.Y.: Cornell University Press, 1980). The most revealing case was the Harvard Linguistics Department's response to a report in the *Harvard Crimson* that women had initiated a linguistic change in the Divinity School, where a class voted to avoid use of masculine pronouns when referring to all people and to God. See Hill, "Pronoun Envy," in *Mother Tongue, Father Time*, pp. 50–65; Casey Miller and Kate Swift, "The Language of Religion," in Miller and Swift, eds., *Words and Women* (Garden City, N.Y.: Doubleday, 1976), esp. pp. 75–77.

20. See, among other statements, Joan Scott, "Women in History: The Modern Period," *Past & Present* 101 (November 1983): 141–157.

21. Mary Daly's *Gyn/Ecology: The Metaethics of Radical Feminism* (Boston: Beacon Press, 1978), pp. 414, 466, contains some odd suggestions about language, including the importance of learning from the nonverbal communications of dumb animals, which Daly claims are "so superior to androcratic speech." Daly reports contributions to her "theory" from a cow, a blackbird, sheep, goats, a monkey, a crab, a dog, and horses, among others.

22. Dale Spender, *Man Made Language* (London: Routledge & Kegan Paul, 1980), pp. 2–4.

23. For cautions about this kind of conception of patriarchy see Rosalind Coward, *Patriarchal Precedents; Sexuality and Social Relations* (London: Routledge & Kegan Paul, 1983); Elizabeth Fox-Genovese, "Culture and Consciousness in the Intellectual History of European Women," *Signs* 12 (1987): 531; Sheila Rowbotham, "The Trouble with 'Patriarchy,'" in Raphael Samuel, ed., *People's History and Socialist Theory* (London: Routledge & Kegan Paul, 1981), pp. 364–369; Scott, "Women in History," p. 151. There have been societies that have been patriarchal. See Stephanie Coontz and Peta Henderson, eds., *Women's Work, Men's Property: The Origins of Gender and Class* (London: Verso, 1986); Gerda Lerner, *The Creation of Patriarchy* (New York: Oxford University Press, 1986). And patriarchy did stretch into the more modern period. Note the discussions in Allan Kulikoff, "The Origins of Domestic Patriarchy among White Families," in *Tobacco and Slaves: The Development of Southern Cultures in the Chesapeake, 1680–1800* (Chapel Hill: University of North Carolina Press, 1986); Katherine Mary Jean McKenna, "The Life of Anne Murray Powell, 1755–1849: A 'Case Study' of the Position of Women in Early Upper Canadian Elite Society" (Ph.D. dissertation, Queen's University, 1987). The indiscriminate use of patriarchy and the adjectival patriarchal among historians has collapsed these terms into a suitable description of any and all gender subordination. This I distance myself from, holding that societies that institutionalize and totalize male dominance over women and children, extending the power relations of the family consciously into the realm of the state and all aspects of civil society, need to be differentiated from other social formations in which gender inequalities and subordination continue but in ways that bear little resemblance to the totalizing confinements of patriarchy. I thus disagree with the definition of patriarchy offered in Lerner's *Creation of Patriarchy*, p. 239.

24. Deborah Cameron, *Feminism and Linguistic Theory* (London: Macmillan, 1985), esp. p. 110.

25. Maria Black and Rosalind Coward, "Linguistic, Social and Sexual Relations," *Screen Education* 39 (1981): esp. 70–78, cited in Cameron, *Feminism and Linguistic Theory*, pp. 115–117, 132.

26. Cameron, *Feminism and Linguistic Theory*, pp. 111, 157, 153, 169–171.

27. Ibid., p. 2.

28. Juliet Mitchell, *Psychoanalysis and Feminism: Freud, Reich, Laing, and Women* (New York: Pantheon, 1974), esp. pp. xv–xxiii; Angela McRobbie, "An Interview with Juliet Mitchell," *New Left Review* 170 (July–August 1988): esp. 80–84. On the early radical Freudians and their repression see Russell Jacoby, *The Repression of Psychoanalysis: Otto Fenichel and the Political Freudians* (New York: Basic Books, 1983). For the anti-Freudianism of sectors of feminism see Firestone, *The Dialectic of Sex*, pp. 41–71; Kate Millett, *Sexual Politics* (New York: Doubleday, 1970), esp. pp. 176–189. For Millett's importance see Chris Weedon, *Feminist Practice and Poststructuralist Theory* (Oxford: Basil Blackwell, 1987), p. 44; Toril Moi, *Sexual/Textual Politics: Feminist Literary Theory* (London: Methuen, 1985), pp. 24–31. See, as well, Roberta Hamilton, "The Collusion with Patriarchy: A Psychoanalytic Account," in Roberta Hamilton and Michèle Barrett, eds., *The Politics of Diversity: Feminism, Marxism, and Nationalism* (London: Verso, 1986), pp. 385–397. Brief current statements on feminism and psychoanalysis can be found in Rose, "Femininity and its Discontents," in *Sexuality in the Field of Vision* (London: Verso, 1986), pp. 83–103; Cameron, *Feminism and Linguistic Theory*, pp. 114–133; Clare Burton, *Subordination: Feminism and Social Theory* (Sydney: George Allen & Unwin, 1985), pp. 86–103.

29. Mitchell, *Psychoanalysis and Feminism*, pp. xxi–xxii. Psychanalyse et Politique later dropped the hierarchical capitalization and renamed itself "politique et psychanalyse" in an effort to clarify its priorities. Here I shall refer to it by its original formulation. See Moi, *Sexual/Textual Politics*, pp. 95–96.

30. Antoinette Fouque, *Le Quotidien des Femmes* (1975), quoted in Duchen, *French Connections*, p. 48.

31. Quoted in Mitchell, *Psychoanalysis and Feminism*, p. xxii.

32. "Interview with Antoinette Fouque," in Duchen, *French Connections*, pp. 50–54.

33. Duchen, *French Connections*, p. 13. Note as well, Duchen, *Feminism in France* (London: Routledge & Kegan Paul, 1986).

34. The key figure in Psych et Po is Hélène Cixous. I have laid less emphasis on Cixous because her influence seems to be waning. But for a treatment of her, Irigaray, and Kristeva, see Tong, *Feminist Thought*, pp. 217–233.

35. For a useful introduction to Kristeva that distinguishes three distinct moments of Kristeva's development—coexistent with the 1960s, the 1970s, and the 1980s—see Alice Jardine, "Opaque Texts and Transparent Contexts: The Political Difference of Julia Kristeva," in Nancy K. Miller, ed., *The Poetics of Gender* (New York: Columbia University Press, 1986), pp. 96–116. I have not followed such a periodization only because I am distilling much and trying to situate Kristeva's work as a whole.

36. For another statement on marginality see Spivak, "Explanation and Culture: Marginalia," *In Other Worlds*, pp. 103–117.

37. Terry Eagleton, *Literary Theory: An Introduction* (Minneapolis: University of Minnesota Press, 1983), p. 190. See Kristeva's statement on Bakhtin in "Word, Dialogue and Novel," and on the semiotic in "Semiotics: A Critical Science and/or a Critique of Science" as well as "Revolution in Poetic Language." All are found in Toril Moi, ed., *The Kristeva Reader* (Oxford: Basil Blackwell, 1986), pp. 34–61, 74–88, 89–135, the latter a translation of some critical passages from *Revolution in Poetic Language*, published in English translation in 1984 from the original French *Doctorat d'Etat* of 1974.

38. The quote is from Julia Kristeva, *Desire in Language: A Semiotic Approach to Literature and Art* (New York: Columbia University Press, 1980), pp. vii–viii. Introductions to Kristeva are the useful opening statement in Moi's invaluably accessible collection of Kristeva's writings, *The Kristeva Reader*, pp. 1–22, which ends with a helpful bibliography on Kristeva and her critics/commentators; Jacqueline Rose, "Julia Kristeva: Take Two," in Rose, *Sexuality in the Field of Vision* (London: Verso, 1986), pp. 141–164; Andrea Nye, "Women Clothed with the Sun: Julia Kristeva and the Escape from/to Language," *Signs* 12 (1987): 664–686.

39. Quoted in Moi, *Sexual/Textual Politics*, p. 168.

40. "Julia Kristeva in Conversation with Rosalind Coward," in Lisa Appignanesi, ed., *Desire* (1984), p. 25, cited in Moi, ed., *Kristeva Reader*, p. 7. For an extended comment on Kristeva's *About Chinese Women* see Spivak, "French Feminism in an International Frame," pp. 136–142.

41. Kristeva, "Woman Can Never Be Defined," in E. Marks and I. de Courtivron, eds., *New French Feminisms* (Brighton: Harvester, 1981), p. 137. Also, Kristeva, "Talking about *Polylogue*," in Toril Moi, ed., *French Feminist Thought: A Reader* (Oxford: Basil Blackwell, 1987), pp. 110–117.

42. See Chris Weedon, *Feminist Pracice and Poststructuralist Theory* (Oxford: Basil Blackwell, 1987), pp. 68–71, 88–91.

43. For a different perspective see Barbara Ehrenreich, Elizabeth Hess, and Gloria Jacobs, *Re-making Love: The Feminization of Sex* (Garden City, N.Y.: Doubleday, 1986).

44. Kristeva, "Women's Time," in Nannerl O. Keohane, Michell Z. Rosaldo, and Barbara C. Gelpi, eds., *Feminist Theory: A Critique of Ideology* (Chicago: University of Chicago Press, 1982), p. 39.

45. See the translated passages of Kristeva's *Histoires d'amour* in Kristeva, "Freud and Love: Treatment and Its Discontents," in Moi, ed., *Kristeva Reader*, pp. 238–271.

46. See Rose, "Julia Kristeva: Take Two," pp. 163–164; Moi, ed., *Kristeva Reader*, "Introduction," pp. 18–19, and Kristeva, "Stabat Mater," pp. 160–186; Kristeva, "Motherhood According to Giovanni Bellini," in *Desire in Language*, pp. 237–270; and, less explicitly, Nye, "Women Clothed with the Sun," p. 674. For another perspective see Heather Jon Maroney, "Embracing Motherhood: New Feminist Theory," in Roberta Hamilton and Michèle Barrett, ed., *The Politics of Diversity: Feminism, Marxism, and Nationalism* (London: Verso, 1986), pp. 398–423.

47. Quote from Cameron, *Feminism and Linguistic Theory*, p. 125.

48. See, for instance, Jennifer Stone, "The Horrors of Power: a Critique of Kristeva," in Francis Barker et al., eds., *The Politics of Theory: Proceedings of the Essex Conference on the Sociology of Literature, July 1982* (Colchester: University of Essex, 1983), pp. 38–48.

49. Kristeva, "Why the United States?" and "A New Type of Intellectual: The Dissident," are relevant here. Both appear in Moi, ed., *Kristeva Reader*, pp. 272–300.

50. See Moi., ed., *Kristeva Reader*, "Introduction," p. 8; Rose, "Julia Kristeva: Take Two," p. 152; although Moi, *Sexual/Textual Politics*, pp. 168–173, is more critical.

51. Kristeva, "A New Type of Intellectual," pp. 299–300.

52. Eagleton, *Literary Theory*, pp. 190–191.

53. The quotes are from Luce Irigaray, "Women's Exile," *Ideology and Consciousness* 1 (May 1977): 62, 71, quoted in Cameron, *Feminism and Linguistic Theory*, pp. 127–129, which provides a succinct introduction to Irigaray. For Irigaray's view of sexual difference see Moi, ed., *French Feminist Thought*, pp. 118–130.

54. From a different tradition note the discussion in Kenneth Burke, "The Thinking of the Body (Comments on the Imagery of Catharsis in Literature)," in *Language as Symbolic Action: Essays on Life, Literature and Method* (Berkeley: University of California Press, 1966), pp. 308–343.

55. Luce Irigaray, *Speculum of the Other Woman* (Ithaca, N.Y.: Cornell University Press, 1985), pp. 124–125, 140.

56. The quote is from Luce Irigaray, *This Sex Which Is Not One* (Ithaca, N.Y.: Cornell University Press, 1985), p. 24. For an introduction to Irigaray's stress on women's autoerotism and the female body's centrality see Janet Sayers, *Sexual Contradictions: Psychology, Psychoanalysis, and Feminism* (London: Tavistock, 1986), pp. 42–48.

57. Luce Irigaray, "When Our Lips Speak Together," *Signs* 6 (Autumn 1980): 76.

58. See Irigaray, "The Blind Spot of an Old Dream of Symmetry," in *Speculum of the Other Woman*, pp. 11–129.

59. Carolyn Burke, "Introduction of Luce Irigaray's 'When our Lips Speak Together,'" *Signs* 6 (Autumn 1980): 68.

60. "Variations on Common Themes," in Marks and de Courtivron, eds., *New French Feminisms*, p. 219, as quoted in Cameron, *Feminism and Linguistic Theory*, p. 130. Note, as well, Mary Jacobus, "The Question of Language: Men of Maxims and the Mill on the Floss," *Critical Inquiry* 8 (1981): 207.

61. See the discussion "Patriarchal Reflections: Luce Irigaray's Looking-Glass," in Moi, *Sexual/Textual Politics*, pp. 127–149.

62. Monique Plaza, "'Phallomorphic Power' and the Psychology of 'Woman,'" *Ideology and Consciousness* 4 (Autumn 1978): 32, cited in ibid., p. 147.

63. Irigaray, *This Sex Which Is Not One*, p. 28.

64. Ibid., pp. 112, 150; Irigaray, "When Our Lips Speak Together," p. 76.

65. See, for another perspective, Mary O'Brien, *The Politics of Reproduction* (London: Routledge & Kegan Paul, 1981).

66. Irigaray, *This Sex Which Is Not One*, pp. 32, 172–173.

67. See Linda J. Nicholson, *Gender and History: The Limits of Social Theory in the Age of the Family* (New York: Columbia University Press, 1986).

68. See Joan Kelly, *Women, History, and Theory: The Essays of Joan Kelly* (Chicago: University of Chicago Press, 1984).

69. Note Firestone, *The Dialectic of Sex*; O'Brien, *The Politics of Reproduction*; and for one of the most explicit statements from MacKinnon, "Feminism, Marxism, Method, and the State: An Agenda for Theory," *Signs* 7 (Spring 1982), reprinted in Keohane, Rosaldo, and Gelpi, eds., *Feminist Theory: A Critique of Ideology*, pp. 1–30. For an historian's qualms about this work see Joan Scott, "Gender: A Useful Category of Historical Analysis," pp. 1058–1059.

70. A host of texts might be considered here. Note, among many: Jeffrey Weeks, *Sex, Politics, and Society: The Regulation of Sexuality Since 1800* (London: Longmans, 1981); John D'Emilio and Estelle B. Freedman, *Intimate Matters: A History of Sexuality in America* (New York: Harper & Row, 1988); Ann Snitow, Christine Stansell, and Sharon Thompson, *Powers of Desire: The Politics of Sexuality* (New York: Monthly Review, 1983); Carol Smith-Rosenberg, *Disorderly Conduct: Visions of Gender in Victorian America* (New York: Oxford University Press, 1985); Mariana Valverde, *Sex Power and Pleasure* (Toronto: Women's Press, 1985); Michael Kaufman, ed., *Beyond Patriarchy: Essays by Men on Pleasure, Power, and Change* (Toronto: Oxford University Press, 1987); Howard Buchbinder et al., *Who's on Top? The Politics of Heterosexuality* (Toronto: Garamond, 1987); Gary Kinsman, *The Regulation of Desire* (Montreal: Black Rose, 1986). For an indication of how traditionally focused studies of male enclaves in the world of work can be scrutinized on the basis of an attention to masculinity/sexuality see Steven Maynard, "A Man's Job? The Social Construction of Masculinity in Working Class History," forthcoming *Labour/le Travail* (1989).

71. See the important recently collected essays in Cora Kaplan, *Sea Changes: Essays in Culture and Feminism* (London: Verso, 1986).

72. See Maria Mies, *Patriarchy and Accumulation on a World Scale* (London: Zed Books, 1986); Mark Rosenfeld, " 'It Was A Hard Life': Dimensions of Class, Gender, and Work in a Railway Community, 1920s–1950s," Paper presented to the Canadian Historical Association Meetings, June 1988; Joy Parr, "Rethinking Work and Kinship in a Canadian Hosiery Town, 1910–1950," *Feminist Studies* 13 (Spring 1987): 137–162.

73. Christine Stansell, *City of Women: Sex and Class in New York, 1789–1860* (New York: Knopf, 1986), pp. 127, 119, among many such examples. In another context Stansell, generally in favor of borrowing loosely from post-structuralism, expresses some inhibitions. See Stansell, "A Response to Joan Scott," *International Labor and Working Class History* 31 (Spring 1987): 28–29.

74. Judy Lown, "Not so much a Factory, More a Form of Patriarchy: Gender and Class during Industrialization," in Eva Gamarnikow et al., eds., *Gender, Class and Work* (London: Heinemann, 1983), pp. 30–33.

75. John D'Emilio and Estelle B. Freedman, *Intimate Matters: A History of Sexuality in America* (New York: Harper and Row, 1988), quote from p. xii.

Foucault appears twice in a four-hundred-page text, and the extensive bibliography has room for Shere Hite, Peter Laslett, and the demographic writings of Daniel Scott Smith and Robert V. Wells, but Derrida and the likes of Lacan get no mention.

76. Judith R. Walkowitz, *Prostitution and Victorian Society: Women, Class, and the State* (New York: Cambridge University Press, 1980), p. 5.

77. See, for instance, Jacques Donzelot, *The Policing of Families* (New York: Pantheon, 1979).

78. Sally Alexander, "Women, Class and Sexual Difference," *History Workshop* 17 (Spring 1984): 125–135, and the comments of Scott, "Gender: A Useful Category of Historical Analysis," pp. 1061–1066.

79. "Editors' Introduction," *Radical History Review* 43 (Winter 1989): 3.

80. Judith Walkowitz, Myra Jehlen, Bell Chevigny, "Patrolling the Borders: Feminist Historiography and the New Historicism," ibid., esp. pp. 25, 27, 28–30, 43.

81. Note as well Lyndal Roper, "Will and Honor: Sex, Words and Power in Augsburg Criminal Trials," ibid., pp. 45–71; Roper, " 'The Common Man,' 'The Common Good,' 'Common Women': Language and Gender in the German Reformation Commune," *Social History* 12 (1987): 1–20.

82. Judith Newton, "Family Fortunes: 'New History' and 'New Historicism,' " *Radical History Review* 43 (Winter 1989): 5–23, esp. 17. This approach, recognizing distinctions but calling for an understanding of their compatabilities, is also embraced by one of the panelists in the exchange, "Patrolling the Borders." See the comment of Bell Chevigny, ibid., pp. 37–40.

83. Myra Jehlen, "Patrolling the Borders," pp. 33–37.

84. Dorinda Outram, "La langage male de la vertu: Women and the Discourse of the French Revolution," in Peter Burke and Roy Porter, eds., *The Social History of Language* (Cambridge: Cambridge University Press, 1987), pp. 120–135, with quotes from pp. 129, 133. For documents relevant to this issue see Darline Gay Levy, Harriet Branson Applewhite, Mary Durham Johnson, eds., *Women in Revolutionary Paris, 1789–1795* (Urbana: University of Illinois Press, 1979). On the later period see Bonnie G. Smith, *Ladies of the Leisure Class: The Bourgeoises of Northern France in the Nineteenth Century* (Princeton, N.J.: Princeton University Press, 1981).

85. The legitimate interrogation of "history" is often undercut by the arrogance and ignorance of discourse theorists who assume historians have, until quite recently, been devoid of theory. Note Spivak, "A Literary Representation of the Subaltern: A Woman's Text from the Third World," *In Other Worlds*, pp. 241–242: "The production of historical accounts is the discursive narrativization of events. When historiography is self-consciously 'nontheoretical,' it sees its task, with respect to rival historical accounts of the same period, as bringing forth 'what really happened' in a value-neutral prose. Since the incursion of 'theory' into the discipline of history, and the uncomfortable advent of Michel Foucault, it is no longer too avant-garde to suspect or admit that 'events' are never not discursively constituted and that the language of historiography is always also language." Note, as well, Linda Hutcheon, "The Postmodern Problematizing of History," *English Studies in Canada* 14 (December 1988): 365–

382, and Len Findlay, "Otherwise Engaged: Postmodernism and the Resistance to History," ibid., pp. 383–399.

86. Denise Riley, *"Am I That Name?" Feminism and the Category of "Women" in History* (London: Macmillan Press, 1988), esp. pp. 1–5.

87. Riley, *"Am I That Name?"* p. 67; Stansell, "Response to Joan Scott," p. 28; E. P. Thompson, "The Poverty of Theory: or an Orrery of Errors," in *The Poverty of Theory and Other Essays* (London: Merlin, 1978), p. 205, a text Riley has little use for.

88. For some suggestion of this, although posed far more sympathetically than need be, see Ann Snitow, "What's in a Name? Denise Riley's Categorical Imperatives," *Voice Literary Supplement* (January–February 1989), pp. 36–37.

89. See, for instance, Irene Diamond and Lee Quinby, eds., *Feminism and Foucault: Reflections on Resistance* (Boston: Northeastern University Press, 1988). This collection of essays opens with Biddy Martin's "Feminism, Criticism, and Foucault," pp. 3–20, a useful statement on both the positive and problematic aspects of Foucault, but the remainder of the text usually avoids a direct critical confrontation with Foucault. Thus the editors' introduction situates feminism within a Foucauldian cycle of waves of power/knowledge, noting that in the twentieth century many "of the tenets of nineteenth-century feminism have been appropriated into operations of disciplinary power—hence the need for a new wave" (p. xi). The interpretive and political message seems to be that what is required is endless waves of mobilization to readdress the capacity of authority to accommodate and incorporate dissent within its endless waves of power/knowledge. Unquestioned is the extent to which incorporation and accommodation proceed on the basis of an incomplete programatic opposition to authority, a political lacuna connected directly to the poststructuralist Foucauldian conception of power itself, which refuses to situate power in a locatable center.

90. See, for instance, Jeffrey Weeks, *Sexuality and Its Discontents: Meanings, Myths, and Modern Sexualities* (London: Routledge & Kegan Paul, 1985), pp. 3, 6, 17; Weeks, *Sexuality* (London: Tavistock, 1986), p. 13.

91. For an indication of a critique of Weeks's radical pluralism see Bryan Bruce, "Modern Diseases: Gay Self-Representation in the Age of AIDS," *cineACTION* 15 (Winter 1988–1989): esp. 30, 37, drawing upon Leo Bersani, "Is the Rectum a Grave," in *October #43* (Cambridge: MIT Press, 1987), esp. pp. 205, 219. My thanks to Steven Maynard for bringing this source to my attention.

92. See especially Weeks, *Sexuality and Its Discontents*, pp. 185–195.

93. Randy Shilts, *And the Band Played On: Politics, People, and the AIDS Epidemic* (New York: St. Martin's Press, 1987). I am aware that this text is not an unproblematic source, weighted down as it is with a kind of journalistic moralism and sensationalism. Nevertheless, it shows clearly the class-ridden character of the gay community and relates these class divisions to the beginnings of the spread of AIDS. For an account of AIDS more amenable to gay activists see Cindy Patton, *Sex and Germs: The Politics of AIDS* (Montreal: Black Rose Books, 1986).

94. To use this kind of language is *not* to lapse into the sensationalized moral panic of the media, but to state a specific kind of reality. That elements of the

gay community have mobilized against AIDS and gone some distance along a path of resistance that is struggling to recoup some gain out of the losses sustained over the course of the past years is undeniable. But so, too, is what has been lost. The issue of the language with which AIDS is addressed is confronted explicitly in John Allemang, "Infectious Innuendo," Toronto *Globe & Mail*, 8 July 1989, and is central to Susan Sontag, *Aids and Its Metaphors* (New York: Farrar, Straus, and Giroux, 1989), a text that many would no doubt use to argue against my choice of words in this paragraph. But simply because the media has used this kind of language to cultivate fear and coerce a kind of resignation is no reason to retreat from the consequences of AIDS and withdraw into the comforts of "the struggle continues," however much it does. This *has* been a moment of defeat, whatever the future, and that defeat was a consequence of capital's essential indifference exacerbated by an inadequate political response on the part of the left and the gay milieu itself. This is not to blame the main North American victims of AIDS, gay males, but to point to the necessity of political responses to threats that are simultaneously material (health and death) and political (heightened homophobia and repression). See the excellent discussion in Simon Watney, *Policing Desire: Pornography, AIDS and the Media* (London: Methuen, 1987).

95. Weeks, *Sexuality and Its Discontents*, pp. 56, 94.

96. Note Weeks, *Sexuality*, pp. 37–38.

97. Weeks, *Sexuality and Its Discontents*, pp. 56, 170. Note the blatant omission of class in Irene Diamond and Lee Quinby, eds., *Feminism and Foucault*, p. xv: "The very achievements of Western humanism have been built on the backs of women and people of color." Other readings appear in Reimut Reiche, *Sexuality and Class Struggle* (London: New Left Books, 1970); Richard Sennett and Jonathan Cobb, *The Hidden Injuries of Class* (New York: Vintage, 1973).

98. Weeks, *Sexuality*, p. 37; Weeks, *Sexuality and Its Discontents*, pp. 170–171, 260. Both Weeks's endorsement of radical sexual pluralism and his unduly voluntarist and overly subjective assessment of what is politically possible relate to positions espoused by Foucault. First, Foucault's political trajectory was toward classical liberalism. See "Polemics, Politics, and Problemizations: An Interview with Michel Foucault," in Paul Rabinow, ed., *The Foucault Reader* (New York: Hill and Wang, 1984). Second, note Foucault's statement that "It is possible that the rough outline of a future society is supplied by the recent experiences with drugs, sex, communes, other forms of consciousness and other forms of individuality. If scientific socialism emerged from the *Utopias* of the nineteenth century, it is possible that a real socialization will emerge, in the twentieth century, from *experiences.*" Michel Foucault, *Language, Counter-Memory, Practice: Selected Essays and Interviews*, ed. by Donald F. Bouchard (Ithaca, N.Y.: Cornell University Press, 1977), p. 231, quoted in J. G. Merquoir, *Foucault* (Berkeley: University of California Press, 1985), pp. 154–155.

99. For an impressionistic tour see David Rieff, *Going to Miami: Exiles, Tourists, and Refugees in the New America* (New York: Penguin, 1987).

100. Program for 27–30 October 1988, in possession of the author.

101. Review of Deborah Gorham, *The Victorian Girl and the Feminine Ideal* (Bloomington: Indiana University Press, 1982), by Dorothy E. Smith, *Labour/Le Travail* 15 (Spring 1985): 248–249.

102. For a sensible critique of some of Dorothy Smith's earlier writings on the construction of meanings within a highly intellectualized tradition (Dorothy Smith, "A Peculiar Eclipsing: Women's Exclusion from Men's Culture," *Women's Studies International Quarterly* 1 [1978]: 281–296) see Cameron, *Feminism and Linguistic Theory*, pp. 110–111.

103. Scott's essays have recently been published in a volume under the title *Gender and the Politics of History* (New York: Columbia University Press, 1988). This publication had not yet appeared at the time of the initial writing of this chapter. I therefore focus mainly on the original versions of Scott's essays, an approach I justify on the grounds that it reveals her development and movement toward discourse. However, I also acknowledge the revisions made in the published collection, where Scott has often deepened her focus on discourse and nuanced her arguments. In few cases does this actually shift ground markedly. A review of the Scott collection by Claudia Koonz, "Post Scripts," *The Women's Review of Books* 6 (January 1989): 19–20, stakes out a position very similiar to that which I develop below. My thanks to Linda Kealey for sending me a copy of the Koonz review.

104. Scott appears to be a particular case of a general phenomenon identified by Peter Dews, *Logics of Disintegration: Post-structuralist Thought and the Claims of Critical Theory* (London: Verso, 1987), p. xv: "For the reception of Derrida's work, perhaps more than that of any other recent French thinker, has been marked by an astonishingly casual and unquestioning acceptance of certain extremely condensed—not to say sloganistic—characterizations of the history of Western thought, as if this history could be dismissed through its reduction to a set of perfunctory dualisms."

105. Lisa Duggan, "Vive la différence: Joan Scott's Historical Imperatives," *Voice Literary Supplement* (January–February 1989): 37.

106. The quote is from Joan Wallach Scott, "Men and Women in the Parisian Garment Trades: Discussions of Family and Work in the 1830s and 1840s," in Pat Thane, Geoffrey Crossick, and Roderick Floud, eds., *The Power of the Past: Essays for Eric Hobsbawm* (Cambridge: Cambridge University Press, 1984), pp. 82–84, 87, and in an endnote on p. 93 she acknowledges the aim of the article: "My greatest debt is to Natalie Zemon Davis who, at an early stage in my research asked me where the female voices were. That was the question that made all the difference." Scott's recognition of the lack of insight from critical theory in earlier publications, up to and including this 1984 article, is found in Joan W. Scott, "Statistical Representations of Work: The Politics of the Chamber of Commerce's *Statistique de l'Industrie à Paris, 1847–48*," in Steven Laurence Kaplan and Cynthia J. Koepp, eds., *Work in France: Representations, Meaning, Organization, and Practice* (Ithaca, N.Y.: Cornell University Press, 1986), p. 337.

107. Scott, *Gender and the Politics of History*, pp. 93–112.

108. Joan Scott, "Women in History: The Modern Period," *Past & Present* 101

(November 1983): 147, 155, rewritten for inclusion in *Gender and the Politics of History*, pp. 15–27.

109. Scott, "Statistical Representations of Work," in Steven Laurence Kaplan and Cynthia J. Koepp, eds., *Work in France: Representation, Meaning, Organization, and Practice* (Ithaca, N.Y.: Cornell University Press, 1986), pp. 361–362.

110. Ibid., p. 363. It is instructive to consider Lenin's discussion of factory statistics, which, though hardly attentive to the social/ideological construction of the data, is at least rigorous in emphasizing the need to assess the material critically and to understand how misrepresentations result in interpretive/political consequences of importance. See V. I. Lenin, *The Development of Capitalism in Russia* (Moscow: Progress Publishers, 1964), esp. pp. 454–484.

111. Karl Marx and Frederick Engels, *The German Ideology* (New York: International, 1947), p. 39.

112. Rancière's discussion is in Jacques Rancière, "The Myth of the Artisan: Critical Reflections on a Category of Social History," *International Labor and Working Class History* 24 (Fall 1983): pp. 8–9, with the essay reprinted in the same collection in which Scott's analysis of the statistical representation of work appeared, and where Scott cites the LaCapra influence. See Kaplan and Koepp, eds., *Work in France*, p. 327 (Rancière) and p. 335 (Scott).

113. See Joan W. Scott, " 'L'ouvrière! Mot impie, sordide . . .': Women Workers in the Discourse of French Political Economy, 1840–1860," in Patrick Joyce, ed., *The Historical Meanings of Work* (New York: Cambridge University Press, 1987), pp. 119–142.

114. Scott, "Representations of Work," in Kaplan and Koepp, eds., *Work in France*, pp. 361–362. This theme is also now developed more rigorously in an essay to be discussed below, "On Language, Gender, and Working-Class History," revised for publication in Scott, *Gender and the Politics of History*, pp. 53–67.

115. Quotes from Scott, *Gender and the Politics of History*, pp. 2, 72. My reading of the one unpublished essay in Scott's collection, "Women in *The Making of the English Working Class*," pp. 68–90, which is discussed in Chapter 2 above, is that it relies on an essentialist reading of women's experience, reifies the expressive content of women's lives, and argues for Thompson's structuring his account of class consciousness along dichotomized masculine/feminine lines without actually establishing that this is what is in the text. There is a large difference between structuring a history around such a dichotomy and being able, for argument's sake, to point to *instances* of such oppositions within the history. For Thompson's text also alludes to these oppositions *within* the supposedly separated sphere of masculinity itself, many of Joanna Southcott's followers being male. Thus, Scott's much discussed gender-based contrast of Paineite rationalist masculinity and Southcottian expressive femininity (see esp. pp. 78–79) is hardly of the importance she suggests. Moreover, it is surely not unproblematic to raise Joanna Southcott to the status of a politicized voice of eighteenth-century women, however fashionable it may be to use her as an example of "representation."

116. Scott, *Gender and the Politics of History*, p. 49.

117. After pages of discussion of gender, consider the questions Scott poses (and the citations that accompany them and often resolve issues of the sexes into implicit concerns with "woman") at the close of her essay. See Joan W. Scott, "Gender: A Useful Category of Historical Analysis," *American Historical Review* 91 (October 1986): esp. 1074–1075.

118. Luce Irigaray, *This Sex Which Is Not One,* pp. 192–193. Cf. Blye Frank, "Hegemonic Heterosexual Masculinity," *Studies in Political Economy* 24 (Autumn 1987): 159–170.

119. Scott, "Gender: A Useful Category of Historical Analysis," p. 1075.

120. There is an emerging literature, highly differentiated in its concerns and often written out of contemporary experience, that addresses working-class masculinity, and it is surprising that this work is not cited, whatever its flaws. Scott does refer in a sentence to two unpublished papers on gender ambivalence and manliness in the Indian colonial experience, but this is surely a rather idiosyncratic choice of material to reference, it being largely inaccessible because of its unpublished status. See Paul Willis, "Shop Floor Culture, Masculinity and the Wage Form," in John Clarke, Chas Critcher, and Richard Johnson, eds., *Working Class Culture: Studies in History and Theory* (London: Hutchinson, 1979), pp. 185–198; Ken Worpole, "The American Connection: The Masculine Style in Popular Fiction," in *Dockers and Detectives—Popular Reading: Popular Writing* (London: Verso, 1983), pp. 29–48. Cynthia Cockburn, *Brothers: Male Dominance and Technological Change* (London: Pluto, 1983); Andrew Tolson, *The Limits of Masculinity* (London: Tavistock, 1977), esp. pp. 51–81; Barbara Ehrenreich, *The Hearts of Men: American Dreams and the Flight from Commitment* (Garden City, N.Y.: Doubleday, 1983), esp. pp. 132–136; David G. Pugh, *Sons of Liberty: The Masculine Mind in Nineteenth-Century America* (Westport, Conn.: Greenwood, 1983); and for other statements that Scott could not have been expected to deal with: Jeff Hearn, *The Gender of Oppression: Men, Masculinity, and the Critique of Marxism* (Brighton: Wheatsheaf, 1987); J. A. Mangan and James Walvin, eds., *Manliness and Morality: Middle-Class Masculinity in Britain and America, 1800–1940* (Manchester: Manchester University Press, 1987); Stan Gray, "Sharing the Shopfloor," in Kaufman, ed., *Beyond Patriarchy,* pp. 216–234; Bryan D. Palmer, " 'What the Hell': or Some Comments on Class Formation and Cultural Reproduction," in Richard Gruneau, ed., *Popular Cultures and Political Practices* (Toronto: Garamond, 1988), pp. 33–42; Rosenfeld, " 'It Was a Hard Life.' " Race also has its writings, indeed an abundance of them relate to race and gender. This area is quite developed in literary criticism. See, as an introduction, Judith Newton and Deborah Rosenfelt, eds., *Feminist Criticism and Social Change: Sex, Class, and Race in Literature and Culture* (London: Methuen, 1985), which offers a number of references in the citations to various articles, and Barbara Smith, "Toward a Black Feminist Criticism," and Deborah E. McDowell, "New Directions for Black Feminist Criticism," both in Elaine Showalter, ed., *The New Feminist Criticism: Essays on Women, Literature, and Theory* (New York: Pantheon, 1985), pp. 168–199.

121. Scott's consideration of "Marxist feminism" is in fact focused on the controversies that develop as a consequence of attempts to merge Marxism and

feminism rather than a sustained discussion of the "Marxist feminist" work itself. She notes that "the English have had greater difficulty in challenging the constraints of strictly deterministic explanations," citing an extensive literature that developed in response to Michèle Barrett's *Women's Oppression Today: Problems in Marxist Feminist Analysis* (London: Verso, 1980). But she neglects substantive contact with Barrett's book itself. See Scott, "Gender: A Useful Category of Historical Analysis," p. 1061. For more explicit feminist confrontations with Marx note the debate around Harold Beneson's "Victorian Sexual Ideology and Marx's Theory of the Working Class," *International Labor and Working-Class History* 25 (Spring 1984): 1–36; and O'Brien, *The Politics of Reproduction*.

122. Scott did not have access to Mitchell's "Reflections on Twenty Years of Feminism" in Juliet Mitchell and Ann Oakley, eds., *What Is Feminism?* (Oxford: Basil Blackwell, 1986), pp. 34–49, but took Mitchell's forceful reassertion of the importance of the material from a set of seminars at Princeton University in 1986. No doubt that essay is a sobering reminder of the need to attend to material conditions, but I do not read it as a rejection of psychoanalysis or a refusal of the possibilities of taking psychoanalytic insight and a Marxist approach to material life and combining them in any understanding of gender. The point of Mitchell's essay is simply that the material must be addressed more rigorously than it often is in feminist circles, a recognition of just how much it determines. It is not a rejection of psychoanalysis, which Mitchell always conceived as a way into the materiality of the unconscious. See, as well, McRobbie, "Interview with Mitchell."

123. Especially Barrett, *Women's Oppression Today*, pp. 84–113. It is perhaps not surprising that the dust-jacket promotion of Scott's *Gender and the Politics of History* (written by Lynn Hunt) concludes with the rather overblown statement, "Our reading of Marx and our understanding of class differentiation will never again be the same." In fact, there is very little sophisticated engagement with Marx or Marxism in Scott's essays.

124. As Koonz's review of Scott's collected essays suggests, Scott's "critique" of Marxism is little more than a caricature. See "Post Scripts," p. 19.

125. Scott, "Gender: A Useful Category of Historical Analysis," pp. 1065–66.

126. Ibid., p. 1067.

127. Geoffrey Kay and James Mott, *Political Order and the Law of Labour* (London: Macmillan, 1982), p. 74.

128. Joan W. Scott, "On Language, Gender, and Working-Class History," *International Labor and Working-Class History* 31 (Spring 1987): 7, revised and presented in far more nuanced, although not substantially theoretically different, form in *Gender and the Politics of History*, pp. 53–67.

129. Scott replied to criticisms, including those of myself, in Joan W. Scott, "A Reply to Criticism," *International Labor and Working-Class History* 32 (Fall 1987): 39–45. The criticisms appeared in ibid. 31 (Spring 1987), by Bryan D. Palmer (pp. 14–23), Christine Stansell (24–29), and Anson Rabinbach (30–36). It would serve no purpose to sustain a lengthy counterreply, but it is worth stating that I refuse Scott's deliberate reconstruction of my own criticisms (which I would not make in the same way at this point) to structure my response into an

unreflective chauvinism. As the tone of Scott's reply to Stansell and myself suggests, Scott, who rejects binary oppositions, lives very much within useful professional oppositions of her own: "junior" colleagues are not to question those of "senior" status, and if they do, they will be slapped down with whatever it takes; "males" are not to challenge "females," and if they do, they will be taken to task for the biological sin of being *him*. On the latter process see as well Sandra M. Gilbert and Susan Gubar, "The Man on the Dump versus the United Dames of America; or, What Does Frank Lentricchia Want?" and Frank Lentricchia, "Andiamo!" both in *Critical Inquiry* 14 (Winter 1988): 387–413.

130. Scott, *Gender and the Politics of History,* p. 2.

131. Scott, "On Language, Gender, and Working-Class History," p. 11; "Reply to Criticism," p. 40.

132. Note, as well, Koonz, "Post Scripts," pp. 19–20.

133. Scott, "Reply to Criticism," p. 40, cited and commented upon in Mari Jo Buhle and Paul Buhle, "The New Labor History at the Cultural Crossroads," *Journal of American History* 75 (June 1988): 154–155.

134. On precisely this problem of perception see the brief comments on Derrida and Marx in Michael Ryan, *Marxism and Deconstruction: A Critical Articulation* (Baltimore: Johns Hopkins University Press, 1982), p. 22.

135. Joan W. Scott, "Deconstructing Equality-Versus-Difference: Or, The Uses of Poststructuralist Theory for Feminism," *Feminist Studies* 14 (Spring 1988): 33–50. Note, as well, Biddy Martin, "Feminism, Criticism, Foucault," *New German Critique* 27 (Fall 1982): 3–30; Jean Bethke Elshtain, "Feminist Discourse and Its Discontents: Language, Power, and Meaning," in Keohane, Rosaldo, and Gelpi, eds., *Feminist Theory: A Critique of Ideology,* pp. 127–145; Jane Flax, "Postmodernism and Gender Relations in Feminist Theory," *Signs* 12 (1987): 621–643, for different approaches and emphases.

136. Scott, "Deconstructing Equality-Versus-Difference," p. 43, quoting Schor, "Reading Double: Sand's Difference," in Miller, ed., *The Poetics of Gender,* p. 256. On the Sears case see also Ruth Milkman, "Women's History and the Sears Case," *Feminist Studies* 12 (Summer 1986): 375–400; Peter Novick, *That Noble Dream: The "Objectivity" Question and the American Historical Profession* (New York: Cambridge University Press, 1988), pp. 502–510; and the commentary and documents in "Women's History Goes to Trial: EEOC v. Sears, Roebuck and Company," *Signs* 11 (Summer 1986): 751–779. For a more general statement on the issues from a radical feminist perspective see Catharine A. MacKinnon, "Difference and Dominance: On Sex Discrimination," in *Feminism Unmodified,* pp. 32–45.

137. As noted earlier in this chapter the radical feminist Catharine A. MacKinnon rejects difference emphatically. See her "Introduction: The Art of the Impossible," in *Feminism Unmodified,* pp. 1–20. Consider as well Flax, "Postmodernism and Gender Relations in Feminist Theory," p. 643.

138. Scott, "Deconstructing Equality-Versus-Difference," pp. 45–46, 48.

139. Scott does allude to this problem and throughout her paper does refer to legal scholarship. But there is no sustained attempt to address legalism through the burgeoning literature in critical legal studies, nor does she address the anti-difference legal scholarship of radical feminist Catharine A. MacKinnon in

Feminism Unmodified. For critical legal studies see David Kairys, ed., *The Politics of Law: A Progressive Critique* (New York: Pantheon, 1982). On the whole question of the ways in which the courts confine testimony, central to Kessler-Harris's failure to convince the judge of the merits of her interpretive framework, see Robyn Penman, "Discourse in Courts: Cooperation, Coercion, and Coherence," *Discourse Processes,* 10 (July–September 1987), pp. 201–218. Much work has been done on legalism and labor. Note Karl Klare, "Judicial Deradicalization of the Wagner Act and the Origins of Modern Legal Consciousness," *Minnesota Law Review* 62 (1978): 265–339; Katherine Van Wezel Stone, "The Post-War Paradigm in American Labor Law," *Yale Law Journal* 90 (June 1981): 1509–1580. See, as well, Bernard Edelman, *Ownership of the Image: Elements for a Marxist Theory of Law* (London: Routledge & Kegan Paul, 1979).

140. Koonz, "Post Scripts," p. 20.

141. Barbara Foley, "The Politics of Deconstruction," in Robert Con and Ronald Schleifer, eds., *Rhetoric and Form: Deconstruction at Yale* (Norman: University of Oklahoma Press, 1985), p. 115. Note, as well, Peter Dews, *The Logics of Disintegration: Post-structuralist Thought and the Claims of Critical Theory* (London: Verso, 1987).

142. Scott, *Gender and the Politics of History,* p. 78, and for the closing essays on equality and difference ("The Sears Case" and "American Women Historians, 1884–1984"), pp. 167–198.

143. Scott, *Gender and the Politics of History,* pp. 5, 2.

144. Scott herself does not eschew these places but has attempted to reinvest them with meaning. See, for instance, Joan Wallach Scott, "New Documents on the Lives of French Women: The Journal of Caroline B., 1864–1868," *Signs* 12 (1987): 568–572.

145. Scott, "Deconstructing Equality-Versus-Difference," pp. 47–48.

146. See Catharine R. Stimpson, "Nancy Reagan Wears a Hat: Feminism and Its Cultural Consensus," *Critical Inquiry* 14 (Winter 1988): 223–243.

147. Koonz, "Post Scripts," p. 19.

148. Juliet Mitchell, "Reflections on Twenty Years of Feminism," in Juliet Mitchell and Ann Oakley, eds., *What Is Feminism?* (Oxford: Basil Blackwell, 1986), pp. 47–48; McRobbie, "Interview with Mitchell," pp. 89–91. For another reflection on feminism that acknowledges the powerful role of sexism but maintains an even more critical stance in relation to feminism see Sheila Delany, "Confessions of an Ex-Handkerchief Head, or Why This Is Not a Feminist Book," in Delany, *Writing Woman: Women Writers and Women in Literature Medieval to Modern* (New York: Shocken, 1983), pp. 1–22. An invaluable discussion is developed in Lynne Segal, *Is the Future Female? Troubled Thoughts on Contemporary Feminism* (London: Virago, 1987).

149. Flax, "Postmodernism and Gender Relations in Feminist Theory," p. 624.

150. This *may* relate to Spivak's concluding paragraph in her essay "Feminism and Critical Theory," where she states, "Feminism lives in the master-text as well as in the pores. It is not the determinant of the last instance." See Spivak, *In Other Worlds,* p. 92.

151. On the social construction of "reality" and feminist theory see Dorothy E. Smith, "The Social Construction of Documentary Reality," *Social Inquiry* 44

(1974): 257–268; Smith, *The Everyday World as Problematic: A Feminist Sociology* (Toronto: University of Toronto Press, 1987); Susan Russell, "The Hidden Curriculum of School: Reproducing Gender and Class Hierarchies," and Jane Gaskell, "Conceptions of Skill and the Work of Women: Some Historical and Political Issues," in Roberta Hamilton and Michèle Barrett, eds., *The Politics of Diversity: Feminism, Marxism, and Nationalism* (London: Verso, 1986), pp. 343–380.

152. The quotes in this paragraph are from Flax, "Postmodernism and Gender Relations in Feminist Theory," pp. 625, 632, 643. For a useful discussion of many of the issues involved here see Barrett, *Women's Oppression Today*.

153. Scott, "Deconstructing Equality-Versus-Difference," p. 47. Contrast Scott's statement with the following, drawn from Cora Kaplan, *Sea Changes: Culture and Feminism* (London: Verso, 1986), p. 11: "In nineteenth century Britain for example, class meaning organizes and orders the split representation of women as good and bad, for women as much as for men. The languages of class, in turn, are steeped in naturalized concepts of sexual difference. In order to understand the boundaries of gendered consciousness in a particular historical moment, we need to examine both the social and psychic elements of difference." If this statement remains a bit opaque in terms of its capacity to address material structural features of economic life, it is at least more open to them than Scott's formulation.

154. But then that is what reification does. See Gajo Petrovic, "Reification," in Tom Bottomore, ed., *A Dictionary of Marxist Thought* (Cambridge: Harvard University Press, 1983), pp. 411–413; Georg Lukacs, "Reification and the Consciousness of the Proletariat," in *History and Class Consciousness: Studies in Marxist Dialectics* (Cambridge: MIT Press, 1971), pp. 83–222.

Chapter 6

1. Cited in Jean Baudrillard, *Forget Foucault* (New York: Foreign Agents/Semiotext(e), 1987), p. 65.

2. See Chris Searle, ed., *The Sunflower of Hope: Poems from the Mozambican Revolution* (London: Allison & Busby, 1982), esp. pp. 104, 68.

3. Lyotard, *Figure* (Paris, 1971), p. 9, quoted in Peter Dews, *Logics of Disintegration: Post-structuralist Thought and the Claims of Critical Theory* (London: Verso, 1987), p. 113, and, for an anlysis of Lyotard, pp. 109–143, 200–219.

4. The following, unless otherwise stipulated, draws upon Jacques Derrida, "Like the Sound of the Sea Deep within a Shell: Paul de Man's War," *Critical Inquiry* 14 (Spring 1988): 590–652. Other sources are cited in Chapter 1, above. The figure on the number of newspaper articles comes from the most recent compilation, Werner Hamacher, Neil Hertz, and Thomas Keenan, eds., *Wartime Journalism, 1939–1943 by Paul de Man* (Lincoln: University of Nebraska Press, 1988), p. vii, while a figure of 169 appears in a comment on the de Man controversy by J. Hans Miller in *Times Literary Supplement*, June 17–23 1988, p. 685. The point is that the count will undoubtedly keep changing as new "discoveries" are made.

5. See James Atlas, "The Case of Paul de Man," *New York Times Magazine*, August 28 1988, p. 68.

6. De Man to Renato Poggioli, Director of the Harvard Society of Fellows, 25 January 1955, from a draft dated September 1954, cited in Derrida, "Paul de Man's War," p. 636.

7. Atlas, "Paul de Man," pp. 68–69.

8. See Derrida, "Paul de Man's War," p. 651; Atlas, "Paul de Man," p. 68.

9. I am reminded of the way in which one rigorous oral biography was constructed. See Peter Friedlander, *The Emergence of a UAW Local, 1936–1939: A Study in Class and Culture* (Pittsburgh: University of Pittsburgh Press, 1975), a text that in its containment of history within its own kind of intertextuality prefigured the potential of critical theory.

10. Derrida, "Paul de Man's War," p. 599.

11. The above paragraphs draw on ibid., pp. 612–613, 616, 621, 623, 631, although the whole article is in fact turning on precisely this kind of dualism in de Man's writings.

12. For the actual text and its surroundings see Hamacher, Hertz, and Keenan, eds., *Wartime Journalism*, pp. 286–292.

13. This problem is addressed interestingly, albeit slightly differently, in Anson Rabinbach, "The Reader, the Popular Novel, and the Imperative to Participate: Reflections on Public and Private Experience in the Third Reich," Paper presented at International Colloquium on Mass Culture and the Working Class, 1914–1970, Paris, 14–15 October 1988, in possession of the author.

14. It has been suggested to me from two different quarters that Derrida's reading of de Man is suspect *as* critical theory. First, those who have no use for Derrida have argued that the article is lucid and historically contextualized precisely because it is a mere exercise in damage control. Second, true critical theory believers have argued that because it is these things, it is not in fact on a par with Derrida's other texts, which remain true to the deconstructionist project. I do not accept these interpretations for in my reading I am struck by the extent to which Derrida's deconstruction of de Man's wartime journalism reveals *both* critical theory's possibilities and severe limitations. If this article is, for various obvious reasons, a text that historians can enter into with more ease than some of Derrida's other works, this is no ground for dismissing it as propaganda or denigrating its importance in comparison to other more profound/pure writings.

15. Derrida, "Paul de Man's War," p. 618.

16. Note that in a text written before the de Man revelations, Peter Dews, *Logics of Disintegration: Post-structuralist Thought and the Claims of Critical Theory* (London: Verso, 1987), p. 35, argues that "when Derrida, during the 1980s, begins to make more explicit statements of social and cultural criticism, he tends to revert" to conventionality.

17. As Trotsky made his way across Finland by train in 1917, en route to the revolution, he found himself lodged in the same compartment with two prominent Belgian socialists, one of whom was Henri de Man. De Man was on his way to Russia to drum up enthusiasm for the war. "Do you recognize us?" asked de

Man. "I do," Trotsky replied, "although people change a lot in time of war." See Ronald Segal, *The Tragedy of Leon Trotsky: Traitor, Hero or Prophet?* (Harmondsworth: Penguin Books, 1983), p. 134.

18. Derrida, "Paul de Man's War," pp. 592, 599, 635–637, 626, 604–606, 600.

19. Ibid., p. 631.

20. Ibid., p. 606.

21. Ibid., pp. 590, 594, 601, 624–625. In a cryptic footnote toward the end of the de Man article (p. 651) Derrida actually comes close to implying that the essay on the Jews and literature is in some ways suspect. I suppose that in a period when we have seen major European publications hoaxed by forgeries of Hitler diaries this is possible. But it seems doubtful. Derrida's raising of this issue in this way appears to me as more important as a sign of his inability to accept de Man's partial complicity in anti-Semitism and accommodation to fascism. This is odd, for Derrida's essay reads the de Man articles rigorously and establishes the extent to which they do espouse the superficial rhetoric and ideology of the Nazi "reconstruction" of Europe. Why is it imperative to reach beyond recognized reality to suggest a de Man untainted by these texts?

22. Ibid., pp. 645, 648, 651.

23. Ibid., pp. 649–650.

24. As Barbara Foley, "The Politics of Deconstruction," in Robert Con and Ronald Schleifer, eds., *Rhetoric and Form: Deconstruction at Yale* (Norman: University of Oklahoma Press, 1985), p. 129, states: "deconstruction cannot—will not—provide the grounds for a rupture that is, finally, anything more than discursive. For to engage in an oppositional *praxis* based upon a determinate analysis and pursuing determinate results would be to grant that binary oppositions are dialectical, rather than static—historical rather than epistemological. And this is an admission that deconstruction cannot make." The de Man controversy, its relationship to deconstruction, and its political meaning is addressed in Denis Donoghue, "The Strange Case of Paul de Man," *New York Review of Books* (29 June 1989), pp. 32–37, a source that came to my attention as this book was in production.

25. E. P. Thompson, "The Politics of Theory," in Raphael Samuel, ed., *People's History and Socialist Theory* (London: Routledge & Kegan Paul, 1981), p. 401, this statement occurring in an article that responded to criticism of Thompson's sustained anti-Althusserian polemic, "The Poverty of Theory: or an Orrery of Errors," in Thompson, *The Poverty of Theory & Other Essays* (London: Merlin, 1978), pp. 193–398.

26. Note, especially, Sande Cohen, *Historical Culture: On the Recoding of an Academic Discipline* (Berkeley: University of California Press, 1986), which includes a "deconstruction" of Thompson's "The Poverty of Theory; or an Orrery of Errors" (pp. 174–229). Thompson's essay is dismissed as "trivializing" by Gayatri Chakravorty Spivak, who considers it little more than a rearguard action to "keep the disciplines going." See Spivak, *In Other Worlds: Essays in Cultural Politics* (New York: Methuen, 1987), pp. 208, 284.

27. A point raised with bluntness and force in Russell Jacoby, *The Last Intellectuals: American Culture in the Age of Academe* (New York: Basic

Books, 1987), pp. 168–173. I will address Jacoby's book and the response to it on the left below.

28. Arthur and Marilouise Kroker, eds., *Body Invaders: Panic Sex in America* (Montreal: New World Perspectives, 1987), from articles by the editors, pp. 21, 19.

29. For statements that expose various aspects of this rejection of class politics and combat this drift in different ways see Michael Buroway, *The Politics of Production* (London: Verso, 1985); Ellen Meiksins Wood, *The Retreat from Class: A New "True" Socialism* (London: Verso, 1986); Ralph Miliband, "The New Revisionism in England," *New Left Review* 150 (March 1985): 5–28.

30. See, for instance, Sheila Rowbotham, Lynne Segal, and Hilary Wainwright, *Beyond the Fragments: Feminism and the Making of Socialism* (London: Merlin Press, 1979).

31. A. Phillips and B. Taylor, "Sex and Skill: Notes Towards a Feminist Economics," *Feminist Review* 6 (1980): 79–83; and, for a general statement, Jane Gaskell, "Conceptions of Skill and Work: Some Historical and Political Issues," in Roberta Hamilton and Michèle Barrett, eds., *The Politics of Diversity: Feminism, Marxism, and Nationalism* (London: Verso, 1986), pp. 361–380.

32. See the important studies: Barbara Taylor, " 'The Men Are as Bad as Their Masters . . .': Socialism, Feminism and Sexual Antagonism in the London Tailoring Trade in the 1830s," in Judith Newton, Mary Ryan, and Judith Walkowitz, eds., *Sex and Class in Women's History* (London: Routledge & Kegan Paul, 1983), pp. 187–220; Joan Wallach Scott, "Men and Women in the Parisian Garment Trades: Discussions of Family and Work in the 1830s and 1840s," in Pat Thane, Geoffrey Crossick, and Roderick Floud, eds., *The Power of the Past: Essays for Eric Hobsbawm* (Cambridge: Cambridge University Press, 1983), pp. 67–94; Christine Stansell, *City of Women: Sex and Class in New York, 1789–1860* (New York: Knopf, 1986), pp. 130–154.

33. Quoted in Gerard Bekerman, *Marx and Engels: A Conceptual Concordance* (Oxford: Blackwell Reference, 1983), pp. 87–88.

34. Karl Marx, *Theories of Surplus Value* (translated by Emile Burns, 3 vols. [Moscow: Progress, 1963–1971], 3: 266–267, quoted in David Montgomery, *The Fall of the House of Labor: The Workplace, the State, and American Labor Activism, 1865–1925* (Cambridge: Cambridge University Press, 1987), p. 45, a text that successfully addresses the two-sidedness of skill.

35. Note the discussions in Mike Holbrook-Jones, *Supremacy and Subordination of Labour: The Hierarchy of Work in the Early Labour Movement* (London: Heinemann, 1982); Craig Heron, *Working in Steel: The Early Years in Canada, 1883–1935* (Toronto: McClelland and Stewart, 1988).

36. Some critiques of parts of this trend remain problematic *and* useful. See, for instance, Tony Judt, "A Clown in Regal Purple: Social History and the Historians," *History Workshop Journal* 7 (Spring 1979): 66–94; Elizabeth Fox-Genovese and Eugene D. Genovese, "The Political Crisis of Social History: Class Struggle as Subject and Object," in *Fruits of Merchant Capital: Slavery and Property in the Rise and Expansion of Capitalism* (Oxford: Oxford University Press, 1983), pp. 179–212.

37. See, among other studies, Gerald M. Sider, *Culture and Class in Anthropology and History: A Newfoundland Illustration* (New York: Cambridge University Press, 1986); Christine Stansell, *City of Women: Sex and Class in New York, 1789–1860* (New York: Alfred A. Knopf, 1986).

38. Jacoby, *The Last Intellectuals*, esp. p. 216.

39. For a taste of the response see Sean Wilentz, "The Cloistering of Radical Minds," *Tikkun* 3 (March–April 1988): 63–66, representative of the more benign challenge; and, worse, Lynn Garafola, "The Last Intellectuals," *New Left Review* 169 (May–June 1988): 122–128. There is an exchange between Jacoby and Garafola in *New Left Review*, 172 (November–December 1988), pp. 125–128.

40. Peter Dews, *The Logics of Disintegration: Post-structuralist Thought and the Claims of Critical Theory* (London: Verso, 1987); Barbara Foley, "The Politics of Deconstruction," in Robert Con Davis and Ronald Schleifer, eds., *Rhetoric and Form: Deconstruction at Yale* (Norman: University of Oklahoma Press, 1985), pp. 113–134. There have been poststructuralist rejoinders to the kinds of criticisms raised by Dews and Foley. See especially Bill Readings, "The Deconstruction of Politics," in Lindsay Waters and Wlad Godzich, eds., *Reading De Man Reading* (Minneapolis: University of Minnesota Press, 1989), pp. 223–243. But note the earlier assessment of Nancy Fraser that a French effort to relate politics and deconstruction imploded in "apolitical liberalism." See Fraser, "The French Derrideans: Politicizing Deconstruction or Deconstructing Politics," *New German Critique* 33 (Fall 1984): 127–154.

41. Charles Taylor, "Logics of Disintegration," *New Left Review*, 170 (July–August 1988), p. 116.

42. Sheila Rowbotham, *Hidden From History: Rediscovering Women in History from the 17th Century to the Present* (New York: Pantheon, 1974).

43. For a survey of some texts of historical materialism drawn up for other purposes, but that nevertheless does reveal the extent to which university-produced and non-university-produced work emerged in this period see Richard Johnson, "Culture and the Historians," in John Clarke, Chas Critcher, and Richard Johnson, eds., *Working Class Culture: Studies in History and Theory* (London: Hutchinson, 1979), pp. 41–71.

44. It is significant that the penultimate chapter of Peter Novick's recent history of the "objectivity question" within the American historical profession is entitled "The Center Does Not Hold" and addresses aspects (albeit quite limited) of the impact of poststructuralism and literary criticism within the discipline. See Peter Novick, *That Noble Dream: The "Objectivity Question" and the American Historical Profession* (New York: Cambridge University Press, 1988), pp. 522–572.

45. See Zygmunt Bauman, *Legislators and Interpreters: On Modernity, Post-Modernity, and Intellectuals* (Ithaca, N.Y.: Cornell University Press, 1987), p. 5; Alice A. Jardine, *Gynesis: Configurations of Woman and Modernity* (Ithaca, N.Y.: Cornell University Press, 1985), pp. 260–261.

46. As an introduction see Jorge Larrain, "Base and Superstructure," in Tom Bottomore et al., eds., *A Dictionary of Marxist Thought* (Cambridge: Harvard University Press, 1983), pp. 42–45; Stephen A. Resnick and Richard D. Wolff,

Knowledge and Class: A Marxian Critique of Political Economy (Chicago: University of Chicago Press, 1987), pp. 38–108; Derek Sayer, *The Violence of Abstraction: The Analytic Foundations of Historical Materialism* (Oxford: Basil Blackwell, 1987); G. A. Cohen, *Karl Marx's Theory of History: A Defence* (Oxford: Clarendon Press, 1978), esp. pp. 134–174, 216–248; Maurice Godelier, *The Mental and the Material: Thought Economy and Society* (London: Verso, 1986).

47. Karl Marx, *Capital: The Process of Capitalist Production as a Whole*, vol. 3 (New York: International, 1967), pp. 791–792.

48. See the not entirely appropriate presentation of this in Richard Johnson, "Culture and the historians," and "Three Problematics: Elements of a Theory of Working-Class Culture," in Clarke, Critcher, and Johnson, eds., *Working-Class Culture*, pp. 41–73, 201–237.

49. E. P. Thompson, "Socialist Humanism: An Epistle to the Philistines," *The New Reasoner: A Quarterly Journal of Socialist Humanism* 1 (Summer 1957): esp. 113–114. Rejection of the base-superstructure metaphor runs through other Thompson writings of this period. See, for instance, "Revolution Again! Or Shut Your Ears and Run," *New Left Review* 6 (November–December 1960): 18–31. For a discussion of this moment of political differentiation and theoretical articulation see Bryan D. Palmer, *The Making of E. P. Thompson: Marxism, Humanism, and History* (Toronto: New Hogtown Press, 1981).

50. E. P. Thompson, *Whigs and Hunters: The Origin of the Black Act* (New York: Pantheon, 1975), p. 260.

51. See E. P. Thompson, "Eighteenth-Century English Society: Class Struggle without Class?" *Social History* 3 (May 1978): 149.

52. Raymond Williams, *Politics and Letters: Interviews with New Left Review* (London: New Left Books, 1979), p. 353.

53. The most explicit statements are Raymond Williams, "Base and Superstructure in Marxist Cultural Theory," in Williams, *Problems in Materialism and Culture* (London: Verso, 1980), pp. 31–49; Williams, *Marxism and Literature* (Oxford: Oxford University Press, 1977), esp. pp. 75–141. But this theme runs throughout works like Williams, *Culture* (London: Fontana, 1981), and is the underlying logic of collections such as Williams, *Writing in Society* (London: Verso, 1986). For another perspective on this whole area see Terry Eagleton, "Two Approaches in the Sociology of Literature," *Critical Inquiry* 14 (Spring 1988): 469–478.

54. R. S. Neale, "Cultural Materialism: A Critique," in Neale, *Writing Marxist History: British Society, Economy, and Culture since 1700* (Oxford: Basil Blackwell, 1988), pp. 277–278.

55. See E. P. Thompson, "Agency and Choice," *New Reasoner* 4 (Summer 1958): 106.

56. While rather too ambiguous, note the comments and practical approach of Wally Seccombe, "Marxism and Demography," *New Left Review* 137 (January–February 1983): 28–31. The issue can be posed, as Nelcya Delanoë has suggested to me, in terms of the easy assimilation of Thompson's *Making of the English Working Class* to almost any possible "reading." We have already noted this in the case of William Reddy's *Money and Liberty in Modern Europe: A*

Critique of Historical Understanding (Cambridge: Cambridge University Press, 1987). François Furet, whose influential studies of the French Revolution were discussed in the context of an earlier chapter's focus on discourse, history, and anti-Marxism, has recently penned a laudatory review of the first French edition of Thompson's *Making*.

57. E. P. Thompson, *The Sykaos Papers* (New York: Pantheon, 1988), pp. 476–478.

58. Ibid., pp. 318–319, 118, 92–93.

59. Ibid., pp. 359–361. For a recent free-wheeling discussion of Thompson that alludes to some of these issues raised by a reading of *The Sykaos Papers,* see Paul Buhle, "Isn't it Romantic: E. P. Thompson's Global Agenda," *Voice Literary Supplement* 76 (July 1989), 24–26.

60. Note S. S. Prawer, *Karl Marx and World Literature* (Oxford: Clarendon Press, 1976). Though by no means unambiguously Marxist in their analyses, note the discussions of peasant economy and resistance in James C. Scott, *The Moral Economy of the Peasant: Rebellion and Subsistence in Southeast Asia* (New Haven: Yale University Press, 1976); Scott, *Weapons of the Weak: Everyday Forms of Peasant Resistance* (New Haven: Yale University Press, 1985).

61. Note the discussion of "The Historicity of Concepts" in Derek Sayer, *The Violence of Abstraction: The Analytic Foundations of Historical Materialism* (Oxford: Basil Blackwell, 1987), pp. 126–149, although Sayer's views on base-superstructure do not necessarily coincide with my own remarks above.

62. In *Theories of Surplus Value* Marx noted, "If material production itself is not grasped in its specific historical form, it is impossible to understand the concrete nature of the intellectual production corresponding to it and the interaction of both factors." Quoted in Prawer, *Karl Marx and World Literature,* p. 314.

63. Most "new" understandings and theories embrace "old" politics, such as popular frontism. Consider the implications of Eric Hobsbawm, "Farewell to the Classic Labour Movement," *New Left Review* 173 (January–February 1989): 69–74.

64. Fox-Genovese and Genovese, "On the Social History of the French Revolution," in *The Fruits of Merchant Capital,* p. 217.

65. Pierre Bourdieu, *Distinction: A Social Critique of the Judgement of Taste* (Cambridge: Harvard University Press, 1984), pp. 462, 463–465.

Index